QUESTIONING

Literary and Rhetorical Analysis for Writers

RICH RAYMOND

FOUNTAINHEAD
PRESS

About the Cover

To the young ravens that cry. . . Psalm 147:9

Many ancient cultures have created a special place in their mythologies for crows and ravens. The Norse God Odin had two ravens named Hugin (thought) and Munin (memory) that supposedly gave him "raven knowledge" of the world. In Scottish lore, this knowledge was referred to as a "second" sense. In British mythology, some believe that if the crows ever leave the Tower of London the British Empire will fall. And the Native Americans of the Pacific Northwest revered the raven to such a degree that they gave it a prominent place in their creation myth. Even today, ravens and crows permeate our pop culture in music, literature and movies. We have chosen to use this ubiquitous bird for the cover of *Questioning* to represent the inquisitive nature that pulses through the veins of every good writer.

Cover design by Doris Bruey
Text design by Patricia Bracken

Books may be purchased for educational purposes.

For information, please call or write:

1-800-586-0330

Fountainhead Press
Southlake, TX 76092

Web site: www.fountainheadpress.com
Email: customerservice@fountainheadpress.com

ISBN 978-1-59871-093-9
Printed in the United States of America

Biography

RICHARD RAYMOND

Rich Raymond teaches composition and literature at Mississippi State University, where he has served as head of the Department of English since 2004. Before coming to MSU, Raymond chaired the Department of Rhetoric and Writing at the University of Arkansas at Little Rock, directed the Little Rock Writing Project, and served as Fulbright Professor of American Literature and Rhetoric at the University of Shkodra in Albania.

You can access Raymond's Fulbright experience in his book *Teaching American Literature at an East European University: Explicating the Rhetoric of Liberty*, Mellen Press, 2006. Also, his article "When Writing Professors Teach Literature: Shaping Questions, Finding Answers, Effecting Change" will soon appear in *College Composition and Communication*.

Preface for Teachers

Rationale and Chapter-by-Chapter Organization

A quick glace at the organization of the first four chapters reveals what looks like a "modes approach" to the teaching of writing: a first chapter on narration; two chapters on exposition, prewriting strategies, and arrangement; then one chapter on persuasion and argumentation. Some of you will find this organizational helpful, a good fit for the catalogue description of the course you teach; others will appreciate that each of these four chapters provides an ongoing subtext on mixed modes, challenging your students to think about the value of narration in expository and persuasive writing, as well as the persuasive edge found in nearly every sample of both narrative and expository writing.

Indeed, your students will find this mixed-modes subtext not only in the discussion of each chapter but also in the imbedded readings and in journaling and writing assignments. In chapter one, for example, your students will find memoirs—excerpts from Frederick Douglass, Esmeralda Santiago, Maxine Hong Kingston, and Maya Angelou—each with a strong persuasive purpose focused on our longings for liberty and the importance of sharing our stories. In like manner, the narrative essays your students will write in the first chapter will carry secondary aims in exposition, explaining the consequences of taking risks or the key influences on their literacy histories.

After building this foundation in narration, exposition, and persuasion, your students will draw on all three modes in the next four chapters. Chapter five focuses on research writing, chapter six on revision, chapter seven on writing about poetry, and chapter eight on preparing portfolios. While each of these chapters provides the focus noted, you'll find, too, that key concepts in each of these chapters thread throughout the entire book. In chapter one, for instance, your students will learn about Cicero and Quintilian, two rhetoricians who referred their students to the poets (the emphasis of chapter seven) as the best source for powerful ideas delivered in narratives. Similarly, while chapter six explores revision and proofreading in depth, each chapter stresses the drafting and revising processes that flow from prewriting strategies. One more example: chapter eight guides your students through the process of constructing a portfolio, but the entire book prepares them for that task by consistently stressing stylistic analysis of others' writings and reflections on their own rhetorical strategies—hence the key phrase in the subtitle of the book, "rhetorical analysis."

That subtitle, you noticed, gives equal billing to "literary analysis," appropriately so, because every chapter couches the study of writing in the best thinking of rhetoricians, poets, novelists, and nonfiction writers. For instance, that first chapter on narration introduces your students not only to Cicero and Quintilian, as noted above, but also to philosophers Plato and John Stuart Mill, to novelists Faulkner and Solzhenitsyn, to poets Seamus Heaney and Maya Angelou, and to mythologist Joseph Campbell—all of whom have much to say about how and why we must tell our stories.

Each chapter will also engage your students in practical applications of rhetorical theories as they write their responses to the readings, each exploring a single theme. In chapter one again, they will learn, for instance, how to use Kenneth Burke's "pentad" theory to guide their reading and writing of narratives on the theme of literacy. Then in chapter two, centered on the theme of personal growth, your students will use Peter Elbow's thinking on the linkage of personal experience to literary analysis to guide their writing on the fiction of Earnest Gaines, Sarah Orne Jewett, or Zora Neale Hurston. In chapter three, focused on the theme of diversity, your students will encounter ancient rhetoric via Professor Edward P. J. Corbett, not only to learn the distinct yet overlapping aims of deliberative, judicial, and ceremonial discourse, but also to apply Aristotle's "common topics" and Cicero's stasis theory as they discover and arrange their ideas on writings by essayist David Brooks, memoir writers Gary Soto and Mary Crow Dog, and Senator John McCain. Next, chapter four, featuring readings on civil and domestic rights, will introduce your students to James Kinneavy to help them reflect further on the overlapping aims of discourse; they will also learn to apply Aristotle's elements of persuasion to Martin Luther King's "Letter from Birmingham Jail," then mediational principles of persuasion to Susan Glaspell's play *Trifles*.

These last four chapters also explore the interface between "literary and rhetorical analysis." Unfolding the theme of literature as a source of personal and social transformation, chapter five will prepare your students to follow Wayne Booth's rhetorical principles on the research process, a process grounded in students discovering their own questions. They will also learn Azar Nafiri's ideas on literature as an agent of social change; they will then apply Booth's processes and Nafiri's ideas to the work of Flannery O'Connor or to another writer of their choice. Then in chapter six, your students will ground their study of "revising and proofing" in Joe Glaser's ideas on "style and voice"; they will then apply those ideas to writings by Jane Austen, Barack Obama, Frank McCourt, Sherwood Anderson, and Alice Walker—all focused on the common theme of parents and children. To prepare your students for writing about poetry, chapter seven will first provide your students an historical sketch on the value and purpose of poetry, a sketch beginning with Plato and ending with contemporary poets Edward Hirsh and Yusef Komunyakaa. They will then learn how imagery and sound effects achieve the poets' rhetorical purposes, lessons they will apply to poems by Robert Frost, William Wordsworth, William Shakespeare, Wilfred Owen, Lawrence Ferlinghetti, Elizabeth Bishop, and Seamus Heaney. Finally, chapter eight will focus on theories of reflective writing provided by Sandra Murphy, Lee Odell, Peter Elbow, and Willa Wolcott; they will also read the reflections of contemporary fiction writers Kevin Brockmeier and Anne Lamott before applying these metacognitive principles in shaping their own portfolios and writing their own reflective essays.

But why, you may be asking, have I insisted on this constant linkage of "literary and rhetorical analysis"? My answer to this question points to the underlying conviction of this book: learning to read literature will give your students the critical savvy and the self-knowledge essential to the meaningful application of rhetorical principles in their own writing. Denis Donoghue puts it this way: If we teach our students "the slow work of reading literature," we will give them the tools they need to shape their own lives (123). David Downing finds this linkage compelling, too: we must heal the "painful splits between literature and writing," he believes, because our students have a right to learn that "the aesthetic and political, the literary and the rhetorical, the textual and the extra-textual are deeply intertwined" (30).

Finally, your students will also read samples of student writing in each of these chapters. These writings will provide models for your students, not models to be copied, just illustrations of other students applying—with varying degrees of success—the concepts each chapter presents.

If you're a new instructor, please turn now to the Instructor's Manual, where you will find tips designed to point out the pitfalls (I have fallen in all of them) and the alternatives for using the reading, prewriting, drafting, and revising strategies described throughout the book.

Preface for Students

By the time you finish this writing course, I hope that you will be able to say that this book has taught you reliable ways to read closely and critically, the kind of reading that all college professors expect of their students. As you practice these reading skills, you will also encounter the reading-writing connection. In other words, you will learn to think of your writing not just as an assignment required by a professor but also as a response to a previous writer, your contribution to an on-going conversation on questions that matter—and have always mattered—to us all. What kinds of questions? Let me list just a few you'll encounter:

- What should we learn, how should we learn, who should learn, and who gets to decide?

- How does our learning shape our roles as citizens?

- What should we do if our leaders corrupt our system of justice?

- What should we think about our parents, their successes and failures?

- On what values should we base our relationships, women to men, women to women, men to men? Why does commitment sometimes liberate, sometimes enslave?

As you wrestle with these immense questions, you will have many great writers to guide your way. Some of these writers fit best in the nonfiction category: Frederick Douglass, Martin Luther King, Barack Obama, Frank McCourt, Azar Nafisi, for example. Others fit better in the fiction category: Ernest Gaines, Jane Austen, Flannery O'Connor, Susan Glaspell, Sarah Orne Jewett, Zora Neale Hurston. Still others have earned the title poet: Robert Frost, Elizabeth Bishop, Seamus Heaney. Sometimes, you will accept these writers' guidance; other times, you will reject it. In either case, however, you will always feel enriched by their "conversation."

Your responses to these writers will be shaped, too, by the strategies you learn to find your topic, to find what you already know, what you need to learn, and to organize your material to serve the needs of your reader. In working through these strategies, you will regularly join yet another conversation, this time with your peers, as you help one another move through the process of revision.

This conversation with your fellow writers will also bring you into conversation with yourself. First, before you write those drafts to share with your peers, you will fill your journal with analyses of others' writing and—just as important—with answers to questions raised by your own heart: Why does Grant Wiggins' abuse of his students anger me so? Would I have the courage to break an unjust law and then accept the penalty, as King urges? I used to be just like Kingston's "silent girl"—how did I get past my fears of language? Where did my fear of language come from in the first place? Why do I feel such a rush when I see Frost's boy "swinging birches," or Jewett's heron soaring above the pines, or Nafisi teaching her Iranian students behind closed doors? You may never find conclusive answers to such questions, but the struggle to find answers will deepen your knowledge of yourself and motivate you to write about the literature that inspired your insights. Finally this conversation with self will follow as well as precede your writing of essays, for you will learn to write reflectively about your own writing: where it works, where it fails, how you can revise it to serve your purpose and to meet your readers' needs.

Enjoy the talk!

Rich Raymond

Works Cited

Donoghue, Denis. "The Practice of Reading." *What's Happened to the Humanities?* Ed. Alvin Kernan. Princeton: Princeton UP, 1997. 122–40.

Downing, David B. "Beyond Disciplinary English: Integrating Reading and Writing by Reforming Academic Labor." *Beyond English, Inc.: Curricular Reform in a Global Economy.* Eds. David B. Downing, Claude Mark Hurlbert, and Paula Mathieu. Portsmouth: Heinemann, 2002. 23–38.

Table of Contents

Chapter 1 Finding the Right Questions: Critical Reading and the Importance of Telling Our Own Stories 1

"Once upon a time"…Asking Questions, Telling Stories 3
Using Burke's Pentad to Ask Questions about Narrative 4
Applying Burke's Pentad to Frederick Douglass' Autobiography 5
 Excerpt from *Narrative of the Life of Frederick Douglass, an American Slave* 5
Journaling on Douglass' Autobiography 9
Recognizing the Qualities of a Narrative Essay........................10
 Student Essay: "Fighting for America" 12
Mastering the Process of Critical Reading and Writing.....................15
Figure: Tree Outlining......................17
 Guidelines for Responding to Draft of Narrative Essay.....................18

Writing Your Own Narrative Essay......................19
Journaling on Esmeralda Santiago's Autobiography.....................19
 Excerpt from *When I Was Puerto Rican*, "A Shot at It".....................20
Journaling on Maxine Hong Kingston's Autobiography 29
 Excerpt from *The Woman Warrior* 30
Journaling on Maya Angelou's Autobiography.....................36
 Excerpt from *I Know Why the Caged Bird Sings*.....................37
Choosing a Topic for Your Narrative Essay.....................43
Works Cited 44

Chapter 2 Finding Your Audience in Your Purpose: Reading Fiction, Writing Exposition.....................45

Identifying Your Audience and Purpose: Why Read? Why Write? And for Whom? 47

Writing the Expository Essay.....................47
Applying Burke's Pentad to Ernest Gaines' Novel.....................48
 Excerpt from *A Lesson Before Dying* 49
Recognizing the Relationship Between Audience and Purpose 64
Writing your Own Expository Essay 65
 Student Essay: "See Me After Class!".....................66
Practicing the Recursive Process of Writing.....................68

Figure: Tree Outline 71
Guidelines for Responding to Draft on *A Lesson Before Dying*................73
Checklist for Revision 73

Writing a Second Expository Essay 74

Using the Elements of Fiction to Interpret Sarah Orne Jewett's Short Story 74
Journaling on Jewett's Short Story 77
    "A White Heron" 78
Journaling on Zora Neale Hurston's Short Story 85
    "Sweat" 86
Choosing a Topic for Your Second Expository Essay...............................95
Works Cited 96

Chapter 3 Serving the Needs of Your Audience: Invention and Arrangement

Invention and Arrangement..97
Understanding The Aims of Discourse.....................................99

Inventing and Arranging 99

Using Invention to Serve the Needs of Your Audience 100
Journaling on David Brooks' Essay..101
    "People Like Us"...102
Freewriting and Outlining 105
Reviewing the Recursive Process of Writing...106
    Student Essay Invented from Stasis Theory: "Are Our Lives Truly Diverse?" 107
Using Arrangement to Serve the Needs of Your Audience 110
Writing an Expository Essay on Diversity 111
    Reader Analysis Worksheet...113

Writing a Second Expository Essay on Diversity.....................115

Journaling on Gary Soto's Essay...115
    "Like Mexicans"...116
Journaling on Mary Crow Dog's Autobiography 119
    Excerpt from *Lakota Woman*, "Civilize Them with a Stick"................120
Journaling on John McCain's Book 126
    Excerpt from *Why Courage Matters* 126
Writing an Expository Essay on Soto, Dog, and McCain 130
Works Cited 131

Chapter 4 Reasoning and Mediating

Reasoning and Mediating 133
Recognizing the Overlapping Aims of Discourse.....................135

Understanding the Elements of Persuasion 136

Journaling on Martin Luther King's Letter 137
    "Letter from Birmingham Jail" 138
Analizing the Persuasive Elements in King's Letter 150
    Student Analysis of King's Ethos, Logos, and Pathos: "An Ecclesiastical
      Fall from Grace" 150
Blending the Inductive and Deductive Processes 153
    Induction 153
    Deduction 154
Blending Deduction and Induction 155
Blending Pathos with Sound Reasoning to Achieve Mediational Goals ...157
Prewriting on King's Letter 158
Choosing a Topic for Your Persuasive Essay 159
Revising to Reveal Sound Reasoning 159
    The Either/Or Fallacy 159
    The Red Herring 160

Writing an Editorial Essay: A Case for Mediation 160

Journaling on Susan Glaspell's Play 161
    Trifles 161
Using Role-Playing to Write the Editorial Essay 172
Works Cited 172

Chapter 5   Finding Answers to Your Questions: Research and Documentation 175

Understanding the Research Process 177

Journaling on Flannery O'Connor's Short Story 178
    "Greenleaf" 178

Analyzing Richard Giannone's Scholarly Article 195

    "'Greenleaf': A Story of Lent" 196
Introduction: the Question and the Problem 203
Arrangement 203
Logos and Pathos: Building Ethos with Examples and Quotations 204
Writing a Proposal Memo on a Literary Topic 207
Shaping a Research Problem 207
Journaling and Freewriting 207
Searching for Secondary Sources 207
Finding a Research Question 207
    Figure 5.1: EBSCO Database 209

Student Proposal Memo on Literary Topic 210
Documenting Your Research 212
   Bibliography Cards 213
      Figure 5.3: Bibliography Card on a Chapter from a Book 213
      Figure 5.3: Bibliography Card on a Journal Article 215
   Note Cards 215
      Figure 5.4: Combination Note Card 216
Writing Summaries 217
Avoiding Academic Dishonesty 218
Analyzing a Literary Research Paper in MLA Style 219
   Student Literary Research Paper: "Saved by the Bull: Grace Versus
     Repressiveness in O'Conner's 'Greenleaf'" 221
Works Cited 226
Analyzing Azar Nafisi's Memoir 226
   Excerpt from *Reading* Lolita *in Tehran* 227
Choosing a Topic for Your Research Writing 243
Works Cited 244

Chapter 6 Revising and Proofing 245

Understanding Style 247

Identifying Jane Austen's Voice 247
   Chapter One of *Pride and Prejudice* 248
Analyzing Austen's Voice 250
Reading a Revised Response to Austen's Novel 252
   Student Essay on Austen: "The Parents' Guilt in *Pride and Prejudice*" 253
Analyzing the Student Essay 255
Revising for Professional Style 256
   Guide to Macro-Issues in Revision 257
   Guide to Micro-Issues in Revision 258
Analyzing Martin Luther King's Style 258
   Paragraph 14 259

Reading More about Parents and Children 262

Journaling on Barack Obama's Memoir 262
   Excerpt from *Dreams from my Father* 264
Journaling on Frank McCourt's Memoir 267
   Excerpt from *Angela's Ashes* 268
Journaling on Sherwood Anderson's Short Story 276
   "The Egg" 277
Journaling on Alice Walker's Essay 284
   "In Search of Our Mothers' Gardens" 285

Writing a Rhetorical Analysis Essay...292

Revising for Micro-Issues..293
   Introduction 293
   Body Paragraphs: Sentence Structure.......................................293
   Body Paragraphs: Diction...294
   Conclusion 294
Checking for Correctness..295
   Subject-Verb Disagreement..295
   Proofreading Solution...296
   Comma Splice 296
   Fragment 297
Works Cited..298

Chapter 7 Writing about Poetry

Chapter 7 Writing about Poetry..299

Learning to Read Poetry...301
Journaling on Edward Hirsch's Advice on Reading Poetry 303
   Excerpt from *How to Read a Poem*..303
Imagining Images: Collaborating on Robert Frost's Poem.............310
   "Birches" 312
Listening for Your Story, Creating Your Own Images....................313
   "The World is Too Much with Us"...314
Analyzing the Figurative Language in Wordsworth's Sonnet...........314
   Personal Response: Student's Narration 315
   Personal Response: Student's Poem..316
Listening for the Song..317
   "That Time of Year"...317
Analyzing Sound Effects and Imagery in Wilfred Owen's War Poem.......320
   "Dulce et Decorum Est"..320
Prewriting for an Essay on Poetry..322
Reading a Critical Response to Ferlinghetti's Poem.........................323
   "In Goya's Greatest Scenes"..324
   Excerpt from Student Essay on "In Goya's Greatest Scenes" 325

Writing on Poetry..326
Journaling on Elizabeth Bishop's Poem...326
   "The Fish"...326
Journaling on Seamus Heaney's Poem...328
   "Digging"..329
Choosing a Topic for Your Essay on Poetry 330
Works Cited..330

Chapter 8 Growing As a Writer: Portfolios and Reflective Writing 333

Practicing Reflective Vision 335
Journaling on Kevin Brockmeiers Essay 336
    "A Kind of Mystery" 337

Creating a Portfolio 343
Selecting Materials for Your Portfolio 343
Writing about Your Writing 344
Workshopping on Reflective Writing and Portfolio Organization 345
Rubric for Rating Portfolios 347
Reading Samples of Reflective Writing 348
Suggestions for Reflective Writing 350
Answering Eight Key Reflective Questions 350
Writing about Anne Lamott's Essay 351
    Excerpt from "The Moral Point of View" 351
Works Cited 354

Glossary 355

CHAPTER 1

Finding the Right Questions:
Critical Reading and the Importance
of Telling Our Own Stories

"What we're learning in our schools is not the wisdom of life. We're learning technologies, we're getting information….Read myths…to put your mind in touch with this experience of being alive. It tells you what the experience is."

JOSEPH CAMPBELL, *The Power of Myth*

"The greatest part of a writer's time is spent in reading, in order to write: a man will turn over half a library to make one book."

DR. SAMUEL JOHNSON, from James Boswell's *Life of Johnson*

"Tell the truth as you understand it. If you're a writer, you have a moral obligation to do this. And it is a revolutionary act—truth is always subversive."

ANNE LAMOTT, *Bird by Bird*

"Once upon a time"...
Asking Questions, Telling Stories

Y ou have probably come to college expecting to expand your knowledge of technologies, knowledge that will help you land a good job and keep you moving apace down the information super hi-way. Because this electronic hi-way runs through the center of our twenty-first century lives—think of your cell phone, your iPod, your laptop, your blog, your Googling, your shopping on eBay—your course work will certainly encourage you to expand your participation in the digital revolution as you master that information and answer professors' questions.

But mythologist Joseph Campbell, quoted above, suggests that you should demand more from college, more than learning to use technology to answer other people's questions. You should also expect to learn how to shape and answer your own questions; you should, therefore, expect to "read myths" and to write stories, the best ways, Campbell says, "to put your mind in touch with the experience of being alive," the best way to wrestle with all the questions raised by your new "experience."

You will experience such purposeful writing at the end of this chapter, as you respond to readings from Frederick Douglass, Esmeralda Santiago, Maxine Hong Kingston, and Maya Angelou, story-tellers who have much to say about our longing for liberty and the importance of sharing our words. Because these writers convey their meanings on these topics through **narration**, story-telling, your first assignment, following the readings, will call for your narrative essay.

When you write your narrative, you will meet an ancient need which, as Joseph Campbell reminds us, has always distinguished our species from other animals: the need to make sense of our lives. We tell stories to frame questions about our origin and destination, about what to do with our time, about how to build and sustain relationships, about how to feed our bellies and our souls. Typically, our stories, whether fictional or non-fictional, provide no simple answers to these questions; instead, the stories create vivid, sometimes unforgettable images—Frederick Douglass' Aunt Hester, strung up and whipped to a bloody pulp by her master for the crime of falling in love; Maxine Hong Kingston as a girl, desperate to wring language from her silent friend—moving pictures of our struggle, our defeats, and our triumphs as we live with questions that have no final answers. Still, we feel compelled to ask our questions. For just this reason, approximately 2,400 years ago, Plato's Socrates urged his friend Meno to devote his life to asking questions. Doing so, Socrates assured Meno, would help him to look behind his unexamined opinions, where he would learn what he does not know; he would also recollect what he does know, the sum of human experience written in our stories and in our souls (69).

Over two hundred years after Plato, as the Roman scholar Cicero taught his students how to speak persuasively, he also taught them to "read the poets," the story-tellers, whose vivid tales, properly woven into their speeches, would help his students to speak persuasively, whether praising a patriot, advising the senators, or defending a client (221). Following his master Cicero, the great teacher Quintilian insisted that his students read "in all the arts," for no speaker or writer can persuade without command of the great stories (333).

This ancient need to read and tell stories, of course, continues to define our modern and postmodern humanity. Quite literally, we cannot live without our stories. Examples? When the nineteenth-century philosopher John Stuart Mill suffered an emotional breakdown, he found his cure in poetry, especially the poetry of William Wordsworth, where he read stories of our common humanity, the imaginative glue that holds us together as we progress through life (103). When the twentieth-century novelist Aleksandr Solzhenitsyn escaped the Communist work camps, he felt compelled to tell his story of Stalinist brutality and oppression, *The Gulag Archipelago* (48–49). When poet Maya Angelou felt the same compulsion to write her story of growing up in rural Arkansas in the Depression era, she knew that a 'caged bird singing' would sustain her readers in the knowledge that "in the struggle lies the joy" (228). When William Faulkner accepted the Nobel Prize for literature in 1949, he urged young writers to tell stories of "the human heart in conflict with itself," the only kind of story "worth telling," the only kind that portrays honestly the agony of living but, at the same time, uplifts us with images of our capacities for intelligence, "compassion, and sacrifice," qualities which ensure that we will "not only endure" but also "prevail." Sharing Faulkner's convictions, Joseph Campbell (see epigraph above) urged us to read old narratives and write new ones so that we might "learn to get back into accord with the wisdom of nature and realize again our brotherhood with the animals and with the water and the sea" (31). Feeling that kinship, when contemporary poet Seamus Heaney contemplated his life's work, he recalled images of his grandfather digging peat for fuel, then of his father cultivating his garden; Heaney then took up his pen—and resolved to "dig with it" (516).

Using Burke's Pentad to Ask Questions about Narrative

Before you read the first narrative, printed below, consider Kenneth Burke's "pentad" theory. As you will see in chapter two, Burke's theory will help you write your rough drafts, but it also provides a powerful tool to guide your critical reading of any narrative, non-fiction or fiction. Basing his theory on the dramatic conflict at the heart of all narratives, Burke gave us a way to read with an eye toward human motivation and the consequences of choices made by those in conflict—with themselves or with others. Specifically, Burke gave us these five questions ("pentad" comes from the Greek word "penta," five) to ask in order to comprehend and interpret any narrative:

1. **Action:** What happened?

2. **Agent:** Who committed the action?

3. **Scene:** Where did the action take place?

4. **Agency:** How was the action performed?

5. **Purpose:** What motivated the action?

If you record your answers to these five questions in your journal (more about journaling below), you will have prepared for class discussion; you will have also taken your first step toward writing a narrative in response to Douglass' story.

Applying Burke's Pentad to Frederick Douglass' Autobiography

With the resolution expressed by Heaney above, Frederick Douglass taught himself to read and write, knowing that literacy would prove him a man, not three-fifths of a human being, the U. S. government's definition of a slave. That determination generated his *Narrative of the Life of Frederick Douglass, an American Slave*; it also led to a distinguished career as lecturer and abolitionist.

Excerpt from *Narrative of the Life of Frederick Douglass, an American Slave*

I lived in Master Hugh's family about seven years. During this time, I succeeded in learning to read and write. In accomplishing this, I was compelled to resort to various stratagems. I had no regular teacher. My mistress, who had kindly commenced to instruct me, had, in compliance with the advice and direction of her husband, not only ceased to instruct, but had set her face against my being instructed by any one else. It is due, however, to my mistress to say of her, that she did not adopt this course of treatment immediately. She at first lacked the depravity indispensable to shutting me up in mental darkness. It was at least necessary for her to have some training in the exercise of irresponsible power, to make her equal to the task of treating me as though I were a brute.

My mistress was, as I have said, a kind and tender-hearted woman; and in the simplicity of her soul she commenced, when I first went to live with her, to treat me as she supposed one human being ought to treat another. In entering upon the duties of a slaveholder, she did not seem to perceive that I sustained to her the relation of a mere chattel, and that for her to treat me as a human being was not only wrong, but dangerously so. Slavery proved as injurious to her as it did to me. When I went there, she was a pious, warm, and tender-hearted woman. There was no sorrow or suffering for which she had not a tear. She had bread for the hungry, clothes for the naked, and comfort for every mourner that came within her reach. Slavery soon proved its ability to divest her of these heavenly qualities. Under its influence, the tender heart became stone, and the lamblike disposition gave way to one of tiger-like fierceness. The first step in her downward course was in her ceasing to instruct me. She now commenced to practice her husband's precepts. She finally became even more violent in her opposition than her husband himself. She was not satisfied with simply doing as well as he had commanded; she seemed anxious to do better. Nothing seemed to make her more angry than to see me with a newspaper. She seemed to think that here lay the danger. I have had her rush at me with a face made all up of fury, and snatch from me a newspaper, in a manner that fully revealed her apprehension. She was an apt woman; and a little experience soon demonstrated, to her satisfaction, that education and slavery were incompatible with each other.

From this time I was most narrowly watched. If I was in a separate room any 3 considerable length of time, I was sure to be suspected of having a book, and was at once called to give an account of myself. All this, however, was too late. The first step had been taken. Mistress, in teaching me the alphabet, had given me the *inch*, and no precaution could prevent me from taking the *ell*.

The plan which I adopted, and the one by which I was most successful, was that of 4 making friends of all the little white boys whom I met in the street. As many of these as I could, I converted into teachers. With their kindly aid, obtained at different times in different places, I finally succeeded in learning to read. When I was sent on errands, I always took my book with me, and by doing one part of my errand quickly, I found time to get a lesson before my return. I used also to carry bread with me, enough of which was always in the house, and to which I was always welcome; for I was much better off in this regard than many of the poor white children in our neighborhood. This bread I used to bestow upon the hungry little urchins, who, in return, would give me that more valuable bread of knowledge. I am strongly tempted to give the names of two or three of those little boys, as a testimonial of the gratitude and affection I bear them; but prudence forbids; —not that it would injure me, but it might embarrass them; for it is almost an unpardonable offence to teach slaves to read in this Christian country. It is enough to say of the dear little fellows, that they lived on Philpot Street, very near Durgin and Bailey's ship-yard. I used to talk this matter of slavery over with them. I would sometimes say to them, I wished I could be as free as they would be when they got to be men. "You will be free as soon as you are twenty-one, *but I am a slave for life!* Have not I as good a right to be free as you have?" These words used to trouble them; they would express for me the liveliest sympathy, and console me with the hope that something would occur by which I might be free.

I was now about twelve years old, and the thought of being a *slave for life* began 5 to bear heavily upon my heart. Just about this time, I got hold of a book entitled "The Columbian Orator." Every opportunity I got, I used to read this book. Among much of other interesting matter, I found in it a dialogue between a master and his slave. The slave was represented as having run away from his master three times. The dialogue represented the conversation which took place between them, when the slave was retaken the third time. In this dialogue, the whole argument in behalf of slavery was brought forward by the master, all of which was disposed of by the slave. The slave was made to say some very smart as well as impressive things in reply to his master—things which had the desired though unexpected effect; for the conversation resulted in the voluntary emancipation of the slave on the part of the master.

In the same book, I met with one of Sheridan's mighty speeches on and in behalf of Catholic emancipation. These were choice documents to me. I read them over and over again with unabated interest. They gave tongue to interesting thoughts of my own soul, which had frequently flashed through my mind, and died away for want of utterance. The moral which I gained from the dialogue was the power of truth over the conscience of even a slaveholder. What I got from Sheridan was a bold denunciation of slavery, and a powerful vindication of human rights. The reading of these documents enabled me to utter my thoughts and to meet the arguments brought forward to sustain slavery; but while they relieved me of one difficulty, they brought on another even more painful than the one of which I was relieved. The more I read, the more I was led to abhor and detest my enslavers. I could regard them in no other light than a band of successful robbers, who had left their homes, and gone to Africa, and stolen us from our homes, and in a strange land reduced us to slavery. I loathed them as being the meanest as well as the most wicked of men. As I read and contemplated the subject, behold! That very discontentment which Master Hugh had predicted would follow my learning to read had already come, to torment and sting my soul to unutterable anguish. As I writhed under it, I would at times feel that learning to read had been a curse rather than a blessing. It had given me a view of my wretched condition, without the remedy. It opened my eyes to the horrible pit, but to no ladder upon which to get out. In moments of agony, I envied my fellow-slaves for their stupidity. I have often wished myself a beast. I preferred the condition of the meanest reptile to my own. Any thing, no matter what, to get rid of thinking! It was this everlasting thinking of my condition that tormented me. There was no getting rid of it. It was pressed upon me by every object within sight or hearing, animate or inanimate. The silver trump of freedom had roused my soul to eternal wakefulness. Freedom now appeared, to disappear no more forever. It was heard in every sound, and seen in every thing. It was ever present to torment me with a sense of my wretched condition. I saw nothing without seeing it, I heard nothing without hearing it, and felt nothing without feeling it. It looked from every star, it smiled in every calm, breathed in every wind, and moved in every storm. 6

I often found myself regretting my own existence, and wishing myself dead; and but for the hope of being free, I have no doubt but that I should have killed myself, or done something for which I should have been killed. While in this state of mind, I was eager to hear any one speak of slavery. I was a ready listener. Every little while, I could hear something about the abolitionists. It was some time before I found what the word meant. It was always used in such connections as to make it an interesting word to me. If a slave ran away and succeeded in getting clear, or if a slave killed his master, set fire to a barn, or did any thing very wrong in the mind of a slaveholder, it was spoken of as the fruit of *abolition*. Hearing the word in this connection very often, I set about learning what it meant. The dictionary afforded me little or no help. I found it was "the act of abolishing;" but then I did not know what was to be abolished. Here I was perplexed. I did not dare to ask any one about its meaning, for I was satisfied that it was something they wanted me to know very little about. After a patient waiting, I got one of our city papers, containing an account of the number of petitions from 7 the north, praying for the abolition of slavery in the District of Columbia, and of the slave trade between the States. From this time I understood the words *abolition* and *abolitionist*, and always drew near when that word was spoken, expecting to hear something of importance to myself and fellow-slaves. The light broke in upon me by degrees. I went one day down on the wharf of Mr. Waters; and seeing two Irishmen unloading a scow of stone, I went, unasked, and helped them. When we had finished, one of them came to me and asked me if I were a slave. I told him I was. He asked, "Are ye a slave for life?" I told him that I was. The good Irishman seemed to be deeply affected by the statement. He said to the other that it was a pity so fine a little fellow as myself should be a slave for life. He said it was a shame to hold me. They both advised me to run away to the north; that I should find friends there, and that I should be free. I pretended not to be interested in what they said, and treated them as if I did not understand them; for I feared they might be treacherous. White men have been known to encourage slaves to escape, and then, to get the reward, catch them and return them to their masters. I was afraid that these seemingly good men might use me so; but I nevertheless remembered their advice, and from that time I resolved to run away. I looked forward to a time at which it would be safe for me to escape. I was too young to think of doing so immediately; besides, I wished to learn how to write, as I might have occasion to write my own pass. I consoled myself with the hope that I should one day find a good chance. Meanwhile, I would learn to write.

The idea as to how I might learn to write was suggested to me by being in Durgin and Bailey's ship-yard, and frequently seeing the ship carpenters, after hewing, and getting a piece of timber ready for use, write on the timber the name of that part of the ship for which it was intended. When a piece of timber was intended for the larboard side, it would be marked thus—"L." When a piece was for the starboard side, it would be marked thus—"S." A piece for the larboard side forward would be marked thus—"L.F." When a piece was for the starboard side forward, it would be marked thus—"S.F." For larboard aft, it would be marked thus—"L.A." For starboard aft, it would be marked thus—"S.A." I soon learned the names of these letters, and for what they were intended when placed upon a piece of timber in the ship-yard. I immediately commenced copying them, and in a short time was able to make the four letters named. After that, when I met with any boy who I knew could write, I would tell him I could write as well as he. The next word would be, "I don't believe you. Let me see you try it." I would then make the letters which I had been so fortunate as to learn, and ask him to beat that. In this way I got a good many lessons in writing, which it is quite possible I should never have gotten in any other way. During this time, my copy-book was the board fence, brick wall, and pavement; my pen and ink was a lump of chalk. With these, I learned mainly how to write. I then commenced and continued copying the Italics in Webster's Spelling Book, until I could make them all without looking on the book. By this time, my little Master Thomas had gone to school, and learned how to write, and had written over a number of copy-books. These had been brought home, and shown to some of our near neighbors, and then laid aside. My mistress used to go to class meeting at the Wilk Street meetinghouse every Monday afternoon and leave me to take care of the house. When left thus, I used to spend the time in writing in the spaces left in Master Thomas's copy-book, copying what he had written. I continued to do this until I could write a hand very similar to that of Master Thomas. Thus, after a long, tedious effort for years, I finally succeeded in learning how to write.

Journaling on Douglass' Autobiography

Whether compiled electronically, conventionally, or both, your journal will serve as a log (or weblog) of your thoughts as you engage the assigned reading. This record of your thinking will foster your growth as a writer in the following ways:

- **Journaling will help you to internalize what you read**. Simply underlining, starring, or high-lighting key passages in your book as you read will help you to concentrate. But journaling will take you a huge step past mere highlighting, for you will find yourself explaining why a passage seems important, well written, absurd, confusing, or inspiring.

- **Journaling will prepare you for online and in-class discussions of the readings**. You'll find that you look forward to exchanges (instead of fearing or dreading them) because you feel prepared. In turn, the discussions will increase your interest in the course. When you're interested in the material, you do better.

- **Journaling will help you to find personal connections to the material**. Again, if you have discovered a personal stake in the issues at hand, you'll pay more attention and write better papers.

- **Journaling will serve as a vital form of prewriting for your essays**. Granted, journaling takes time, but when you factor in journaling as prewriting, you actually use time more efficiently than does the person who must read everything twice, and then spend hours staring at a blank monitor because he/she has not internalized the material.

Now that you've read Douglass' narrative and answered Burke's five questions, try answering the following questions, too. You'll immediately notice that these questions grow from the pentad: What? Who? Where? How? Why? But these questions will also help you to dig deeper as readers, focusing not only on the conflicts and motivations of young Douglass prior to his run to freedom, but also on the motivations and techniques of Douglass the writer. Once again, record your answers in your journal, precisely where you'll need them as you begin to contemplate your own narrative.

1. What details in the first four paragraphs convey the circumstances under which Douglass learned to read? How do these details shape Douglass' ethos, his credibility as an intelligent human being and as an advocate for liberty?

2. How does Douglass' "plan" for learning to read further develop his ethos? What does he tell you about the contents of the books he secretly read?

3. What image (picture painted with words) does he use to explain why knowing how to read proved to be a "curse"?

4. Great writers often use parallel sentence structure to stress key ideas and to color those ideas with emotional intensity. Dr. Martin Luther King once wrote, for example, that he dreamed of a day when his children would be "judged not by the color of their skin but by the content of their character." Where do you see Douglass using parallel sentence structures to define the "torment" of this curse of literacy?

5. Great writers also use the rhetorical device **of irony** to stress the difference between what we expect in life and what we get. What irony do you see emerging in paragraph seven as Douglass further contemplates the "torment" of his literacy?

6. Why does his decision to run away from slavery—a crime that would lead, were he caught, to a brutal whipping, perhaps even to death—lead to his decision to teach himself to write? What do his strategies for learning to write tell you about his character and his intelligence?

7. How has reading this excerpt from Douglass' narrative affected the way you think about your own ways of reading and writing? How has writing on this reading affected your views on the purposes of developing your literacy?

8. By learning to read and write, then running away, young Douglass breaks many laws. Yet we now celebrate Frederick Douglass—and rightly so—as an American patriot, a great advocate of liberty for all. Do you know any patriots? How can a patriot know when to uphold and defend the law, and when to challenge and resist the law?

Recognizing the Qualities of a Narrative Essay

Having now practiced **critical reading**—that is, reading that analyzes and interprets—you've probably begun to form a clear idea of the qualities that make a narrative essay work as a story. At the simplest level, you have seen that a narrative usually finds its organization in **chronological order**, the order of time. True, some narratives, such as Lawrence Sterne's eighteenth-century novel *Tristram Shandy*, deliberately violate chronology, making the point that, thanks to our abilities to remember the past and anticipate the future, our past and future profoundly color our experience of each present moment.

Still, traditionally, most narratives present a beginning, where we meet characters and learn what situation they face; a middle, where characters make choices to deal with their situation, invariably coming in conflict in the process; and an end, where the conflicts resolve. You saw this chronological structure in the chapter from Douglass' narrative: In the beginning, you learn of Douglass' problem: his master and his once "kind-hearted" mistress determine that young Frederick, a slave, must not achieve literacy. Had Douglass accepted this dehumanizing policy, we would have no conflict and therefore no story. However, even though "nothing seemed to make [his mistress] more angry than to see [Douglass] with a newspaper," he decides to resist their policy with a secret plan to learn reading, then writing. Notice, too, that before he launches into the middle, the story of his "plan," he offers a thesis about slavery: "Slavery proved as injurious to her as it did to me." In fictional narratives—short stories and novels—you will rarely see a thesis statement; instead, the key idea will be implied. But narrative essays, like all other essays, usually do explicitly state a point, a claim—a thesis.

Having stated his thesis about the dehumanizing effect of slavery on owners as well as on slaves, Douglass moves into the middle of his story, where he relates chronologically the steps in his plan: using bread to bribe white "urchins" to teach him words whenever he went out on errands; reading *The Columbian Orator*, then "Sheridan's mighty speeches on and in behalf of Catholic emancipation"; learning to write at the shipyard by copying letters that carpenters wrote on timbers. Notice, too, that this three-part plan provides an outline of the story, but Douglass puts meat on these chronological bones by using dialogue so that his readers can hear his simmering outrage as he coaxes other boys to help him toward literacy: "You will be free as soon as you are twenty-one, but I am a slave for life." He also uses description so that his readers can understand his feelings—"The more I read, the more I was led to abhor and detest my enslavers"—and see his cleverness in learning to read from the carpenter's etchings on lumber: "For larboard aft, it would be marked thus—'L.A.' For starboard aft, it would be marked thus—'S.A.' I soon learned the names of these letters, and for what they were intended when placed upon a piece of timber in the ship-yard."

Additionally, Douglass breathes more life into his narrative with **figurative language**— the language of comparison—and with parallel sentence rhythms. For instance, when Douglass wants his readers to understand the ironic misery of learning to read without any prospect of freedom, he compares slavery to a "horrible pit" and literacy to a "ladder" that will not free him from the pit until he dares to run to the North:

> Learning to read had been a curse rather than a blessing. It had given me a
> view of my wretched condition, without a remedy. It opened my eyes to the
> *horrible pit,* but to no *ladder* upon which to get out.

With the same emotional intensity, Douglass uses parallel sentence structure to help readers hear the anguish of seeing freedom just beyond his reach:

> I saw *nothing* without seeing it [freedom], I heard *nothing* without hearing it,
> and felt *nothing* without feeling it. It looked from every star, it smiled in every
> calm, breathed in every wind, and moved in every storm.

Note that the repetition of "nothing" begins his chant of despair over the elusive liberty that he "saw" and "heard" everywhere, and then the parallel verbs (looked, smiled, breathed, moved) help us to hear the torment of living with freedom all about—"in every calm…in every wind…in every storm"—but forever out of reach.

A strong narrative essay, then, will have these characteristics:

- Chronological Order, including a beginning, which identifies the people and the problems they face; a middle, which develops the conflicts between and among the people wrestling with their common problems; and ending, which resolves the conflicts.

- A **thesis**, which states a conclusion drawn from the resolved conflicts. In a narrative essay, the thesis may be stated at the end of the introduction (the beginning) or at the end of the essay (in a concluding paragraph).

- Vivid description and occasionally **dialogue** so that readers can *see* and *hear* the "characters" in conflict.

- Figurative language and parallel sentence structures to add emotional intensity to the narrator's voice.

With this list of narrative characteristics in mind, read the student essay printed below, a narrative response to question #8 above. After you have read this sample narrative, we will review the prewriting processes that led to a rough draft, then to this revised narrative. Finally, you'll get to try your own hand at writing a personal narrative essay in response to Douglass' narrative.

Student Essay: "Fighting for America"

CHARLES GRANGER

Patriotism is the love of one's country, a fervent belief in the underlying ideals of the government that controls it and the society it governs. It can then be inferred that patriotism is the art of changing your mind. How else can one honor the founding fathers who wrote that "all men are created equal," and then passed the three-fifths compromise, defining slaves as less than human? How else can one uphold the integrity of the Supreme Court that handed down both the enslaving decision on *Dred Scott* and the liberating ruling on *Brown vs. the Board of Education*? In a country that has and is constantly reevaluating its positions on what is right and proper, a country that is today apologizing for the unquestioned necessities of yesterday, staying "patriotic" appears to be nothing more than simple agreement with the government, just nodding "yes" or "no" when prodded. But patriotism doesn't have to be agreement; the dissenters of every decision in US history had good reason and good intentions behind their protests. Might doesn't always make right—the change from what was to what is acceptable is often, if not always, wrought from the outside, from those dissatisfied with the government's decisions. Unpatriotic, one might call them. Patriotism, then, is the act of looking beyond the current and the political to find the true meaning and integrity of a country, and working towards it, precisely what Frederick Douglass did from the moment, armed with literacy, he decided to run for his freedom. To be an American patriot is to say that democracy must be defended.

It is interesting to note that the concept of patriotism is almost synonymous with war. "Give me liberty or give me death," Patrick Henry said, unknowingly setting the standard by which all patriotism would be judged. Take the 2004 presidential election, for example. George W. Bush, Kerry supporters claimed, is not a true patriot because he never fought in a war *and* missed some of his National Guard service. John Kerry, Bush supporters retorted, is not a true patriot because he did not fully support the war in Iraq *and* threw away his medals from Vietnam. Kerry's service in Vietnam, a war which ended over thirty years ago, received as much airtime as his position on the current Iraq war, and certainly more than his views on other issues.

From this perspective on patriotism, I belong to a patriotic family: My grandfather on my mother's side, Virgil Baylis, enlisted in the Marines at 22. Following rudimentary training, he was shipped off to fight the Nazis. His service occurred toward the end of the war in Europe, so he was shipped directly to the Franco-German border and worked his way in, all the way to Berlin. He lived there, following the war's conclusion, for three years on a military base with his wife, where she gave birth to three daughters. Preceding these events he was shipped to Japan, where he island-hopped for two months. He told me the names of the islands he visited once, but I was young and can't remember them, and now neither can he. He received a Purple Heart for a wound, shrapnel in the shoulder.

My father, Tommy Wimberley, was drafted at 19 and sent to Vietnam. He considered running, but his family was poor and Canada is far from Jackson, Mississippi. He doesn't know the names of the places he marched through; once he told me that he wasn't sure if even the commanders knew where they were some of the time. He stayed for about a year, and was sent home with an injury, for which he also received a Purple Heart.

My grandfather knew the reasons his country was at war: we had been attacked, Pearl Harbor; Nazis were invading Europe and threatening our allies, threatening us. So he signed up and shipped out and marched, marched through burned-out fields and bombed buildings, the remnants of cities. He lay in trenches with hundreds of other men in the mud and rain; he felt the dust and the rumble of exploding bombs, and heard the zip of bullets over his head. And later he stormed islands and shot and stabbed Japanese civilians fighting with bamboo spears and with tooth and nail, shot them because they wouldn't surrender. My grandfather hated Nazis, hated what they stood for, and is today not fond of Germany, but he always respected the Japanese. On the few occasions I have heard him speak of the war; he always commends the Japanese fighters, even the kamikaze pilots riding missiles and ramming their jets into boats. Bravery, he called it, patriotism. "They knew what their situation was and stood strong in defense of their country, even when they knew they couldn't win. Like the Alamo," he said.

My father knew why we were going to Vietnam: the French. It wasn't about communism, not at the beginning—that was just a convenient justifier. It was the

French, and Vietnam belonged to them, and so when it revolted and they couldn't handle it, we stepped in, because that's what had to be done to keep the powerful in power. And so for the French my father waded through jungles and rice patties and bogs up to his shoulders, carrying his rifle over his head. For imperialism he saw men trigger land mines and explode and smelled napalm burning trees and houses. For the government, for political credibility, he saw men (and maybe himself) do horrible things, things he won't speak about but, when I ask about the realism of some movie set there, will say, "It was worse." And we lost, but he kept his medal.

My grandfather has never wavered in his convictions about the war; his black and white view has been largely unchallenged. When he finally arrived back home, he was a hero, a member of the greatest generation. He got his job and his house in the country and the support and thanks of the world.

My father came back from Vietnam despised; he was called "baby killer" and spit and jeered at; he watched the country dismiss and disown what he'd done. Not that he'd cared—he didn't want to go over there anyway, he was forced into it, so he began to protest with the rest of the college-age kids. He still speaks of it with contempt. On a trip to Washington DC two years ago, we visited the Vietnam Memorial. He showed me the name of a friend who'd died; there was anger in his voice. That was the last of his touring there.

Patriotism is fighting for the good of your country, but what kind of country would ask its men, its boys, to go and kill and die for it? In World War II the enemy was real; in Vietnam the enemy was unnecessary; today in Iraq we're divided. Some say that the threat is real and they signed up and went to war, or stayed home and lobbied for it and worked to support it. Others argue that Iraq is the new Vietnam, and they protest and march against it. Who, then, is more of a patriot, the defector fighting for withdrawal or the men like my father, fighting and dying for their country, yes, but not for what they believe in?

I think—I hope—that it can be both, because patriotism is such a fickle idea, and who knows who will be seen as patriotic in twenty years? If the American Revolution failed, wouldn't the Loyalists have been seen as patriotic? If my grandfather can find patriotism, not fanaticism, in Japanese kamikazes, maybe both protestors and soldiers are right. Love of country, like any type of love, has many means of expression. Sometimes it means signing up, sometimes backing down, but always with the idea of the country's intentions at heart. My father hated Vietnam not because of the fighting but because of why he was sent. Many protestors feel that way today about the US's reasons for being in the Middle East. Their quarrel isn't with America but with its government's reasons for invasion. Others, like my grandfather, view the war as noble and necessary and perfectly justified. Sadaam was evil and dangerous; he had to go, they say. Only time will tell who's right. Until then, to both sides: keep fighting.

Mastering the Process of Critical Reading and Writing

No doubt, you readily discovered the student writer's purpose, to challenge conventional definitions of patriotism, and his equally strong sense of audience beyond the teacher, his desire to be understood. You heard this purposefulness in his introduction, where he challenges readers with thought-provoking definitions: "patriotism is the art of changing your mind…the act of looking beyond the current and the political to find the true meaning and integrity of a country." But you also found the student's purposefulness in his body paragraphs, where he shows his readers not just what his grandfather and father had to endure for love of country—fighting from mud-filled trenches, wading through jungle bogs, watching mines blow up friends—but also where he describes the capacity of both patriots to change their minds, to honor patriotism in the enemy, to protest hypocrisy in the government.

But where did this student find the passion you heard throughout his paper? What made the writing of the essay much more than completing an assignment to write a narrative essay on patriotism? What made him want to read his paper aloud before all his peers? The answer to these questions, as suggested above, lies in a process of critical reading and writing that preceded the writing of the essay, a process that allowed the student to own the topic and to care about being understood. Let's look at his process now so that you can apply it, master it. Doing so, you will find, will transform you from a student taking a composition course into a writer.

First, this student learned the truth of the quote from Samuel Johnson above: writers must be readers. While he did not have to "turn over half a library" to find information on patriotism, you can tell from his **allusions**—his literary and historical references— that he has read widely on the subject of liberty. In addition to his reading of Douglass' *Narrative*, he shares his reading of American history, stressing the documents (Declaration of Independence), the court cases (*Dred Scott, Brown v. the Board of Education*), the wars (WWII, Vietnam, Iraq), and the presidential elections (1968, 2004) which have shaped our thinking on patriotism.

Second, this student drew from his memory of his grandfather's and father's words about their wars, stories shared in bits and pieces over the years. As you will see directly below, he gathered these memories through the **freewriting** process, a process that also led to interviewing.

Third, this student and his classmates used their journals to explore the reading on Douglass and to find their personal connections to Douglass' narrative. As noted above, the essay on patriotism grew directly from the student's journaling on question #8. He also posted his response to #8 on the Discussion board found on the WebCT homepage for the class; others posted on the same patriotic topic; still others posted on #7, the question about one's own acquisition of literacy. If your class has no WebCT or Blackboard site, you can achieve the same objective—communal journaling—by posting your comments on your personal blog, inviting your classmates to read and respond.

Following this electronic discussion, our student and his classmates undertook a **freewriting** exercise. Such writing follows no rules and totally ignores "correctness" issues like spelling, punctuation, and pronoun usage. Instead, the readers "freely" respond to a focused prompt, writing furiously, non-stop, for 10 minutes to learn, in this case, what they already knew, believed, and felt about "patriots." More specifically, the students freewrote on the following prompts:

- List 5–10 people and historical events that come immediately to mind when you hear the word "patriot" or "patriotism"—one minute.

- Pick one of the persons or events and freewrite for two minutes on the patriot's appearance.

- Freewrite for seven minutes on what the patriot did and said that qualifies as patriotism.

Having finished their freewriting, the students rested their weary hands, happily marveling over how much they had written in just ten minutes. Next, they shared their results. Some did so eagerly, others seemed apologetic about the lack of polish to such rule-less freewriting, but all read about patriotic people and events, such as grandfathers fighting in German trenches and on Japanese islands, and fathers wading through the horror of Vietnam.

After this exchange among members of this writing community, our student writer and his peers took home additional prewriting assignments. First, they completed two additional ten-minute freewrites, focusing on other patriots from their initial list. This process increased the probability that they would write on patriots they knew the best, cared about the most. Next, they constructed **tree outlines**, showing the patriots they would describe and, as sub-branches, the sequence of events—the stories—that would bring to life each student's definition of patriotism. Our student author's tree outline below features the two primary branches, his grandfather and his father, then the sub-branches that collectively tell their patriotic stories.

For the student writer featured above, this freewriting led to another step. Knowing that memory can be selective, that we sometimes misunderstand, misremember, he interviewed his father and grandfather, asking his own questions, not just to complete an assignment, but also to preserve the record of his beloved patriots, to clarify his own thinking on the sometimes conflicting duties of patriots, the duty to serve, the duty to protest or disobey. These intellectual and emotional needs generated predictable but urgent questions:

- Where did you serve? Why did you serve?

- What did you have to do?

- What did you see?

- How did you service affect your view of the enemy, your view of your country, your view of yourself?

- How were you received when you returned? How did that reception confirm or alter your feelings about your country and about your service?

Patriots Searching for the Meaning of One's Country

Figure: Tree Outlining

In completing this outline before he attempted a rough draft, our writer could see at a glance that his narrative essay would, like most stories, move chronologically—getting drafted, then going to Vietnam, then coming back to criticism instead of praise—yet he could also see that his narrative essay would also be an **expository essay**, one that explains to readers the ambiguity of the word patriotism, comparing the heroism of each soldier, yet contrasting their views of their respective wars—the justice, the injustice—and the hero's welcome for his grandfather versus the anti-hero's welcome for his father. See chapter two for further discussion of exposition and its relation to narration.

Having completed this critical reading, journaling, discussing, freewriting, and outlining, the writer and his classmates proceeded with a rough draft of their essays on patriotism. With the draft completed, they then met in writing groups of three to respond to each other's drafts. As you will see below in Guidelines for Responding to Draft of Narrative Essay, this process began with each author reading the draft aloud, then responders stating where they found the draft engaging and persuasive, and, conversely, where they felt confused or unconvinced. Notice, too, that this process calls for *written comments* as well as discussion, so that each student writer could leave the session with written praise to enjoy and written suggestions to consider before revising the draft and submitting it.

Guidelines for Responding to Draft of Narrative Essay

Name of Author:

Names of Readers:

Procedure:

1. The first reader should distribute a copy of the draft to each responder and proceed to read the draft aloud.

2. Responders should then comment on the draft (using the questions below as a guide) and write a brief comment in response to the questions under "Overall." That comment might also address this question: What audience—other than our writing community—might like to read this narrative, and how might that audience affect the writer's word choice and depth/range of examples?

3. Repeat 1–3 for each member of the group.

Introduction

1. Does the introductory paragraph quote other writers on patriotism to give a social context to the essay?

2. Does the student use various methods of defining—synonyms, etymology, negation— to set up for the story?

3. Does the introduction state a thesis (definition) and forecast the organization of the paper?

Body Paragraphs

1. Does each body paragraph begin with a transition (from the previous paragraph) and a topic sentence which ties into the thesis, identifying one of the qualities or characteristics of a patriot?

2. Does each topic sentence receive support from narrated examples and vivid description?

3. Do you find examples of figurative language and parallel sentence structures that add emotional intensity to the story?

Conclusion

1. Does the essay end with a fresh re-statement of the thesis, a summary of key points about patriotism?

2. Does the student/writer sound like she or he means what she or he says (voice)?

Overall

What is the greatest strength of the draft? The greatest weakness? How would you recommend improving the paper?

Writing Your Own Narrative Essay

You should be ready now to try your own hand at writing an essay like the one on patriotism, but you need a place to start. To find that starting point, re-read the selection from Douglass, and then try the three readings below. Each will invite you into a rich conversation, one that began before the founding of our republic. This historic conversation focuses on the intimate connections between our growth as users of language and our growth as human beings. The first selection comes from Esmeralda Santiago's autobiography, *When I Was Puerto Rican*; the second comes from Maxine Hong Kingston's memoir, *The Woman Warrior*; the third, from Maya Angelou's autobiography, *I Know Why the Caged Bird Sings*.

By trying the reading and pre-writing strategies described below, you will find in each of these selections a purposeful writer with a keen sense of audience, readers who need to see and hear the anguish and joy of acquiring language in a culture that demands the narrator's silence. You will also find your own message, your own purpose, your own sense of readers who need to hear your story.

Before each of the readings below, you'll find some brief remarks on the context of each reading, as well as journaling suggestions. As mentioned above, such journaling prompts will help you to internalize the reading; they will also help you to find a limited topic, one you actually want to explore. Also, after these three sections you will find suggestions for writing in response to all four selections.

Journaling on Esmeralda Santiago's Autobiography

The first selection above dramatized how the acquisition of literacy persuaded Frederick Douglass to run for his life, to run for liberty. Santiago's autobiography, *When I Was Puerto Rican*, recounts another odyssey, beginning in rural Puerto Rico, moving to the barrios of New York and Brooklyn, then ending on the commencement stage of Harvard University, where Santiago received the college degree which—as an immigrant and a woman—no one expected her to earn. Our excerpt, titled "A Shot at It," tells the story of fourteen-year-old Esmeralda auditioning for a position at an exclusive high school for the performing arts. Though well-rehearsed and patiently coached by her teachers, Esmeralda yields to her panic before her Anglo judges, delivering her three-minute monologue in "one minute flat," all in Spanglish, not in the formal English she had memorized. Though the chapter ends with Santiago acknowledging that she "failed the audition," we learn in the "Epilogue: One of these Days," that she won admission to this school for arts, the place that opened the door to Harvard and her life as a writer.

As you read Santiago's reflections on this turning point in her life, answer the following questions in your journal. Your answers will also prepare you to write an essay that will allow you to join in this conversation on the importance of self-expression and taking risks:

1. To ensure that you have a firm grip on the story, write two or three sentences answering each of Burke's pentad questions.

2. Though Santiago admits that she "couldn't speak English very well," she also mentions that as a ninth-grader she "read and wrote at the tenth-grade level." Do these literacy skills serve her well in her preparations for the audition? Explain.

3. Esmeralda tells her guidance counselor, Mr. Barone, that she does not want "to teach." Still, Mr. Barone, her English teacher Mr. Gatti, and her judges at the audition recognize her gift for language and her potential to achieve her dreams and to escape the barrio. Describe specifically how these two teachers help her. What qualities, other than her gift for language, do these adults perceive in her? What does this story imply about the role of teachers outside of the classroom?

4. Study closely the descriptions of Mr. Barone and the three judges at the audition. What details help us to see these people? Why does Santiago want us to see them so clearly?

5. Describe the mixed emotions of Mami as she contemplates her daughter "leaving the neighborhood." What insight to the experience of immigrant parents does this story provide?

6. Though this autobiography ends with Santiago's graduation from Harvard, most of this 270-page book focuses on her family and the life she left behind. What do you infer from this fact about the feelings of immigrants who achieve 'the American Dream'?

Excerpt from *When I was Puerto Rican*, "A Shot at It"

Esmeralda Santiago

Te conozco bacalao, aunque vengas disfrazao.
I recognize you salted codfish, even if you're in disguise.

While Francisco was still alive, we had moved to Ellery Street. That meant I had to change schools, so Mami walked me to P.S. 33, where I would attend ninth grade. The first week I was there I was given a series of tests that showed that even though I couldn't speak English very well, I read and wrote it at the tenth-grade level. So they put me in 9-3, with the smart kids.

One morning, Mr. Barone, a guidance counselor, called me to his office. He was short, with a big head and large hazel eyes under shapely eyebrows. His nose was long and round at the tip. He dressed in browns and yellows and often perched his tortoiseshell glasses on his forehead, as if he had another set of eyes up there.   2

"So," he pushed his glasses up, "what do you want to be when you grow up?"   3

"I don't know."   4

He shuffled through some papers. "Let's see here...you're fourteen, is that right?"   5

"Yes, sir."   6

"And you've never thought about what you want to be?"   7

When I was very young, I wanted to be a *jíbara*. When I was older, I wanted to be a cartographer, then a topographer. But since we'd come to Brooklyn, I'd not thought about the future much.   8

"No, sir."   9

He pulled his glasses down to where they belonged and shuffled through the papers again.   10

"Do you have any hobbies?" I didn't know what he meant. "Hobbies, hobbies," he flailed his hands, as if he were juggling, "things you like to do after school."   11

"Ah, yes." I tried to imagine what I did at home that might qualify as a hobby. "I like to read."   12

He seemed disappointed. "Yes, we know that about you." He pulled out a paper and stared at it. "One of the tests we gave you was an aptitude test. It tells us what kinds of things you might be good at. The tests show that you would be good at helping people. Do you like to help people?"   13

I was afraid to contradict the tests. "Yes, sir."   14

"There's a high school we can send you where you can study biology and chemistry which will prepare you for a career in nursing."   15

I screwed up my face. He consulted the papers again.   16

"You would also do well in communications. Teaching maybe."   17

I remembered Miss Brown standing in front of a classroom full of rowdy teenagers, some of them taller than she was.   18

"I don't like to teach."   19

Mr. Barone pushed his glasses up again and leaned over the stack of papers on his desk. "Why don't you think about it and get back to me," he said, closing the folder   20 with my name across the top. He put his hand flat on it, as if squeezing something out. "You're a smart girl, Esmeralda. Let's try to get you into an academic school so that you can have a shot at college."

On the way home, I walked with another new ninth grader, Yolanda. She had been in New York for three years but knew as little English as I did. We spoke in Spanglish, a combination of English and Spanish in which we hopped from one language to the other depending on which word came first. 21

"*Te preguntó el* Mr. Barone, you know, *lo que querías hacer* when you grow up?" I asked. 22

"*Sí, pero,* I didn't know. *¿Y tú?*" 23

"*Yo tampoco.* He said, *que* I like to help people. *Pero,* you know, *a mí no me gusta mucho la gente.*" When she heard me say I didn't like people much, Yolanda looked at me from the corner of her eye, waiting to become the exception. 24

By the time I said it, she had dashed up the stairs of her building. She didn't wave as she ducked in, and the next day she wasn't friendly. I walked around the rest of the day in embarrassed isolation, knowing that somehow I had given myself away to the only friend I'd made at Junior High School 33. I had to either take back my words or live with the consequences of stating what was becoming the truth. I'd never said that to anyone, not even to myself. It was an added weight, but I wasn't about to trade it for companionship. 25

A few days later, Mr. Barone called me back to his office. 26

"Well?" Tiny green flecks burned around the black pupils of his hazel eyes. 27

The night before, Mami had called us into the living room. On the television "fifty of America's most beautiful girls" paraded in ruffled tulle dresses before a tinsel waterfall. 28

"Aren't they lovely?" Mami murmured, as the girls, escorted by boys in uniform, floated by the camera, twirled, and disappeared behind a screen to the strains of a waltz and an announcer's dramatic voice calling their names, ages, and states. Mami sat mesmerized through the whole pageant. 29

"I'd like to be a model," I said to Mr. Barone. 30

He stared at me, pulled his glasses down from his forehead, looked at the papers inside the folder with my name on it, and glared. "A model?" His voice was gruff, as if he were more comfortable yelling at people than talking to them. 31

"I want to be on television." 32

"Oh, then you want to be an actress," in a tone that said this was only a slight improvement over my first career choice. We stared at one another for a few seconds. He pushed his glasses up to his forehead again and reached for a book on the shelf in back of him. "I only know of one school that trains actresses, but we've never sent them a student from here." 33

Performing Arts, the write-up said, was an academic, as opposed to a vocational, public school that trained students wishing to pursue a career in theater, music, and dance.

34

"It says here that you have to audition." He stood up and held the book closer to the faint gray light coming through the narrow window high on his wall. "Have you ever performed in front of an audience?"

35

"I was announcer in my school show in Puerto Rico," I said. "And I recite poetry. There, not here."

36

He closed the book and held it against his chest. His right index finger thumped a rhythm on his lower lip. "Let me call them and find out exactly what you need to do. Then we can talk some more."

37

I left his office strangely happy, confident that something good had just happened, not knowing exactly what.

38

"I'm not afraid...I'm not afraid...I'm not afraid." Every day I walked home from school repeating those words. The broad streets and sidewalks that had impressed me so on the first day we had arrived had become as familiar as the dirt road from Macún to the highway. Only my curiosity about the people who lived behind these walls ended where the facades of the buildings opened into dark hallways or locked doors. Nothing good, I imagined, could be happening inside if so many locks had to be breached to go in or step out.

39

It was on these tense walks home from school that I decided I had to get out of Brooklyn. Mami had chosen this as our home, and just like every other time we'd moved, I'd had to go along with her because I was a child who had no choice. But I wasn't willing to go along with her on this one.

40

"How can people live like this?" I shrieked once, desperate to run across a field, to feel grass under my feet instead of pavement.

41

"Like what?" Mami asked, looking around our apartment, the kitchen and living room crisscrossed with sagging lines of drying diapers and bedclothes.

42

"Everyone on top of each other. No room to do anything. No air."

43

"Do you want to go back to Macún, to live like savages, with no electricity, no toilets..."

44

"At least you could step outside every day without somebody trying to kill you."

45

"Ay, Negi, stop exaggerating!"

46

"I hate my life!" I yelled.

47

"Then do something about it," she yelled back.

48

Until Mr. Barone showed me the listing for Performing Arts High School, I hadn't known what to do.

49

"The auditions are in less than a month. You have to learn a monologue, which you will perform in front of a panel. If you do well, and your grades here are good, you might get into the school." 50

Mr. Barone took charge of preparing me for my audition to Performing Arts. He selected a speech from *The Silver Cord*, a play by Sidney Howard, first performed in 1926, but whose action took place in a New York drawing room circa 1905. 51

"Mr. Gatti, the English teacher," he said, "will coach you....And Mrs. Johnson will talk to you about what to wear and things like that." 52

I was to play Christina, a young married woman confronting her mother-in-law. I learned the monologue phonetically from Mr. Gatti. It opened with "You belong to a type that's very common in this country, Mrs. Phelps—a type of self-centered, self-pitying, son-devouring tigress, with unmentionable proclivities suppressed on the side." 53

"We don't have time to study the meaning of every word," Mr. Gatti said. "Just make sure you pronounce every word correctly." 54

Mrs. Johnson, who taught Home Economics, called me to her office. 55

"Is that how you enter a room?" she asked the minute I came in. "Try again, only this time, don't barge in. Step in slowly, head up, back straight, a nice smile on your face. That's it." I took a deep breath and waited. "Now, sit. No, not like that. Don't just plop down. Float down to the chair with your knees together." She demonstrated, and I copied her. "That's better. What do you do with your hands? No, don't hold your chin like that; it's not ladylike. Put your hands on your lap, and leave them there. Don't use them so much when you talk." 56

I sat stiff as a cutout while Mrs. Johnson and Mr. Barone asked me questions they thought the panel at Performing Arts would ask. 57

"Where are you from?" 58

"Puerto Rico." 59

"No," Mrs. Johnson said, "Porto Rico. Keep your *r*'s soft. Try again." 60

"Do you have any hobbies?" Mr. Barone asked. Now I knew what to answer. 61

"I enjoy dancing and the movies." 62

"Why do you want to come to this school?" 63

Mrs. Johnson and Mr. Barone had worked on my answer if this question should come up. 64

"I would like to study at Performing Arts because of its academic program and so that I may be trained as an actress." 65

"Very good, very good!" Mr. Barone rubbed his hands together, twinkled his eyes at Mrs. Johnson. "I think we have a shot at this." 66

CHAPTER 1

"Remember," Mrs. Johnson said, "when you shop for your audition dress, look for something very simple in dark colors."

Mami bought me a red plaid wool jumper with a crisp white shirt, my first pair of stockings, and penny loafers. The night before, she rolled up my hair in pink curlers that cut into my scalp and made it hard to sleep. For the occasion, I was allowed to wear eye makeup and a little lipstick.

"You look so grown up!" Mami said, her voice sad but happy, as I twirled in front of her and Tata.

"*Toda una señorita*," Tata said, her eyes misty.

We set out for the audition on an overcast January morning heavy with the threat of snow.

"Why couldn't you choose a school close to home?" Mami grumbled as we got on the train to Manhattan. I worried that even if I were accepted, she wouldn't let me go because it was so far from home, one hour each way by subway. But in spite of her complaints, she was proud that I was good enough to be considered for such a famous school. And she actually seemed excited that I would be leaving the neighborhood.

"You'll be exposed to a different class of people," she assured me, and I felt the force of her ambition without knowing exactly what she meant.

Three women sat behind a long table in a classroom where the desks and chairs had been pushed against a wall. As I entered I held my head up and smiled, and then I floated down to the chair in front of them, clasped my hands on my lap, and smiled some more.

"Good morning," said the tall one with hair the color of sand. She was big boned and solid, with intense blue eyes, a generous mouth, and soothing hands with short fingernails. She was dressed in shades of beige from head to toe and wore no makeup and no jewelry except for the gold chain that held her glasses just above her full bosom. Her voice was rich, modulated, each word pronounced as if she were inventing it.

Next to her sat a very small woman with very high heels. Her cropped hair was pouffed around her face, with bangs brushing the tips of her long false lashes, her huge dark brown eyes were thickly lined in black all around, and her small mouth was carefully drawn in and painted cerise. Her suntanned face turned toward me with the innocent curiosity of a lively baby. She was dressed in black, with many gold chains around her neck, big earrings, several bracelets, and large stone rings on the fingers of both hands.

The third woman was tall, small boned, thin, but shapely. Her dark hair was pulled flat against her skull into a knot in back of her head. Her face was all angles and light, with fawnlike dark brown eyes, a straight nose, full lips painted just a shade pinker than their natural color. Silky forest green cuffs peeked out from the sleeves of her burgundy suit. Diamond studs winked from perfect earlobes.

25

I had dreamed of this moment for several weeks. More than anything, I wanted to impress the panel with my talent, so that I would be accepted into Performing Arts and leave Brooklyn every day. And, I hoped, one day I would never go back. 78

But the moment I faced these three impeccably groomed women, I forgot my English and Mrs. Johnson's lessons on how to behave like a lady. In the agony of trying to answer their barely comprehensible questions, I jabbed my hands here and there, forming words with my fingers because the words refused to leave my mouth. 79

"Why don't you let us hear your monologue now?" the woman with the dangling glasses asked softly. 80

I stood up abruptly, and my chair clattered onto its side two feet from where I stood. I picked it up, wishing with all my strength that a thunderbolt would strike me dead to ashes on the spot. 81

"It's all right," she said. "Take a breath. We know you're nervous." 82

I closed my eyes and breathed deeply, walked to the middle of the room, and began my monologue. 83

"Ju bee lonh 2 a type dats berry como in dis kuntree, Meesees Felps. A type off selfcent red self pee tee in sun de boring tie gress wid on men shon ah ball pro klee bee tees on de side." 84

In spite of Mr. Gatti's reminders that I should speak slowly and enunciate every word, even if I didn't understand it, I recited my three-minute monologue in one minute flat. 85

The small woman's long lashes seemed to have grown with amazement. The elegant woman's serene face twitched with controlled laughter. The tall one dressed in beige smiled sweetly. 86

"Thank you, dear," she said. "Could you wait outside for a few moments?" 87

I resisted the urge to curtsy. The long hallway had narrow wainscoting halfway up to the ceiling. Single bulb lamps hung from long cords, creating yellow puddles of light on the polished brown linoleum tile. A couple of girls my age sat on straight chairs next to their mothers, waiting their turn. They looked up as I came out and the door shut behind me. Mami stood up from her chair at the end of the hall. She looked as scared as I felt. 88

"What happened?" 89

"Nothing," I mumbled, afraid that if I began telling her about it, I would break into tears in front of the other people, whose eyes followed me and Mami as we walked to the EXIT sign. "I have to wait here a minute." 90

"Did they say anything?" 91

"No. I'm just supposed to wait." 92

We leaned against the wall. Across from us there was a bulletin board with newspaper clippings about former students. On the ragged edge, a neat person had printed in blue ink, "P.A." and the year the actor, dancer, or musician had graduated. I closed my eyes and tried to picture myself on that bulletin board, with "P.A. '66" across the top.

93

The door at the end of the hall opened, and the woman in beige poked her head out.

94

"Esmeralda?"

95

"*Sí*, I mean, here." I raised my hand.

96

She led me into the room. There was another girl in there, whom she introduced as Bonnie, a junior at the school.

97

"Do you know what a pantomime is?" The woman asked. I nodded. "You and Bonnie are sisters decorating a Christmas tree."

98

Bonnie looked a lot like Juanita Marin, whom I had last seen in Macún four years earlier. We decided where the invisible Christmas tree would be, and we sat on the floor and pretended we were taking decorations out of boxes and hanging them on the branches.

99

My family had never had a Christmas tree, but I remembered how once I had helped Papi wind colored lights around the eggplant bush that divided our land from Dona Ana's. We started at the bottom and wound the wire with tiny red bulbs around and around until we ran out; then Papi plugged another cord to it and we kept going until the branches hung heavy with light and the bush looked like it was on fire.

100

Before long I had forgotten where I was, and that the tree didn't exist and Bonnie was not my sister. She pretended to hand me a very delicate ball, and just before I took it, she made like it fell to the ground and shattered. I was petrified that Mami would come in and yell at us for breaking her favorite decoration. Just as I began to pick up the tiny fragments of nonexistent crystal, a voice broke in. "Thank you."

101

Bonnie got up, smiled, and went out.

102

The elegant woman stretched her hand out for me to shake.

103

"We will notify your school in a few weeks. It was very nice to meet you."

104

I shook hands all around then backed out of the room in a fog, silent, as if the pantomime had taken my voice and the urge to speak.

105

On the way home Mami kept asking what had happened, and I kept mumbling, "Nothing. Nothing happened," ashamed that, after all the hours of practice with Mrs. Johnson, Mr. Barone, and Mr. Gatti, after the expense of new clothes and shoes, after Mami had to take a day off from work to take me into Manhattan, after all that, I had failed the audition and would never, ever, get out of Brooklyn.

106

El mismo jíbaro con diferente caballo.
Same jíbaro, different horse.

107

A decade after my graduation from Performing Arts, I visited the school. I was by then living in Boston, a scholarship student at Harvard University. The tall, elegant woman of my audition had become my mentor through my three years there. Since my graduation, she had married the school principal.

108

"I remember your audition," she said, her chiseled face dreamy, her lips toying with a smile that she seemed, still, to have to control.

109

I had forgotten the skinny brown girl with the curled hair, wool jumper, and lively hands. But she hadn't. She told me that the panel had had to ask me to leave so that they could laugh, because it was so funny to see a fourteen-year-old Puerto Rican girl jabbering out a monologue about a possessive mother-in-law at the turn of the century, the words incomprehensible because they went by so fast.

110

"We admired," she said, "the courage it took to stand in front of us and do what you did."

111

"So you mean I didn't get into the school because of my talent, but because I had chutzpah?" We both laughed.

112

"Are any of your sisters and brothers in college?"

113

"No, I'm the only one, so far."

114

"How many of you are there?"

115

"By the time I graduated from high school there were eleven of us."

116

"Eleven!" She looked at me for a long time, until I had to look down. "Do you ever think about how far you've come?" she asked.

117

"No." I answered. "I never stop to think about it. It might jinx the momentum."

118

"Let me tell you another story, then," she said. "The first day of your first year, you were absent. We called your house. You said you couldn't come to school because you had nothing to wear. I wasn't sure if you were joking. I asked to speak to your mother, and you translated what she said. She needed you to go somewhere with her to interpret. At first you wouldn't tell me where, but then you admitted you were going to the welfare office. You were crying, and I had to assure you that you were not the only student in this school whose family received public assistance. The next day you were here, bright and eager. And now here you are, about to graduate from Harvard."

119

"I'm glad you made that phone call," I said.

120

"And I'm glad you came to see me, but right now I have to teach a class." She stood up, as graceful as I remembered. "Take care."

121

Her warm embrace, fragrant of expensive perfume, took me by surprise. "Thank you," I said as she went around the corner to her classroom.

122

I walked the halls of the school, looking for the room where my life had changed. 123
It was across from the science lab, a few doors down from the big bulletin board where
someone with neat handwriting still wrote the letters "P.A." followed by the graduating
year along the edges of newspaper clippings featuring famous alumni.

"P.A. '66," I said to no one in particular. "One of these days." 124

Journaling on Maxine Hong Kingston's Autobiography

Another immigrant, Maxine Hong Kingston published *The Woman Warrior* in 1976,
eighteen years before Santiago's autobiography. In our selection, Kingston describes her
adolescent self as "arrogant with talk" and full of hatred for another Chinese girl who could
"read aloud" but who "would not talk," an abiding silence that Kingston resolves to end.
Once again, answer the following questions in your journal; your answers will serve you well
as prewriting for an essay on the role of language in building tolerance for the Other and in
coming to fuller knowledge of self.

1. Again, start your journaling by briefly answering Burke's pentad questions.

2. Though Kingston's talkativeness contrasts starkly with the other girl's silence, they have
   much in common beyond their Chinese parentage: both "were similar in sports," inept
   at baseball, confused by basketball, always the last chosen for their respective teams.
   Additionally, protective mothers monitor the talker and the silent one; neither girl has
   friends of her own. With so much that bonds them in friendship, what need or
   emotion, other than "hatred," might explain Kingston's angry contempt for this quiet
   girl?

3. Just before Kingston corners the girl and says, "I am going to make you talk, you sissy-
   girl," we see Kingston's vivid imagination as she, the poor athlete, flips off a fire escape,
   runs "across the schoolyard," and disappears "into the sun." Given this capacity to
   fantasize about being "different," how do you interpret her admitting—as she glares
   into the silent girl's face "so I could hate it close up"—that "I did not want to look at
   her face anymore; I hated fragility....I hated her weak neck....I grew my hair long to
   hide it in case it was a flower-stem neck"?

4. Kingston describes the silent girl's features, even the quality of her skin, in vivid detail.
   What details, both literal and figurative, help us to see the silent girl as Kingston saw
   her? Can you relate these physical traits to behavioral ones that Kingston doesn't
   "like" in this girl?

5. As Kingston begins to blend her own crying with the "quarts of tears" she has squeezed
   out of the silent girl, Kingston shouts out the consequences of the girl's continued
   silence. What do these statements reveal about Kingston's fears and aspirations?

6. What irony do you see in Kingston offering to give the silent girl candy if she talks? What irony do you see when Kingston returns to school after the long illness brought on by her encounter with this silent one?

Excerpt from *The Woman Warrior*

MAXINE HONG KINGSTON

She was a year older than I and was in my class for twelve years. During all those years she read aloud but would not talk. Her older sister was usually beside her; their parents kept the older daughter back to protect the younger one. They were six and seven years old when they began school. Although I had flunked kindergarten, I was the same age as most other students in our class; my parents had probably lied about my age, so I had had a head start and came out even. My younger sister was in the class below me; we were normal ages and normally separated. The parents of the quiet girl, on the other hand, protected both daughters. When it sprinkled, they kept them home from school. The girls did not work for a living the way we did. But in other ways we were the same.

We were similar in sports. We held the bat on our shoulders until we walked to first base. (You got a strike only when you actually struck at the ball.) Sometimes the pitcher wouldn't bother to throw to us. "Automatic walk," the other children would call, sending us on our way. By fourth or fifth grade, though, some of us would try to hit the ball. "Easy out," the other kids would say. I hit the ball a couple of times. Baseball was nice in that there was a definite spot to run to after hitting the ball. Basketball confused me because when I caught the ball I didn't know whom to throw it to. "Me. Me," the kids would be yelling. "Over here." Suddenly it would occur to me I hadn't memorized which ghosts were on my team and which were on the other. When the kids said "Automatic walk," the girl who was quieter than I kneeled with one end of the bat in each hand and placed it carefully on the plate. Then she dusted her hands as she walked to first base, where she rubbed her hands softly, fingers spread. She always got tagged out before second base. She would whisper-read but not talk. Her whisper was as soft as if she had no muscles. She seemed to be breathing from a distance. I heard no anger or tension.

I joined in at lunchtime when the other students, the Chinese too, talked about whether or not she was mute, although obviously she was not if she could read aloud. People told how *they* had tried *their* best to be friendly. *They* said hello, but if she refused to answer, well, they didn't see why they had to say hello anymore. She had no friends of her own but followed her sister everywhere, although people and she herself probably thought I was her friend. I also followed her sister about, who was fairly normal. She was almost two years older and read more than anyone else.

I hated the younger sister, the quiet one. I hated her when she was the last chosen for her team and I, the last chosen for my team. I hated her for her China doll hair cut. I hated her at music time for the wheezes that came out of her plastic flute.

One afternoon in the sixth grade (that year I was arrogant with talk, not knowing there were going to be high school dances and college seminars to set me back). I and my little sister and the quiet girl and her big sister stayed late after school for some reason. The cement was cooling, and the tetherball poles made shadows across the gravel. The hooks at the rope ends were clinking against the poles. We shouldn't have been so late; there was laundry work to do and Chinese school to get to by 5:00. The last time we had stayed late, my mother had phoned the police and told them we had been kidnapped by bandits. The radio stations broadcast our descriptions. I had to get home before she did that again. But sometimes if you loitered long enough in the schoolyard, the other children would have gone home and you could play with the equipment before the office took it away. We were chasing one another through the playground and in and out of the basement, where the playroom and lavatory were. During air raid drills (it was during the Korean War, which you knew about because every day the front page of the newspaper printed a map of Korea with the top part red and going up and down like a window shade), we curled up in this basement. Now everyone was gone. The playroom was army green and had nothing in it but a long trough with drinking spigots in rows. Pipes across the ceiling led to the drinking fountains and to the toilets in the next room. When someone flushed you could hear the water and other matter, which the children named. Running inside the big pipe above the drinking spigots. There was one playroom for girls next to the girls' lavatory and one playroom for boys next to the boys' lavatory. The stalls were open and the toilets had no lids, by which we knew that ghosts have no sense of shame or privacy.

Inside the playroom the lightbulbs in cages had already been turned off. Daylight came in x-patterns through the caging at the windows. I looked out and, seeing no one in the schoolyard, ran outside to climb the fire escape upside down, hanging on to the metal stairs with fingers and toes.

I did a flip off the fire escape and ran across the schoolyard. The day was a great eye, and it was not paying much attention to me now. I could disappear with the sun; I could turn quickly sideways and slip into a different world. It seemed I could run faster at this time, and by evening I would be able to fly. As the afternoon wore on we could run into the forbidden places—the boys' big yard, the boys' playroom. We could go into the boys' lavatory and look at the urinals. The only time during school hours I had crossed the boys' yard was when a flatbed truck with a giant thing covered with canvas and tied down with ropes had parked across the street. The children had told one another that it was a gorilla in captivity; we couldn't decide whether the sign said "Trail of the Gorilla" or "Trial of the Gorilla." The thing was as big as a house. The teachers couldn't stop us from hysterically rushing to the fence and clinging to the wire mesh. Now I ran across the boys' yard clear to the Cyclone fence and thought about the hair that I had seen sticking out of the canvas. It was going to be summer soon, so you could feel that freedom coming on too.

I ran back into the girls' yard, and there was the quiet sister all by herself. I ran past her, and she followed me into the girls' lavatory. My footsteps rang hard against cement and tile because of the taps I had nailed into my shoes. Her footsteps were soft, padding after me. There was no one in the lavatory but the two of us. I ran all around the rows of twenty-five open stalls to make sure of that. No sisters. I think we must have been playing hide-and-go-seek. She was not good at hiding by herself and usually followed her sister; they'd hide in the same place. They must have gotten separated. In the growing twilight, a child could hide and never be found.

I stopped abruptly in front of the sinks, and she came running toward me before she could stop herself, so that she almost collided with me. I walked closer. She backed away, puzzlement, then alarm in her eyes.

9

"You're going to talk," I said, my voice steady and normal, as it is when talking to the familiar, the weak, and the small. "I am going to make you talk, you sissy-girl." She stopped backing away and stood fixed.

10

I looked into her face so I could hate it close up. She wore black bangs, and her cheeks were pink and white. She was baby-soft. I thought that I could put my thumb on her nose and push it bonelessly in, indent her face. I could poke dimples into her cheeks. I could work her face around like dough. She stood still, and I did not want to look at her face anymore; I hated fragility. I walked around her, looked her up and down the way the Mexican and Negro girls did when they fought, so tough. I hated her weak neck, the way it did not support her head but let it droop; her head would fall backward. I stared at the curve of her nape. I wished I was able to see what my own neck looked like from the back and sides. I hoped it did not look like hers; I wanted a stout neck. I grew my hair long to hide it in case it was a flower-stem neck. I walked around to the front of her to hate her face some more.

11

I reached up and took the fatty part of her cheek, not dough, but meat, between my thumb and finger. This close, and I saw no pores. "Talk," I said. "Are you going to talk?" Her skin was fleshy, like squid out of which the glassy blades of bones had been pulled. I wanted tough skin, hard brown skin. I had callused my hands; I had scratched dirt to blacken the nails, which I cut straight across to make stubby fingers. I gave her face a squeeze. "Talk." When I let go, the pink rushed back into my white thumbprint on her skin. I walked around to her side. "Talk!" I shouted into the side of her head. Her straight hair hung, the same all these years, no ringlets or braids or permanents. I squeezed her other cheek. "Are you? Huh? Are you going to talk?" She tried to shake her head, but I had hold of her face. She had no muscles to jerk away. Her skin seemed to stretch. I let go in horror. What if it came away in my hand? "No, huh?" I said, rubbing the touch of her off my fingers. "Say 'No,' then," I said. I gave her another pinch and a twist. "Say, 'No.'" She shook her head, her straight hair turning with her head, not swinging side to side like the pretty girls'. She was so neat. Her neatness bothered me. I hated the way she folded the wax paper from her lunch; she did not wad her brown paper bag and her school papers. I hated her clothes—the blue pastel cardigan, the white blouse with the collar that lay flat over the cardigan, the homemade flat, cotton skirt she wore when everybody else was wearing flared skirts. I hated pastels; I would wear black always. I squeezed again, harder, even though her cheek had a weak rubbery feeling I did not like. I squeezed one cheek, then the other, back and forth until the tears ran out of her eyes as if I had pulled them out. "Stop crying," I said, but although she habitually followed me around, she did not obey. Her

12

eyes dripped; her nose dripped. She wiped her eyes with her papery fingers. The skin on her hands and arms seemed powdery-dry, like tracing paper, onion paper. I hated her fingers. I could snap them like breadsticks. I pushed her hands down. "Say 'Hi,'" I said. "Hi. Like that. Say your name. Go ahead. Say it. Or are you stupid? You're so stupid, you don't know your own name, is that it? When I say, 'What's your name?' you just blurt it out, O.K.? What's your name?" Last year the whole class had laughed at a boy who couldn't fill out a form because he didn't know his father's name. The teacher sighed, exasperated and was very sarcastic, "Don't you notice things? What does your mother call him?" she said. The class laughed at how dumb he was not to notice things. "She calls him father of me," he said. Even we laughed although we knew that his mother did not call his father by name, and a son does not know his father's name. We laughed and were relieved that our parents had had the foresight to tell us some names we could give the teachers. "If you're not stupid," I said to the quiet girl, "what's your name?" She shook her head, and some hair caught in the tears; wet black hair stuck to the side of the pink and white face. I reached up (she was taller than I) and took a strand of hair. I pulled it. "Well, then, let's honk your hair," I said. "Honk. Honk." Then I pulled the other side—"ho-o-n-nk"—a long pull; "ho-o-n-n-nk"—a longer pull. I could see her little white ears, like white cutworms curled underneath the hair. "Talk!" I yelled into each cutworm.

I looked right at her. "I know you talk," I said. "I've heard you." Her eyebrows flew up. Something in those black eyes was startled, and I pursued it. "I was walking past your house when you didn't know I was there. I heard you yell in English and in Chinese. You weren't just talking. You were shouting. I heard you shout. You were saying, 'Where are you?' Say that again. Go ahead, just the way you did at home." I yanked harder on the hair, but steadily, not jerking. I did not want to pull it out. "Go ahead. Say, 'Where are you?' Say it loud enough for your sister to come. Call her. Make her come help you. Call her name. I'll stop if she comes. So call. Go ahead."

She shook her head, her mouth curved down, crying. I could see her tiny white teeth, baby teeth. I wanted to grow big strong yellow teeth. "You do have a tongue," I said. "So use it." I pulled the hair at her temples, pulled the tears out of her eyes. "Say, 'Ow'" I said. "Just 'Ow.' Say, 'Let go.' Go ahead. Say it. I'll honk you again if you don't say, 'Let me alone.' Say, 'Leave me alone,' and I'll let you go. I will. I'll let go if you say it. You can stop this anytime you want to, you know. All you have to do is tell me to stop. Just say, 'Stop.' You're just asking for it, aren't you? You're just asking for another honk. Well then, I'll have to give you another honk. Say, 'Stop.'" But she didn't. I had to pull again and again.

Sounds did come out of her mouth, sobs, chokes, noises that were almost words. Snot ran out of her nose. She tried to wipe it on her hands, but there was too much of it. She used her sleeve. "You're disgusting," I told her. "Look at you, snot streaming down your nose, and you won't say a word to stop it. You're such a nothing." I moved behind her and pulled the hair growing out of her weak neck. I let go. I stood silent for a long time. Then I screamed, "Talk!" I would scare the words out of her. If she had had little bound feet, the toes twisted under the balls, I would have jumped up and landed

33

on them—crunch!—stomped on them with my iron shoes. She cried hard, sobbing aloud. "Cry, 'Mama,'" I said. "Come on. Cry, 'Mama.' Say, 'Stop it.'"

I put my finger on her pointed chin. "I don't like you. I don't like the weak little toots you make on your flute. Wheeze. Wheeze. I don't like the way you don't swing at the ball. I don't like the way you're the last one chosen. I don't like the way you can't make a fist for tetherball. Why don't you make a fist? Come on. Get tough. Come on. Throw fists." I pushed at her long hands; they swung limply at her sides. Her fingers were so long, I thought maybe they had an extra joint. They couldn't possibly make fists like other people's. "Make a fist," I said. "Come on. Just fold those fingers up; fingers on the inside, thumbs on the outside. Say something. Honk me back. You're so tall, and you let me pick on you. 16

"Would you like a hanky? I can't get you one with embroidery on it or crocheting along the edges, but I'll get you some toilet paper if you tell me to. Go ahead. Ask me. I'll get it for you if you ask." She did not stop crying. "Why don't you scream, 'Help'?" I suggested. "Say, 'Help.' Go ahead." She cried on. "O.K., O.K. Don't talk. Just scream, and I'll let you go. Won't that feel good? Go ahead. Like this." I screamed not too loudly. My voice hit the tile and rang it as if I had thrown a rock at it. The stalls opened wider and the toilets wider and darker. Shadows leaned at angles I had not seen before. I was very late. Maybe a janitor had locked me in with this girl for the night. Her black eyes blinked and stared, blinked and stared. I felt dizzy from hunger. We had been in the lavatory together forever. My mother would call the police again if I didn't bring my sister home soon. "I'll let you go if you say just one word," I said. "You can even say 'a' or 'the,' and I'll let you go. Come on. Please." She didn't shake her head anymore, only cried steadily, so much water coming out of her. I could see the two duct holes where the tears welled out. Quarts of tears but no words. I grabbed her by the shoulder. I could feel bones. The light was coming in queerly through the frosted glass with the chicken wire embedded in it. Her crying was like an animal's—a seal's—and it echoed around the basement. "Do you want to stay here all night?" I asked. "Your mother is wondering what happened to her baby. You wouldn't want to have her mad at you. You'd better say something." I shook her shoulder. I pulled her hair again. I squeezed her face. "Come on! Talk! Talk! Talk!" She didn't seem to feel it anymore when I pulled her hair. "There's nobody here but you and me. This isn't a classroom or a playground or a crowd. I'm just one person. You can talk in front of one person. Don't make me pull harder and harder until you talk." But her hair seemed to stretch; she did not say a word. "I'm going to pull harder. Don't make me pull anymore, or your hair will come out and you're going to be bald. Do you want to be bald? You don't want to be bald, do you?" 17

Far away, coming from the edge of town, I heard whistles blow. The cannery was changing shifts, letting out the afternoon people, and still we were here at school. It was a sad sound—work done. The air was lonelier after the sound died. 18

"Why won't you talk?" I started to cry. What if I couldn't stop, and everyone would want to know what happened? "Now look what you've done," I scolded. "You're going to pay for this. I want to know why. And you're going to tell me why. You don't see I'm trying to help you out, do you? Do you want to be like this, dumb (do you know what 19 dumb means?), your whole life? Don't you ever want to be a cheerleader? Or a pompon girl? What are you going to do for a living? Yeah, you're going to have to work because you can't be a housewife. Somebody has to marry you before you can be a housewife. And you, you are a plant. Do you know that? That's all you are if you don't talk. If you don't talk, you can't have a personality. You'll have no personality and no hair. You've got to let people know you have a personality and a brain. You think somebody is going to take care of you all your stupid life? You think you'll always have your big sister? You think somebody's going to marry you, is that it? Well, you're not the type that gets dates, let alone gets married. Nobody's going to notice you. And you have to talk for interviews, speak right up in front of the boss. Don't you know that? You're so dumb. Why do I waste my time on you?" Sniffing and snorting, I couldn't stop crying and talking at the same time. I kept wiping my nose on my arm, my sweater lost somewhere (probably not worn because my mother said to wear a sweater). It seemed as if I had spent my life in that basement, doing the worst thing I had yet done to another person. "I'm doing this for your own good," I said. "Don't you dare tell anyone I've been bad to you. Talk. Please talk."

I was getting dizzy from the air I was gulping. Her sobs and my sobs were bouncing wildly off the tile, sometimes together, sometimes alternating. "I don't understand why you won't say just one word," I cried, clenching my teeth. My knees were shaking, and I hung on to her hair to stand up. Another time I'd stayed too late, I had had to walk around two Negro kids who were bonking each other's head on the concrete. I went back later to see if the concrete had cracks in it. "Look. I'll give you something if you talk. I'll give you my pencil box. I'll buy you some candy. O.K.? What do you want? Tell me. Just say it, and I'll give it to you. Just say, 'yes,' or, 'O.K.,' or, 'Baby Ruth.'" But she didn't want anything.

I had stopped pinching her cheek because I did not like the feel of her skin. I would go crazy if it came away in my hands. "I skinned her," I would have to confess.

Suddenly I heard footsteps hurrying through the basement, and her sister ran into the lavatory calling her name. "Oh, there you are," I said. "We've been waiting for you. I was only trying to teach her to talk. She wouldn't cooperate, though." Her sister went into one of the stalls and got handfuls of toilet paper and wiped her off. Then we found my sister, and we walked home together. "Your family really ought to force her to speak," I advised all the way home. "You mustn't pamper her."

The world is sometimes just, and I spent the next eighteen months sick in bed with a mystery illness. There was no pain and no symptoms, though the middle line in my left palm broke in two. Instead of starting junior high school, I lived like the Victorian recluses I read about. I had a rented hospital bed in the living room, where I watched soap operas on TV, and my family cranked me up and down. I saw no one but my family, who took good care of me. I could have no visitors, no other relatives, no villagers. My bed was against the west window, and I watched the seasons change the peach tree. I had a bell to ring for help. I used a bedpan. It was the best year and a half of my life. Nothing happened.

But one day my mother, the doctor, said, "You're ready to get up today. It's time to 24 get up and go to school." I walked about outside to get my legs working, leaning on a staff I cut from the peach tree. The sky and trees, the sun were immense—no longer framed by a window, no longer grayed with a fly screen. I sat down on the sidewalk in amazement—the night, the stars. But at school I had to figure out again how to talk. I met again the poor girl I had tormented. She had not changed. She wore the same clothes, hair cut, and manner as when we were in elementary school, no make-up on the pink and white face, while the other Asian girls were starting to tape their eyelids. She continued to be able to read aloud. But there was hardly any reading aloud anymore, less and less as we got into high school....

Journaling on Maya Angelou's Autobiography

Published in 1970, *I Know Why the Caged Bird Sings* tells Maya Angelou's story of growing up in the 1930s, first in rural Arkansas, then in St. Louis, San Francisco, and southern California. Our selection features a nine-year-old Maya (then named Marguerite Johnson), just one year after being raped by her mother's St. Louis boyfriend. Having returned to Stamps, Arkansas to live with "Momma," her illiterate but extremely intelligent paternal grandmother, Angelou has resumed her studies but taken a vow of silence, considering herself unworthy to communicate with anyone. Our selection also focuses on Mrs. Flowers, a well-read African American woman who teaches Maya to reclaim her voice. Answering the following questions in your journal will draw you into conversation with Angelou's powerful voice:

1. Once again, summarize the narrative by answering Burke's pentad questions.

2. Angelou begins this narrative with figurative language, comparing herself to "an old biscuit, dirty and inedible." What does this simile suggest about the post-rape psychology of victims?

3. Select at least three descriptive words or phrases, and explain how each helps us to *see* Mrs. Flowers and to understand her power over Maya.

4. During their visit, Mrs. Flowers teaches Maya to be "intolerant of ignorance but understanding of illiteracy." How does this advice relate to Maya's earlier embarrassment over Momma's omission of verbs when talking to the educated Mrs. Flowers?

5. Explain how Mrs. Flowers combines actions with words to lure Maya away from her vow of silence. In doing so, include at least three quotations from this "lesson in living."

Excerpt from *I Know Why the Caged Bird Sings*

Maya Angelou

For nearly a year, I sopped around the house, the Store, the school and the church, like an old biscuit, dirty and inedible. Then I met, or rather got to know, the lady who threw me my first life line. 1

Mrs. Bertha Flowers was the aristocrat of Black Stamps. She had the grace of control to appear warm in the coldest weather, and on the Arkansas summer days it seemed she had a private breeze which swirled around, cooling her. She was thin without the taut look of wiry people, and her printed voile dresses and flowered hats were as right for her as denim overalls for a farmer. She was our side's answer to the richest white woman in town. 2

Her skin was a rich black that would have peeled like a plum if snagged, but then no one would have thought of getting close enough to Mrs. Flowers to ruffle her dress, let along snag her skin. She didn't encourage familiarity. She wore gloves too. 3

I don't think I ever saw Mrs. Flowers laugh, but she smiled often. A slow widening of her thin black lips to show even, small white teeth, then the slow effortless closing. When she chose to smile on me, I always wanted to thank her. The action was so graceful and inclusively benign. 4

She was one of the few gentlewomen I have ever known, and has remained throughout my life the measure of what a human being can be. 5

Momma had a strange relationship with her. Most often when she passed on the road in front of the Store, she spoke to Momma in that soft yet carrying voice, "Good Day, Mrs. Henderson." Momma responded with "How you, Sister Flowers?" 6

Mrs. Flowers didn't belong to our church, nor was she Momma's familiar. Why on earth did she insist on calling her Sister Flowers? Shame made me want to hide my face. Mrs. Flowers deserved better than to be called Sister. Then, Momma left out the verb. Why not ask, "How are you Mrs. Flowers?" With the unbalanced passion of the young, I hated her for showing her ignorance to Mrs. Flowers. It didn't occur to me for many years that they were as alike as sisters, separated only by formal education. 7

Although I was upset, neither of the women was in the least shaken by what I thought an unceremonious greeting. Mrs. Flowers would continue her easy gait up the hill to her little bungalow, and Momma kept on shelling peas or doing whatever had brought her to the front porch. 8

Occasionally, though, Mrs. Flowers would drift off the road and down to the Store and Momma would say to me, "Sister, you go on and play." As I left I would hear the beginning of an intimate conversation. Momma persistently using the wrong verb, or none at all. 9

"Brother and Sister Wilcox is sho'ly the meanest—" "Is," Momma? "Is"? Oh, please, not "is," Momma, for two or more. But they talked, and from the side of the 10 building where I waited for the ground to open up and swallow me, I heard the soft-voiced Mrs. Flowers and the textured voice of my grandmother merging and melting. They were interrupted from time to time by giggles that must have come from Mrs. Flowers (Momma never giggled in her life). Then she was gone.

She appealed to me because she was like people I had never met personally. Like women in English novels who walked the moors (whatever they were) with their loyal dogs racing at a respectful distance. Like the women who sat in front of roaring fireplaces, drinking tea incessantly from silver trays full of scones and crumpets. Women who walked over the "heath" and read morocco-bound books and had two last names divided by a hyphen. It would be safe to say that she made me proud to be Negro, just by being herself. 11

She acted just as refined as whitefolks in the movies and books and she was more beautiful, for none of them could have come near that warm color without looking gray by comparison. 12

It was fortunate that I never saw her in the company of powwhitefolks. For since they tend to think of their whiteness as an evenizer, I'm certain that I would have had to hear her spoken to commonly as Bertha, and my image of her would have been shattered like the unmendable Humpty-Dumpty. 13

One summer afternoon, sweet-milk fresh in my memory, she stopped at the Store to buy provisions. Another Negro woman of her health and age would have been expected to carry the paper sacks home in one hand, but Momma said, "Sister Flowers, I'll send Bailey up to your house with these things." 14

She smiled that slow dragging smile, "Thank you, Mrs. Henderson. I'd prefer Marguerite, though." My name was beautiful when she said it. "I've been meaning to talk to her, anyway." They gave each other age-group looks. 15

Momma said, "Well, that's all right then. Sister, go and change your dress. You going to Sister Flowers's." 16

The chifforobe was a maze. What on earth did one put on to go to Mrs. Flowers' house? I knew I shouldn't put on a Sunday dress. It might be sacrilegious. Certainly not a house dress, since I was already wearing a fresh one. I chose a school dress, naturally. It was formal without suggesting that going to Mrs. Flowers' house was equivalent to attending church. 17

I trusted myself back into the Store. 18

"Now, don't you look nice." I had chosen the right thing, for once. 19

"Mrs. Henderson, you make most of the children's clothes, don't you?" 20

"Yes, ma'am. Sure do. Store-bought clothes ain't hardly worth the thread it take to stitch them." 21

"I'll say you do a lovely job, though, so neat. That dress looks professional." 22

Momma was enjoying the seldom-received compliments. Since everyone we knew (Except Mrs. Flowers, of course) could sew competently, praise was rarely handed out for the commonly practiced craft. 23

"I try, with the help of the Lord, Sister Flowers, to finish the inside just like I does the outside. Come here, Sister." 24

I had buttoned up the collar and tied the belt, apronlike, in back. Momma told me to turn around. With one hand she pulled the strings and the belt fell free at both sides of my waist. Then her large hands were at my neck, opening the button loops. I was terrified. What was happening? 25

"Take it off, Sister." She had her hands on the hem of the dress. 26

"I don't need to see the inside, Mrs. Henderson, I can tell..." But the dress was over my head and my arms were stuck in the sleeves. Momma said, "That'll do. See here, Sister Flowers, I French-seams around the armholes." Through the cloth film, I saw the shadow approach. "That makes it last longer. Children these days would bust out of sheet-metal clothes. They so rough." 27

"That is a very good job, Mrs. Henderson. You should be proud. You can put your dress back on, Marguerite." 28

"No ma'am. Pride is a sin. And 'cording to the Good Book, it goeth before a fall." 29

"That's right. So the Bible says. It's a good thing to keep in mind." 30

I wouldn't look at either of them. Momma hadn't thought that taking off my dress in front of Mrs. Flowers would kill me stone dead. If I had refused, she would have thought I was trying to be "womanish" and might have remembered St. Louis. Mrs. Flowers had known that I would be embarrassed and that was even worse. I picked up the groceries and went out to wait in the hot sunshine. It would be fitting if I got a sunstroke and died before they came outside. Just dropped dead on the slanting porch. 31

There was a little path beside the rocky road, and Mrs. Flowers walked in front swinging her arms and picking her way over the stones. 32

She said, without turning her head, to me, "I hear you're doing very good school work, Marguerite, but that it's all written. The teachers report that they have trouble getting you to talk in class." We passed the triangular farm on our left and the path widened to allow us to walk together. I hung back in the separate unasked and unanswerable questions. 33

"Come along and walk along with me, Marguerite." I couldn't have refused even if I wanted to. She pronounced my name so nicely. Or more correctly, she spoke each word with such clarity that I was certain a foreigner who didn't understand English could have understood her. 34

"Now no one is going to make you talk—possibly no one can. But bear in mind, language is man's way of communicating with his fellow man and it is language alone which separates him from the lower animals." That was a totally new idea to me, and I 35 would need time to think about it.

"Your grandmother says you read a lot. Every chance you get. That's good, but not 36
good enough. Words mean more than what is set down on paper. It takes the human
voice to infuse them with the shades of deeper meaning."

I memorized the part about the human voice infusing words. It seemed so valid 37
and poetic.

She said she was going to give me some books and that I not only must read 38
them, I must read them aloud. She suggested that I try to make a sentence sound in as
many different ways as possible.

"I'll accept no excuse if you return a book to me that has been badly handled." My 39
imagination boggled at the punishment I would deserve if in fact I did abuse a book of
Mrs. Flowers'. Death would be too kind and brief.

The odors in the house surprised me. Somehow I had never connected Mrs. 40
Flowers with food or eating or any other common experience of common people.
There must have been an outhouse, too, but my mind never recorded it.

The sweet scent of vanilla had met us as she opened the door. 41

"I made tea cookies this morning. You see, I had planned to invite you for cookies 42
and lemonade so we could have this little chat. The lemonade is in the icebox."

It followed that Mrs. Flowers would have ice on an ordinary day, when most 43
families in our town bought ice late on Saturdays only a few times during the summer
to be used in the wooden ice-cream freezers.

She took the bags from me and disappeared through the kitchen door. I looked 44
around the room that I had never in my wildest fantasies imagined I would see.
Browned photographs leered or threatened from the walls and the white, freshly done
curtains pushed against themselves and against the wind. I wanted to gobble up the
room entire and take it to Bailey, who would help me analyze and enjoy it.

"Have a seat, Marguerite. Over there by the table." She carried a platter covered 45
with a tea towel. Although she warned that she hadn't tried her hand at baking sweets
for some time, I was certain that like everything else about her the cookies would be
perfect.

They were flat round wafers, slightly browned on the edges and butter-yellow in 46
the center. With the cold lemonade they were sufficient for childhood's lifelong diet.
Remembering my manners, I took nice little lady-like bits off the edges. She said that
she had made them expressly for me and that she had a few in the kitchen that I could
take home to my brother. So I jammed one whole cake in my mouth and the rough
crumbs scratched the insides of my jaws, and if I hadn't had to swallow, it would have
been a dream come true.

As I ate she began the first of what we later called "my lessons in living." She 47
said that I must always be intolerant of ignorance but understanding of illiteracy. That

some people, unable to go to school, were more educated and even more intelligent than college professors. She encouraged me to listen carefully to what country people called mother wit. That in those homely sayings was couched the collective wisdom of generations.

When I finished the cookies she brushed off the table and brought a thick, small book from the bookcase. I had read *A Tale of Two Cities* and found it up to my standards as a romantic novel. She opened the first page and I heard poetry for the first time in my life. 48

"It was the best of times and the worst of times..." Her voice slid in and curved down through and over the words. She was nearly singing. I wanted to look at the pages. Were they the same that I had read? Or were there notes, music, lined on the pages, as in a hymn book? Her sounds began cascading gently. I knew from listening to a thousand preachers that she was nearing the end of her reading, and I hadn't really heard, heard to understand, a single word. 49

"How do you like that?" 50

It occurred to me that she expected a response. The sweet vanilla flavor was still on my tongue and her reading was a wonder in my ears. I had to speak. 51

I said, "Yes, ma'am." It was the least I could do, but it was the most also. 52

"There's one more thing. Take this book of poems and memorize one for me. Next time you pay me a visit, I want you to recite." 53

I have tried often to search behind the sophistication of years for the enchantment I so easily found in those gifts. The essence escapes but its aura remains. To be allowed, no, invited, into the private lives of strangers, and to share their joys and fears, was a chance to exchange the Southern bitter worm-wood for a cup of mead with Beowulf or a hot cup of tea and milk with Oliver Twist. When I said aloud, "It is a far, far better thing that I do, than I have ever done..." tears of loved filled my eyes at my selflessness. 54

On that first day, I ran down the hill and into the road (few cars ever came along it) and had the good sense to stop running before I reached the Store. 55

I was liked, and what a difference it made. I was respected not as Mrs. Henderson's grandchild or Bailey's sister but for just being Marguerite Johnson. 56

Childhood's logic never asks to be proved (all conclusions are absolute). I didn't question why Mrs. Flowers had singled me out for attention, nor did it occur to me that Momma might have asked her to give me a little talking to. All I cared about was that she made tea cookies for *me* and read to *me* from her favorite book. It was enough to prove that she liked me. 57

Momma and Bailey were waiting inside the Store. He said, "My, what did she give you?" He had seen the books, but I held the paper sack with his cookies in my arms shielded by the poems. 58

Momma said, "Sister, I know that you acted like a little lady. That do my heart 59 good to see settled people take to you all. I'm trying my best, the Lord knows, but these days..." Her voice trailed off. "Go on in and change your dress."

In the bedroom it was going to be a joy to see Bailey receive his cookies. I said, "By the way, Bailey, Mrs. Flowers sent you some tea cookies—" 60

Momma shouted, "What did you say, Sister? You, Sister, what did you say?" Hot anger was crackling in her voice. 61

Bailey said, "She said Mrs. Flowers sent me some—" 62

"I ain't talking to you, Ju." I heard the heavy feet walk across the floor toward our bedroom. "Sister, you heard me. What's that you said?" She swelled to fill the doorway. 63

Bailey said, "Momma." His pacifying voice—"Momma, she—" 64

"You shut up, Ju. I'm talking to your sister." 65

I didn't know what sacred cow I had bumped, but it was better to find out than to hang like a thread over an open fire. I repeated, "I said, 'Bailey, by the way, Mrs. Flowers sent you—" 66

"That's what I thought you said. Go on and take off your dress. I'm going to get a switch." 67

At first I thought she was playing. Maybe some heavy joke that would end with "You sure she didn't send me something?" but in a minute she was back in the room with a long, ropy, peach-tree switch, the juice smelling bitter at having been torn loose. She said, "Get down on your knees. Bailey, Junior, you come on too." 68

The three of us knelt as she began, "Our Father, you know the tribulations of your humble servant. I have with your help raised two grown boys. Many's the day I thought I wouldn't be able to go on, but you gave me the strength to see my way clear. Now, Lord, look down on this heavy heart today. I'm trying to raise my son's children in the way they should go, but, oh, Lord, the Devil try to hinder me on every hand. I never thought I'd live to hear cursing under this roof, what I try to keep dedicated to the glorification of God. And cursing out of the mouths of babes. But you said, in the last days brother would turn against brother, and children against their parents. That there would be a gnashing of teeth and a rendering of flesh. Father, forgive this child, I beg you, on bended knee." 69

I was crying loudly now. Momma's voice had risen to a shouting pitch, and I knew that whatever wrong I had committed was extremely serious. She had even left the Store untended to take up my case with God. When she finished we were all crying. She pulled me to her with one hand and hit me only a few times with the switch. The shock of my sin and the emotional release of her prayer had exhausted her. 70

Momma wouldn't talk right then, but later in the evening I found that my violation lay in using the phrase "by the way." Momma explained that "Jesus was the Way, the Truth and the Light," and anyone who says "by the way" is really saying, "by Jesus," or "by God" and the Lord's name would not be taken in vain in her house. 71

When Bailey tried to interpret the words with: 72

"Whitefolks use 'by the way' to mean while we're on the subject," Momma   73
reminded us that "whitefolks" mouths were most in general loose and their words were
an abomination before Christ.

Choosing a Topic for Your Narrative Essay

Now that you have read all four of these selections and answered the journaling questions
above, you should feel ready to write. Before doing so, however, you would be wise to
complete the process illustrated above in the analysis of the narrative on patriotism:

- Listing

- Freewriting

- Tree Outlining

- Writing a draft and sharing with a peer-response group or with a
  Writing Center intern

More specifically, your prewriting process will look something like this:

- **Listing:** Lessons you have learned here about the relationship between literacy and
  liberty; or your memories of learning to read and write

- **Freewriting:** Ten-minute writings on several prompts drawn from your list. You
  might write, for example, on people who discouraged and encouraged your growth
  as reader and writer—10 minutes on each person, recalling their appearances, their
  language, their actions, their effects on you.

- **Tree Outlining:** Drawing on material from your freewriting to sketch the major
  branches of your essay and sub-branches that grow from them

- **Writing a Rough Draft:** If you don't have a chance to share your rough draft with a
  peer-response group in class, you can visit your university or college Writing Center
  to deepen your sense of audience before revising the draft.

These other forms of prewriting will complement your journaling, helping you to find a
limited topic as well as your purpose and audience. In other words, as Anne Lamott puts
it at the beginning of this chapter, you will be ready to commit a "revolutionary act," telling
your "truth as you understand it." The topics below may help you in deciding on the scope
as well as the focus of your paper:

1. Write a narrative essay, focusing on your own experiences with taking risks, with
   disappointing parents' plans for you, or with coming to accept the self that you dislike
   in others. Did the experience lead to growth? Did you find joy in the struggle? Would
   you "go back" if you could? Be sure to quote from Douglass, Santiago, Kingston, or

Angelou in setting up your narrative and introducing the theme you will explore.

2. Write your own narrative, telling the history of your literacy, the formation of your attitudes toward reading and writing. Who are the heroes and heroines in your story? Who are the villains? What responsibility (credit or blame) can you take for your attitudes and abilities? Be sure to quote from at least one of the four readings to set up your narration and/or to comment on its significance.

Works Cited

Angelou, Maya. *I Know Why the Caged Bird Sings*. New York: Bantam, 1970.

Boswell, James. *Life of Johnson*. Ed. R. W. Chapman. Oxford: Oxford UP, 1980.

Burke, Kenneth. *A Grammar of Motives*. Berkeley: University of California Press, 1969.

Campbell, Joseph, with Bill Moyers. *The Power of Myth*. New York: Doubleday, 1988.

Cicero. *Of Oratory*. *The Rhetorical Tradition: Readings from Classical Times to the Present*. Eds. Patricia Bizzell and Bruce Herzberg. Boston: St. Martin's, 1990. 200–50.

Douglass, Frederick. *Narrative of the Life of Frederick Douglass: An American Slave*. New York: Signet, 1997.

Faulkner, William. "The Stockholm Address." *The Craft of Prose*. 4th ed. Eds. Robert H. Woodward and H. Wendell Smith. Belmont: Wadsworth, 1977. 294–95.

Granger, Charles. "Fighting for America." Student essay.

Heaney, Seamus. "Digging." *Imagining Worlds*. Eds. Marjorie Ford and Jon Ford. New York: McGraw-Hill, 1995.

Kingston, Maxine Hong. *The Woman Warrior*. New York: Knopf, 1976.

Lamott, Anne. *Bird by Bird: Some Instructions on Writing and Life*. New York: Anchor, 1994.

Mill, John Stuart. *Autobiography of John Stuart Mill*. New York: Columbia UP, 1966.

Plato. *Meno*. *Classics of Philosophy*. Ed. Louis P. Pojman. New York: Oxford UP, 1998.

Santiago, Esmeralda. *When I Was Puerto Rican*. New York: Vintage, 1993.

Solzhenitsyn, Aleksandr I. *The Gulag Archipelago*. New York: Harper and Row, 1973.

Quintilian. *Institutes of Oratory*. *The Rhetorical Tradition*. Eds. Patricia Bizzell and Bruce Herzberg. Boston: St. Martin's, 1990. 297–363.

CHAPTER 2

Finding Your
Audience in Your Purpose:
Reading Fiction,
Writing Exposition

"And he started to read. My words! He was reading my words out loud to the entire class. What's more, the entire class was listening. Listening attentively....I was feeling...pure ecstasy at this startling demonstration that my words had...power."

RUSSELL BAKER, *Growing Up*

"Expository writing...has a few very clear rules....The first and most fundamental of all those rules is simple: Make yourself understood."

STEPHEN WHITE, *The Written Word*

Identifying Your Audience and Purpose: Why Read? Why Write? And for Whom?

Have you ever experienced the "pure ecstasy" that Russell Baker describes above, the joy of hearing your writing read aloud, of seeing your words capture your audience, moving them to see what you want them to see, to believe what you want them to believe, or to do what you want them to do?

You might not expect to experience such joy in a college writing classroom, where you anticipate one reader, the professor, and one purpose, a good grade. But you should expect much more. As you discovered in chapter one, you should expect to learn reading and pre-writing strategies that will help you find a purpose beyond that passing grade and an audience beyond your professor. Indeed, according to Dr. Peter Elbow, a writing professor at the University of Massachusetts, you should always expect reading and writing assignments that help you to make sense of your "lives and feelings" (538). Such writing will always seem deeply purposeful, always worth sharing.

Your reading and writing in chapter one focused on non-fiction narratives, true stories about this same struggle to understand our feelings and thoughts, particularly on the interrelated subjects of literacy and liberty. Another kind of narrative, the novel or the short story, provides fictional accounts of this same life-long search for meaning in our lives. Rarely, however, will a novel or short story include a thesis statement, the explicit claim which all essays include. Instead, fiction writers show us their meanings through description, they let us hear their meanings through dialogue, but they leave us free to infer, to interpret what we saw and heard. Notice that I used the plural form, meanings. Most serious works of fiction carry multiple meanings, precisely because they deal with the complexities of human motivation and the uncertainties of our lives. Consequently, because of these multiple meanings, fictional narratives often inspire another kind of writing, the **expository essay**, which aims to explain at least one of those meanings, one of those interpretations derived from the story. To put it another way, expository writing aims to account for our experience as readers, to inform our audience how we made sense of the complex fiction.

Writing the Expository Essay

This chapter, then, will offer readings in fiction, a selection from Ernest Gaines' novel *A Lesson Before Dying*, then two short stories, Sarah Orne Jewett's "A White Heron" and Zora Neale Hurston's "Sweat." All three fictions focus on the subject of personal growth, but you'll find not a single thesis statement on this topic anywhere. Instead, you'll be invited to write an **expository essay** on these works, explaining to your readers what inferences you make from the stories about the subject of personal growth. To assist you in moving from reading fiction to writing exposition, the chapter will provide another sample of student writing, an expository essay on *A Lesson Before Dying*. The chapter will also build on what you learned in chapter one about asking questions about the stories, about journaling on your reflections, about moving from reflections to a draft, about collaborating with other writers to revise your exposition, making it clearer to your reader how you arrived at your meaning. You will also learn the elements of fiction, giving you the vocabulary you will need to write expositions of literature.

Applying Burke's Pentad to Ernest Gaines' Novel

Before you read the excerpt from Gaines' novel, printed below, consider the historical and fictional contexts of the excerpt. Publishing *A Lesson Before Dying* in 1993, Gaines sets his novel in 1948, fifteen years before Martin Luther King found himself in Birmingham jail for challenging his country to live up to its promise of justice for all (see chapter four). Though Grant Wiggins has escaped his rural Louisiana home long enough to earn a teacher's degree in California, this teacher has returned to the St. Charles River, a pull that every Louisianan understands.

However, after six years of teaching in a one-room school, Grant regrets his decision, driven to despair by a chronic shortage of textbooks and by a white superintendent of schools, who tolerates no whining for frills like paper, pencils and chalk, and who inspects the teeth of black children as though they were cattle, as though they were slaves.

Though desperate to leave such hopelessness, this "vicious circle" of racism (62), Grant feels compelled to stay, at least until his lover Vivian wins her freedom from a loveless marriage. Grant also gets caught up in the life of Jefferson, a twenty-one-year old black man who finds himself on death row for a crime he did not commit. After Jefferson's trial, Grant finds he must also stay long enough to attempt the impossible, to teach an innocent "boy" to die with dignity. Specifically, Grant's aunt and Jefferson's godmother insist that he teach Jefferson to walk to the electric chair like a man, even though Jefferson's culture has never affirmed that status, even though his attorney publicly called him a brainless "hog" in order to win a 'life' sentence instead of a death sentence (7–8). Additionally, Reverend Ambrose demands that Grant teach Jefferson to kneel before God, asking forgiveness, overlooking the fact of Jefferson's innocence. In short, Grant has been asked to "change everything that has been going on for three hundred years" (167).

In the excerpt that follows below, you will overhear the struggle between the minister and the teacher; you will then hear the life-saving lessons that Grant teaches in Jefferson's cell; finally, you will read Jefferson's diary, the illiterate but eloquent record of his new manhood, his personal growth. After you have read this selection, you will return to Kenneth Burke's pentad (see chapter one), answering questions that will help you to pin down who did what, where, how, and why. Once again, as you fill your journal with answers to these and other questions, you will be preparing to write on the topic suggested in the next section.

Excerpt from *A Lesson Before Dying*

Ernest Gaines

Chapter 27

After church, the minister came back to the house with my aunt, Miss Eloise, Miss Emma, and Inez for coffee and cake. I lay across the bed in my room, looking out the window at the stack of bean poles in the garden. As far back as I could remember, my aunt would pull up the rows of poles at the end of each season and stack them in that same corner of the garden, until a new crop of beans was ready to be poled. Beyond the poles, on the other side of the road, I could see the tops of the pecan trees in Farrell Jarreau's backyard. The trees had begun to bud again. The buds looked black from this distance. I could see above the trees how heavy, low, and gray the sky was. I had intended to go for a drive, but I was afraid it might rain while I was gone, making the road too muddy for me to drive back down the quarter. Anyway, I had work to do. But as usual, I ended up doing only a little, because of the singing and praying up at the church. After Tante Lou and her company had been at the house awhile, she came into my room. 1

"You 'sleep?" she asked. 2

"I'm awake." 3

"Reverend Ambrose like to talk to you." 4

"What about?" 5

I lay on my back, gazing up at the ceiling, my hands clasped behind my head so that my arms stuck out, forming a cross. 6

"I done told you that's bad luck," my aunt said. 7

Without shifting my eyes from the ceiling, I unclasped my hands from behind my head and clasped them on my chest. Tante Lou stood there looking at me. 8

"He can come in?" 9

"Sure. He can come in." 10

"You go'n put on your shoes and tuck in that shirt?" she asked. 11

"I'll put on my shoes and tuck in my shirt," I said. 12

She stood there watching me awhile, then she left the room. I sat up on the bed and passed my hands over my face. When the minister came into the room, I had tucked in my shirt and put on my shoes, and I was standing at the window looking out at the garden. My aunt had prepared a half-dozen rows about thirty feet long for spring planting. She would start her planting the week after Easter if the ground was dry enough. 13

The minister stood behind me, and I turned from the window to look at him. 14

"Care to sit down, Reverend?" 15

There were only two chairs in the room, the one at my desk and a rocker by the 16
fireplace.

"You go'n sit down?" he asked me. 17

"I don't mind standing." 18

He looked at my desk. 19

"I see you been working." 20

"I tried to. Afraid I didn't get too much done." 21

He sat down in the chair and looked up at me. 22

"They learning anything?" 23

"I do my best, Reverend." 24

He nodded his bald head. "I do the same. My best." 25

My back to the window, I waited to hear what he wanted to talk to me about. He 26
looked down at his hands and rubbed them together. For a man his size, he had really
big hands. He rubbed them again before raising his eyes to me.

"There ain't much time." 27

"Jefferson?" 28

"Yes." 29

"Three weeks." 30

"Not quite." 31

"Minus a couple days," I said. 32

He nodded his head, a small, tired little man. He had preached a long sermon 33
today, and it showed in his face.

"He ain't saved." 34

"I can't help you there, Reverend." 35

"That's where you wrong. He listen to you." 36

I turned my back on him and looked out on the garden. 37

"You ever think of anybody else but yourself?" 38

I didn't answer him. 39

"I ask you, 'You ever think of anybody but yourself?'" 40

"I have my work to do, Reverend, you have yours," I said, without looking around 41
at him. "Mine is reading, writing, and arithmetic, yours is saving souls."

"He don't need no more reading, writing, and 'rithmetic." 42

"That's where you come in, Reverend." 43

I stared beyond the garden toward the budding pecan trees in Farrell Jarreau's 44
backyard. The sky was so low the trees seemed nearly to touch it.

"When you going back?" Reverend Ambrose asked behind me. 45

"I don't know. One day next week, I suppose." 46

"And what you go'n talk about?" 47

"I don't know, Reverend." 48

"I'm going back with Sis' Emma tomorrow. I'm go'n talk about God." 49

"I'm sure he needs to hear that, Reverend." 50

"You sure you sure?" 51

"Maybe not. Maybe I'm not sure about anything." 52

"I know I'm sure," he said. "Yes, I know I'm sure." 53

I looked out at the newly turned rows of earth, and I wished I could just lie down 54
between the rows and not hear and not be a part of any of this.

"This is a mean world. But there is a better one. I wish to prepare him for that 55
better world. But I need your help."

"I don't believe in that other world, Reverend." 56

"Don't believe in God?" 57

"I believe in God, Reverend," I said, looking beyond the rows of turned-up earth, 58
toward the budding pecan trees across the road. "I believe in God. Every day of my life
I believe in God."

"Just not that other world?" 59

I didn't answer him. 60

"And how could they go on? You ever thought about that?" 61

I looked at the buds on the trees, and I did not answer him. 62

"Well?" he said to my back. 63

I turned from the window and looked at him where he sat at my desk. School 64
papers, notebooks, textbooks, and pencils were spread out on the table behind him.

"She told me to help him walk to that chair like a man—not like a hog—and I'm 65
doing the best I can, Reverend. The rest is up to you."

He got up from the chair and came toward me. He peered at me intently, his face 66
showing pain and confusion. He stopped at arm's distance from me, and I could smell

in his clothes the sweat from his preaching.

"You think you educated?" 67

"I went to college." 68

"But what did you learn?" 69

"To teach reading, writing, and arithmetic, Reverend." 70

"What did you learn about your own people? What did you learn about her—her 71 'round there?" he said, gesturing toward the other room and trying to keep his voice down.

I didn't answer him. 72

"No, you not educated, boy," he said shaking his head. "You far from being 73 educated. You learned your reading, writing, and 'rithmetic, but you don't know nothing. You don't even know yourself. Well?"

"You're doing the talking, Reverend." 74

"And educated, boy," he said, thumping his chest. "I'm the one that's educated. 75 I know people like you look down on people like me, but"—he touched his chest again—"I'm the one that's educated."

He stared at me as if he could not make up his mind whether to hit me or scream. 76

"Grief, oh, Grief." He muffled his cry. "When will you cease? Oh, when?" He drew 77 a deep breath, then he began to speak faster. "When they had nothing else but grief, where was the release? None, none till He rose. And He said there's relief from grief across the river, and she believed, and there was relief from grief. Do you know what I'm trying to say to you, boy?"

"I hear you talking, Reverend." 78

"You hear me talking. But are you listening? No, you ain't listening." 79

His eyes examined me, from the top of my head to my chest, and I could see the 80 rage in his face, see his mouth trembling. He was doing all he could to control his voice so that the others, back in the kitchen, would not hear him.

"I won't let you send that boy's soul to hell," he said. "I'll fight you with all the 81 strength I have left in this body, and I'll win."

"You don't have to fight me, Reverend," I told him. "You can have him all to 82 yourself. I don't even have to go back up there, if that's all you want."

"You going back," he said, nodding his bald head, and still trying hard to control 83 his voice. "You owe her much as I owe her. And long as I can stand on my feet, I owe her and all the others every ounce of my being. And you do too."

"I don't owe anybody anything, Reverend," I said, and turned toward the window. 84

I felt his hand gripping my shoulder and pulling me around to face him. 85

"Don't you turn your back on me, boy." 86

"My name is Grant," I said. 87

"When you act educated, I'll call you Grant. I'll even call you Mr. Grant, when 88
you act like a man." His hand still grasped my shoulder, and I needed all my willpower
to keep from knocking it off. He could see what I was thinking, and he slowly released
his grip and brought his hand to his side. "You think you the only one ever felt this
way?" he asked. "You think I never felt this way? You think she never felt this way?
Every last one of them back there one time in they life wanted to give up. She want to
give up now. You know that? You got any idea how sick she is? Soon after he go, she's
going too. I won't give her another year. I want her to believe he'll be up there waiting
for her. And you can help me do it. And you the only one."

"How?" 89

"Tell him to fall down on his knees 'fore he walk to that chair. Tell him to fall 90
down on his knees 'fore her. You the only one he'll listen to. He won't listen to me."

"No," I said. "I won't tell him to kneel. I'll tell him to listen to you—but I won't tell 91
him to kneel. I will try to help him stand."

"You think a man can't kneel and stand?" 92

"It hasn't helped me." 93

The minister drew back from me. His head was shining; so was his face. I could 94
see his mouth working as though he wanted to say something but didn't know how to
say it.

"You're just lost," he said. "That's all. You're just lost." 95

"Yes, sir, I'm lost. Like most men, I'm lost." 96

"Not all men," he said. "Me, I'm found." 97

"Then you're one of the lucky ones, Reverend." 98

"And I won't let you lose his soul in hell." 99

"I want him in heaven as much as you do, Reverend." 100

"A place you can't believe in?" 101

"No, I don't believe in it, Reverend." 102

"And how can you tell him to believe in it?" 103

"I'll never tell him not to believe in it." 104

"And suppose he ask you if it's there, then what? Suppose he write on that tablet 105
you give him, is it there? Then what?"

"I'll tell him I don't know." 106

"You the teacher." 107

"Yes. But I was taught to teach reading, writing, and arithmetic. Not the gospel. I'd tell him I heard it was there, but I don't know." 108

"And suppose he ask you if you believe in heaven? Then what?" 109

"I hope he doesn't, Reverend." 110

"Suppose he do?" 111

"I hope he doesn't." 112

"You couldn't say yes?" 113

"No, Reverend, I couldn't say yes. I couldn't lie to him at this moment. I will never tell him another lie, no matter what." 114

"No for her sake?" 115

"No, sir." 116

The minister nodded his bald head and grunted to himself. His dark-brown eyes in that tired, weary face continued to stare back at me. 117

"You think you educated, but you not. You think you the only person ever had to lie? You think I never had to lie?" 118

"I don't know, Reverend." 119

"Yes, you know. You know, all right. That's why you look down on me, because you know I lie. At wakes, at funerals, at weddings——yes, I lie. I lie at wakes and funerals to relieve pain. 'Cause reading, writing, and 'rithmetic is not enough. You think that's all they sent you to school for? They sent you to school to relieve pain, to relieve hurt—and if you have to lie to do it, then you lie. You lie and you lie and you lie. When you tell yourself you feeling good when you sick, you lying. You tell them that 'cause they have pain too, and you don't want to add yours—and you lie. She been lying every day of her life, your aunt in there. That's how you got through that university—cheating herself here, cheating herself there, but always telling you she's all right. I've seen her hands bleed from picking cotton. I've seen the blisters from the hoe and the cane knife. At that church, crying on her knees. You ever looked at the scabs on her knees, boy? Course you never. 'Cause she never wanted you to see it. And that's the difference between me and you, boy; that make me the educated one, and you the gump. I know my people. I know what they gone through. I know they done cheated themself, lied to themself—hoping that one they all love and trust can come back and help relieve the pain." 120

Chapter 28

I went into the cell with a paper bag full of baked sweet potatoes. The deputy locked the heavy door behind me. 121

"How's it going, partner?" 122

Jefferson nodded. 123

"How do you feel?"

124

"I'm all right."

125

"I brought you a little something."

126

Jefferson was sitting on the bunk, with his hands clasped together. I put the bag beside him on the bunk and sat down. I could hear the radio, on the floor against the wall, playing a sad cowboy song. I saw the notebook and the pencil on the floor, next to the radio. This was my first visit since I'd given him the notebook and pencil, and I could see that the lead on the pencil was worn down to the wood. I could also see that he had used the eraser a lot. We were quiet awhile.

127

"Hungry?" I asked.

128

"Maybe later."

129

"I see you've been writing."

130

He didn't answer.

131

"Personal, or can I look at it?"

132

"It ain't nothing."

133

"Do you mind?" I asked.

134

"If you want."

135

I got the notebook and came back to the bunk. The fellow on the radio was saying what a beautiful day it was in Baton Rouge.

136

Jefferson had filled three quarters of the first page. The letters were large and awkward, the way someone would write who could barely see. He had written across the lines instead of above them. He had used the eraser so much that in some places the paper was worn through. Nothing was capitalized, and there were no punctuation marks. The letters were thin at the beginning, but became broader as the lead was worn down. As closely as I could figure, he had written: *I dreampt it again last night. They was taking me somewhere. I wasn't crying. I wasn't begging. I was just going, going with them. Then I woke up. I couldn't go back to sleep. I didn't want to go back to sleep. I didn't want dream no more.* There was a lot of erasing, then he wrote: *If I ain't nothing but a hog, how come they just don't knock me in the head like a hog? Starb me like a hog?* More erasing, then: *Man walk on two foots; hogs on four hoofs.*

137

The last couple of words were barely visible, because the lead had been worn down all the way to the wood. I read it over a second time before closing the notebook. I didn't know what to say to him. He was staring at the wall, his hands clasped together.

138

"Do you want me to bring you a pencil sharpener?" I asked after a while. "The little ones you hold in your hand?"

139

"If you can find one."

140

"I'm sure I can," I said. "You know, Paul would have sharpened this pencil for you. He wouldn't mind."   141

Jefferson had unclasped his hands, and now he was scraping the ends of his left fingernails with the index finger of the right hand. His fingernails were hard and purplish.   142

"When's Easter?" he asked.   143

"Tomorrow is Good Friday."   144

"That's when He rose?"   145

"No. He rose on Easter."   146

"That's when He died," Jefferson said to himself. "Never said a mumbling word. That's right. Not a word."   147

"Did you talk to Reverend Ambrose when he came to visit you?" I asked Jefferson.   148

"Some."   149

"You ought to talk to him. It's good for your nannan. She wants you to talk to him."   150

"He told me to pray."   151

"Do you?"   152

"No."   153

"It would be good for your nannan."   154

He looked at me. His eyes were large and sad and reddened.   155

"You think I'm going to heaven?" he asked.   156

"I don't know."   157

"You think Mr. Grope went to heaven? You think Brother and Bear went to heaven?"   158

"I don't know."   159

"Then what I'm go'n pray for?"   160

"For your nannan."   161

"Nannan don't need me to help her get to heaven. She'll make it if it's up there."   162

"She wants you there with her, where there's no pain and no sorrow."   163

He grinned at me, a brief cynical grin.   164

"You pray, Mr. Wiggins?"   165

"No, Jefferson, I don't."   166

He grunted. 167

"But then I'm lost, Jefferson," I said, looking at him closely. "At this moment I don't believe in anything. Like your nannan does, like Reverend Ambrose does, and like I want you to believe. I want you to believe so that one day maybe I will." 168

"In heaven, Mr. Wiggins?" 169

"If it helps others down here on earth, Jefferson." 170

"Reverend Ambrose say I have to give up what's down here. Say there ain't nothing down here on this earth for me no more." 171

"He meant possessions, Jefferson. Cars, money, clothes—thinks like that." 172

"You ever seen me with a car, Mr. Wiggins?" 173

"No." 174

"With more than a dollar in my pocket?" 175

"No." 176

"More than two pair shoes, Mr. Wiggins? One for Sunday, one for working in?" 177

"No, Jefferson." 178

"Then what on earth I got to give up, Mr. Wiggins?" 179

"You've never had any possessions to give up, Jefferson. But there is something greater than possessions—and that is love. I know you love her and would do anything for her. Didn't you eat the gumbo when you weren't hungry, just to please her? That's all we're asking for now, Jefferson—do something to please her." 180

"What about me, Mr. Wiggins? What people done done to please me?" 181

"Hasn't she done many things to please you, Jefferson? Cooked for you, washed for you, taken care of you when you were sick? She is sick now, Jefferson, and she is asking for only one thing in this world. Walk like a man. Meet her up there." 182

"Y'all asking a lot, Mr. Wiggins, from a poor old nigger who never had nothing." 183

"She would do it for you." 184

"She go to that chair for me, Mr. Wiggins? You? Anybody?" 185

He waited for me to answer him. I wouldn't. 186

"No, Mr. Wiggins, I got to go myself. Just me, Mr. Wiggins. Reverend Ambrose say God'd be there if I axe Him. You think He be there if I axe Him, Mr. Wiggins?" 187

"That's what they say, Jefferson." 188

"You believe in God, Mr. Wiggins?" 189

"Yes, Jefferson, I believe in God." 190

"How?" 191

"I think it's God that makes people care for people, Jefferson. I think it's God 192
makes children play and people sing. I believe it's God that brings loved ones together.
I believe it's God that makes trees bud and food grow out of the earth."

"Who make people kill people, Mr. Wiggins?" 193

"They killed His Son, Jefferson." 194

"And He never said a mumbling word." 195

"That's what they say." 196

"That's how I want to go, Mr. Wiggins. Not a mumbling word." 197

Another cowboy song was playing on the radio, but it was quiet and not 198
disturbing. I could hear inmates down the cellblock calling to one another. Jefferson sat
forward on the bunk, his big hands clasped together again. I still had the notebook. I
had started to open it, but changed my mind.

"You need anything, Jefferson?" 199

"No, I don't need nothing, Mr. Wiggins. Reverend Ambrose say I don't need 200
nothing down here no more."

"I'll get you that sharpener," I said. 201

"I ain't got nothing more to say, Mr. Wiggins." 202

"I'm sure you have." 203

"I hope the time just hurry up and get here. Cut out all this waiting." 204

"I wish I knew what to do, Jefferson." 205

"I'm the one got to do everything, Mr. Wiggins. I'm the one." 206

He got up from the bunk and went to the window and looked up at the buds on 207
the higher branches of the sycamore tree. Through the branches of the tree I could see
the sky, blue and lovely and clear. "You Are My Sunshine" was playing on the radio.
Jefferson turned his back to the window and looked at me. "Me, Mr. Wiggins. Me. Me
to take the cross. Your cross, nannan's cross, my own cross. Me, Mr. Wiggins. This old
stumbling nigger. Y'all axe a lot, Mr. Wiggins." He went to the cell door and grasped
it with both hands. He started to jerk on the door, but changed his mind and turned
back to look at me. "Who ever car'd my cross, Mr. Wiggins? My mama? My daddy?
They dropped me when I wasn't nothing. Still don't know where they at this minute. I
went in the field when I was six, driving that old water cart. I done pulled that cotton
sack, I done cut cane, load cane, swung that ax, chop ditch banks, since I was six." He
was standing over me now. "Yes, I'm youman, Mr. Wiggins. But nobody didn't know
that 'fore now. Cuss for nothing. Beat for nothing. Work for nothing. Grinned to get
by. Everybody thought that's how it was s'pose to be. You too, Mr. Wiggins. You never
thought I was nothing else. I didn't neither. Thought I was doing what the Lord had

put me on this earth to do." He went to the window and turned to look at me. "Now all y'all want me to be better than ever'body else. How, Mr. Wiggins? You tell me."

"I don't know, Jefferson." 208

"What I got left, Mr. Wiggins—two weeks?" 209

"I think it's something like that—if nothing happens." 210

"Nothing go'n happen, Mr. Wiggins. And it ain't 'something like that.' That's all I got on this here earth. I got to face that, Mr. Wiggins. It's all right for y'all to say 'something like that.' For me, it's 'that'—'that,' that's all. And like Reverend Ambrose say, then I'll have to give up this old earth. But ain't that where I'm going, Mr. Wiggins, back in the earth?" 211

My head down, I didn't answer him. 212

"You can look at me, Mr. Wiggins; I don't mind." 213

I raised my head, and I saw him standing there under the window, big and tall, and not stooped as he had been in chains. 214

"I'm go'n do my best, Mr. Wiggins. That's all I can promise. My best." 215

"You're more a man than I am, Jefferson." 216

"'Cause I'm go'n die soon? That make me a man, Mr. Wiggins?" 217

"My eyes were closed before this moment, Jefferson. My eyes have been closed all my life. Yes, we all need you. Every last one of us." 218

He studied me awhile, then he turned his back and looked up at the window. 219

"So pretty out there," he said. "So pretty. I ain't never seen it so pretty." I looked at him standing there big and tall, his broad back toward me. "What it go'n be like, Mr. Wiggins?" 220

I thought I knew what he was talking about, but I didn't answer him. He turned around to face me. 221

"What it go'n feel like, Mr. Wiggins?" 222

I shook my head. I felt my eyes burning. 223

"I hope it ain't long." 224

"It's not long, Jefferson," I said. 225

"How you know, Mr. Wiggins?" 226

"I read it." 227

I was not looking at him. I was looking at the wall. It had been in the newspaper. The first jolt, if everything is right, immediately knocked a person unconscious. 228

He came back and sat down on the bunk. 229

"I'm all right, Mr. Wiggins." 230

I nodded without looking at him. 231

"Care for a 'tato, Mr. Wiggins?" he said, opening the paper bag. 232

"Sure," I said. 233

Chapter 29

Jefferson's Diary

mr wigin you say rite somethin but I dont kno what to rite an you say i must be 234
thinkin bout things i aint telin nobody an i order put it on paper but i dont kno what
to put on paper cause i aint never rote nothin but homework i aint never rote a leter in
all my life cause nanan use to get other chiren to rite her leter an read her leter for her
not me so i cant think of too much to say but maybe nex time

its evenin an i done eat my rice an beans an i done had my cup of milk an the sun 235
comin in the windo cause i can see it splashin on the flo and i can yer ned an them
talkin an thats bout all for now

i coudn sleep las nite cause i kept dreamin it and i dont want dreem it cause im 236
jus walkin to somwher but i dont kno wher its at an fore i get to the door i wake up an
i want to rite in the tablet las nite but you aint got no lite in yer but the moon so im
ritin this monin soon is sunup but now i done fogot what i want to say

nanan brot me some easter egg an i et one an nanan et one an reven ambros he 237
et one an reven ambros ax me if i know why the lord die an he say he die for me so i
can meet him in heven an all he want me to do is say i want be up ther wit him an the
angels an say if i mean it wit all my heart an sol ill go to heven an nanan start cryin
again an mis lou got to hug her an nanan say all i need to do an make her life wors
livin is ax the lord forgiv me in the pardn of my sin an her an reven ambros was on
they knee an mis lou was still in the cher huggin her an i was glad when paul come an
got me

i dont kno what day it is but las nite i coudn sleep an i cud yer ned down the way 238
snoin an i laid ther and thot bout samson sayin if the lord love me how com he let
my wife die an leave me an them chiren an how come he dont come here an take way
people like them matin brothers on the st charl river stead of messin wit po ol foks
who aint never done nothin but try an do all they kno how to serv him

it look like the lord just work for wite folks cause ever sens i wasn nothin but a 239
litle boy i been on my on haulin water to the fiel on that ol water cart wit all them
dime bukets an that dipper jus hittin an old dorthy just trottin and trottin an me up
their hittin her wit that rope an all them dime bukets an that dipper just hittin an
hittin gainst that bal of water so i can git the peple they food an they water on time
an the peple see me an drop they hoe an come and git they buket cause they kno they
string or they mark on the top an boo sittin under a bloodweed wit his wite beans an
rice and goin wher he at wher he at this yer very minit an how com he dont giv a man

a little breeze if he so mercful an mis rachel wit her rice an grens sayin keep it up jus keep it up an see if a clap of litenin dont come ther an nok the fool out you an boo sayin let him i dont care cause a ded niger is beter of an a live one any weekday an saddy im gittin drunk an say it agin an saddy standin in the midle the road hollin up in the air sayin com on an git me com on an git me see if i care an fallin down in the dich an rollin back in the dich an rollin back in the road an drinkin and holin the botle up so the lord could see it an sayin i kno you dont love nobody but wite folks cause you they god not mine an com on an tho you litenin if you want cause no niger aint got no god an the church goin people closin they doors an windos to keep from herin boo blasfemin the lord but me an the rest of the chiren in the quarter like boo cause he always boght us candy an cake

i jus cant sleep no mo cause evertime i shet my eyes i see that door an fore i git 240
ther i wake up an i dont go back to sleep cause i dont want walk to that door no mo cause i dont know what back o ther f its wher they gon put that cher or if it spose to mean def or the grave or heven i dont know i wonder if boo went to heven cause i know he didn git religin firs

mr wigin you say you like what i got here but you say you still cant giv me a a jus 241
a b cause you say i aint gone deep in me yet an you kno i can if i try hard an when i ax you what you mean deep in me you say jus say whats on my mind so one day you can be save an you can save the chiren and i say i don't kno what you mean an you say i do kno what you mean an you look so tied sometime mr wigin i just feel like tellin you i like you but i dont kno how to say this cause i aint never say it to nobody before an nobody aint never say it to me

i kno i care for nanan but i dont kno if love is care cause cuttin wood and haulin 242
water and things like that i dont know if thats love or jus work to do an you say thats love but you say you kno i got mo an jus that to say an when i lay ther at nite and ant sleep i try an think what you mean i got mo cause i aint done this much thinkin and this much writin in all my life befor

its munday an i aint got but just a few days lef an i hope i see my nanan jus one 243
mo time cause mis lou and reven ambros say she aint fairin too good an coudn make it wit them this time but the lord kno mr wigin i hope i can see her one mo time on this earth fore i go is that love mr wigin when you want to see sombody bad bad mr wigin thank you for sayin im doin b+ work an you know the a aint too far

the shef an mr picho and mr mogan come in the cell today an mr picho ax me 244
how im doin an i tell him im doin all rite an he say yes he can see im all rite an he ax me if he can do somthin for me an i tell him nosir im all rite and he ax if i want a brand new pencil wit a penny erase on it an i tol him i wud take the pencil but i dont need the erase cause you tol me to jus put down anything come in my hed an if it aint rite jus scratch over it an go on an he say yes he can see that an he ax me if i want him to shopen my pencil an i say yesir and he shopen the pencil on a teeny perl hanle nife an i look at the nife an i seen mr picho look up at shef guiry an mr mogan an the shef look back at him but mr mogan never stop lookin at me like he was tryin to figer me

an me an mr picho ax me if i want the litle nife an i tell him yesir i didn mind an he unhook the litle gole chan from his belt lope an han me the nife an the chan an he say it was all mine an i say just for a few days an you can hav it back an i helt the litle nife in my han an the chan in my other han an jus look at it an i yer mr picho say well an i yer mr mogan say it aint fridy yet an mr picho say you want double that bet you want add that troter an mr mogan say it still aint fridy yet

ole clark been comin roun too tryin to act like a youman but i can see in his face   245 he aint no good an i dont even look at him when he ax me if im doin all rite and can he git me somthin no i jus go on ritin in my tablet an i dont care if he do see it after im dead and gone

paul trying to be hod when he aint like he dont want get too close to me no mo   246 an all the time he is the only one rond yer kno how to talk like a youman to people i kno you paul an i kno ole clark an i kno you too shef guiry and you mr picho and mr mogan an all the rest of yall i jus never say non of this befor but i know yall ever las one of yall

lord have merce sweet jesus mr wigin where all them peple come from when you   247 ax me if some chiren can com up here an speak to me i didn kno you was meanin all them chiren in yo clas an jus sitin ther on the flo all quite in they clean close lookin at me an i coud see som was scard o me but mos was brave an spoke an my litle cosin estel even com up an kiss me on the jaw an i coudn hol it back no mo

then after the chiren here com the ole folks an look like everbody from the quarter   248 was here mis julia an joe an mis haret an ant agnes an mr noman an mis sara an mis lilia an mr harry an mis lena an god kno who all an mr ofal an mis felia wit her beeds an jus prayin an all the peple sayin how good i look an lord hav merce sweet jesus mr wigin how you got bok yer in that suit that suit look like it half bog siz cause i member mis rita got him that suit way back ten leben yers back an bok babbin ther like he kno me an mis rita sayin he want to say glad to see me an he want to give me one of hiss aggis an me jus lookin at bok shakin my head an shakin my hed an i cant stop sayin ole bok ole bok you want giv me one o you aggis but ole bok woudn turn it loose til mis rita had to tell him let go bok few times an still bok woudn turn loose till mis rita pri it out his han and han it to me an bok start babbin ther til mis rita had to reach out her han of me to give it back to her an she giv it back to bok an bok put it back in his pocket an start rattlin it wit all the others in ther an mis rita say she was sho he want to giv me somthin thats why he want to com an i tol her it was all rite i didn't need nothin but she say bok woudn res tonite if he didn giv me somethin an she tol him to giv me a diffen one if he didn want give me the aggi an ole bok lookin way over yonder kep rattlin the marbles in his pocket an jus kep on lookin way over yonder rattlin the marbles til he fond the litles one he had in his pocket an han me that

this was the firs time i cry when they lok that door bahind me the very firs time an   249 i jus set on my bunk cryin but not let them see or yer me cause i didn want them think rong but i was cryin cause of bok an the marble he giv me and cause o the peple com to see me cause they hadn never done nothin lik that for me befor i dont want to sleep at nite no mo jus catnap in the day while they got lite and they got noise cause i dont want drem bout that door ever time i shet my eyes

250

when they brot me in the room an i seen nanan at the table i seen how ole she look an how tied she look an i tol her i love her an i tol her i was strong an she just look ole and tied an pull me to her an kiss me an it was the firs time she never done that an i felt good an i let her hol me long is she want cause you say it was good for her an i tol her i was strong an she didn need to come back no mo cause i was strong an she just set ther wit her eyes mos shet like she want to go to sleep lookin at me all the time til reven and mis lou have to hep her up an take her back home

251

mr wigin when i see you girlfren an yall together i see how pretty she is an im sorry how i talk that day when i was mad at you an say them nasty thing bout her cause she so pretty an smil so pretty when she look at peple an you can see she aint putin on airs an its jus kwaly in her an she talk so nice to peple an all the time i want to look at her but scare to cause she so pretty an im so ugly an she got on a pretty dress with pretty flowers an my close dont smell good and i aint took a baf sens sady but i still want look at her an she say she think im lookin good an strong an when she put her han on my sholder i start tremblin an she lean close an kiss me and i feel hot an i could smell her poder cent an i felt good an scare an hot cause thats the firs lady that pretty ever tech me an nobody that pretty never kiss me an when yall left i come to the door an i look at her long long as i coud and coud smell her poder cent and still feel her mof on my face

252

im sory i cry mr wigin im sory i cry when you say you aint comin back tomoro im strong an reven ambros gon be yer wit me an mr harry comin to an reson i cry cause you been so good to me mr wigin an nobody aint never been that good to me an make me think im sombody

253

shef guiry ax me what i want for my super an i tol him i want nanan to cook me som okra an rice an some pok chop an a cornbred an som claba an he say he gon see what he can do an say what i want for desert an i tol him jus a little ice crme in a cup an a moon pie

254

they took me an let me stan under the shoer wit a new bar a sope an they giv me a big wite clen tower an brot me back an i put on some clen close an set down cause my food was yer an i et it ever bit an it was the bes meal i kno my nanan ever cook

255

sun goin down an i kno this the las one im gon ever see but im gon see one mo sunrise cause i aint gon sleep tonite

256

im gon sleep a long time after tomoro

257

shef guiry come by after i et an ax me how im doin an i say im doin all right an he ax me he say i aint never pik up yo tablet an look in it an he ax me what all i been ritin an i tol him jus things an he say aint he done tret me rite an i tol him yesir an he say aint his deptis done tret me fair an i tol him yesir an he say aint he done let peple vist me anytime an i say yesir an he say didn he let the chiren an all the peple from the quarter com an visit me jus two days ago an i say yesir an he say good put that down in

258

yo tablet i tret you good all the tiem you been yer an he say he had to go hom cause he hadn et his super yet but for me to call a depty if i need somthin an he ax me if i want the lite to stay on all nite in case i want rite som mo an i tol him yesir an he say all rite i coud have all the lite i want

my lite on but they aint no mo lite on in the place an the place is quite quite but nobody sleepin 259

they got a moon out ther an i can see the leves on the tree but i aint gon see no mo leves after tomoro 260

i dont know if they got a heven cause samson say they cant be an boo say they aint non of no niger but reven ambros say they is one for all men an bok dont kno 261

i been shakin an shakin but im gon stay strong 262

i aint had no bisnes goin ther wit brother an bear cause they aint no good an im gon be meetin them soon 263

its quite quite an i can yer my teefs hitin an i can yer my heart 264

when i was a litle boy i was a waterboy an rode the cart but now i got to be a man an set in a cher 265

dont kno if you can read this mr wigin my han shakin and i can yer my hart 266

i can yer randy but i aint listnin no mo cause he for the livin and not for me 267

its late an i dont know what time it is but i kno its late an i jus went to the tolet an i jus wash my face 268

day breakin 269

sun comin up 270

the bird in the tre soun like a blu bird 271

sky blu blu mr wigin 272

good by mr wigin tell them im strong tell them im a man good by mr wigin im gon ax paul if he can bring you this 273

sincely jefferson 274

Recognizing the Relationship Between Audience and Purpose

If you answered Burkean questions in your journal as you read this excerpt from Gaines' novel, you have already made significant discoveries about the close relationship of audience to purpose. For example, when you answered the "what happened?" question about chapter 27, you noted that Reverend Ambrose commands Grant to tell Jefferson to get on his knees and pray for forgiveness before his execution. In answering this question, you probably bumped into "why?" recognizing that the Reverend's jealousy over Grant's influence on

Jefferson motivates him at least as much as his desire to save souls. At the same time, you probably realized the relevance of "where does the action happen?" Since Ambrose has the audacity to give these orders in Grant's bedroom, you no doubt also addressed Burke's agency question—how does Ambrose try to manipulate Grant to follow his orders? In answering this question, you realized that Ambrose bases his daring command on the authority of God (Jefferson "ain't saved"), on Grant's apparent insensitivity to the needs of Jefferson's dying godmother ("Soon after he go, she's going too"), and on Grant's alleged incompetence ("you don't know nothing"). Realizing that his manipulations have failed, that his "audience" hasn't budged, Ambrose tries to change Grant's mind by confessing his own willingness to lie to "relieve pain" of his grieving parishioners.

In answering these questions on Reverend Ambrose, you inescapably encountered a key question about Grant's motivations: Why won't Grant oblige Reverend Ambrose by telling Jefferson to "kneel" to God? As you discovered in the dialogue the answer to this question, you also discovered Grant's purpose: to help Jefferson "walk to the chair like a man....I'll tell him to listen to you—but I won't tell him to kneel. I will try to help him stand." Because Grant has come to embrace this dignity-saving purpose, he knows that he must resist the demands of his audience, Reverend Ambrose.

With these understandings about dramatic conflict in mind, you positioned yourself well to discover in chapter 28 that *a change in one's audience does not change one's purpose but does change one's language.* Facing now an increasingly receptive student instead of a well-intended but hostile, manipulative preacher, Grant dramatically changes his tone. When Jefferson responds to Grant's request that he please his godmother by talking with Reverend Ambrose, Grant responds honestly once again to questions about religion; however, instead of dismissing such questions of faith as he did in Reverend Ambrose's presence (religion "is up to you"), this time he acknowledges his doubts but endorses the seriousness and the validity of questions of belief:

> "You think I'm going to heaven?" he asked.
> "I don't know....I want you to believe so that one day maybe I will."
> "You believe in God, Mr. Wiggins?"
> "Yes, Jefferson, I believe in God....I think it's God that makes people
> care for people, Jefferson."

This gentle testimony also validates Grant's request, on behalf of the godmother, that Jefferson claim his worth in the manly way that he dies: "She is asking only one thing in this world. Walk like a man. Meet her up there."

Writing Your Own Expository Essay

With this analysis and your own journaling in front of you, you are now ready to try your hand at exposition. Explain to your readers how the excerpt that you read from Frederick Douglass' autobiography affects your view of Grant Wiggins as a teacher. As you inform your readers how you "read" Grant Wiggins, be sure that you consider how he defines his teacherly role in chapter 27, how he motivates Jefferson to learn in chapter 28, and what we see of his effectiveness as a teacher in chapter 29. Suggestion: Before you begin your draft, try freewriting for 10 minutes on each of these questions:

1. What does Jefferson's diary teach you about Jefferson?

2. What does Jefferson's diary teach you about writing?

After you have finished a rough draft drawn from these freewrites and from your journaling, begin the revision process by sharing your work with writing group members or with a tutor at your university Writing Center, as described at the end of chapter one and this chapter. In the meantime, consider the following expository essay on Gaines' novel, an essay which also explores the teacher-student relationship between Grant and Jefferson but draws on the entire novel, not just on the three chapters you have read. As you read this exposition, identify the student's *purpose* and determine where she seems to be addressing an audience beyond her obvious reader, the professor.

Student Essay: "See Me After Class!"

Amanda Beard

Teachers and students sometimes develop love-hate relationships. In Earnest Gaines' novel *A Lesson before Dying,* teacher Grant Wiggins and his student-prisoner Jefferson experience a bitter relationship that later blossoms into a gentle and loving friendship. Initially, Grant reluctantly agrees to teach Jefferson, a twenty-one-year-old on death row for a crime he did not commit, to go to his execution like a man, not like a "hog," the label he receives at his trial. Ironically, because Jefferson angrily resists Grant's teachings, the student ends up schooling the teacher as well as learning this lesson in self-respect.

Shortly after Jefferson's conviction for murder, Grant's Aunt and her friend Miss Emma urge Grant to go to the jailhouse and teach Jefferson how to become a man. Though they know they can't appeal the verdict reached by the racist jury, they hope that Grant, a college-educated teacher in this small Cajun town, can teach Jefferson to walk straight to the chair on his execution day, his self-respect restored. Though a dedicated teacher, Grant resists this charge, believing that he cannot reverse the destructive effects of racism in a few weeks:

Tante Lou, Miss Emma, Jefferson is dead. It is only a matter of weeks…but he's already dead. The past twenty-one years, we've done all we could for Jefferson. He's dead now. And I can't raise the dead. All I can do is try to keep the others from ending up like this. (14)

However, Grant has also fallen in love with Vivian, and she succeeds in persuading him to go to Jefferson, even though he is "screaming inside" (14).

After Grant's first several visits to Jefferson's cell, he believes that he was right, that his attempts to transform the hog into a man are useless. Filled with resentment and fear, Jefferson sits on his bunk, stares at the wall, and refuses to talk. Eventually, hoping to drive Grant away, Jefferson mocks Vivian in the crudest language he knows. Grant responds with controlled rage, a turning point for the angry student and the equally angry teacher:

> *That lady you speak of, boy, cares a lot about you. She's waiting at that school right now for me to bring her news about you. That's a lady you spoke of, boy. That's a lady. Because it's she who keeps me coming here. Not your nannan, not my aunt. Vivian. If I didn't have Vivian, I wouldn't be in this damn hole. Because I know damn well I'm not doing any good, for you or for any of the others. (130)*

This outburst from his teacher brings some "tears" into the hog's eyes, the first sign that he has begun to learn the lesson that will make him a man before dying.

This emotional breakthrough leads to many other lessons before Jefferson dies. Though Jefferson's defense attorney broke his spirits, trying to get him a lesser sentence by calling him a "hog" and a "fool," less than a man, Grant's persistence and anger, as we have seen, begin to penetrate Jefferson's despair. Next, Grant's generosity, in the shape of a radio, lures Jefferson back into life through the magic of music. But finally, Jefferson finds his manhood through language, filling the diary that Grant left with him. As Jefferson spends his last few days in his cell, his thoughts and emotions pour out into his diary. He expresses his newly found self worth by writing in semi-literate eloquence that "this was the firs time I cry….I jus set on my bunk cryin but not let them see or yer me cause I didn want them think rong but I was cryin cause…the peple com to see me cause they hadn never done nothing lik that for me befor" (231). In their following meetings, Grant helps Jefferson to realize that the entire town is behind him, admiring his efforts to be a man, to be braver and stronger than any of them. This strong man cries again, as his diary records, because "aint never been that good to me and make me think im somebody" (232).

Along with finding himself, Jefferson finds God, again with Grant's help. Reverend Ambrose had wanted Grant to persuade Jefferson to kneel down to God, but Grant refuses. In a furious attempt to deny Reverend Ambrose's soul-crushing request, Grant states, "No, I won't tell him to kneel. I'll tell him to listen to you—but I won't tell him to kneel. I will try to help him stand" (216). Though Grant is agnostic, he also teaches Jefferson that God "makes people care for people" (223), a lesson that strengthens Jefferson so that he can return his grandmother's love and walk to the electric chair with the dignity of a man: "Tell Nannan I walked" (254).

Jefferson the new man also teaches his teacher to value his educational skills. Before he begins to get through to Jefferson, Grant longs to give up his teaching—in the classroom as well as in the jail. Though Vivian tries to convince Grant that she sees "something is changing" (141), Grant denies it, until Jefferson's tears, as we have seen, confirm Vivian's perception. This one success revives the loving and compassionate teacher long dormant in Grant. He shows this kindness not only in bringing a radio, a diary, and ice cream to Jefferson, but also in teaching Jefferson that "a hero does for others. He would do anything for people he loves, because he knows it would make their lives better. I am not that kind of person, but I want you to be. You could give something to her, to me, to those children in the quarter" (191). Though Grant denies any heroics on his own part, his actions now certainly fit his definition of heroism, a lesson Grant needed to learn.

Grant and Jefferson's tension-filled relationship, then, evolves into a great success. Both teacher and student learn the power of words to change others, and both men learn self-respect by learning to accept others' love.

Practicing the Recursive Process of Writing

In reading the student's introduction, you readily discovered her purpose, to explain how and why Grant teaches Jefferson to be a man, and her equally strong sense of audience beyond the teacher, her desire, as journalist Stephen White puts it above, to be "understood" by her classmates. You also heard her purposefulness when she asserts that "the student ends up schooling the teacher." But you also found the student's purposefulness in her body paragraphs, where she lets her readers see and hear the transformations of teacher and student.

To prepare for writing this purposeful expository essay, the student moved through the process you practiced in chapter one, a process that works effectively in preparing expository essays as well as narrative essays:

- Journaling in response to her reading
- Sharing her journaling in class and on the WebCT Discussion board
- Listing and Freewriting in class
- Growing a Tree Outline
- Writing a rough draft
- Sharing her draft with members of her writing group
- Revising her draft based on responses from her peers

The paragraphs below will expand on each of the steps in this process, but you'll discover in taking each step that you often have to back-up. For example, as you draw the branches of your outline, you might discover a major branch for which you have no off-shoots, a clear signal that you have a gap in your reading, that you need to go back to the novel and find the evidence—the examples, quotes, details—that will enable you to complete your outline and to write a full draft. Similarly, if your writing group members suggest that one of your ideas lacks clarity because it lacks development, you may decide to go back to the freewriting stage or to the reading stage to find the examples, details, and quotations which will make your point clearly. Writing theorists use the term **recursiveness** to describe this back-and-forth nature of the writing process. Don't fight it. Instead, enjoy the adventure of finding your meaning through reading, asking questions, writing, asking more questions, reading again, and revising. In other words, if you resist going back-and-forth, marching mechanically from step one to step two, and so on, you will likely never discover your purpose or your audience; as a result, you will produce thin writing that engages neither you nor your readers.

First, as she read the novel, the student began her recursive process by answering reading prompts in her journal. She also shared her answers with other writers, sometimes in class, other times at the WebCT discussion site. Though she filled her journal with responses to questions on all 31 chapters, the questions listed below center on the Grant-Jefferson relationship, one that caught her interest early and kept her turning pages eagerly. Notice as you read these questions their Burkean nature, their focus not only on what happened but also on how and where Grant and Jefferson come in conflict, and why their conflict resolves.

1. How does the defense attorney's case affect your feelings for Jefferson? (7–8)

2. How do you explain Grant's anger—as a black man and as a teacher—when Miss Emma's face (12) and Tante Lou's words (13–14) urge him to talk to Henri about visiting Jefferson?

3. How do Grant's feelings for Vivian and for the town (29) explain his reluctance to intervene in Jefferson's case?

4. Describe Grant's teaching and disciplining methods. Do they seem effective? Explain. How do Grant's situation and the students' lives influence and explain Grant's harshness (29)?

5. What similarity do you see between the attorney's defense of Jefferson (ch. 1) and the way Mr. Pichot and Sheriff Guidry treat Grant (ch. 6)?

6. How does Grant use language to assert his manhood in this chapter?

7. At the top of p. 62, Grant compares the "old men" laborers to the student woodchoppers. What do his thoughts reveal about his goals as a teacher? Why had his former teacher urged Grant to "run"?

8. Why does Grant believe his aunt is "stripping" him of "everything you sent me to school for"?

9. Give two reasons why Grant tells Jefferson that he will "lie" to Emma about Jefferson's refusal to eat.

10. Why do Grant's memories of Joe Louis and the old men's talk of Jackie Robinson—both black heroes—make Grant think of Jefferson? What irony do you see in the achievement of these heroes?

11. How do you explain the tension and anger between Grant and his Aunt, Grant and Reverend Ambrose?

12. What does Grant mean when he says he is "unable to accept what used to be my life, unable to leave it"?

13. This novel on racism and injustice is also a love story. How does Grant's tenderness for Vivian affect your view of him? What effect might their love have on Grant's ability to "teach" Jefferson to be a man?

14. At the end of ch. 18, Grant wants to give up on Jefferson, but Vivian insists that "something is changing" (141). What evidence do you see in 16–18 that suggests that Grant and Jefferson are both changing?

15. What historical significance does Grant see in what Emma "wants" from Jefferson, what his Aunt wants from him? (166–167)

16. What connection do you see between Jefferson's crime and Grant's seeking money for Jefferson's radio (174)?

17. Why does Reverend Ambrose object to the "sin box" (181)?

18. What does Grant's defense of the radio tell you about the "change" in him and in Jefferson (182–183)?

19. What lesson does Grant teach Jefferson on 190–193? How does he use definitions and metaphors to teach the lesson?

20. What lesson does Grant learn about himself in chapters 25–26?

21. Why won't Grant oblige Reverend Ambrose by telling Jefferson to "kneel" to God? (216)

22. Given Grant's conflicts with Reverend Ambrose, what irony do you see in what he teaches Jefferson (222–225)?

23. What does Jefferson's diary teach you about Jefferson?

24. What does Jefferson's diary teach you about writing?

25. What thoughts, feelings, did you have in reading the description of the Chair and of Jefferson meeting his death?

26. How do Paul's comments and Grant's responses affect your view of Grant and Jefferson (254–256)?

If your professor assigns the entire novel, you'll find, as did the author of the expository essay above, that writing on all these questions will help you to generate information on both Grant and Jefferson. In any case, seeing all these questions here serves to remind you that good readers (chapter 1) must ask questions, and that such journaling focuses your reading, helping you to find key quotes and significant actions which, in turn, help you to discover what you want to say about the characters. Such discoveries inspire purposeful writing.

In sharing her journaling with her fellow students, in class and online, the student also renewed her membership in a community of writers, her audience. Further, journaling prepared her for other pre-writing activities. Having read each other's WebCT postings online and shared some journaling in class, the students undertook a **freewriting** exercise. As you recall from chapter one, such writing follows no rules and totally ignores "correctness" issues like spelling, punctuation, and pronoun usage. Instead, the reader "freely" responds to a focused prompt, writing furiously, non-stop, for 10 minutes to learn, in this case, what he or she believes about Gaines' characters, what conclusions and convictions the writer wants to convey to readers. More specifically, the students freewrote on the following prompts:

- List at least three characters from Gaines' novel who have captured your interest. Next to each name, in one sentence or even a phrase, write the reason(s) for your interest—one minute.

- Pick one of the characters and freewrite for two minutes on the conflicts or problems that character faces.

- Freewrite for seven minutes on what that character has done to resolve his or her conflicts, and on how you respond to those efforts.

Once they completed this freewriting, the students shared their views on the characters and issues that command their attention: Grant, on his conflicts with his aunt and with Reverend Ambrose, on his love-making with Vivian, on the lawyers and jail keepers, on the superintendent of schools, on Grant's students.

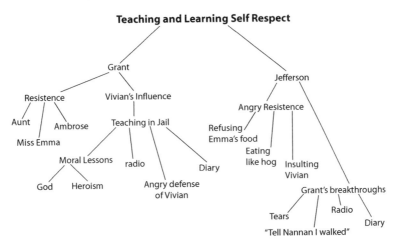

Figure: Tree Outline

After this exchange among members of this writing community, the students took home additional prewriting assignments. First, they completed two additional ten-minute freewrites, focusing on other characters from their initial list. This process increased the probability that they would write on characters they cared about the most. Next, they constructed tree outlines, (see figure) showing the characters they would describe and, as sub-branches, the sequence of events—the stories—that would support their emerging claims about the characters. The tree outline drawn by our student writer above featured the two primary branches, Grant and Jefferson, then the sub-branches that trace their interdependence as they move from anger and despair to self-respect and hope.

In completing this outline before she attempted a rough draft, the student could see at a glance that her essay would trace causes to effects, using quotes and examples from the novel to show how each man taught the other and learned from the other.

Having completed this critical reading, journaling, discussing, freewriting, and outlining, the student and her classmates proceeded with a rough draft of their essays on Gaines' novel. With the draft completed, they then met in writing groups of three to respond to each other's drafts, the same process you learned and practiced in chapter one. As you will note below in Guidelines for Responding to Draft on *A Lesson Before Dying*, this process calls for each author to read the draft aloud, then on responders to explain where they found the draft engaging and persuasive, and, on the other hand, where they felt confused or unconvinced. Notice, again, that this process calls for written comments as well as discussion. These comments provide both encouragement—praise for achieving a purpose, reaching an audience—and suggestions for doing so consistently.

Guidelines for Responding To Draft on *A Lesson Before Dying*

Name of Author:

Names of Readers:

Procedure:

1. The first reader should distribute a copy of the draft to each responder, state his or her purpose, and then proceed to read the draft aloud.

2. Responders should comment orally on the draft, using the questions under "Reader's Responses." Then, each responder should write those comments on a separate piece of paper so that the writer can use them in pondering revision.

3. Repeat 1–3 for each member of the group.

Reader's Responses—*Describe your experience reading the draft:*

1. Where does the essay "work" for you? Explain and be specific, relating the passage to the student's purpose.

2. Where does the draft need further work? Explain and be specific, connecting the problem(s) to the needs of the audience.

Checklist for Revision

Introduction

1. Does the introductory paragraph mention the name of the author and the title of the novel?

2. Does the introductory paragraph identify the problem to be explored? Does it make a claim (thesis) and forecast the organization of the analysis?

Body Paragraphs

1. Does each body paragraph begin with a transition (from the previous paragraph) and a topic sentence which ties into the thesis and moves the analysis forward?

2. Does each topic sentence receive support from examples and quotations? Are those examples sufficiently explained?

Conclusion

1. Have I achieved my purpose? Does the essay end with a fresh re-statement of the thesis, a summary of key points about the character(s) or theme?

2. Have I met the needs and expectations of my audience? Do I sound like I mean what I say (voice)?

Writing a Second Expository Essay

Having written a short expository paper on Grant and Jefferson's relationship, then studied a longer exposition on the same topic, you should be ready now to try a another expository piece, this time in response to Sarah Orne Jewett's "A White Heron," or Zora Neale Hurston's "Sweat." Both short stories, like Gaines' novel, explore the subject of personal growth; they also focus on a female character who breaks free of the man who smothers her.

Before Jewett's story, you will find a brief paragraph contextualizing her work, then a brief discussion of the story in terms of the elements of fiction: the cause-and-effect relationship between characterization and plot, the importance of setting in clarifying the problems that characters face, the value of imagery and symbolism in helping you to grasp a character's motives and the author's theme, the importance of narrative point of view in shaping your responses to the characters and their choices (see below for definitions of these terms).

Next, you'll find a list of questions—drawn from Burke's pentad—to help you get started on journaling. No doubt, your answers will generate other questions as well as lists of potential focal points, each providing a perfect prompt for a freewriting session. Such prewriting activities should then move to outlining, drafting, peer exchanges, then revision, the recursive process you have seen and practiced above.

Following Jewett's story, you'll find a paragraph describing the context of Hurston's story, then journaling questions on her powerful story, "Sweat," which follows the questions.

Using the Elements of Fiction to Interpret
Sarah Orne Jewett's Short Story

Published in 1886, Sarah Orne Jewett's "A White Heron" reflects the rural beauty on the coast of Maine, where Jewett lived most of her life surrounded by the ocean, the forests, and the birds that populate both realms. But the story also reveals a late-nineteenth-century Maine in transition, with "manufacturing towns" encroaching on the splendor of nature. According to critic Elizabeth Ammons, this tension between industrial progress and natural beauty parallels other "competing sets of values" in the story: "scientific/empathetic, masculine/feminine, adult/juvenal." Ammons claims, too, that the story "offers a highly critical perspective on heterosexual romantic love" (Ammons 131).

Before you tackle the following questions, each focused on conflicts caused by these "competing sets of values," consider the technical terms listed below. Understanding these elements of fiction will help you to answer the questions and, consequently, to understand the story.

Characterization: Most great fiction features neither heroes nor heroines but rather flawed characters who bear striking resemblances to flawed human beings, complicated bundles of virtues and vices who show themselves capable of intelligence and stupidity, courage and cowardice, compassion and cruelty. When these characters have differing motives, they come in **conflict**. In Jewett's story, for instance, you will see the main character, nine-year-old Sylvia, come into conflict with a young man: though they both love birds, Sylvia loves them in flight; he loves them stuffed. Therefore, we may call Sylvia the **protagonist** and the young hunter the **antagonist**; however, you should not necessarily see the protagonist as "the good guy" and the antagonist as "the bad guy." Think of them, rather, as two human beings with differing motivations. You'll see, too, that characters sometimes come in conflict with external forces—like the expanding of industry—and other times with themselves, which we will see when Sylvia struggles with the confusion created by her love for birds and her infatuation with the hunter.

Plot: Most plots exhibit chronological order (see chapter one), though readers often encounter **flashbacks**, tripping back in time with the characters as they remember the events that profoundly color their present. Sometimes, too, the action may begin at the end, with the entire story line representing a looking back as the narrator struggles to make sense of what happened and what that event means. Even as we allow for these structural innovations, we can think of most plots as having four parts:

- In a short story, the **exposition** may be one sentence or several paragraphs; in a novel, it may be the entire first chapter. Whatever the length, the exposition usually orients the reader to the main character and the situation he or she faces. In "A White Heron," for example, we meet Sylvia, a nine-year-old girl with no greater problem than herding her cow home before darkness falls in the woods. However, by the end of the second paragraph, we find her recalling her first eight years of life spent in a "crowded manufacturing town," then at the end of the third paragraph thinking that "she never should wish to go home again," implying the potential for conflict, should she ever have to leave her grandmother's country home. While such seeds for conflict often get planted in the exposition, you will see no conflict because the main character hasn't fully discovered a problem, hasn't made a choice to solve the problem, and hasn't encountered an adversary, an antagonist, a person or force that opposes the main character's desires.

- After the exposition comes the **rising action**, a section that begins at the point of initial conflict, when the main character encounters a problem and an opponent, sometimes simultaneously. You will find a question below that asks you to find that point in "A White Heron." The rising action ends at the point of **climax**, the point at which the conflict reaches its highest pitch and the protagonist stands on the brink of a major choice. Again, you will find a question below that asks you to identify the point of crisis, when Sylvia and her birds seem in jeopardy, then the climax, when Sylvia makes a choice to resolve her conflict with the hunter.

- Following the point of climax, the story enters a section of **falling action**, then a final **resolution**, when the consequences of the character's choice become clear. In these same sections, you will see most clearly that character drives plot, that what happens grows directly from characters' motives and actions. When those actions work a great change in a character, you can fairly describe that character as **dynamic**; when a character has made no life-changing choice and therefore undergoes no change, you can accurately describe that character as **static**. Expect questions below on Sylvia's choices and their significance.

Setting: Setting refers to where and when the action takes place; it also refers to the range of societal values that color that historical period. When you realize, for instance, that Jewett sets her story in the late nineteenth century and her main character in the Maine woods, not far from an expanding industrial center, then you realize that Sylvia's determination to preserve birds and the splendor of nature will eventually face adversaries far more formidable than the young hunter. When you further recall that in the late nineteenth century men still dominated all organizations and relationships, then you further appreciate Sylvia's courage in resisting the handsome hunter.

Imagery and Symbolism: As you follow the conflicts between characters, you will notice that certain concrete nouns—either through their constant presence or through repetition—take on significance beyond their face value. In "A White Heron," for example, the woods, for Sylvia, represent more than trees; they represent freedom, escape from a stifling urban area. In other words, such prominent images take on symbolic value, suggesting a range of meanings that help us to understand the importance of the conflict and its resolution. Expect several questions below on such images—and on actions that take on symbolic importance.

Theme: While short stories have no thesis statements, they definitely carry themes. Think of a theme as the author's implied comment on one of the subjects explored in the story. What implied comment, for example, does Jewett's story offer on the subject of preserving nature, on the subject of pre-adolescent love, on the subject of male domination? Expect thematic questions below as well as a writing assignment that invites your thoughts on theme.

Point of View: At the simplest level, you can think of point-of-view as a grammatical issue: Does the author tell the story from the main character's point of view, using the first-person pronoun "I" throughout, or does a narrator tell the story of the main character using the third-person pronoun "he" or "she"? While this grammatical distinction may seem pointless at first, consider how Jewett's story would change if written from the point of view of nine-year-old Sylvia. Would Sylvia have the language to describe her ecstasy and pain atop the pine tree as she watches the heron? Expect questions below on Jewett's adult narrator, who seems to have almost god-like *omniscience*, knowing everyone's thoughts, knowing the future. Of course, as you listen to the comments of narrators, you should pay equal heed to **dialogue**, the actual words spoken by the characters in conflict. Sometimes, the dialogue will illustrate the accuracy of the narrator's comments; other times, the dialogue will suggest that you should not rely on the narrator as a guide to theme.

Journaling on Jewett's Short Story

Answer the following questions in your journal as you read "A White Heron." Also, be sure to blend key quotations with your answers. Doing so ensures that your journaling functions as prewriting for your essay.

1. Consult your dictionary on the word "sylvan." How does this definition relate to Sylvia and the details that describe her setting in the first three paragraphs?

2. Why do you think that Jewett placed a double space between the third and fourth paragraphs?

3. What descriptive details explain why the pre-adolescent Sylvia would "tremble" as the young man emerges from the shadows? What information concerning his intentions for the night and next day adds to her anxiety?

4. What information about Sylvia, provided by her grandmother, makes Sylvia interesting to the young man?

5. Why does Sylvia's heart give "a wild beat" when the young man, an ornithologist, announces his hopes to kill and stuff the rare white heron which he has seen?

6. Given Sylvia's love for the heron and her aversion to guns, how do you explain her temptation to guide him to his prey? Give your answer in terms of "conflict" and "rising action," as defined above. As you consider the nature of her temptations and inner conflicts, account for the significance of the white space before the last two paragraphs of section I.

7. Jewett uses Roman numerals to suggest the two-part structure of her plot. At the end of section I, Sylvia has been only following the ornithologist. What shift in her purpose do you observe in section II? What, precisely, motivates her dangerous climbing of the pine tree?

8. What details does the narrator provide to stress the physical pains and the emotional ecstasy caused by climbing the giant pine? Be sure to note the figurative language (comparisons) as well as the literal details.

9. Identify Sylvia's point of crisis, then the point of climax, in the four paragraphs

following Sylvia's adventure in the pine. How do her experiences in the tree help you to understand her resistance of her grandmother, then her resistance of the young man? How, precisely, has Sylvia changed as a result of this conflict?

10. Describe the symbolic value of the tree and the heron. How do you know that Jewett wants us to see the tree as more than just a tree? How do you know that she wants us to understand that the heron is more than just a bird? How does the last paragraph affect the heron's symbolic value? What implied comments—themes—emerge from Sylvia's conflict and its resolution?

"A White Heron"

SARAH ORNE JEWETT

I

The woods were already filled with shadows one June evening, just before eight o'clock, though a bright sunset still glimmered faintly among the trunks of the trees. A little girl was driving home her cow, a plodding, dilatory, provoking creature in her behavior, but a valued companion for all that. They were going away from the western light, and striking deep into the dark woods, but their feet were familiar with the path, and it was no matter whether their eyes could see it or not.

There was hardly a night the summer through when the old cow could be found waiting at the pasture bars; on the contrary, it was her greatest pleasure to hide herself away among the high huckleberry bushes, and though she wore a loud bell she had made the discovery that if one stood perfectly still it would not ring. So Sylvia had to hunt for her until she found her, and call Co'! Co'! with never an answering Moo, until her childish patience was quite spent. If the creature had not given good milk and plenty of it, the case would have seemed very different to her owners. Besides, Sylvia had all the time there was, and very little use to make of it. Sometimes in pleasant weather it was a consolation to look upon the cow's pranks as an intelligent attempt to play hide and seek, and as the child had no playmates she lent herself to this amusement with a good deal of zest. Though this chase had been so long that the wary animal herself had given an unusual signal of her whereabouts, Sylvia had only laughed when she came upon Mistress Moolly at the swamp-side, and urged her affectionately homeward with a twig of birch leaves. The old cow was not inclined to wander farther, she even turned in the right direction for once as they left the pasture, and stepped along the road at a good pace. She was quite ready to be milked now, and seldom stopped to browse. Sylvia wondered what her grandmother would say because they were so late. It was a great while since she had left home at half past five o'clock, but everybody knew the difficulty of making this errand a short one. Mrs. Tilley had chased the horned torment too many summer evenings herself to blame any one else for lingering, and was only thankful as she waited that she had Sylvia, nowadays, to give such valuable assistance. The good woman suspected that Sylvia loitered occasionally on her own account; there never was such a child for straying about out-of-doors since the world was made! Everybody said that it was a good change for a little maid who had tried to grow for eight years in a crowded manufacturing town, but, as for Sylvia herself, it seemed as if she never had been alive at all before she came to live at the farm. She thought often with wistful compassion of a wretched dry geranium that belonged to a town neighbor.

"Afraid of folks," old Mrs. Tilley said to herself, with a smile, after she had made the unlikely choice of Sylvia from her daughter's houseful of children, and was returning to the farm. "'Afraid of folks,' they said! I guess she won't be troubled no great with 'em up to the old place!" When they reached the door of the lonely house and stopped to unlock it, and the cat came to purr loudly, and rub against them, a deserted pussy, indeed, but fat with young robins, Sylvia whispered that this was a beautiful place to live in, and she never should wish to go home. 3

The companions followed the shady woodroad, the cow taking slow steps, and the child very fast ones. The cow stopped long at the brook to drink, as if the pasture were not half a swamp, and Sylvia stood still and waited, letting her bare feet cool themselves in the shoal water, while the great twilight moths struck softly against her. She waded on through the brook as the cow moved away, and listened to the thrushes with a heart that beat fast with pleasure. There was a stirring in the great boughs overhead. They were full of little birds and beasts that seemed to be wide-awake, and going about their world, or else saying good-night to each other in sleepy twitters. Sylvia herself felt sleepy as she walked along. However, it was not much farther to the house, and the air was soft and sweet. She was not often in the woods so late as this, and it made her feel as if she were part of the gray shadows and the moving leaves. She was just thinking how long it seemed since she first came to the farm a year ago, and wondering if everything went on in the noisy town just the same as when she was there; the thought of the great red-faced boy who used to chase and frighten her made her hurry along the path to escape from the shadow of the trees. 4

Suddenly this little woods-girl is horror-stricken to hear a clear whistle not very far away. Not a bird's whistle, which would have a sort of friendliness, but a boy's whistle, determined, and somewhat aggressive. Sylvia left the cow to whatever sad fate might await her, and stepped discreetly aside into the bushes, but she was just too late. The enemy had discovered her, and called out in a very cheerful and persuasive tone, "Halloa, little girl, how far is it to the road?" and trembling Sylvia answered almost inaudibly, "A good ways." 5

She did not dare to look boldly at the tall young man, who carried a gun over his shoulder, but she came out of her bush and again followed the cow, while he walked alongside. 6

"I have been hunting for some birds," the stranger said kindly, "and I have lost my way, and need a friend very much. Don't be afraid," he added gallantly. "Speak up and tell me what your name is, and whether you think I can spend the night at your house, and go out gunning early in the morning." 7

Sylvia was more alarmed than before. Would not her grandmother consider her much to blame? But who could have foreseen such an accident as this? It did not appear 8 to be her fault, and she hung her head as if the stem of it were broken, but managed to answer "Sylvy," with much effort when her companion again asked her name.

Mrs. Tilley was standing in the doorway when the trio came into view. The cow gave a loud moo by way of explanation. 9

"Yes, you'd better speak up for yourself, you old trial! Where'd she tucked herself away this time, Sylvy?" Sylvia kept an awed silence; she knew by instinct that her grandmother did not comprehend the gravity of the situation. She must be mistaking the stranger for one of the farmer-lads of the region. 10

The young man stood his gun beside the door, and dropped a heavy game-bag beside it; then he bade Mrs. Tilley good-evening, and repeated his wayfarer's story, and asked if he could have a night's lodging. 11

"Put me anywhere you like," he said. "I must be off early in the morning, before day; but I am very hungry, indeed. You can give me some milk at any rate, that's plain." 12

"Dear sakes, yes," responded the hostess, whose long slumbering hospitality seemed to be easily awakened. "You might fare better if you went out on the main road a mile or so, but you're welcome to what we've got. I'll milk right off, and you make yourself at home. You can sleep on husks or feathers," she proffered graciously. "I raised them all myself. There's good pasturing for geese just below here towards the ma'sh. Now step round and set a plate for the gentleman, Sylvy!" And Sylvia promptly stepped. She was glad to have something to do, and she was hungry herself. 13

It was a surprise to find so clean and comfortable a little dwelling in this New England wilderness. The young man had known the horrors of its most primitive housekeeping, and the dreary squalor of that level of society which does not rebel at the companionship of hens. This was the best thrift of an old-fashioned farmstead, though on such a small scale that it seemed like a hermitage. He listened eagerly to the old woman's quaint talk, he watched Sylvia's pale face and shining gray eyes with ever growing enthusiasm, and insisted that this was the best supper he had eaten for a month; then, afterward, the new-made friends sat down in the doorway together while the moon came up. 14

Soon it would be berry-time, and Sylvia was a great help at picking. The cow was a good milker, though a plaguy thing to keep track of, the hostess gossiped frankly, adding presently that she had buried four children, so that Sylvia's mother, and a son (who might be dead) in California were all the children she had left. "Dan, my boy, was a great hand to go gunning," she explained sadly. "I never wanted for pa'tridges or gray squer'ls while he was to home. He's been a great wand'rer, I expect, and he's no hand to write letters. There, I don't blame him, I'd ha' seen the world myself if it had been so I could. 15

"Sylvia takes after him," the grandmother continued affectionately, after a minute's pause. "There ain't a foot o'ground she don't know her way over, and the wild creatur's counts her one o' themselves. Squer'ls she'll tame to come an' feed right out o' her hands, and all sorts o' birds. Last winter she got the jay-birds to bangeing here, and I believe she'd a' scanted herself of her own meals to have plenty to throw out amongst 16 'em, if I hadn't kep' watch. Anything but crows, I tell her, I'm willin' to help support,—though Dan he went an' tamed one o' them that did seem to have reason same as folks. It was round here a good spell after he went away. Dan an' his father they didn't hitch,—but he never held up his head ag'in after Dan had dared him an' gone off."

The guest did not notice this hint of family sorrows in his eager interest in something else. **17**

"So Sylvy knows all about birds, does she?" he exclaimed, as he looked round at the little girl who sat, very demure but increasingly sleepy, in the moonlight. "I am making a collection of birds myself. I have been at it ever since I was a boy." (Mrs. Tilley smiled.) "There are two or three very rare ones I have been hunting for these five years. I mean to get them on my own ground if they can be found." **18**

"Do you cage 'em up?" asked Mrs. Tilley doubtfully, in response to this enthusiastic announcement. **19**

"Oh, no, they're stuffed and preserved, dozens and dozens of them," said the ornithologist, "and I have shot or snared every one myself. I caught a glimpse of a white heron three miles from here on Saturday, and I have followed it in this direction. They have never been found in this district at all. The little white heron, it is," and he turned again to look at Sylvia with the hope of discovering that the rare bird was one of her acquaintances. **20**

But Sylvia was watching a hop-toad in the narrow footpath. **21**

"You would know the heron if you saw it," the stranger continued eagerly. "A queer tall white bird with soft feathers and long thin legs. And it would have a nest perhaps in the top of a high tree, made of sticks, something like a hawk's nest." **22**

Sylvia's heart gave a wild beat; she knew that strange white bird, and had once stolen softly near where it stood in some bright green swamp grass, away over at the other side of the woods. There was an open place where the sunshine always seemed strangely yellow and hot, where tall, nodding rushes grew, and her grandmother had warned her that she might sink in the soft black mud underneath and never be heard of more. Not far beyond were the salt marshes and beyond those was the sea, the sea which Sylvia wondered and dreamed about, but never had looked upon, though its great voice could often be heard above the noise of the woods on stormy nights. **23**

"I can't think of anything I should like so much as to find that heron's nest," the handsome stranger was saying. "I would give ten dollars to anybody who could show it to me," he added desperately, "and I mean to spend my whole vacation hunting for it if need be. Perhaps it was only migrating, or had been chased out of its own region by some bird of prey." **24**

Mrs. Tilley gave amazed attention to all this, but Sylvia still watched the toad, not divining, as she might have done at some calmer time, that the creature wished to get to its hole under the doorstep, and was much hindered by the unusual spectators at that hour of the evening. No amount of thought, that night, could decide how many wished-for treasures the ten dollars, so lightly spoken of, would buy. **25**

The next day the young sportsman hovered about the woods, and Sylvia kept him company, having lost her first fear of the friendly lad, who proved to be most kind and sympathetic. He told her many things about the birds and what they knew and where they lived and what they did with themselves. And he gave her a jack-knife, which she thought as great a treasure as if she were a desert-islander. All day long he did not once make her troubled or afraid except when he brought down some unsuspecting singing creature from its bough. Sylvia would have liked him vastly better without his gun; she could not understand why he killed the very birds he seemed to like so much. But as the day waned, Sylvia still watched the young man with loving admiration. She had never seen anybody so charming and delightful; the woman's heart, asleep in the child, was vaguely thrilled by a dream of love. Some premonition of that great power stirred and swayed these young foresters who traversed the solemn woodlands with soft-footed silent care. They stopped to listen to a bird's song; they pressed forward again eagerly, parting the branches—speaking to each other rarely and in whispers; the young man going first and Sylvia following, fascinated, a few steps behind, with her gray eyes dark with excitement. 26

She grieved because the longed-for white heron was elusive, but she did not lead the guest, she only followed, and there was no such thing as speaking first. The sound of her own unquestioned voice would have terrified her,—it was hard enough to answer yes or no when there was need of that. At last evening began to fall, and they drove the cow home together, and Sylvia smiled with pleasure when they came to the place where she heard the whistle and was afraid only the night before. 27

II

Half a mile from home, at the farther edge of the woods, where the land was highest, a great pine-tree stood, the last of its generation. Whether it was left for a boundary mark, or for what reason, no one could say; the woodchoppers who had felled its mates were dead and gone long ago, and a whole forest of sturdy trees, pines and oaks and maples, had grown again. But the stately head of this old pine towered above them all and made a landmark for sea and shore miles and miles away. Sylvia knew it well. She had always believed that whoever climbed to the top of it could see the ocean; and the little girl had often laid her hand on the great rough trunk and looked up wistfully at those dark boughs that the wind always stirred, no matter how hot and still the air might be below. Now she thought of the tree with a new excitement, for why, if one climbed it at break of day, could not one see all the world, and easily discover whence the white heron flew, and mark the place, and find the hidden nest? 28

What spirit of adventure, what wild ambition! What fancied triumph and delight and glory for the later morning when she could make known the secret! It was almost too real and too great for the childish heart to bear. 29

All night the door of the little house stood open, and the whippoorwills came and sang upon the very step. The young sportsman and his old hostess were sound asleep, but Sylvia's great design kept her wide awake and watching. She forgot to 30 think of sleep. The short summer night seemed as long as the winter darkness, and at last when the whippoorwills ceased, and she was afraid the morning would after all come too soon, she stole out of the house and followed the pasture path through the woods, hastening toward the open ground beyond, listening with a sense of comfort and companionship to the drowsy twitter of a half-awakened bird, whose perch she had jarred in passing. Alas, if the great wave of human interest which flooded for the first time this dull little life should sweep away the satisfactions of an existence heart to heart with nature and the dumb life of the forest!

There was the huge tree asleep yet in the paling moonlight, and small and hopeful Sylvia began with utmost bravery to mount to the top of it, with tingling, eager blood coursing the channels of her whole frame,with her bare feet and fingers, that pinched and held like bird's claws to the monstrous ladder reaching up, up, almost to the sky itself. First she must mount the white oak tree that grew alongside, where she was almost lost among the dark branches and the green leaves heavy and wet with dew; a bird fluttered off its nest, and a red squirrel ran to and fro and scolded pettishly at the harmless housebreaker. Sylvia felt her way easily. She had often climbed there, and knew that higher still one of the oak's upper branches chafed against the pine trunk, just where its lower boughs were set close together. There, when she made the dangerous pass from one tree to the other, the great enterprise would really begin. 31

She crept out along the swaying oak limb at last, and took the daring step across into the old pine-tree. The way was harder than she thought; she must reach far and hold fast, the sharp dry twigs caught and held her and scratched her like angry talons, the pitch made her thin little fingers clumsy and stiff as she went round and round the tree's great stem, higher and higher upward. The sparrows and robins in the woods below were beginning to wake and twitter to the dawn, yet it seemed much lighter there aloft in the pine-tree, and the child knew that she must hurry if her project were to be of any use. 32

The tree seemed to lengthen itself out as she went up, and to reach farther and farther upward. It was like a great main-mast to the voyaging earth; it must truly have been amazed that morning through all its ponderous frame as it felt this determined spark of human spirit creeping and climbing from higher branch to branch. Who knows how steadily the least twigs held themselves to advantage this light, weak creature on her way! The old pine must have loved his new dependent. More than all the hawks, and bats, and moths, and even the sweet-voiced thrushes, was the brave, beating heart of the solitary gray-eyed child. And the tree stood still and held away the winds that June morning while the dawn grew bright in the east. 33

Sylvia's face was like a pale star, if one had seen it from the ground, when the last thorny bough was past, and she stood trembling and tired but wholly triumphant, high in the tree-top. Yes, there was the sea with the dawning sun making a golden dazzle over it, and toward that glorious east flew two hawks with slow-moving pinions. How low they looked in the air from that height when before one had only seen them far up, and dark against the blue sky. Their gray feathers were as soft as moths; they seemed only a little way from the tree, and Sylvia felt as if she too could go flying away 34 among the clouds. Westward, the woodlands and farms reached miles and miles into the distance; here and there were church steeples, and white villages; truly it was a vast and awesome world.

The birds sang louder and louder. At last the sun came up bewilderingly bright.   35
Sylvia could see the white sails of ships out at sea, and the clouds that were purple and rose-colored and yellow at first began to fade away. Where was the white heron's nest in the sea of green branches, and was this wonderful sight and pageant of the world the only reward for having climbed to such a giddy height? Now look down again, Sylvia, where the green marsh is set among the shining birches and dark hemlocks; there where you saw the white heron once you will see him again; look, look! a white spot of him like a single floating feather comes up from the dead hemlock and grows larger, and rises, and comes close at last, and goes by the landmark pine with steady sweep of wing and outstretched slender neck and crested head. And wait! wait! do not move a foot or a finger, little girl, do not send an arrow of light and consciousness from your two eager eyes, for the heron has perched on a pine bough not far beyond yours, and cries back to his mate on the nest, and plumes his feathers for the new day!

The child gives a long sigh a minute later when a company of shouting catbirds   36
comes also to the tree, and vexed by their fluttering and lawlessness the solemn heron goes away. She knows his secret now, the wild, light, slender bird that floats and wavers, and goes back like an arrow presently to his home in the green world beneath. Then Sylvia, well satisfied, makes her perilous way down again, not daring to look far below the branch she stands on, ready to cry sometimes because her fingers ached and her lamed feet slipped. Wondering over and over again what the stranger would say to her, and what he would think when she told him how to find his way straight to the heron's nest.

"Sylvy, Sylvy!" called the busy old grandmother again and again, but nobody   37
answered, and the small husk bed was empty, and Sylvia had disappeared.

The guest waked from a dream, and remembering his day's pleasure hurried to   38
dress himself that it might sooner begin. He was sure from the way the shy little girl looked once or twice yesterday that she had at least seen the white heron, and now she must really be persuaded to tell. Here she comes now, paler than ever, and her worn old frock is torn and tattered, and smeared with pine pitch. The grandmother and the sportsman stand in the door together and question her, and the splendid moment has come to speak of the dead hemlock-tree by the green marsh.

But Sylvia does not speak after all, though the old grandmother fretfully rebukes   39
her, and the young man's kind appealing eyes are looking straight in her own. He can make them rich with money; he has promised it, and they are poor now. He is so well worth making happy, and he waits to hear the story she can tell.

No, she must keep silence! What is it that suddenly forbids her and makes her   40
dumb? Has she been nine years growing, and now, when the great world for the first time puts out a hand to her, must she thrust it aside for a bird's sake? The murmur of the pine's green branches is in her ears, she remembers how the white heron came

flying through the golden air and how they watched the sea and the morning together, and Sylvia cannot speak; she cannot tell the heron's secret and give its life away.

Dear loyalty, that suffered a sharp pang as the guest went away disappointed later in the day, that could have served and followed him and loved him as a dog loves! Many a night Sylvia heard the echo of his whistle haunting the pasture path as she came home with the loitering cow. She forgot even her sorrow at the sharp report of his gun and the piteous sight of the thrushes and sparrows dropping silent to the ground, their songs hushed and their pretty feathers stained and wet with blood. Were the birds better friends than their hunter might have been,—who can tell? Whatever treasures were lost to her, woodlands and summer-time, remember! Bring your gifts and graces and tell your secrets to this lonely country child!

Journaling on Zora Neale Hurston's Short Story

Published in 1926, Zora Neale Hurston's "Sweat" added a woman's voice to the Harlem Renaissance, the cultural and literary movement that celebrated African American heritage and the liberating spirit of the arts. The story also reflects Hurston's childhood in Florida at the turn of the twentieth century, when African Americans struggled with poverty, the legacy of slavery. Additionally, "Sweat" focuses on Delia Jones, a hard-working woman fed spiritually by her church but starved emotionally and brutalized physically by her husband Sykes.

Once again, as you read Hurston's story, answer the following questions in your journal. Your answers will tighten your grip on the elements of fiction and partially prepare you to write an expository essay on "Sweat."

1. What details in the first paragraph create your first impression of Delia?

2. Would you say that the exposition ends in paragraph 2, where the narrator hints of a potential conflict as Delia wonders "where Sykes, her husband had gone"? Or does the exposition end in paragraphs 18–21, which end with the raised skillet? As you consider your answer, note the details of her physical appearance prior to the raised skillet.

3. Compare Sykes' behavior with the bull whip in paragraph 3 to his response to the skillet in paragraph 21. What inference do you draw about his character?

4. How do paragraphs 25–28 add to your understanding of Delia's marriage and her anger? What details cause you to sympathize with Delia? What details cause you to admire her?

5. How does the dialogue among Jim Merchant, Joe Lindley, Dave Carter, and Joe Clark in section II add to your sympathy and admiration for Delia?

6. In section III, Sykes brings home the rattle snake to drive Delia from her house.

What initial responses from Delia (through paragraph 81) suggest that his strategy may backfire? Can you pinpoint the moment of crisis, the place where you see that Delia will not give in again to Sykes' brutal intimidation?

7. Can you pinpoint the climax, the place where you realize that Delia will win this conflict?

8. Explain to what extent you hold Delia responsible for Sykes' death.

9. What thematic comment on marriage emerges from this chilling ending? Do the repeated images—the house, the cart and pony, the whip, the snake—take on symbolic meaning, guiding your thematic interpretation?

10. Explain to what extent this 80-year-old story offers valid insights for partners in any relationship.

"Sweat"

Zora Neale Hurston

It was eleven o'clock of a Spring night in Florida. It was Sunday. Any other night, Delia Jones would have been in bed for two hours by this time. But she was a washwoman, and Monday morning meant a great deal to her. So she collected the soiled clothes on Saturday when she returned the clean things. Sunday night after church, she sorted and put the white things to soak. It saved her almost a half-day's start. A great hamper in the bedroom held the clothes that she brought home. It was so much neater than a number of bundles lying around.

She squatted on the kitchen floor beside the great pile of clothes, sorting them into small heaps according to color, and humming a song in a mournful key, but wondering through it all where Sykes, her husband, had gone with her horse and buckboard.[1]

Just then something long, round, limp, and black fell upon her shoulders and slithered to the floor beside her. A great terror took hold of her. It softened her knees and dried her mouth so that it was a full minute before she could cry out or move. Then she saw that it was the big bull whip her husband liked to carry when he drove.

She lifted her eyes to the door and saw him standing there bent over with laughter at her fright. She screamed at him.

"Sykes, what you throw dat whip on me like dat? You know it would skeer me— looks just like a snake, an' you knows how skeered Ah is of snakes."

"Course Ah knowed it! That's how come Ah done it." He slapped his leg with his hand and almost rolled on the ground in his mirth. "If you such a big fool dat you got to have a fit over a earth worm or a string, Ah don't keer how bad Ah skeer you."

"You ain't got no business doing it. Gawd knows it's a sin. Some day Ah'm gointuh

1 A four-wheeled open carriage with the seat resting on a spring platform.

drop dead from some of yo' foolishness. 'Nother thing, where you been wid mah rig? Ah feeds dat pony. He ain't fuh you to be drivin' wid no bull whip."

"You sho' is one aggravatin' nigger woman!" he declared and stepped into the room. 8
She resumed her work and did not answer him at once. "Ah done tole you time and again to keep them white folks' clothes outa dis house."

He picked up the whip and glared at her. Delia went on with her work. She went 9
out into the yard and returned with a galvanized tub and set it on the washbench. She saw that Sykes had kicked all of the clothes together again, and now stood in her way truculently, his whole manner hoping, *praying*, for an argument. But she walked calmly around him and commenced to re-sort things.

"Next time, Ah'm gointer kick 'em outdoors," he threatened as he struck a match 10
along the leg of his corduroy breeches.

Delia never looked up from her work, and her thin, stooped shoulders sagged 11
further.

"Ah ain't for no fuss t'night Sykes. Ah just come from taking sacrament at the 12
church house."

He snorted scornfully. "Yeah, you just come from de church house on a Sunday 13
night, but heah you is gone to work on them clothes. You ain't nothing but a hypocrite. One of them amen-corner Christians—sing, whoop, and shout, then come home and wash white folks' clothes on the Sabbath."

He stepped roughly upon the whitest pile of things, kicking them helter-skelter 14
as he crossed the room. His wife gave a little scream of dismay, and quickly gathered them together again.

"Sykes, you quite grindin' dirt into these clothes. How can Ah git through by 15
Sat'day if Ah don't start on Sunday?"

"Ah don't keer if you never git through. Anyhow, Ah done promised Gawd and 16
a couple of other men, Ah ain't gointer have it in mah house. Don't gimme no lip neither, else Ah'll throw 'em out and put mah fist up side yo' head to boot."

Delia's habitual meekness seemed to slip from her shoulders like a blown scarf. 17
She was on her feet; her poor little body, her bare knuckly hands bravely defying the strapping hulk before her.

"Looka heah, Sykes, you done gone too far. Ah been married to you fur fifteen 18
years, and Ah been takin' in washin' fur fifteen years. Sweat, sweat, sweat! Work and sweat, cry and sweat, pray and sweat!"

"What's that got to do with me?" he asked brutally. 19

"What's it got to do with you, Sykes? Mah tub of suds is filled yo' belly with vittles 20
more times than yo' hands is filled it. Mah sweat is done paid for this house and Ah reckon Ah kin keep on sweatin' in it."

She seized the iron skillet from the stove and struck a defensive pose, which act 21
surprised him greatly, coming from her. It cowed him and he did not strike her as he
usually did.

"Naw you won't," she panted, "that ole snaggle-toothed black woman you runnin' 22
with ain't comin' heah to pile up on *mah* sweat and blood. You ain't paid for nothin' on
this place, and Ah'm gointer stay right heah till Ah'm toted out foot foremost."

"Well, you better quit gittin' me riled up, else they'll be totin' you out sooner than 23
you expect. Ah'm so tired of you Ah don't know what to do. Gawd! How Ah hates
skinny wimmen!"

A little awed by this new Delia, he sidled out of the door and slammed the back 24
gate after him. He did not say where he had gone, but she knew too well. She knew
very well that he would not return until nearly daybreak also. Her work over, she went
on to bed but not to sleep at once. Things had come to a pretty pass!

She lay awake, gazing upon the debris that cluttered their matrimonial trail. 25
Not an image left standing along the way. Anything like flowers had long ago been
drowned in the salty steam that had been pressed from her heart. Her tears, her sweat,
her blood. She had brought love to the union and he had brought a longing after the
flesh. Two months after the wedding, he had given her the first brutal beating. She
had the memory of his numerous trips to Orlando with all of his wages when he had
returned to her penniless, even before the first year had passed. She was young and soft
then, but now she thought of her knotty, muscled limbs, her harsh knuckly hands, and
drew herself up into an unhappy little ball in the middle of the big feather bed. Too
late now to hope for love, even if it were not Bertha it would be someone else. This
case differed from the others only in that she was bolder than the others. Too late for
everything except her little home. She had built it for her old days, and planted one by
one the trees and flowers there. It was lovely to her, lovely.

Somehow, before sleep came, she found herself saying aloud: "Oh well, whatever 26
goes over the Devil's back, is got to come under his belly. Sometime or ruther, Sykes,
like everybody else, is going to reap his sowing." After that she was able to build
a spiritual earthworks[2] against her husband. His shells could no longer reach her.
AMEN. She went to sleep and slept until he announced his presence in bed by kicking
her feet and rudely snatching the covers away.

"Gimme some kivah heah, an' git yo' damn foots over on yo' own side! Ah oughter 27
mash you in yo' mouf fuh drawing dat skillet on me."

Delia went clear to the rail without answering him. A triumphant indifference to 28
all that he was or did.

II

The week was full of work for Delia as all other weeks, and Saturday found her 29

---

[2] Earthworks are military fortifications made of earth; here Hurston uses it metaphorically to mean Delia's
emotional defenses.

behind her little pony, collecting and delivering clothes.

It was a hot, hot day near the end of July. The village men on Joe Clarke's porch even chewed cane listlessly. They did not hurl the cane knots as usual. They let them dribble over the edge of the porch. Even conversation had collapsed under the heat. 30

"Heah come Delia Jones," Jim Merchant said, as the shaggy pony came 'round the bend of the road toward them. The rusty buckboard was heaped with baskets of crisp clean laundry. 31

"Yep," Joe Lindsay agreed. "Hot or col', rain or shine, jes' ez reg'lar ez de weeks roll roun' Delia carries 'em an' fetches 'em on Sat'day." 32

"She better if she wanter eat," said Moss. "Syke Jones ain't wuth de shot an' powder it would tek tuh kill 'em. Not to *huh* he ain't." 33

"He sho' ain't," Walter Thomas chimed in. "It's too bad, too, cause she wuz a right pretty li'l trick when he got huh. Ah'd uh mah'ied huh mahself if he hadnter beat me to it." 34

Delia nodded briefly at the men as she drove past. 35

"Too much knockin' will ruin *any* 'oman. He done beat huh 'nough tuh kill three women, let 'lone change they looks," said Elijah Moseley. "How Syke kin stommuck dat big black greasy Mogul he's layin' roun' wid, gits me. Ah swear dat eight-rock couldn't kiss a sardine can Ah done thowed out de back do' 'way las' yeah." 36

"Aw, she's fat, thass how come. He's allus been crazy 'bout fat women," put in Merchant. "He'd a' been tied up wid one long time ago if he could a' found one tuh have him. Did Ah tell yuh 'bout him come sidlin' roun' *mah* wife—bringin' her a basket uh pecans outa his yard fuh a present? Yessir, mah wife! She tol' him tuh take 'em straight back home, 'cause Delia works so hard ovah dat washtub she reckon everything on de place taste lak sweat an' soapsuds. Ah jus' wisht Ah'd a' caught 'im 'roun' dere! Ah'd a' made his hips ketch on fiah down dat shell road." 37

"Ah know he done it, too. Ah seems 'im grinnin' at every 'oman dat passes," Walter Thomas said. "But even so, he useter eat some mighty big hunks uh humble pie tuh git dat li'l oman he got. She wuz ez pritty ez a speckled pup! Dat wuz fifteen years ago. He useter be so skeered uh losin' huh, she could make him do some parts of a husband's duty. Dey never wuz de same in de mind." 38

"There oughter be a law about him," said Lindsay. "He ain't fit tuh carry guts tuh a bear." 39

Clarke spoke for the first time. "Tain't no law on earth dat kin make a man be decent if it ain't in 'im. There's plenty men dat takes a wife lak dey do a joint uh sugar-cane. It's round, juicy, an' sweet when dey gits it. But dey squeeze an' grind, squeeze an' grind an' wring tell dey wring every drop uh pleasure dat's in 'em out. When dey's satisfied dat dey is wrung dry, dey treats 'em jes' lak dey do a cane-chew. Dey thows 'em away. Dey knows whut dey is doin' while dey is at it, an' hates theirselves fuh it but they 40

89

keeps on hangin' after huh tell she's empty. Den dey hates huh fuh bein' a cane-chew an' in de way."

"We oughter take Syke an' dat stray 'oman uh his'n down in Lake Howell swamp an' lay on de rawhide till they cain't say Lawd a'mussy. He allus wuz uh ovahbearin niggah, but since dat white 'oman from up north done teached 'im how to run a automobile, he done got too beggety to live—an' we oughter kill 'im," Old Man Anderson advised. 41

A grunt of approval went around the porch. But the heat was melting their civic virtue and Elijah Moseley began to bait Joe Clarke. 42

"Come on, Joe, git a melon outa dere an' slice it up for yo' customers. We'se all sufferin' wid de heat. De bear's done got me!" 43

"Thass right, Joe, a watermelon is jes' whut Ah needs tuh cure de eppizudicks," Walter Thomas joined forces with Moseley. "Come on dere, Joe. We all is steady customers an' you ain't set us up in a long time. Ah chooses dat long, bowlegged Floridy favorite." 44

"A god, an' be dough. You all gimme twenty cents and slice away," Clarke retorted. "Ah needs a col' slice m'self. Heah, everybody chip in. Ah'll lend y'all mah meat knife." 45

The money was all quickly subscribed and the huge melon brought forth. At that moment, Sykes and Bertha arrived. A determined silence fell on the porch and the melon was put away again. 46

Merchant snapped down the blade of his jackknife and moved toward the store door. 47

"Come on in, Joe, an' gimme a slab uh sow belly an' uh pound uh coffee—almost fuhgot 'twas Sat'day. Got to git on home." Most of the men left also. 48

Just then Delia drove past on her way home, as Sykes was ordering magnificently for Bertha. It pleased him for Delia to see. 49

"Git whatsoever yo' heart desires, Honey. Wait a minute, Joe. Give huh two bottles uh strawberry soda-water, uh quart parched ground-peas, an' a blok uh chewin' gum." 50

With all this they left the store, with Sykes reminding Bertha that this was his town and she could have it if she wanted it. 51

The men returned soon after they left, and held their watermelon feast. 52

"Where did Syke Jones git da 'oman from nowhow?" Lindsay asked. 53

"Ovah Apopka. Guess dey musta been cleanin' out de town when she lef. She don't look lak a thing but a hunk uh liver wid hair on it." 54

"Well, she sho' kin squall," Dave Carter contributed. "When she gits ready tuh laff, she jes' opens huh mouf an' latches it back tuh de las' notch. No ole granpa alligator down in Lake Bell ain't got nothin' on huh." 55

III

Bertha had been in town three months now. Sykes was still paying her room-rent at Della Lewis'—the only house in town that would have taken her in. Sykes took her frequently to Winter Park to "stomps." He still assured her that he was the swellest man in the state. 56

"Sho' you kin have dat li'l ole house soon's Ah git dat 'oman outadere. Everything b'longs tuh me an' you sho' kin have it. Ah sho' 'bominates uh skinny 'oman. Lawdy, you sho' is got one portly shape on you! You kin git *anything* you wants. Dis is *mah* town an' you sho' kin have it." 57

Delia's work-worn knees crawled over the earth in Gethsemane[3] and up the rocks of Calvary[4] many, many times during these months. She avoided the villagers and meeting places in her efforts to be blind and deaf. But Bertha nullified this to a degree, by coming to Delia's house to call Sykes out to her at the gate. 58

Delia and Sykes fought all the time now with no peaceful interludes. They slept and ate in silence. Two or three times Delia had attempted a timid friendliness, but she was repulsed each time. It was plain that the breaches must remain agape. 59

The sun had burned July to August. The heat streamed down like a million hot arrows, smiting all things living upon the earth. Grass withered, leaves browned, snakes went blind in shedding, and men and dogs went mad. Dog days! 60

Delia came home one day and found Sykes there before her. She wondered, but started to go on into the house without speaking, even though he was standing in the kitchen door and she must either stoop under his arm or ask him to move. He made no room for her. She noticed a soap box beside the steps, but paid no particular attention to it, knowing that he must have brought it there. As she was stooping to pass under his outstretched arm, he suddenly pushed her backward, laughingly. 61

"Look in de box dere Delia, Ah done brung yuh somethin'!" 62

She nearly fell upon the box in her stumbling, and when she saw what it held, she all but fainted outright. 63

"Syke! Syke, mah Gawd! You take dat rattlesnake 'way from heah! You gottuh. Oh, Jesus, have mussy!" 64

"Ah ain't got tuh do nuthin' uh de kin'—fact is Ah ain't got tuh do nothin' but die. Tain't no use uh you puttin' on airs makin' out lak you skeered uh dat snake—he's gointer stay right heah tell he die. He wouldn't bit me cause Ah knows how tuh handle 'im. Nohow he wouldn't risk breakin' out his fangs 'gin yo skinny laigs." 65

"Naw, now Syke, don't keep dat thing 'round tryin' tuh skeer me tuh death. You knows Ah'm even feard uh earth worms. Thass de biggest snake Ah evah did see. Kill 'im Syke, please." 66

---

[3] The garden outside Jerusalem that was the scene of Jesus' agony and arrest (see Matthew 26:36–57); hence, a scene of great suffering.

[4] The hill outside Jerusalem where Jesus was crucified.

"Doan ast me tuh do nothin' fuh yuh. Goin' 'round tryin' tuh be so damn   67
asterperious[5]. Naw, Ah ain't gonna kill it. Ah think uh damn sight mo' uh him dan you!
Dat's a nice snake an' anybody doan lak 'im kin jes' hit de grit."

The village soon heard that Sykes had the snake, and came to see and ask   68
questions.

"How de hen-fire did you ketch dat six-foot rattler, Syke?" Thomas asked.   69

"He's full uh frogs so he cain't hardly move, thass how Ah eased up on 'im. But   70
Ah'm a snake charmer an' knows how tuh handle 'em. Shux, dat ain't nothin'. Ah could
ketch one eve'y day if Ah so wanted tuh."

"Whut he needs is a heavy hick'ry club leaned real heavy on his head. Dat's de bes'   71
way tuh charm a rattlesnake."

"Naw, Walt, y'all jes' don't understand dese diamon'backs lak Ah do," said Sykes in   72
a superior tone of voice.

The village agreed with Walter, but the snake stayed on. His box remained by the   73
kitchen door with its screen wire covering. Two or three days later it had digested its
meal of frogs and literally came to life. It rattled at every movement in the kitchen
or the yard. One day as Delia came down the kitchen steps she saw his chalky-white
fangs curved like scimitars hung in the wire meshes. This time she did not run away
with averted eyes as usual. She stood for a long time in the doorway in a red fury that
grew bloodier for every second that she regarded the creature that was her torment.

That night she broached the subject as soon as Sykes sat down to the table.   74

"Syke, Ah wants you tuh take dat snake 'way fum heah. You done starved me   75
an' Ah put up widcher, you done beat me an Ah took dat, but you done kilt all mah
insides bringin' dat varmint heah."

Sykes poured out a saucer full of coffee and drank it deliberately before he   76
answered her.

"A whole lot Ah keer 'bout how you feels inside uh out. Dat snake ain't goin' no   77
damn wheah till Ah gits ready fuh 'im tuh go. So fur as beatin' is concerned, yuh ain't
took near all dat you gointer take ef yuh stay 'round me."

Delia pushed back her plate and got up from the table. "Ah hates you, Sykes," she   78
said calmly. "Ah hates you tuh de same degree dat Ah useter love yuh. Ah done took
an' took till mah belly is full up tuh mah neck. Dat's de reason Ah got mah letter fum
de church an' moved mah membership tuh Woodbridge—so Ah don't haftuh take no
sacrament wid yuh. Ah don't wantuh see yuh 'round me atall. Lay 'round wid dat 'oman all
yuh wants tuh, but gwan 'way fum me an' mah house. Ah hates yuh lak uh suck-egg dog."

Sykes almost let the huge wad of corn bread and collard greens he was chewing   79
fall out of his mouth in amazement. He had a hard time whipping himself up to the
proper fury to try to answer Delia.

[5] Haughty.

92

"Well, Ah'm glad you does hate me. Ah'm sho' tiahed uh you hangin' ontuh me. Ah don't want yuh. Look at yuh stringey ole neck! Yo' rawbony laigs an arms is enough tuh cut uh man tuh death. You looks jes' lak de devvul's dollbaby tuh me. You cain't hate me no worse dan Ah hates you. Ah been hatin' you fuh years." 80

"Yo' ole black hide don't look lak nothin' tuh me, but uh passle uh wrinkled up rubber, wid yo' big ole yeahs flappin' on each side lak uh paih uh buzzard wings. Don't think Ah'm gointuh be run 'way fum mah house neither. Ah'm goin' tuh de white folks 'bout you, mah young man, de very nex' time you lay yo' han's on me. Mah cup is done run ovah." Delia said this with no signs of fear and Sykes departed from the house threatening her, but made not the slightest move to carry out any of them. 81

That night he did not return at all, and the next day being Sunday, Delia was glad she did not have to quarrel before she hitched up her pony and drove the four miles to Woodbridge. 82

She stayed to the night service—"love feast"—which was very warm and full of spirit. In the emotional winds her domestic trials were borne far and wide so that she sang as she drove homeward, 83

> Jurden water,[6] black an' col 84
> Chills de body, not de soul
> An' Ah wahtah cross Jurden in uh calm time.

She came from the barn to the kitchen door and stopped. 85

"Whut's de mattah, ol' Satan, you ain't kickin' up yo' racket?" She addressed the snake's box. Complete silence. She went on into the house with a new hope in its birth struggles. Perhaps her threat to go to the white folks had frightened Sykes! Perhaps he was sorry! Fifteen years of misery and suppression had brought Delia to the place where she would hope anything that looked towards a way over or through her wall of inhibitions. 86

She felt in the match-safe behind the stove at once for a match. There was only one there. 87

"Dat niggah wouldn't fetch nothin' heah tuh save his rotten neck, but he kin run thew whut Ah brings quick enough. Now he done toted off nigh on tuh haff uh box uh matches. He done had dat 'oman heah in mah house, too." 88

Nobody but a woman could tell how she knew this even before she struck the match. But she did and it put her into a new fury. 89

Presently she brought in the tubs to put the white things to soak. This time she decided she need not bring the hamper out of the bedroom; she would go in there and do the sorting. She picked up the pot-bellied lamp and went in. The room was small and the hamper stood hard by the foot of the white iron bed. She could sit and reach through the bedposts—resting as she worked. 90

---

[6] Black Southern dialect for the River Jordan, which represents the last boundary before entering heaven. It comes from the Old Testament, when the Jews had to cross the River Jordan to reach the Promised Land.

"Ah wantah cross Jurden in uh calm time." She was singing again. The mood of the "love feast" had returned. She threw back the lid of the basket almost gaily. Then, moved by both horror and terror, she sprang back toward the door. There lay the snake in the basket! He moved sluggishly at first, but even as she turned round and round, jumped up and down in an insanity of fear, he began to stir vigorously. She saw him pouring his awful beauty from the basket upon the bed, then she seized the lamp and ran as fast as she could to the kitchen. The wind from the open door blew out the light and the darkness added to her terror. She sped to the darkness of the yard, slamming the door after her before she thought to set down the lamp. She did not feel safe even on the ground, so she climbed up in the hay barn. 91

There for an hour or more she lay sprawled upon the hay a gibbering wreck. 92

Finally she grew quiet, and after that came coherent thought. With this stalked through her a cold, bloody rage. Hours of this. A period of introspection, a space of retrospection, then a mixture of both. Out of this an awful calm. 93

"Well, Ah done de bes' Ah could. If things ain't right, Gawd knows tain't mah fault." 94

She went to sleep—a twitch sleep—and woke up to a faint gray sky. There was a loud hollow sound below. She peered out. Sykes was at the wood-pile, demolishing a wire-covered box. 95

He hurried to the kitchen door, but hung outside there some minutes before he entered, and stood some minutes inside before he closed it after him. 96

The gray in the sky was spreading. Delia descended without fear now, and crouched beneath the low bedroom window. The drawn shade shut out the dawn, shut in the night. But the thin walls held back no sound. 97

"Dat ol' scratch[7] is woke up now!" She mused at the tremendous whirr inside, which every woodsman knows, is one of the sound illusions. The rattler is a ventriloquist. His whirr sounds to the right, to the left, straight ahead, behind, close under foot—everywhere but where it is. Woe to him who guesses wrong unless he is prepared to hold up his end of the argument! Sometimes he strikes without rattling at all. 98

Inside, Sykes heard nothing until he knocked a pot lid off the stove while trying to reach the match-safe in the dark. He had emptied his pockets at Bertha's. 99

The snake seemed to wake up under the stove and Sykes made a quick leap into the bedroom. In spite of the gin he had had, his head was clearing now. 100

"Mah Gawd!" he chattered, "ef Ah could on'y strack uh light!" 101

The rattling ceased for a moment as he stood paralyzed. He waited. It seemed that the snake waited also. 102

"Oh, fuh de light! Ah thought he'd be too sick"—Sykes was muttering to himself 103

[7] A folk expression for the devil.

when the whirr began again, closer, right underfoot this time. Long before this, Sykes' ability to think had been flattened down to primitive instinct and he leaped—onto the bed.

Outside Delia heard a cry that might have come from a maddened chimpanzee, a stricken gorilla. All the terror, and the horror, all the rage that man could possibly express, without a recognizable human sound.   104

A tremendous stir inside there, another series of animal screams, the intermittent whirr of the reptile. The shade torn violently down from the window, letting in the red dawn, a huge brown hand seizing the window stick, great dull blows upon the wooden floor punctuating the gibberish of sound long after the rattle of the snake had abruptly subsided. All this Delia could see and hear from her place beneath the window, and it made her ill. She crept over to the four o'clocks and stretched herself on the cool earth to recover.   105

She lay there. "Delia, Delia!" She could hear Sykes calling in a most despairing tone as one who expected no answer. The sun crept on up, and he called. Delia could not move—her legs had gone flabby. She never moved, he called, and the sun kept rising.   106

"Mah Gawd!" She heard him moan, "Mah Gawd fum Heben!" She heard him stumbling about and got up from her flower-bed. The sun was growing warm. As she approached the door she heard him call out hopefully, "Delia, is dat you Ah heah?"   107

She saw him on his hands and knees as soon as she reached the door. He crept an inch or two toward her—all that he was able, and she saw his horribly swollen neck and his one open eye shining with hope. A surge of pity too strong to support bore her away from that eye that must, could not, fail to see the tubs. He would see the lamp. Orlando with its doctors was too far. She could scarcely reach the chinaberry tree, where she waited in the growing heat while inside she knew the cold river was creeping up and up to extinguish that eye which must know by now that she knew.   108

Choosing a Topic for Your Second Expository Essay

If you re-read your journaling in response to the questions above, you will find plenty of raw material on the first two topics listed below. Reading your journal will also reveal which issues you found most interesting, which ideas you found most exciting. In turn, these responses may spark ideas for topic 3, one that invites you to find your own topic in your interests. But remember: to find your purpose and your audience, you will need to engage in the recursive writing process described above, a process that only begins with journaling.

1. Focusing on either "A White Heron" or "Sweat," explain how repeated images take on symbolic meaning, helping you understand the fears, the longings, and the personal growth of Sylvia or Delia. You might consider, for example, the gun, the pine tree, and

the heron in Jewett's story, or the whip, the house, and the snake in Hurston's story.

2. At the points of climax, both Sylvia and Delia make choices rarely condoned, usually condemned by social custom and criminal law: Sylvia defies adults and suppresses the truth; Delia waits in silence, letting Sykes fall into the snake trap he set for her. Explain to what extent that setting, dialogue, and description persuade you to understand and even admire Sylvia's defiance or Delia's crime.

3. Devise your own topic in response to either story, focusing on any character, conflict, image pattern, or thematic concern that has aroused your interest. Whatever your choice of topics, your expository purpose will remain the same: to explain to your readers how you read the story.

Works Cited

Ammons, Elizabeth. Commentary on Sarah Orne Jewett's "A White Heron." *The Heath Anthology of American Literature*. 3rd ed. Volume 2. Boston: Houghton, 1998. 131–138.

Baker, Russell. *Growing Up*. New York: Penguin, 1982.

Beard, Amanda. "See Me After Class." Student essay.

Elbow, Peter. "The Cultures of Literature and Composition: What Could Each Learn from the Other." *College English* 64 (May 2002): 533–546.

Gaines, Ernest. *A Lesson Before Dying*. New York: Vintage, 1994.

Hurston, Zora Neale. "Sweat." *The Literature of the American South*. Ed. William L. Andrews. New York: Norton, 1998. 407–415.

White, Stephen. *The Written Word: Associated Digressions Concerned with the Writer as Craftsman*. New York: Harper and Row, 1984.

CHAPTER 3

Serving the Needs of Your Audience: Invention and Arrangement

"One of the chief values of rhetoric, conceived as a system for gathering, selecting, arranging, and expressing our material, is that it represents a positive approach to the problems of writing."

EDWARD P. J. CORBETT, *Classical Rhetoric for the Modern Student*

"Students who want a systematic way of asking questions about rhetorical situations can use stasis theory. This means of invention provides rhetors with a set of questions that, when asked systematically, can help them to determine where the disagreement between themselves and their audience begins."

SHARON CROWLEY AND DEBRA HAWHEE, *Ancient Rhetorics for Contemporary Students*

Understanding the Aims of Discourse

When Professor Edward P. J. Corbett defines "rhetoric" as "the art or the discipline that deals with the use of discourse, either spoken or written, to inform or persuade or motivate an audience" (1), his use of the word "audience" reminds us that rhetoric began as oral discourse, one person speaking to fellow citizens. Sometimes, those citizens may be receptive; often, they will be indifferent, even hostile, reluctant to accept new information, change their beliefs, or act in a way that carries risks.

Well over 2,000 years ago, when ancient Greeks gathered to bury the dead or to laud a hero, an orator—the *rhetor*—would make a speech, praising the person's virtues, perhaps even blaming others for not properly valuing the great one. Such discourse, Professor Corbett reminds us, the ancients termed epideictic or **ceremonial discourse** (23), which aims to persuade the audience that the person described should be honored for her/his virtue, or dishonored for her/his vice (126). In November 2004, when the United States buried its 40th president, you heard Democrats as well as Republicans praise the character and achievements of Ronald Reagan. These contemporary examples of ceremonial discourse aimed at honoring the man and motivating the audience's patriotism.

When those ancients gathered in the senate to debate and set policy for their democracy, they practiced **deliberative discourse**, advising colleagues to adopt one course of action and dissuading them from adopting another. When you heard Senator Kerry in 2004 advise Americans to elect a president with a coherent strategy for creating jobs, you heard deliberative discourse; you heard the same kind of discourse when President Bush dissuaded Americans from electing a president who changes his views with each new poll. Such discourse aims to persuade an audience that one course of action should be chosen because it will make people happy, another avoided because it will generate misery; that one policy should be adopted because it is practical, another avoided because it is impractical; that one plan will yield inherently good results, another avoided for its inherent evils.

When those same Athenians met Socrates in a court of law, the philosopher spoke forensic or **judicial discourse**, defending himself against Meletus and other citizens who had accused him of corrupting the youth with his allegedly atheistic teachings (Corbett 195–209). When you heard prosecuting attorneys in 2005 present evidence showing that Scott Peterson murdered his wife Lacey and their unborn child, you heard them call on the jury—their audience—for justice, the aim of judicial discourse.

Inventing and Arranging

To succeed in any of these three modes of discourse, then, you must analyze your audience. What does your reader need to know in order to believe or act as you would have the reader believe or act? How much does the reader already know? What previous beliefs does the reader likely hold on your topic? Will the reader likely be interested in your topic? Indifferent? Hostile? How will the age, gender, and educational level of your readers affect their openness to your topic and your thesis?

Before you can analyze your audience, however, you must gather ideas on your subject. In turn, those ideas—and the evidence that shapes them—will help you to clarify your purpose and to identify your audience—the people who need to know what you have learned.

But you may be wondering where and how you can gather ideas. You know, of course, that you can gather ideas on a subject through your reading, sometimes, too, through your experimenting in the lab or through interviewing experts. Yet you also realize that you cannot read, experiment, or interview at random; you need a question-asking system, one that will help you to organize the evidence you find and, eventually, to arrange your findings for your readers.

Using Invention to Serve the Needs of Your Audience

Ancient rhetoricians provided us just such a system. The Greeks called this question-asking system *heuresis*; their Latin counterparts used the term *inventio*; both terms, as Professor Corbett explains, mean methods of "discovery" (17). Aristotle, for example, sent his rhetoric students to the **topoi** or "common topics" to discover "lines of argument" (Corbett 87) to persuade their audiences on a given subject:

- **Definition**: What do key terms mean?
- **Comparison**: What similarities and differences emerge in your study?
- **Relationship**: What cause-effect patterns have you discovered?
- **Circumstance**: What solutions to problems seem feasible?
- **Testimony**: What do the experts say?

By systematically answering these questions, Aristotle taught, a speaker or writer can find lines of argument, key claims about the subject which has captured the speaker/writer's interest.

Over 200 years after Aristotle's *Rhetoric*, Roman lawyer and professor of rhetoric, Marcus Tullius Cicero, sent his students to the same "topics" to find deliberative and judicial arguments, essential skills for young men who would join Cicero in resisting the rise of tyranny and the decline of republican government. With these highest political and moral stakes in mind, Cicero thought of the *topoi* more as **stases,** places to "stand" relative to those with opposing views. More specifically, as Sharon Crowley and Debra Hawhee have explained, Cicero taught his students to invent their arguments by systematically attending to "four stases" and the questions each stasis generates:

- **Conjecture**: Does it exist? Did it happen?
- **Definition**: What kind of thing or event is it?
- **Quality**: Was it right or wrong?
- **Procedure**: What should we do? (48)

Notice that this version of Aristotle's topics stresses the places where disagreement begins. Two persons, for instance, might agree that the USA population exemplifies diversity, but they may well disagree about the nature of that diversity, whether or not patterns of diversity seem healthy, whether or not we should strive to know the Other. Any or all of these points of disagreement can become places where writers stand to share what they have learned and to urge others to adopt those views.

In the essay that follows, for instance, *New York Times* columnist David Brooks takes the stand that our apparent national diversity disappears at local levels. His essay, titled "People Like Us," published in *The Atlantic Monthly* in September 2003, argues that "we don't really care about diversity all that much in America." He also thinks that we should care more. Indeed, he finds it "appalling" (stasis of quality) that we "know so little about one another," so much so that he suggests such reaching-out procedures (fourth stasis, above) as "national service" as a "rite of passage for young people in this country."

Journaling on David Brooks' Essay

As you read Brooks' essay, answer the following questions in your journal. Your answers will give you a strong grasp on stasis theory and prepare you to write your own essay on diversity:

1. How does the third sentence of Brooks' first paragraph challenge the conjecture that we value and have achieved diversity in the US?

2. Comment on the effectiveness of Brooks' use of examples and testimony in paragraphs 2–3 to support his claim that we prefer to live in homogeneous neighborhoods.

3. Comment on the effectiveness of Brooks' use of examples and testimony in paragraphs 7–9 to support his claim that marketers know and exploit the fact of our geographical homogeneity.

4. How does Brooks signal his transition in paragraph 10 from our geographical homogeneity to our habit of choosing media and churches based on our preference for "people like us"?

"People Like Us"

DAVID BROOKS

Maybe it's time to admit the obvious. We don't really care about diversity all that much in America, even though we talk about it a great deal. Maybe somewhere in this country there is a truly diverse neighborhood in which a black Pentecostal minister lives next to a white anti-globalization activist, who lives next to an Asian short-order cook, who lives next to a professional golfer, who lives next to a postmodern-literature professor and a cardiovascular surgeon. But I have never been to or heard of that neighborhood. Instead, what I have seen all around the country is people making strenuous efforts to group themselves with people who are basically like themselves.

Human beings are capable of drawing amazingly subtle social distinctions and then shaping their lives around them. In the Washington, D.C., area Democratic lawyers tend to live in suburban Maryland, and Republican lawyers tend to live in suburban Virginia. If you asked a Democratic lawyer to move from her $750,000 house in Bethesda, Maryland, to a $750,000 house in Great Falls, Virginia, she'd look at you as if you had just asked her to buy a pickup truck with a gun rack and to shove chewing tobacco in her kid's mouth. In Manhattan the owner of a $3 million SoHo loft would feel out of place moving into a $3 million Fifth Avenue apartment. A West Hollywood interior decorator would feel dislocated if you asked him to move to Orange County. In Georgia a barista from Athens would probably not fit in serving coffee in Americus.

It is a common complaint that every place is starting to look the same. But in the information age, the late writer James Chapin once told me, every place becomes more like itself. People are less often tied down to factories and mills, and they can search for places to live on the basis of cultural affinity. Once they find a town in which people share their values, they flock there, and reinforce whatever was distinctive about the town in the first place. Once Boulder, Colorado, became known as congenial to politically progressive mountain bikers, half the politically progressive mountain bikers in the country (it seems) moved there; they made the place so culturally pure that it has become practically a parody of itself.

But people love it. Make no mistake—we are increasing our happiness by segmenting off so rigorously. We are finding places where we are comfortable and where we feel we can flourish. But the choices we make toward that end lead to the very opposite of diversity. The United States might be a diverse nation when considered as a whole, but block by block and institution by institution it is a relatively homogenous nation.

When we use the word *diversity* today we usually mean racial integration. But even here our good intentions seem to have run into the brick wall of human nature. Over the past generation reformers have tried heroically, and in many cases successfully, to end housing discrimination. But recent patterns aren't encouraging:

according to an analysis of the 2000 census data, the 1990s saw only a slight increase in the racial integration of neighborhoods in the United States. The number of middle-class and upper-middle-class African American families is rising, but for whatever reasons—racism, psychological comfort—these families tend to congregate in predominantly black neighborhoods.

In fact, evidence suggests that some neighborhoods become more segregated over time. New suburbs in Arizona and Nevada, for example, start out reasonably well integrated. These neighborhoods don't yet have reputations, so people choose their houses for other, mostly economic reasons. But as neighborhoods age, they develop personalities (that's where the Asians live, and that's where the Hispanics live), and segmentation occurs. It could be that in a few years the new suburbs in the Southwest will be nearly as segregated as the established ones in the Northeast and the Midwest.

6

Even though race and ethnicity run deep in American society, we should in theory be able to find areas that are at least culturally diverse. But here, too, people show few signs of being truly interested in building diverse communities. If you run a retail company and you're thinking of opening new stores, you can choose among dozens of consulting firms that are quite effective at locating your potential customers. They can do this because people with similar tastes and preferences tend to congregate by ZIP code.

7

The most famous of these precision marketing firms is Claritas, which breaks down the U.S. population into sixty-two psycho-demographic clusters, based on such factors as how much money people make, what they like to read and watch, and what products they have bought in the past. For example, the "suburban sprawl" cluster is composed of young families making about $41,000 a year and living in fast-growing places such as Burnsville, Minnesota, and Bensalem, Pennsylvania. These people are almost twice as likely as other Americans to have three-way calling. They are two and a half times as likely to buy Light n' Lively Kid Yogurt. Members of the "towns & gowns" cluster are recent college graduates in places such as Berkeley, California, and Gainesville, Florida. They are big consumers of DoveBars and *Saturday Night Live*. They tend to drive small foreign cars and to read *Rolling Stone* and *Scientific American*.

8

Looking through the market research, one can sometimes be amazed by how efficiently people cluster—and by how predictable we all are. If you wanted to sell imported wine, obviously you would have to find places where rich people live. But did you know that the sixteen counties with the greatest proportion of imported-wine drinkers are all in the same three metropolitan areas (New York, San Francisco, and Washington, D.C.)? If you tried to open a motor-home dealership in Montgomery County, Pennsylvania, you'd probably go broke, because people in this ring of the Philadelphia suburbs think RVs are kind of uncool. But if you traveled just a short way north, to Monroe County, Pennsylvania, you would find yourself in the fifth motor-home-friendliest county in America.

9

Geography is not the only way we find ourselves divided from people unlike us. Some of us watch Fox News, while others listen to NPR. Some like David Letterman,

10

and others—typically in less urban neighborhoods—like Jay Leno. Some go to charismatic churches; some go to mainstream churches. Americans tend more and more often to marry people with education levels similar to their own, and to befriend people with backgrounds similar to their own.

My favorite illustration of this latter pattern comes from the first, noncontroversial 11 chapter of *The Bell Curve*. Think of your twelve closest friends, Richard J. Hernstein and Charles Murray write. If you had chosen them randomly from the American population, the odds that half of your twelve closest friends would be college graduates would be six in a thousand. The odds that half of the twelve would have advanced degrees would be less than one in a million. Have any of your twelve closest friends graduated from Harvard, Stanford, Yale, Princeton, Caltech, MIT, Duke, Dartmouth, Cornell, Columbia, Chicago, or Brown? If you chose your friends randomly from the American population, the odds against your having four or more friends from those schools would be more than a billion to one.

Many of us live in absurdly unlikely groupings, because we have organized our 12 lives that way.

It's striking that the institutions that talk the most about diversity often practice it 13 the least. For example, no group of people sings the diversity anthem more frequently and fervently than administrators at just such elite universities. But elite universities are amazingly undiverse in their values, politics, and mores. Professors in particular are drawn from a rather narrow segment of the population. If faculties reflected the general population, 32 percent of professors would be registered Democrats and 31 percent would be registered Republicans. Forty percent would be evangelical Christians. But a recent study of several universities by the conservative Center for the Study of Popular Culture and the American Enterprise Institute found that roughly 90 percent of those professors in the arts and sciences who had registered with a political party had registered Democratic. Fifty-seven professors at Brown were found on the voter-registration rolls. Of those, fifty-four were Democrats. Of the forty-two professors in the English, history, sociology, and political-science departments, all were Democrats. The results at Harvard, Penn State, Maryland, and the University of California at Santa Barbara were similar to the results at Brown.

What we are looking at here is human nature. People want to be around others 14 who are roughly like themselves. That's called community. It probably would be psychologically difficult for most Brown professors to share an office with someone who was pro-life, a member of the National Rifle Association, or an evangelical Christian. It's likely that hiring committees would subtly—even unconsciously—screen out any such people they encountered. Republicans and evangelical Christians have sensed that they are not welcome at places like Brown, so they don't even consider working there. In fact, any registered Republican who contemplates a career in academia these days is both a hero and a fool. So, in a semi-self-selective pattern, brainy people with generally liberal social mores flow to academia, and brainy people with generally conservative mores flow elsewhere.

The dream of diversity is like the dream of equality. Both are based on ideals we celebrate even as we undermine them daily. (How many times have you seen someone renounce a high-paying job or pull his child from an elite college on the grounds that these things are bad for equality?) On the one hand, the situation is appalling. It is appalling that Americans know so little about one another. It is appalling that many of us are so narrow-minded that we can't tolerate a few people with ideas significantly different from our own. It's appalling that evangelical Christians are practically absent from entire professions, such as academia, the media, and filmmaking. It's appalling that people should be content to cut themselves off from everyone unlike themselves. 15

The segmentation of society means that often we don't even have arguments across the political divide. Within their little validating communities, liberals and conservatives circulate half-truths about the supposed awfulness of the other side. These distortions are believed because it feels good to believe them. 16

On the other hand, there are limits to how diverse any community can or should be. I've come to think that it is not useful to try to hammer diversity into every neighborhood and institution in the United States. Sure, Augusta National should probably admit women, and university sociology departments should probably hire a conservative or two. It would be nice if all neighborhoods had a good mixture of ethnicities. But human nature being what it is, most places and institutions are going to remain culturally homogenous. 17

It's probably better to think about diverse lives, not diverse institutions. Human beings, if they are to live well, will have to move through a series of institutions and environments, which may be individually homogenous but, taken together, will offer diverse experiences. It might also be a good idea to make national service a rite of passage for young people in this country; it would take them out of their narrow neighborhood segment and thrust them in with people unlike themselves. Finally, it's probably important for adults to get out of their own familiar circles. If you live in a coastal, socially liberal neighborhood, maybe you should take out a subscription to the *Door*, the evangelical humor magazine; or maybe you should visit Branson, Missouri. Maybe you should stop in at a megachurch. Sure, it would be superficial familiarity, but it beats the iron curtains that now separate the nation's various cultural zones. 18

Look around at your daily life. Are you really in touch with the broad diversity of American life? Do you care? 19

Freewriting and Outlining

Now that you have dug deep into Brooks' essay, try freewriting in response to these prompts:

1. Brooks says that "elite universities are amazingly undiverse," that most professors are democrats. Does Brooks' comment apply to your university? Do your professors try to force their political views on you, or do they—regardless of their political

affiliations—encourage you to think for yourself and to examine a wide spectrum of views on social issues? Focus on specific examples to uncover the quality of the classroom experience.

2. Do you agree with Brooks' stand that young adults can come to value diversity through required "national service" in the military or in non-military service organizations? Explain.

3. Do you find diversity anywhere on your campus? In your hometown? In your workplace? In your church? Freewrite on each of these "neighborhoods," focusing on causes and effects, similarities and differences.

4. Can you think of specific procedures, solutions, to the homogeneity problem? Freewrite, focusing on the harmony you have observed when diverse peoples live and work together.

With these freewritings complete, sketch a tentative outline for an expository essay on this topic:

Topic: Paint a portrait of your neighborhood to reveal its identity and the degree of its diversity. You may focus on just one of your neighborhoods—your hometown, your sorority or fraternity, your campus, your workplace, your church—or you may compare and contrast two or three of the places where you live and work.

Tentative Purpose: To comment on that identity—praising, blaming, or both—and on the diversity or the lack of diversity you find.

Your Tentative Audience: Inhabitants of the "neighborhood(s)" that you describe and the newspaper they usually read.

Reviewing the Recursive Process of Writing

Armed now with your freewritings and your sketch outline, you're no doubt eager to begin your draft, but please put your project aside for a few minutes so that you can read first the student essay below, another stand on the topic of diversity in America. Can you identify her use of stasis theory in shaping her paper? Following this essay, you'll also find a full account of the recursive process (see chapter two) this student and her peers completed to write on this complicated topic. This account should clarify for you the process you're about to undertake.

Student Essay Invented from Stasis Theory: "Are Our Lives Truly Diverse?"

Mary Beth Eiland

Diversity is usually considered the number of different races or lifestyles present in an area. However, it is extremely common for members of an ethnically diverse community to lead lives with little variety. My hometown is a prime example of this enigma. In Columbus, Mississippi, the two main races are Caucasian and African American. The races are about even in numbers. Strangely, however, the black people and white people do not often attempt to intermingle, to bridge the economic and educational gaps that separate them. Most human beings, especially Americans, gravitate toward individuals similar to them, creating homogeneity in our everyday lives. In his article "People Like Us," David Brooks, a columnist for the *New York Times*, states that "the United States might be a diverse nation when considered as a whole, but block by block and institution by institution it is a relatively homogenous nation."

The social separation of the races in Columbus is strictly voluntary. No school, business, or church bans specific races. However, certain places have developed reputations for being 'for' a certain race. For example, many upper-class white kids attend private school in Columbus, while most black kids attend the public school. Hate is not to blame for this racial tension; fear is the only culprit. The extreme racial tension of the South's past still haunts many Southerners, who, like most Americans, fear stepping out of our comfort zones.

This Southern tradition of being slow to change our ways carries over into economic issues, as well. The most obvious type of diversity in Columbus is the economic diversity of the residents, illustrated in the homes of people of different economic levels. The poor condition of many homes is obvious. Many are in need of numerous repairs and painting, and the yards need mowing. When I drive by these homes, I feel so sorry for the inhabitants. In contrast, there are also a relatively high number of wealthy people in Columbus. Most of these extremely wealthy families live in gorgeous antebellum homes and lead lavish lifestyles. I have visited many of these homes, and I am absolutely amazed at their beauty. I worked in an antebellum home, which boasts over one million dollars in furniture. Like most of the furniture in these homes, each piece in this home is a beautiful, hand-carved antique. These people can afford the best in life, including extravagant parties and balls that are always covered by the local newspaper. The poorer residents, however, are usually ignored by the same newspaper. Many of the rich people simply choose to ignore the fact that our town is home to an increasing number of poverty-stricken people. This reality illustrates the fact that most people, especially wealthy people, tend to exclude and ignore people unlike themselves.

The wealthy and the poor are not only separated by economic issues, but usually by levels of education as well. Many wealthy people in Columbus are doctors or lawyers.

In contrast, a relatively high number of residents lack high school diplomas; as a result, they often lack jobs and live on welfare. Of course, when a poor person becomes ill, he or she must visit a doctor; when someone cannot defend himself in a lawsuit, he must employ a lawyer. Although forced to intermingle on this professional level, the relationships stop there. These people could theoretically form close friendships, taking the time to get to know one another on a personal basis, but, of course, they do not. They simply retreat to their respective groups, never challenging the homogeneity of their lives.

In Columbus, Mississippi, then, like so many places, diversity shows up in population figures but not in the ways people live. If we could look past the color, wealth, and education of our fellow Columbus residents, maybe our town would be less sharply divided. Instead of refusing to experience diversity, we need to enrich our lives by striving to know people who are different from us, a decision that rests in our own hands.

In reading this student essay, you probably noticed that her title signals a paper generated by the first stasis, conjecture: Does diversity exist? "Are Our Lives Truly Diverse?" You probably noted, too, that Aristotle's "topics" and Cicero's other "stases" generate the arrangement of her arguments:

- Her introduction acknowledges the diversity of the population of Columbus but claims that differences (topic of comparison) in income and education cause (topic of relationship) the races to live separately, a separation reinforced by fear.

- In supporting this stand, the student provides support paragraphs that stress the quality of this segregated society: school children and their parents "fear" to "intermingle"; rich people "ignore" the growing numbers of "poverty-stricken people"; doctors and lawyers and their clients fear to relate on a personal level.

- Finally, the student ends with the stasis of procedure, recommending that we "enrich our lives" by looking "past the color, wealth, and education" of those unlike ourselves.

Though you may agree with her views on our superficial diversity, you probably have seen or heard of exceptions to her claims: a working-class neighborhood neatly kept; a neighborhood with educated, prosperous persons, both black and white, living together peacefully; occasions when citizens of both races worked together to attend to the needs of the homeless or victims of disaster. Each of these challenges to this student's views, then, suggests places to stand, places where arguments may fruitfully begin. Indeed, you might agree with her final conclusion, that we should always strive to "enrich our lives" by experiencing diversity, yet strenuously disagree with her claim that we live "sharply divided," separated by fears.

Whichever "stands" on this issue of diversity you would take, you may readily conclude from this brief critique of her essay that writers need to provide solid evidence to support each of their lines of argument. Of course, as noted above, writers often turn to other writers to corroborate their experience. You saw above, for example, that the student quoted David

Brooks' essay, "People Like Us," to bolster her claim about our homogenous neighborhoods. After reading Brooks' testimony, the student also analyzed his article in her journal, where she praised his examples of our willful homogeneity: "In paragraph nine, Brooks explains how one Pennsylvania county thinks 'RVs are kind of uncool,' while a nearby county 'is the fifth motor-home-friendliest county in America.'"

In addition to reading and journaling on Brooks, the student and her classmates used stasis theory in class to brainstorm on this diversity topic. First, they used the white board to record their conjectures on the places where they have found—or did not find—diversity: hometown, church, workplace, campus—sorority/fraternity, classrooms, cafeteria, library, gym. Next, they moved toward definitions of diversity by brainstorming on the kinds of diversity they might find in these places: race, age, gender, educational level, political affiliations, religious affiliations.

Before beginning their rough drafts, the students next freewrote on the quality of the diversity or homogeneity in one of these "neighborhoods" of their experience, then on the procedure they would recommend to sustain the diversity or to create diversity where they found homogeneity. These high-speed, ten-minute freewrites, with spelling and punctuation issues thrown to the wind, led to some sharp images and some emotional shared readings: some students read of their all-white sororities; others read of their slowly integrating churches; several read about Katrina, the hurricane that seemed to tear apart the lives of mainly African Americans, but also brought together blacks, whites, indeed, persons of all ages, colors, genders, church groups, and political persuasions, working hard to save lives and rebuild homes. One student spoke of volunteers working 10 hours straight, dragging soaked carpets out of coastal homes; another praised Habitat for Humanity as the best "procedure" he knew to celebrate unity and diversity.

After this prewriting in class, the students completed more freewriting at home to ensure that they had found evidence to support their stands on diversity. They next wrote their rough drafts and brought them to class to share with members of their Writing Groups, using the procedure described in the first and second chapters. They also used Aristotle's topics and Cicero's stasis theory to guide their responses to one another's drafts:

- **Conjecture:** Does the writer use narration and description to bring to life examples of diversity or homogeneity in a given neighborhood?

- **Definition:** Does the writer define diversity and identify the kinds of neighborhoods he or she will examine?

- **Quality:** Does the writer clarify why the diversity or homogeneity is desirable or problematic, right or wrong?

- **Comparison:** Does the writer explore diversity—or the lack of it—in varied neighborhoods—such as workplace, church, campus—stressing key similarities and differences?

- **Relationships:** Does the writer explain the causes of the diversity (or homogeneity) and its effects?

- **Procedures:** Did the writer specify why and how diversity should be sought or sustained?

Using Arrangement to Serve the Needs of Your Audience

In answering these questions on invention, responders commented, too, on the arrangement of the draft:

- Does (do) the introductory paragraph(s) identify a problem to solve, relative to "diversity"? Does it provide any expert testimony to stress the importance of the issue? Does it narrow the focus, telling us the scope of the analysis, the sites of diversity or homogeneity to be explored? Does it include a claim on the importance of sustaining or building diversity?

- Do the body paragraphs trace the causes of diversity or homogeneity to their effects?

- Do the transitional phrases, clauses, or sentences stress the similarities or differences in the degree of diversity found in the sites examined?

- Does the conclusion repeat the claim and summarize the causes and effects, the similarities and differences? Does it specify how lack of diversity can be rectified?

- Did the writer identify potential audiences (beyond the teacher and the members of the Writing Group) for the paper? Does the overall arrangement of the paper seem suited to capture and sustain the interest of that audience?

With oral and written answers to these questions provided by two peers, the students took home their rough drafts and began revision.

Before you practice these strategies for inventing and arranging a draft on diversity, let's reflect a few more moments on the "arrangement" questions above and their value to writers.

The first four bullets above derive—just like the material on invention—from classical rhetorical theory. Aristotle, Cicero, and their followers taught their students the importance of *dispositio* (arrangement) and its interrelationship with invention. Any oration, they taught, must begin with an **exordium,** an introduction, one that identifies the deliberative, judicial, or ceremonial issue to be explored. To do so in an engaging way, the orator would often have to include a **narratio,** a narration, a brief story that dramatizes the importance of the subject at hand. Additionally, a speaker would provide the audience with **divisio,** a statement that spells out the order of key points to be addressed, knowing that audiences want to know where the speaker will take them. Having stated his or her claim on the subject, the orator would next launch into the **confirmatio** and/or the **confutatio,** confirming points of agreement with the opposing speaker, but then refuting other claims, presenting instead more compelling points to the contrary. Finally, the orator must conclude with a **peroratio**, summarizing key points and urging action (Corbett 17–23).

But before that conclusion, what should come first, paragraphs that confirm or paragraphs that refute? No writer can answer this question meaningfully without thinking about the readers—their views, their sensitivities, their willingness to listen. In other words, the processes of invention provide you immense help in generating a first draft, but your meaningful revision can start only when you begin making decisions about arrangement in terms of your readers' attitudes and needs.

Let's say, for example, that one of the student's class mates has written a draft praising the diversity in his college classrooms but deploring the voluntary segregation she has observed in the cafeteria, library, and workout center, as well as the lack of diversity in sorority houses. The order of these points, let's imagine further, seemed irrelevant to this student's peer responders—until the writer explained that she intended to offer this essay for publication in the university student newspaper. The responders might well suggest that her sorority sisters would take offense at this apparent attack, especially because it comes last, making the paper end with this negative point, one that seems to imply racism on the part of the sororities.

Helpful responders might then suggest some solutions: acknowledging that the sorority's national headquarters mandates multi-racial membership, that the same fears separating races at the food court prevent "other" races from attending rush functions at sororities where all the faces are the "other" color. The responders might also suggest focusing on ways to overcome these barriers to diversity on campus, such as racially mixed groups of students and faculty working together to clean up the Mississippi coast after hurricane Katrina. Whether or not to accept these suggestions remains the writer's decision, but such comments from a live audience of peers leaves the writer thinking about arrangement not as a fixed formula but as a strategic plan to be heard.

Writing an Expository Essay on Diversity

With these guidelines on process before you, go ahead now and write your draft on this diversity topic, using the materials you generated above. Once you finish the draft, share it, either with your Writing Group or with an intern in your university Writing Center. Such responses will help you determine if you invented enough material to serve your audience and purpose. Before you revise your rough draft, use the worksheet below to ensure that you have reconsidered your content and arrangement relative to the needs and attitudes of your readers.

Reader Analysis Worksheet

1. **Who is (are) my reader(s)?**

   - Age and Gender
   - Educational Level
   - Socio-economic Level

2. **What is my reader's attitude toward my subject?**

3. **How much does my reader already know about my topic?**

4. **What is my reader's attitude toward me?**

5. **How likely will my reader believe my claim, accept my proposal, or change her/his beliefs or behavior?**

6. **Based on the information above, what decisions should I make about the content of my essay?**

   - **Limiting my focus**: What scope fits my reader's needs?

   - **Choosing evidence**: What range and depth of evidence—facts, statistics, examples, testimony, quotations—will I need to support my claim? In other words, what degree of specificity must I achieve to be persuasive?

   - **Arranging my points**: What order should my supporting points take? Which point should come first? Do I have a "clincher," a "big gun" that I want to fire at the end?

   - **Choosing my words, building my sentences**: What tone and "voice" does my reader expect?

Writing a Second Expository Essay on Diversity

Both David Brooks' essay and the student essay above may have disturbed you, for both essays suggest that we impoverish our lives and our culture by allowing our fears of difference to prevent us from living up to the motto still printed on the backs of our quarters: "e pluribus unum," unity in many. Reading the following essays will not make those disturbing feelings go away, but in doing so you will reflect further on the consequences of seeing diversity as a curse or a blessing.

In the first piece, Gary Soto's "Like Mexicans," you will read the entertaining account of Soto defying his Mexican American grandmother's advice that he "should marry a Mexican girl," courting instead a Japanese girl, whose family teaches him the liberating lesson that her "people were like Mexicans, only different."

In the second essay, you will read Mary Crow Dog's painful account of receiving an education in a 1950's mission school, where the faculty believed that American Indian children should be civilized "with a stick."

In the third selection, a chapter from Senator John McCain's book *Why Courage Matters*, you will read the story of Roy Benavidez, who grew up hearing himself described as a "dirty Mexican" but who later risked his life to save other soldiers, regardless of their color or race.

Before each of these readings, you will once again find a few contextualizing remarks, then some journaling questions to help you get started on the process of writing in response to these powerful essays. Finally, you will receive one more invitation to write an expository essay, this time explaining what you have learned—about diversity and about writing—from these three writers.

Journaling on Gary Soto's Essay

Born in 1952, Gary Soto grew up in Fresno, California, where his parents and their parents had long labored in the fields. Wanting to escape his family's poverty, Soto earned a BA from Fresno State University, then a Master of Fine Arts degree from the University of California, Irvine, which led to a professorship in creative writing and eventually to a career in writing poetry, fiction, and nonfiction.

Read Soto's essay on diversity in marriages and answer the following questions in your journal:

1. Explain how Soto uses humor in his first paragraph to draw you into his essay. Focus particularly on his grandmother's recognizing just four ethnic groups: Mexicans, blacks, Asians, and "Okies" (a reference to the poor white people from Oklahoma who migrated to California during the Great Depression). Do you see a serious concern, a fear, behind her definition of Mexican girls by their three "virtues"? What

assumption does she make about racially or ethnically mixed marriages?

2. In paragraph five, the adolescent Soto and his friend Scott survey "Mexican and Okie" girls as they pass by. How does this scene add to the humor of the essay? Though we can readily find humor in the scene, what does the paragraph suggest about our methods—often learned in childhood—for categorizing people?

3. Soto frequently uses figurative language, usually similes, to help you see his world and understand his thinking processes. Find the similes in paragraphs 4, 8, and 9, and explain how these comparisons enrich the description and narration.

4. In paragraph eight, what does the twenty-year-old Soto realize about his grandmother and mother's preference that he marry a Mexican woman?

5. Explain how paragraphs nine through thirteen alter the Soto family conjecture about ethnic differences and validate Soto's plan to marry a non-Mexican.

"Like Mexicans"

GARY SOTO

My grandmother gave me bad advice and good advice when I was in my early teens. For the bad advice, she said that I should become a barber because they made good money and listened to the radio all day. "Honey, they don't work como burros," she would say every time I visited her. She made the sound of donkeys braying. "Like that, honey!" For the good advice, she said that I should marry a Mexican girl. "No Okies, hijo"—she would say—"Look, my son. He marry one and they fight every day about I don't know what and I don't know what." For her, everyone who wasn't Mexican, black, or Asian were Okies. The French were Okies, the Italians in suits were Okies. When I asked about Jews, whom I had read about, she asked for a picture. I rode home on my bicycle and returned with a calendar depicting the important races of the world. "Pues si, son Okies tambien!" she said, nodding her head. She waved the calendar away and we went to the living room where she lectured me on the virtues of the Mexican girl: first, she could cook and, second, she acted like a woman, not a man, in her husband's home. She said she would tell me about a third when I got a little older.

I asked my mother about it—becoming a barber and marrying a Mexican. She was in the kitchen. Steam curled from a pot of boiling beans, the radio was on, looking as squat as a loaf of bread. "Well, if you want to be a barber—they say they make good money." She slapped a round steak with a knife, her glasses slipping down with each strike. She stopped and looked up. "If you find a good Mexican girl, marry her of course." She returned to slapping the meat and I went to the backyard where my brother and David King were sitting on the lawn feeling the inside of their cheeks.

"This is what girls feel like," my brother said, rubbing the inside of his cheek. David put three fingers inside his mouth and scratched. I ignored them and climbed the back fence to see my best friend, Scott, a second-generation Okie. I called him and his mother pointed to the side of the house where his bedroom was, a small aluminum trailer, the kind you gawk at when they're flipped over on the freeway, wheels spinning in the air. I went around to find Scott pitching horseshoes.

I picked up a set of rusty ones and joined him. While we played, we talked about school and friends and record albums. The horseshoes scuffed up dirt, sometimes ringing the iron that threw out a meager shadow like a sundial. After three argued-over games we pulled two oranges apiece from his tree and started down the alley still talking school and friends and record albums. We pulled more oranges from the alley and talked about who we would marry. "No offense, Scott," I said with an orange slice in my mouth, "but I would never marry an Okie." We walked in step, almost touching, with a sled of shadows dragging behind us. "No offense, Gary," Scott said, "but I would *never* marry a Mexican." I looked at him: a fang of orange slice showed from his munching mouth. I didn't think anything of it. He had his girl and I had mine. But our seventh-grade vision was the same: to marry, get jobs, buy cars and maybe a house if we had money left over.

We talked about our future lives until, to our surprise, we were on the downtown mall, two miles from home. We bought a bag of popcorn at Penneys and sat on a bench near the fountain watching Mexican and Okie girls pass. "That one's mine," I pointed with my chin when a girl with eyebrows arched into black rainbows ambled by. "She's cute," Scott said about a girl with yellow hair and a mouthful of gum. We dreamed aloud, our chins busy pointing out girls. We agreed that we couldn't wait to become men and lift them onto our laps.

But the woman I married was not Mexican but Japanese. It was a surprise to me. For years, I went about wide-eyed in my search for the brown girl in a white dress at a dance. I searched the playground at the baseball diamond. When the girls raced for grounders, their hair bounced like something that couldn't be caught. When they sat together in the lunchroom, heads pressed together, I knew they were talking about us Mexican guys. I saw them and dreamed them. I threw my face into my pillow, making up sentences that were good as in the movies.

But when I was twenty, I fell in love with this other girl who worried my mother, who had my grandmother asking once again to see the calendar of the Important Races of the World. I told her I had thrown it away years before. I took a much-glanced-at snapshot from my wallet. We looked at it together, in silence. Then grandma reclined in her chair, lit a cigarette, and said, "Es pretty." She blew and asked with all her worry pushed up to her forehead: "Chinese?"

I was in love and there was no looking back. She was the one. I told my mother who was slapping hamburger into patties. "Well, sure if you want to marry her," she said. But the more I talked, the more concerned she became. Later I began to worry. Was it all a mistake? "Marry a Mexican girl," I heard my mother say in my mind. I heard it at breakfast. I heard it over math problems, between Western Civilization and cultural geography. But then one afternoon while I was hitchhiking home from school, it struck me like a baseball in the back: my mother wanted me to marry someone of my own social class—a poor girl. I considered my fiancée, Carolyn, and she didn't look poor, though I knew she came from a family of farm workers and pull-yourself-up-by-your-bootstraps ranchers. I asked my brother who was marrying Mexican poor that fall, if I should marry a poor girl. He screamed "Yeah" above his terrible guitar playing in his bedroom. I considered my sister who had married a Mexican. Cousins were dating Mexican. Uncles were remarrying poor women. I asked Scott, who was still my best friend, and he said, "She's too good for you, so you better not." 9

I worried about it until Carolyn took me home to meet her parents. We drove in her Plymouth until the houses gave way to farms and ranches and finally her house fifty feet from the highway. When we pulled into the drive, I panicked and begged Carolyn to make a U-turn and go back so we could talk about it over a soda. She pinched my cheek, calling me a "silly boy." I felt better, though, when I got out of the car and saw the house: the chipped paint, a cracked window, boards for a walk to the brick door. There were rusting cars near the barn. A tractor with a net of spiderwebs under a mulberry. A field. A bale of barbed wire like children's scribbling leaning against an empty chicken coop. Carolyn took my hand and pulled me to my future mother-in-law who was coming out to greet us. 10

We had lunch: sandwiches, potato chips, and iced tea. Carolyn and her mother talked mostly about neighbors and the congregation at the Japanese Methodist Church in West Fresno. Her father, who was in khaki work clothes, excused himself with a wave that was almost a salute and went outside. I heard a truck start, a dog bark, and then the truck rattled away. 11

Carolyn's mother offered another sandwich, but I declined with a shake of my head and a smile. I looked around when I could, when I was not saying over and over that I was a college student, hinting that I could take care of her daughter. I shifted my chair, I saw newspapers piled in corners, dusty cereal boxes and vinegar bottles in corners. The wallpaper was bubbled from rain that had come in from a bad roof. Dust. Dust lay on lamp shades and window sills. These people are just like Mexicans, I thought. Poor people. 12

Carolyn's mother asked me through Carolyn if I would like a *sushi*. A plate of black and white things were held in front of me. I took one, wide-eyed, and turned it over like a foreign coin. I was biting into one when I saw a kitten crawl up the window screen over the sink. I chewed and the kitten opened its mouth of terror as she crawled higher, wanting in to paw the leftovers from our plates. I looked at Carolyn who said that the cat was just showing off. I looked up in time to see it fall. It crawled up, then fell again. 13

We talked for an hour and had apple pie and coffee, slowly. Finally, we got up with Carolyn taking my hand. Slightly embarrassed, I tried to pull away but her grip held me. I let her have her way as she led me down the hallway with her mother right behind me. When I opened the door, I was startled by a kitten clinging to the screen door, its mouth screaming "cat food, dog biscuits, sushi...." I opened the door and the kitten, still holding on, whined in the language of hungry animals. When I got into Carolyn's car, I looked back: the cat was still clinging. I asked Carolyn if it were 14 possibly hungry, but she said the cat was being silly. She started the car, waved to her mother, and bounced us over the rain-poked drive, patting my thigh for being her lover baby. Carolyn waved again. I looked back, waving then gawking at a window screen where there were now three kittens clawing and screaming to get in. Like Mexicans, I thought. I remembered the Molinas and how the cats clung to their screens—cats they shot down with squirt guns. On the highway, I felt happy, pleased by it all. I patted Carolyn's thigh. Her people were like Mexicans, only different.

Journaling on Mary Crow Dog's Autobiography

This selection comes from Mary Crow Dog's autobiography *Lakota Woman*, which tells the story of her growing up as a Sioux woman in a society still dominated by white people. Though "Civilize Them with a Stick" narrates her girlhood in a Catholic school in the 1950's, you will hear an anger that traces back to the Battle of Wounded Knee, South Dakota, where American troops crushed the Sioux in 1890.

As you follow Dog's story, answer the following questions in your journal:

1. Dog acknowledges in her first paragraph that boarding schools now are "much improved" over those in the 1950s, and that such schools today feature professional staffs trained in psychology. What else do you learn in the first paragraph that explains why, in spite of these improvements, Dog still must tell her story and we should listen?

2. List the details and examples in paragraphs 2–11 that document the brutality of the teachers and staff and the extreme suffering of Dog and her classmates. Collectively, what do these paragraphs teach you about the effects of racism on oppressors?

3. Explain how Dog uses parallel sentence structure in paragraph 12 to vent her outrage and to assert her dignity.

4. In paragraph 19, what "boy-girl stuff" seems characteristic of young people of any ethnic group?

5. Focusing on Dog's conflict with the priest in paragraphs 21–28, explain how the encounter eventually helps Dog and the priest to see each other more clearly and to accept one another's full humanity.

Excerpt from *Lakota Woman*, "Civilize Them With a Stick"

MARY CROW DOG AND RICHARD ERDOES

Gathered from the cabin, the wickiup, and the tepee,
partly by cajolery and partly by threats,
partly by bribery and partly by force,
they are induced to leave their kindred
to enter these schools and take upon themselves
the outward appearance of civilized life.

-ANNUAL REPORT OF THE DEPARTMENT OF INTERIOR, 1901

It is almost impossible to explain to a sympathetic white person what a typical old Indian boarding school was like; how it affected the Indian child suddenly dumped into it like a small creature from another world, helpless, defenseless, bewildered, trying desperately and instinctively to survive and sometimes not surviving at all. I think such children were like the victims of Nazi concentration camps trying to tell average, middle-class Americans what their experience had been like. Even now, when these schools are much improved, when the buildings are new, all gleaming steel and glass, the food tolerable, the teachers well trained and well intentioned, even trained in child psychology—unfortunately the psychology of white children, which is different from ours—the shock to the child upon arrival is still tremendous. Some just seem to shrivel up, don't speak for days on end, and have an empty look in their eyes. I know of an eleven-year-old on another reservation who hanged herself, and in our school, while I was there, a girl jumped out of the window, trying to kill herself to escape an unbearable situation. That first shock is always there....

The mission school at St. Francis was a curse for our family for generations. My grandmother went there, then my mother, then my sisters and I. At one time or other every one of us tried to run away. Grandma told me once about the bad times she had experienced at St. Francis. In those days they let students go home only for one week every year. Two days were used up for transportation, which meant spending just five days out of three hundred and sixty-five with her family. And that was an improvement. Before grandma's time, on many reservations they did not let the students go home at all until they had finished school. Anybody who disobeyed the nuns was severely punished. The building in which my grandmother stayed had three floors, for girls only. Way up in the attic were little cells, about five by five by ten feet. One time she was in church and instead of praying she was playing jacks. As punishment they took her to one of those little cubicles where she stayed in darkness because the windows had been boarded up. They left her there for a whole week with only bread and water for nourishment. After she came out she promptly ran away, together with three other girls. They were found and brought back. The nuns stripped them naked and whipped them. They used a horse buggy whip on my grandmother. Then she was put back into the attic for two weeks.

120

My mother had much the same experiences but never wanted to talk about them, and then there I was, in the same place. The school is now run by the BIA—the Bureau of Indian Affairs—but only since about fifteen years ago. When I was there, during the 1960s, it was still run by the Church. The Jesuit father ran the boys' wing and the Sisters of the Sacred Heart ran us—with the help of the strap. Nothing had changed since my grandmother's days. I have been told recently that even in the '70s they were still beating children at that school. All I got out of school was being taught how to pray. I learned quickly that I would be beaten if I failed in my devotions or, God forbid, prayed the wrong way, especially prayed in Indian to Wakan Tanka, the Indian Creator. 3

The girls' wing was built like an F and was run like a penal institution. Every morning at five o'clock the sisters would come into our large dormitory to wake us up, and immediately we had to kneel down at the sides of our beds and recite the prayers. At six o'clock we were herded into the church for more of the same. I did not take kindly to the discipline and to marching by the clock, left-right, left-right. I was never one to like being forced to do something. I do something because I feel like doing it. I felt this way always, as far as I can remember, and my sister Barbara felt the same way. An old medicine man once told me: "Us Lakotas are not like dogs who can be trained, who can be beaten and keep on wagging their tails, licking the hand that whipped them. We are like cats, little cats, big cats, wildcats, bobcats, mountain lions. It doesn't matter what kind, but cats who can't be tamed, who scratch if you step on their tails." But I was only a kitten and my claws were still small. 4

Barbara was still in the school when I arrived and during my first year or two she could still protect me a little bit. When Barb was a seventh-grader, she ran away together with five other girls, early in the morning before sunrise. They brought them back in the evening. The girls had to wait for two hours in front of the mother superior's office. They were hungry and cold, frozen through. It was wintertime and they had been running the whole day without food, trying to make good their escape. The mother superior asked each girl, "Would you do this again?" She told them that as punishment they would not be allowed to visit home for a month and that she'd keep them busy on work details until the skin on their knees and elbows had worn off. At the end of her speech she told each girl, "Get up from this chair and lean over it." She then lifted the girls' skirts and pulled down their underpants. Not little girls either, but teenagers. She had a leather strap about a foot long and four inches wide fastened to a stick, and beat the girls, one after another, until they cried. Barb did not give her that satisfaction but just clenched her teeth. There was one girl, Barb told me, the nun kept on beating and beating until her arm got tired. 5

I did not escape my share of the strap. Once, when I was thirteen years old, I refused to go to Mass. I did not want to go to church because I did not feel well. A nun grabbed me by the hair, dragged me upstairs, made me stoop over, pulled my dress up (we were not allowed at the time to wear jeans), pulled my panties down, and gave me what they called "swats"—twenty-five swats with a board around which Scotch tape had been wound. She hurt me badly. 6

My classroom was right next to the principal's office and almost every day I could   7
hear him swatting the boys. Beating was the common punishment for not doing one's
homework, or for being late to school. It had such a bad effect upon me that I hated
and mistrusted every white person on sight, because I met only one kind. It was not
until much later that I met sincere white people I could relate to and be friends with.
Racism breeds racism in reverse.

The routine at St. Francis was dreary. Six a.m., kneeling in church for an hour or   8
so; seven o'clock, breakfast; eight o'clock, scrub the floor, peel spuds, make classes. We
had to mop the dining room twice every day and scrub the tables. If you were caught
taking a rest, doodling on the bench with a fingernail or knife, or just rapping, the nun
would come up with a dish towel and just slap it across your face, saying, "You're not
supposed to be talking, you're supposed to be working!" Monday mornings we had
cornmeal mush, Tuesday oatmeal, Wednesday rice and raisins, Thursday cornflakes,
and Friday all the leftovers mixed together or sometimes fish. Frequently the food had
bugs or rocks in it. We were eating hot dogs that were weeks old, while the nuns were
dining on ham, whipped potatoes, sweet peas, and cranberry sauce. In winter our dorm
was icy cold while the nuns' rooms were always warm.

I have seen little girls arrive at the school, first-graders, just fresh from home and   9
totally unprepared for what awaited them, little girls with pretty braids, and the first
thing the nuns did was chop their hair off and tie up what was left behind their ears.
Next they would dump the children into tubs of alcohol, a sort of rubbing alcohol, "to
get the germs off." Many of the nuns were German immigrants, some from Bavaria,
so that we sometimes speculated whether Bavaria was some sort of Dracula country
inhabited by monsters. For the sake of objectivity I ought to mention that two of the
German fathers were great linguists and that the only Lakota-English dictionaries and
grammars which are worth anything were put together by them.

At night some of the girls would huddle together for comfort and reassurance.   10
Then the nun in charge of the dorm would come in and say, "What are the two of
you doing in bed together? I smell evil in this room. You girls are evil incarnate. You
are sinning. You are going to hell and burn forever. You can act that way in the devil's
frying pan." She would get them out of bed in the middle of the night, making them
kneel and pray until morning. We had not the slightest idea what it was all about. At
home we slept two and three in a bed for animal warmth and a feeling of security.

The nuns and the girls in the two top grades were constantly battling it out   11
physically with fists, nails, and hair-pulling. I myself was growing from a kitten into
an undersized cat. My claws were getting bigger and were itching for action. About
1969 or 1970 a strange young white girl appeared on the reservation. She looked
about eighteen or twenty years old. She was pretty and had long, blond hair down
to her waist, patched jeans, boots, and a backpack. She was different from any other
white person we had met before. I think her name was Wise. I do not know how she
managed to overcome our reluctance and distrust, getting us into a corner, making us
listen to her, asking us how we were treated. She told us that she was from New York.
She was the first real hippie or Yippie we had come across. She told us of people called

the Black Panthers, Young Lords, and Weathermen. She said, "Black people are getting it on. Indians are getting it on in St. Paul and California. How about you?" She also said, "Why don't you put out an underground paper, mimeograph it. It's easy. Tell it like it is. Let it all hang out." She spoke a strange lingo but we caught on fast.

Charlene Left Hand Bull and Gina One Star were two full-blood girls I used to hang out with. We did everything together. They were willing to join me in a Sioux uprising. We put together a newspaper which we named the Red Panther. In it we wrote how bad the school was, what kind of slop we had to eat—slimy, rotten, blackened potatoes for two weeks—the way we were beaten. I think I was the one who wrote the worst article about our principal of the moment, Father Keeler. I put all my anger and venom into it. I called him a goddam wasicun son of a bitch. I wrote that he knew nothing about Indians and should go back to where he came from, teaching white children whom he could relate to. I wrote that we knew which priests slept with which nuns and that all they ever could think about was filling their bellies and buying a new car. It was the kind of writing which foamed at the mouth, but which also lifted a great deal of weight from one's soul. 12

On Saint Patrick's Day, when everybody was at the big powwow, we distributed our newspapers. We put them on windshields and bulletin boards, in desks and pews, in dorms and toilets. But someone saw us and snitched on us. The shit hit the fan. The three of us were taken before a board meeting. Our parents, in my case my mother, had to come. They were told that ours was a most serious matter, the worst thing that had ever happened in the school's long history. One of the nuns told my mother, "Your daughter really needs to be talked to." "What's wrong with my daughter?" my mother asked. She was given one of our Red Panther newspapers. The nun pointed out its name to her and then my piece, waiting for mom's reaction. After a while she asked, "Well, what have you got to say to this? What do you think?" 13

My mother said, "Well, when I went to school here, some years back, I was treated a lot worse then these kids are. I really can't see how they can have any complaints, because we was treated a lot stricter. We could not even wear skirts halfway up our knees. These girls have it made. But you should forgive them because they are young. And it's supposed to be a free country, free speech and all that. I don't believe what they done is wrong." So all I got out of it was scrubbing six flights of stairs on my hands and knees, every day. And no boy-side privileges. 14

The boys and girls were still pretty much separated. The only time one could meet a member of the opposite sex was during free time, between four and five-thirty, in the study hall or on benches or the volleyball court outside, and that was strictly supervised. One day Charlene and I went over to the boys' side. We were on the ball team and they had to let us practice. We played three extra minutes, only three minutes more than we were supposed to. Here was the nuns' opportunity for revenge. We got twenty-five swats. I told Charlene, "We are getting too old to have our bare asses whipped that way. We are old enough to have babies. Enough of this shit. Next time we fight back." Charlene only said, "Hoka-hay!" 15

We had to take showers every evening. One little girl did not want to take her panties off and one of the nuns told her, "You take those underpants off—or else!" But the child was ashamed to do it. The nun was getting her swat to threaten the girl. I went up to the sister, pushed her veil off, and knocked her down. I told her that if she wanted to hit a little girl she should pick on me, pick one her own size. She got herself transferred out of the dorm a week later. 16

In a school like this there is always a lot of favoritism. At St. Francis it was strongly tinged with racism. Girls who were near-white, who came from what the nuns called "nice families," got preferential treatment. They waited on the faculty and got to eat ham or eggs and bacon in the morning. They got the easy jobs while the skins, who did not have the right kind of background—myself among them—always wound up in the laundry room sorting out ten bushel baskets of dirty boys' socks every day. Or we wound up scrubbing the floors and doing all the dishes. The school therefore fostered fights and antagonism between whites and breeds, and between breeds and skins. At one time Charlene and I had to iron all the robes and vestments the priests wore when saying Mass. We had to fold them up and put them into a chest in the back of the church. In a corner, looking over our shoulders, was a statue of the crucified Savior, all bloody and beaten up. Charlene looked up and said, "Look at that poor Indian. The pigs sure worked him over." That was the closest I ever came to seeing Jesus. 17

I was held up as a bad example and didn't mind. I was old enough to have a boyfriend and promptly got one. At the school we had an hour and a half for ourselves. Between the boys' and the girls' wings were some benches where one could sit. My boyfriend and I used to go there just to hold hands and talk. The nuns were very uptight about any boy-girl stuff. They had an exaggerated fear of anything having even the faintest connection with sex. One day in religion class, an all-girl class, Sister Bernard singled me out for some remarks, pointing me out as a bad example, an example that should be shown. She said that I was too free with my body. That I was holding hands which meant that I was not a good example to follow. She also said that I wore unchaste dresses, skirts which were too short, too suggestive, shorter than regulations permitted, and for that I would be punished. She dressed me down before the whole class, carrying on and on about my unchastity. 18

I stood up and told her, "You shouldn't say any of those things, miss. You people are a lot worse than us Indians. I know all about you, because my grandmother and my aunt told me about you. Maybe twelve, thirteen years ago you had a water stoppage here in St. Francis. No water could get through the pipes. There are water lines right under the mission, underground tunnels and passages where in my grandmother's time only the nuns and priests could go, which were off-limits to everybody else. When the water backed up they had to go through all the water lines and clean them out. And in those huge pipes they found the bodies of newborn babies. And they were white babies. They weren't Indian babies. At least when our girls have babies, they don't do away with them that way, like flushing them down the toilet, almost. 19

"And that priest they sent here from Holy Rosary in Pine Ridge because he molested a little girl. You couldn't think of anything better than dump him on us. All 20 he does is watch young women and girls with that funny smile on his face. Why don't you point him out for an example?"

Charlene and I worked on the school newspaper. After all we had some practice. Every day we went down to Publications. One of the priests acted as the photographer, doing the enlarging and developing. He smelled of chemicals which had stained his hands yellow. One day he invited Charlene into the darkroom. He was going to teach her developing. She was developed already. She was a big girl compared to him, taller too. Charlene was nicely built, not fat, just rounded. No sharp edges anywhere: All of a sudden she rushed out of the darkroom, yelling to me, "Let's get out of here! He's trying to feel me up. That priest is nasty." So there was this too to contend with— sexual harassment. We complained to the student body. The nuns said we just had a dirty mind. 21

We got a new priest in English. During one of his first classes he asked one of the boys a certain question. The boy was shy. He spoke poor English, but he had the right answer. The priest told him, "You did not say it right. Correct yourself. Say it over again." The boy got flustered and stammered. He could hardly get out a word. But the priest kept after him: "Didn't you hear? I told you to do the whole thing over. Get it right this time." He kept on and on. 22

I stood up and said, "Father, don't be doing that. If you go into an Indian's home and try to talk Indian, they might laugh at you and say, 'Do it over correctly. Get it right this time!'" 23

He shouted at me, "Mary, you stay after class. Sit down right now!" 24

I stayed after class, until after the bell. He told me, "Get over here!" 25

He grabbed me by the arm, pushing me against the blackboard, shouting, "Why are you always mocking us? You have no reason to do this." 26

I said, "Sure I do. You were making fun of him. You embarrassed him. He needs strengthening, not weakening. You hurt him. I did not hurt you." 27

He twisted my arm and pushed real hard. I turned around and hit him in the face, giving him a bloody nose. After that I ran out of the room, slamming the door behind me. He and I went to Sister Bernard's office. I told her, "Today I quit school. I'm not taking any more of this, none of this shit anymore. None of this treatment. Better give me my diploma. I can't waste any more time on you people." 28

Sister Bernard looked at me for a long, long time. She said, "All right, Mary Ellen, go home today. Come back in a few days and get your diploma." And that was that. Oddly enough, that priest turned out okay. He taught a class in grammar, orthography, composition, things like that. I think he wanted more respect in class. He was still young and unsure of himself. But I was in there too long. I didn't feel like hearing it. Later he became a good friend of the Indians, a personal friend of myself and my husband. He stood up for us during Wounded Knee and after he stood up to his superiors, stuck his neck way out, became a real people priest. He even learned our language. He died prematurely of cancer. It is not only the good Indians who die 29 young, but the good whites, too. It is the timid ones who know how to take care of themselves who grow old. I am still grateful to that priest for what he did for us later and for the quarrel he picked with me—or did I pick it with him?—because it ended a situation which had become unendurable for me. The day of my fight with him was my last day in school.

Journaling on John McCain's Book

You're probably well aware that Senator John McCain sought the Republican nomination for president in 2004 and 2008, and has served as Congressman, then Senator from Arizona for over 30 years. He also served as a naval officer in Vietnam, including four years imprisoned in North Vietnam's "Hanoi Hilton." This selection from McCain's new book introduces us to a man who values all human life, regardless of ethnicity.

As you read McCain's chapter on Sergeant Benavidez, answer the following questions in your journal:

1. McCain combines definition and testimony in his first paragraph to secure his readers' interest. Explain why you think that McCain succeeds or fails in this purpose.

2. How does McCain use contrast in paragraph two to narrow the focus of this chapter?

3. What conclusions about Benavidez' character do you draw from the brief narrative in paragraph 3?

4. Paragraphs 4–10 narrate Benavidez' heroics in 1968. Explain how effectively McCain uses facts, description, and action verbs to support his claim about Benavidez' "superhuman heroics."

5. How does McCain use conjecture in paragraphs 10–13 to modify his definition of courage?

6. In paragraph 14, McCain says that we can "emulate" Benavidez' "character," even if we cannot duplicate his superhuman courage. Explain how McCain clarifies this idea of emulation in his peroration, paragraphs 16–18.

Excerpt from *Why Courage Matters*

John McCain

"A kind of madness" is how a friend of mine, a Marine Corps veteran of the Vietnam War, described the courage displayed by men whose battlefield heroics had earned them the Medal of Honor. "It's impossible to comprehend, really, even if you witness it....It's one mad moment. You never think anyone you know is really capable of it. Not even the toughest, bravest, best men in the company. They're as surprised as anyone to see it. And if someone does do it, and lives, they probably never do it again. You might think the guy who's always running around in a fight, exposing himself to enemy fire, yelling a lot, might do it. But that's not what happens. They just get killed usually."

Select at random a dozen Medal of Honor recipients and read the citations that accompany their decorations. Some will describe a single lonely act of heroism, one man's self-sacrifice that saved the lives of his comrades, who will remember the act for the rest of their lives with feelings of gratitude and lasting obligation mixed with something that feels much like shame—shame that one's life, no matter how good and useful, no matter how honorable, might not deserve to have been ransomed at such a cost. All the citations will record acts of great heroism, of course. But some might seem plausible, if just barely so. The reader might even fantasize himself capable of such heroism, under extreme circumstances, without feeling too ashamed of the presumption. Maybe you are. At least one, however, will tell of such incredible daring, such epic courage, that no witness to it could imagine himself, or anyone he knows, capable of it. It might be the story of Roy Benavidez. [2]

Special Forces master sergeant Roy Benavidez was the son of a Texas sharecropper. Orphaned at a young age, quiet and mistaken as slow, derided as a "dumb Mexican" by his classmates, he left school in the eighth grade to work in the cotton fields. He joined the army at nineteen. On his first tour in Vietnam, in 1964, he stepped on a land mine. Army doctors thought the wound would be permanently crippling. It wasn't. He recovered and became a Green Beret. [3]

During his second combat tour, in the early morning of May 2, 1968, in Loc Ninh, Vietnam, Sergeant Benavidez monitored by radio a twelve-man reconnaissance patrol. Three Green Berets, friends of his, and nine Montagnard tribesmen had been dropped in the dense jungle west of Loc Ninh, just inside Cambodia. No man aboard the low-flying helicopters beating noisily toward the landing zone that morning could have been unaware of how dangerous the assignment was. Considered an enemy sanctuary, the area was known to be vigilantly patrolled by a sizable force of the North Vietnamese army intent on keeping it so. Once on the ground, the twelve men were almost immediately engaged by the enemy and soon surrounded by a force that grew to a battalion. [4]

The mission had been a mistake, and three helicopters were ordered to evacuate the besieged patrol. Fierce small arms and antiaircraft fire, wounding several crew members, forced the helicopters to return to base. Listening on the radio, Benavidez heard one of his friends scream, "Get us out of here!" and, "So much shooting it sounded like a popcorn machine." He jumped into one of the returning helicopters, volunteering for a second evacuation attempt. When he arrived at the scene, he found that none of the patrol had made it to the landing zone. Four were already dead, including the team leader, and the other eight were wounded and unable to move. Carrying a knife and a medic bag, Benavidez made the sign of the cross, leapt from the helicopter hovering ten feet off the ground, and ran seventy yards to his injured comrades. Before he reached them, he was shot in the leg, face, and head. He got up and kept moving. [5]

When he reached their position, he armed himself with an enemy rifle, began to treat the wounded, reposition them, distribute ammunition, and call in air strikes. He threw smoke grenades to indicate their location and ordered the helicopter pilot to come in close to pick up the wounded. He dragged four of the wounded aboard, and then, while under intense fire and returning fire with his captured weapon, he ran alongside the helicopter as it flew just a few feet off the ground toward the others. He got the rest of the wounded aboard, as well as the dead, except for the fallen team leader. As he raced to retrieve his body, and the classified documents the dead man had carried, he was shot in the stomach and grenade fragments cut into his back.

Before he could make his way back toward the helicopter, the pilot was fatally wounded and the aircraft crashed upside down. He helped the wounded escape the burning wreckage and organized them in a defensive perimeter. He called for air strikes and fire from circling gunships to suppress the ever increasing enemy fire enough to allow another evacuation attempt. Critically wounded, Benavidez moved constantly along the perimeter, bringing water and ammunition to the defenders, treating their wounds, encouraging them to hold on. He sustained several more gunshot wounds, but he continued to fight. For six hours.

When another extraction helicopter landed, he helped the wounded toward it, one and two at a time. On his second trip, an enemy solider ran up behind him and struck him with his rifle butt. Sergeant Benavidez turned to close with the man and his bayonet and fought him, hand to hand, to the death. Wounded again, he recovered the rest of his comrades. As the last were lifted onto the helicopter, he exchanged more gunfire with the enemy, killing two more Vietnamese soldiers, and then ran back to collect the classified documents before at last climbing aboard and collapsing, apparently dead.

The army doctor back at Loc Ninh thought him dead anyway. Bleeding profusely, his intestines spilling from his stomach wounds, completely immobile, and unable to speak, Benavidez was placed into a body bag. As the doctor began to pull up the black shroud's zipper, Roy Benavidez spit in his face. They flew him to Saigon for surgery, where he began a year in hospitals recovering from seven serious gunshot wounds, twenty-eight shrapnel wounds, and bayonet wounds in both arms.

Hard to believe, isn't it, what this one man did? And why? Because his buddies called out to him? Because the training just took over? Because it was automatic, he was in the moment, aware of what was required of him but senseless to the probable futility of his efforts? These are the sort of explanations you usually hear from someone who has distinguished himself in battle. They really don't help us understand. They mean something, but as an explanation for that kind of heroism, they are as unenlightening to me as haiku poetry. What kind of training prepares you to do that? What kind of unit solidarity, how great the love and trust for the man to your right and your left, inspires you to the superhuman heroics of Roy Benavidez?

I'll be damned if I know. I was trained to be an aviator, not a Special Forces commando. But how does anyone—Green Beret, navy SEAL, whatever—learn to be that brave? How do you build that kind of courage in someone? It certainly appears to be superhuman and incomprehensible to those with a more human-size supply, brave and resourceful though they may be. I can't explain it. No one I know can.

We are taught to understand, correctly, that courage is not the absence of fear, but the capacity for action despite our fears. Does anyone have that great a store of courage that he would think himself capable of meaningful action with the eruption of fear that any one of us would have felt rise in our throats and burn our hearts were we to find ourselves in the hopeless situation of Roy Benavidez? I wouldn't. I don't know anyone who would, and I've known some very brave men. I doubt very much Roy Benavidez thought he would. I would challenge the sanity of any reader who imagines the possibility of possessing such mastery over fear. It's not to be expected in anyone. No courage could contend with such fear, and animate our limbs, and control our minds. Fear would have to be vanquished completely. 12

Roy Benavidez jumped off the helicopter, acutely aware of the situation, perhaps, of the enemy's strength, of their location, of the circumstances of his comrades, of what needed to be done, but somehow insensate to the hopelessness of it all, to the gravity of his wounds, to the futility of fighting on. What pushed him? A tsunami of adrenaline? What carried him through? A sublime fatalism, driven by love or sense of duty to resign himself completely to the situation, whatever its horrors, and make his last hour his greatest? We can't know. All we can know is that in one moment of madness, six hours long, Roy Benavidez became to the men he saved, and maybe to himself, an avenging angel of God, masterful, indomitable, and utterly fearless. 13

If we can't comprehend his heroism or imagine possessing his courage, can it offer our own lives any instruction? I believe it can. Roy's life won't teach us how to save eight men while sustaining several dozen wounds. An act of heroism, of extraordinary courage, the grandeur of it, won't easily inspire us to act in imitation, but it can inspire us to emulate its author. For that, we should learn what we can of the whole experience of the subject, the hero's life, as it was before and after, and believe that trying to emulate the character it reveals is one tried way to prepare for the tests that might await us and gain hope that our courage will not be wanting in the moment. 14

We must accept the fact that some heroes, whether their courage was momentary or constant, might have led less than admirable lives. I don't think, however extraordinary the courage, that it will attain the grandeur of the inspirational to a sound mind were it motivated by selfish or malevolent purposes, or exercised by someone whose life, on the whole, was contemptible. Unless, of course, an act of heroism was an anomaly in the life that preceded it and character changing thereafter. The stories cherished most by all sinners whose consciences are not permanently mute concern the life-redeeming act of courage. They're not, however, as abundant in real life as they are in fiction. Better to look to the lives of good men and women who in a crucible risked or sacrificed their own security for someone else. 15

What do we know of Roy Benavidez's life before and after that moment of madness? We know that he was a good man. The straitened circumstances of his 16 youth did not embitter him or lead him astray. The constant, life-long pain of his wounds didn't undo him. His valor was not properly recognized for thirteen years. In 1981, Ronald Reagan—who said of his heroism that were it a movie script "you wouldn't believe it"—replaced the Distinguished Service Cross that General William Westmoreland had given Roy in 1968 with the Medal of Honor. The delay didn't seem to bother Roy. "I don't like to be called a hero," he complained, and then, in familiar refrain of veterans from all wars, he offered observation, "The real heroes are the ones who gave their lives for their country." That kind of humility from surviving veterans who distinguished themselves in combat is so commonplace that we've come to expect it from them. We don't take it seriously. We even suspect that it's false. We don't see how remarkable it is. They mean it. Every word.

Roy stayed in the army until he retired in 1976. Then he lived on his pension and disability pay and spent his time speaking at schools and to youth groups, counseling troubled kids, encouraging them to stay in school and off drugs. In 1998, on his deathbed, with two pieces of shrapnel still in his heart, he proclaimed: "I'm proud to be an American." 17

The navy named a ship after him and the army a building. His hometown erected a statue. But Hollywood never made a movie about him. No one would have believed it. 18

Writing an Expository Essay on Soto, Dog, and McCain

Now that you have analyzed Soto's, Dog's, and McCain's uses of invention and arrangement to move their readers toward accepting their claims on diversity, try freewriting in response to these prompts to invent your own material on this subject. Spend at least 15 minutes freewriting on each prompt:

1. How does each author help us to see the dignity of individual human beings?

2. How does each author teach us to respect ethnic groups other than our own?

3. What would you say is the primary aim of each essay? That is, does the aim of each piece seem deliberative, advising us to change our view, dissuading us from keeping our eyes closed? Or is the aim primarily judicial, accusing and/or defending the people discussed in the essay? See the first page of this chapter to review definitions of these terms.

After reflecting on your responses to the questions above, sketch a tentative outline for an expository essay on the following topic:

Focusing on each author's use of description and on the arrangement of each essay, discuss the effectiveness of each essay in exposing our fears of diversity and the importance of overcoming those fears. Assume that many of your readers consider "diversity" to be a non-issue or an issue of little importance. Your purpose, then, will be deliberative, urging your readers to listen to these writers whose lives testify to the importance of the diversity issue.

Once you have written your rough draft, begin the recursive process you practiced above, including peer responses, further analysis of your readers, and revision.

Works Cited

Brooks, David. "People Like Us." *The Atlantic Monthly* 292.2 (September 2003): 29–32.

Corbett, Edward P. J., and Robert J. Connors. *Classical Rhetoric for the Modern Student.* 4th ed. Oxford: Oxford UP, 1999.

Crowley, Sharon, and Debra Hawhee. *Ancient Rhetorics for Contemporary Students.* 2nd ed. New York: Longman, 1999.

Eiland, Mari Beth. "Are Our Lives Truly Diverse?" Student essay.

McCain, John. *Why Courage Matters.* New York: Random House, 2004.

Dog, Mary Crow, and Richard Erdoes. "Civilize them with a Stick." *Lakota Woman.* New York: Grove Weidenfeld, 1990.

Soto, Gary. "Like Mexicans." *The Essay Connection.* 6th ed. Ed. Lynn Z. Bloom. Boston: Houghton Mifflin, 2001. 436–40.

Reasoning and Mediating

"So let Rhetoric be defined as the faculty of discovering in the particular case what are the available means of persuasion."

ARISTOTLE, *The Rhetoric*

With mediation, "the goal has changed: it is no longer to win but to arrive at a solution…acceptable to both sides."

CATHERINE E. LAMB, "Beyond Argument in Feminist Composition"

Recognizing The Overlapping Aims of Discourse

In working through the first chapter, you read narratives by Douglass, Santiago, Kingston, and Angelou, which examined the causes and effects of their aspirations for literacy and liberty. You then wrote your own narrative essay, telling the story of learning to take risks or learning to read and write. Then in chapter two, you read fiction by Gaines, Jewett, and Hurston, stories on the joys and the pains of personal growth; you then wrote an expository essay, explaining how you read one of these pieces. In both of your first two essays, you learned to write with a purpose in mind, a purpose beyond completing an assignment; you also learned to write with an audience in mind, an audience beyond your professor.

Similarly, in working through chapter three, you maintained this dual focus on audience and purpose, learning ways to invent and arrange ideas and supporting evidence to engage readers. After examining the invention and arrangement strategies used by student and professional writers, you employed these same strategies in writing your own expository essays, first sharing your reflections on the diversity of American culture, and then your views on the effectiveness of Soto, Dog, and McCain in teaching their readers to see the Other with respect.

As you completed these readings and writings, you learned that theorist James Kinneavy rightly stressed the "overlap" of the "aims of discourse" (Kinneavy 60). In other words, when you write a narrative essay, your primary aim, to tell a story, almost always includes secondary aims, to inform and persuade your reader. When Frederick Douglass narrated his clever methods of learning to read and write (chapter 1), for example, he also sought to inform you about the inequities of slavery and to persuade you of its evil. Similarly, when you write an expository essay, your primary aim, to inform or explain, almost always carries a secondary aim, to persuade, and often those primary and secondary aims receive key support from narration, a story imbedded in the exposition. For instance, when John McCain explained the nature of courage (chapter 3), he told the story of Sergeant Benavidez' unusual sacrifice, trying to persuade us to "emulate" such selflessness and to honor the ethnicity of the hero. Sometimes, however, persuasion becomes your primary aim.

In this chapter, you will learn the elements of persuasion and mediation, focusing on Dr. Martin Luther King's famous "Letter from Birmingham Jail." After reading a student's analysis of King's argument and writing your own rhetorical analysis of King's persuasive strategies, you will have a chance to try your hand at mediation in response to Susan Glaspell's one-act play, *Trifles*.

Understanding The Elements of Persuasion

When you employ language, spoken or written, to change readers' minds on urgent social issues, when you select your words to inspire action and, in turn, to rectify a serious problem, then you can't settle for exposition. Instead, you must try to persuade. In such situations, you may still tell stories, you will certainly include the same facts and examples needed in expository writing, but, as medieval rhetorician St. Augustine wrote, you will try to convey your stories and your information in the most "grand" language you can muster (*The Rhetorical Tradition*, 411). "Grand," here, does not mean pompous; rather, it means elevating your language to the level that matches the seriousness of your subject; it means blending Aristotle's elements of persuasion so seamlessly that your reader experiences simultaneously the strength of your **ethos, logos, and pathos**:

Ethos: Credible Image

- Informed

- Generous

- Honest

Logos: Managed Ideas

- Evidence: facts, statistics, case histories, expert testimony, personal experience

- Reasoning: induction and deduction

Pathos: Emotional Appeal

- Parallel Sentence Structure

- Connotative Word Choice

- Arrangement

Why must you be so careful to blend these elements if you hope to persuade? Consider the case of Dr. Martin Luther King in 1963, when he sat in the Birmingham jail with his followers, their demonstration for integration having violated the city's ordinance against parading without a permit. He knew that he must write an expository letter to the eight fellow clergymen, who condemned him in the local newspaper for his "unwise" and "untimely" demonstrations; he would have to explain why he had to leave Atlanta for Birmingham, why he had to break a law, why he could wait no longer for freedom. But he also knew that mere exposition would not be enough; he would need to persuade the clergymen, his immediate audience, and the American people, his extended audience, that "injustice anywhere is a threat to justice everywhere," that the "stinging darts" of segregation have made it impossible to wait any longer for liberty.

To achieve this persuasive goal, he would have to provide plenty of logos, plenty of facts about his nonviolent movement, plenty of examples of lunch counters closed to black men and amusement parks closed to black children, plenty of cases of lynchings and drownings, plenty of testimony from prominent theologians who define segregation as "sin." He would also have to temper his outrage over such cruelties with cool reason, stressing the illogic of writing laws that apply to some but not to all. Such logos, he knew, would build his ethos, his credibility, showing his skeptical audience that he knows the facts of injustice (informed), that he cares about his people's long sufferings (generous), that he has told the truth about the brutal police. As a preacher, he knew, too, that he could further build his ethos with pathos, the appeal created by emotionally charged words and vivid imagery imbedded in rhythmic sentences, calling us all, black and white, to rise from "the dark depths of prejudice and racism to the majestic heights of understanding and brotherhood."

Journaling on Martin Luther King's Letter

As you read Dr. King's letter below, answer the following questions in your journal. In doing so, you will recognize questions drawn from Kenneth Burke's pentad (chapter 1), stressing what happened in Birmingham, how it happened, why it happened, who created the racial problem, who did and did not contribute to the just solution. You will also recognize questions informed by stasis theory (chapter three), focusing on definitions of racism and justice, on the qualities of the segregation experience and the nonviolent protest experience, on procedures for change, on the consequences of resisting change. Additionally, you will begin your prewriting process on your persuasive essay in response to King.

1. How does King establish his ethos in paragraphs 1–3?

2. What is King's purpose in paragraphs 6–11? How do these paragraphs build his ethos?

3. In paragraph 16, King uses the most sophisticated form of figurative language, allusion, to motivate the cooperation of his clergymen-critics. Specifically, he alludes to the Jewish philosopher Martin Buber and to the Christian theologian Paul Tillich, knowing that his fellow ministers will recognize these learned names. He hopes, too, that they will be moved by Buber's call for "I-thou" relationships between blacks and whites, that they will agree with Tillich that segregation, a cruel form of "separation," counts as a "sin."

   With these two allusions as your models, find at least five more allusions (references to famous people, events, or literary works). After listing each allusion and the paragraph where you found it, explain how each allusion builds King's ethos and bolsters his logos.

4. According to King's philosophy of non-violent direct action, what must those who commit civil disobedience be willing to do (paragraphs eight through ten, 20–22)? How does King's explanation of this willingness build his ethos?

5. In addition to his many allusions, King uses more common forms of figurative language, **metaphor** and **simile**, to add pathos to his argument. Remembering that a metaphor offers an implied comparison ("garment of destiny") and that a simile states the comparison explicitly by using "like" or "as," list other examples of figurative language in paragraphs 24–26. After each example of metaphor or simile, explain why the comparison clarifies King's displeasure with the "white moderate" and his eagerness for action.

6. Explain how King blends logos and pathos in paragraph 25, focusing on white moderates, and in paragraph 45, focusing on the Birmingham police.

"Letter from Birmingham Jail"

Martin Luther King Jr.
April 16, 1963
My Dear Fellow Clergymen:

While confined here in the Birmingham city jail, I came across your recent statement calling my present activities "unwise and untimely." Seldom do I pause to answer criticism of my work and ideas. If I sought to answer all the criticisms that cross my desk, my secretaries would have little time for anything other than such correspondence in the course of the day, and I would have no time for constructive work. But since I feel that you are men of genuine good will and that your criticisms are sincerely set forth, I want to try to answer your statement in what I hope will be patient and reasonable terms.

I think I should indicate why I am here in Birmingham, since you have been influenced by the view which argues against "outsiders coming in." I have the honor of serving as president of the Southern Christian Leadership Conference, an organization operating in every southern state, with headquarters in Atlanta, Georgia. We have some eighty-five affiliated organizations across the South, and one of them is the Alabama Christian Movement for Human Rights. Frequently we share staff, educational, and financial resources with our affiliates. Several months ago the affiliate here in Birmingham asked us to be on call to engage in a nonviolent direct-action program if such were deemed necessary. We readily consented, and when the hour came we lived up to our promise. So I, along with several members of my staff, am here because I was invited here. I am here because I have organizational ties here.

But more basically, I am in Birmingham because injustice is here. Just as the prophets of the eighth century B.C. left their villages and carried their "thus saith the Lord" far beyond the boundaries of their home towns, and just as the Apostle Paul left his village of Tarsus and carried the gospel of Jesus Christ to the far corners of the Greco-Roman world, so am I compelled to carry the gospel of freedom beyond my own home town. Like Paul, I must constantly respond to the Macedonian call for aid.

Moreover, I am cognizant of the interrelatedness of all communities and 4
states. I cannot sit idly by in Atlanta and not be concerned about what happens in
Birmingham. Injustice anywhere is a threat to justice everywhere. We are caught in an
inescapable network of mutuality, tied in a single garment of destiny. Whatever affects
one directly, affects all indirectly. Never again can we afford to live with the narrow,
provincial "outside agitator" idea. Anyone who lives inside the United States can never
be considered an outsider anywhere within its bounds.

You deplore the demonstrations taking place in Birmingham. But your statement, 5
I am sorry to say, fails to express a similar concern for the conditions that brought
about the demonstrations. I am sure that none of you would want to rest content
with the superficial kind of social analysis that deals merely with effects and does not
grapple with underlying causes. It is unfortunate that demonstrations are taking place
in Birmingham, but it is even more unfortunate that the city's white power structure
left the Negro community with no alternative.

In any nonviolent campaign there are four basic steps: collection of the facts to 6
determine whether injustices exist; negotiation; self-purification; and direct action.
We have gone through all these steps in Birmingham. There can be no gainsaying the
fact that racial injustice engulfs this community. Birmingham is probably the most
thoroughly segregated city in the United States. Its ugly record of brutality is widely
known. Negroes have experienced grossly unjust treatment in the courts. There have
been more unsolved bombings of Negro homes and churches in Birmingham than in
any other city in the nation. These are the hard, brutal facts of the case. On the basis of
these conditions, Negro leaders sought to negotiate with the city fathers. But the latter
consistently refused to engage in good-faith negotiation.

Then, last September, came the opportunity to talk with leaders of Birmingham's 7
economic community. In the course of the negotiations, certain promises were made
by the merchants—for example, to remove the stores' humiliating racial signs. On
the basis of these promises, the Reverend Fred Shuttlesworth and the leaders of the
Alabama Christian Movement for Human Rights agreed to a moratorium on all
demonstrations. As the weeks and months went by, we realized that we were the victims
of a broken promise. A few signs, briefly removed, returned; the others remained.

As in so many past experiences, our hopes had been blasted, and the shadow of 8
deep disappointment settled upon us. We had no alternative except to prepare for
direct action, whereby we would present our very bodies as a means of laying our
case before the conscience of the local and the national community. Mindful of the
difficulties involved, we decided to undertake a process of self-purification. We began
a series of workshops on nonviolence, and we repeatedly asked ourselves: "Are you
able to accept blows without retaliating?" "Are you able to endure the ordeal of jail?"
We decided to schedule our direct-action program for the Easter season, realizing that
except for Christmas, this is the main shopping period of the year. Knowing that a
strong economic-withdrawal program would be the by-product of the direct action, we
felt that this would be the best time to bring pressure to bear on the merchants for the
needed change.

Then it occurred to us that Birmingham's mayoral election was coming up in March, and we speedily decided to postpone action until after election day. When we discovered that the Commissioner of Public Safety, Eugene "Bull" Connor, had piled up enough votes to be in the run-off, we decided again to postpone action until the day after the run-off so that the demonstrations could not be used to cloud the issues. Like many others, we waited to see Mr. Connor defeated, and to this end we endured postponement after postponement. Having aided in this community need, we felt that our direct-action program could be delayed no longer.

9

You may well ask: "Why direct action? Why sit-ins, marches and so forth? Isn't negotiation a better path?" You are right in calling for negotiation. Indeed, this is the very purpose of direct action. Nonviolent direct action seeks to create such a crisis and foster such a tension that a community which has constantly refused to negotiate is forced to confront the issue. It seeks so to dramatize the issue that it can no longer be ignored. My citing the creation of tension as part of the work of the nonviolent-resister may sound rather shocking. But I must confess that I am not afraid of the word "tension." I have earnestly opposed violent tension, but there is a type of constructive, nonviolent tension which is necessary for growth. Just as Socrates felt that it was necessary to create a tension in the mind so that individuals could rise from the bondage of myths and half-truths to the unfettered realm of creative analysis and objective appraisal, so must we see the need for nonviolent gadflies to create the kind of tension in society that will help men rise from the dark depths of prejudice and racism to the majestic heights of understanding and brotherhood.

10

The purpose of our direct-action program is to create a situation so crisis-packed that it will inevitably open the door to negotiation. I therefore concur with you in your call for negotiation. Too long has our beloved Southland been bogged down in a tragic effort to live in monologue rather than dialogue.

11

One of the basic points in your statement is that the action that I and my associates have taken in Birmingham is untimely. Some have asked: "Why didn't you give the new city administration time to act?" The only answer that I can give to this query is that the new Birmingham administration must be prodded about as much as the outgoing one, before it will act. We are sadly mistaken if we feel that the election of Albert Boutwell as mayor will bring the millennium to Birmingham. While Mr. Boutwell is a much more gentle person than Mr. Connor, they are both segregationists, dedicated to maintenance of the status quo. I have hope that Mr. Boutwell will be reasonable enough to see the futility of massive resistance to desegregation. But he will not see this without pressure from devotees of civil rights. My friends, I must say to you that we have not made a single gain in civil rights without determined legal and nonviolent pressure. Lamentably, it is an historical fact that privileged groups seldom give up their privileges voluntarily. Individuals may see the moral light and voluntarily give up their unjust posture; but, as Reinhold Niebuhr has reminded us, groups tend to be more immoral than individuals.

12

We know through painful experience that freedom is never voluntarily given by the oppressor; it must be demanded by the oppressed. Frankly, I have yet to engage

13

in a direct-action campaign that was "well timed" in the view of those who have not suffered unduly from the disease of segregation. For years now I have heard the word "Wait!" It rings in the ear of every Negro with piercing familiarity. This "Wait" has almost always meant "Never." We must come to see, with one of our distinguished jurists, that "justice too long delayed is justice denied."

We have waited for more than 340 years for our constitutional God-given rights. The nations of Asia and Africa are moving with jetlike speed toward gaining political independence, but we still creep at horse-and-buggy pace toward gaining a cup of coffee at a lunch counter. Perhaps it is easy for those who have never felt the stinging darts of segregation to say, "Wait." But when you have seen vicious mobs lynch your mothers and fathers at will and drown your sisters and brothers at whim; when you have seen hate-filled policemen curse, kick, and even kill your black brothers and sisters; when you see the vast majority of your twenty million Negro brothers smothering in an airtight cage of poverty in the midst of an affluent society; when you suddenly find your tongue twisted and your speech stammering as you seek to explain to your six-year-old daughter why she can't go to the public amusement park that has just been advertised on television, and see tears welling up in her eyes when she is told that Funtown is closed to colored children, and see ominous clouds of inferiority beginning to form in her little mental sky, and see her beginning to distort her personality by developing an unconscious bitterness toward white people; when you have to concoct an answer for a five-year-old son who is asking: "Daddy, why do white people treat colored people so mean?"; when you take a cross-country drive and find it necessary to sleep night after night in the uncomfortable corners of your automobile because no motel will accept you; when you are humiliated day in and day out by nagging signs reading "white" and "colored"; when your first name becomes "nigger," your middle name becomes "boy" (however old you are), and your last name becomes "John," and your wife and mother are never given the respected title "Mrs."; when you are harried by day and haunted by night by the fact that you are a Negro, living constantly at tiptoe stance, never quite knowing what to expect next, and are plagued with inner fears and outer resentments; when you are forever fighting a degenerating sense of "nobodiness"—then you will understand why we find it difficult to wait. There comes a time when the cup of endurance runs over, and men are no longer willing to be plunged into the abyss of despair. I hope, sirs, you can understand our legitimate and unavoidable impatience.

You express a great deal of anxiety over our willingness to break laws. This is certainly a legitimate concern. Since we so diligently urge people to obey the Supreme Court's decision of 1954 outlawing segregation in the public schools, at first glance it may seem rather paradoxical for us consciously to break laws. One may well ask: "How can you advocate breaking some laws and obeying others?" The answer lies in the fact that there are two types of laws: just and unjust. I would be the first to advocate obeying laws. Conversely, one has a moral responsibility to disobey unjust laws. I would agree with St. Augustine that "an unjust law is no law at all."

Now, what is the difference between the two? How does one determine whether a law is just or unjust? A just law is a man-made code that squares with the moral law

14

15

16

141

or the law of God. An unjust law is a code that is out of harmony with the moral law. To put it in the terms of St. Thomas Aquinas: An unjust law is a human law that is not rooted in eternal law and natural law. Any law that uplifts human personality is just. Any law that degrades human personality is unjust. All segregation statutes are unjust because segregation distorts the soul and damages the personality. It gives the segregator a false sense of superiority and the segregated a false sense of inferiority. Segregation, to use the terminology of the Jewish philosopher Martin Buber, substitutes an "I-it" relationship for an "I-thou" relationship and ends up relegating persons to the status of things. Hence, segregation is not only politically, economically, and sociologically unsound, it is morally wrong and sinful. Paul Tillich has said that sin is separation. Is not segregation an existential expression of man's tragic separation, his awful estrangement, his terrible sinfulness? Thus it is that I can urge men to obey the 1954 decision of the Supreme Court, for it is morally right; and I can urge them to disobey segregation ordinances, for they are morally wrong.

Let us consider a more concrete example of just and unjust laws. An unjust law is a code that a numerical or power majority group compels a minority group to obey but does not make binding on itself. This is difference made legal. By the same token, a just law is a code that a majority compels a minority to follow and that it is willing to follow itself. This is sameness made legal. 17

Let me give another explanation. A law is unjust if it is inflicted on a minority that, as a result of being denied the right to vote, had no part in enacting or devising the law. Who can say that the legislature of Alabama which set up that state's segregation laws was democratically elected? Throughout Alabama all sorts of devious methods are used to prevent Negroes from becoming registered voters, and there are some counties in which, even though Negroes constitute a majority of the population, not a single Negro is registered. Can any law enacted under such circumstances be considered democratically structured? 18

Sometimes a law is just on its face and unjust in its application. For instance, I have been arrested on a charge of parading without a permit. Now, there is nothing wrong in having an ordinance which requires a permit for a parade. But such an ordinance becomes unjust when it is used to maintain segregation and to deny citizens the First-Amendment privilege of peaceful assembly and protest. 19

I hope you are able to see the distinction I am trying to point out. In no sense do I advocate evading or defying the law, as would the rabid segregationist. That would lead to anarchy. One who breaks an unjust law must do so openly, lovingly, and with a willingness to accept the penalty. I submit that an individual who breaks a law that conscience tells him is unjust, and who willingly accepts the penalty of imprisonment in order to arouse the conscience of the community over its injustice, is in reality expressing the highest respect for law. 20

Of course, there is nothing new about this kind of civil disobedience. It was evidenced sublimely in the refusal of Shadrach, Meshach, and Abednego to obey the laws of Nebuchadnezzar, on the ground that a higher moral law was at stake. It was practiced superbly by the early Christians, who were willing to face hungry lions and 21 the excruciating pain of chopping blocks rather than submit to certain unjust laws of the Roman Empire. To a degree, academic freedom is a reality today because Socrates practiced civil disobedience. In our own nation, the Boston Tea Party represented a massive act of civil disobedience.

We should never forget that everything Adolf Hitler did in Germany was "legal" and everything the Hungarian freedom fighters did in Hungary was "illegal." It was "illegal" to aid and comfort a Jew in Hitler's Germany. Even so, I am sure that, had I lived in Germany at the time, I would have aided and comforted my Jewish brothers. If today I lived in a Communist country where certain principles dear to the Christian faith are suppressed, I would openly advocate disobeying that country's antireligious laws.

I must make two honest confessions to you, my Christian and Jewish brothers. First, I must confess that over the past few years I have been gravely disappointed with the white moderate. I have almost reached the regrettable conclusion that the Negro's great stumbling block in his stride toward freedom is not the White Citizens' Counciler or the Ku Klux Klanner, but the white moderate, who is more devoted to "order" than to justice; who prefers a negative peace which is the presence of tension to a positive peace which is the presence of justice; who constantly says: "I agree with you in the goal you seek, but I cannot agree with your methods of direct action"; who paternalistically believes he can set the timetable for another man's freedom; who lives by a mythical concept of time and who constantly advises the Negro to wait for a "more convenient season." Shallow understanding from people of good will is more frustrating than absolute misunderstanding from people of ill will. Lukewarm acceptance is much more bewildering than outright rejection.

I had hoped that the white moderate would understand that law and order exist for the purpose of establishing justice and that when they fail in this purpose they become the dangerously structured dams that block the flow of social progress. I had hoped that the white moderate would understand that the present tension in the South is a necessary phase of the transition from an obnoxious negative peace, in which the Negro passively accepted his unjust plight, to a substantive and positive peace, in which all men will respect the dignity and worth of human personality. Actually, we who engage in nonviolent direct action are not the creators of tension. We merely bring to the surface the hidden tension that is already alive. We bring it out in the open, where it can be seen and dealt with. Like a boil that can never be cured so long as it is covered up but must be opened with all its ugliness to the natural medicines of air and light, injustice must be exposed, with all the tension its exposure creates, to the light of human conscience and the air of national opinion before it can be cured.

In your statement you assert that our actions, even though peaceful, must be condemned because they precipitate violence. But is this a logical assertion? Isn't this like condemning a robbed man because his possession of money precipitated the evil act of robbery? Isn't this like condemning Socrates because his unswerving commitment to truth and his philosophical inquiries precipitated the act by

22

23

24

25

143

the misjudged populace in which they made him drink hemlock? Isn't this like condemning Jesus because his unique God-consciousness and never-ceasing devotion to God's will precipitated the evil act of crucifixion? We must come to see that, as the federal courts have consistently affirmed, it is wrong to urge an individual to cease his efforts to gain his basic constitutional rights because the quest may precipitate violence. Society must protect the robbed and punish the robber.

I had also hoped that the white moderate would reject the myth concerning   26
time in relation to the struggle for freedom. I have just received a letter from a white brother in Texas. He writes: "All Christians know that the colored people will receive equal rights eventually, but it is possible that you are in too great a religious hurry. It has taken Christianity almost two thousand years to accomplish what it has. The teachings of Christ take time to come to earth." Such an attitude stems from a tragic misconception of time, from the strangely irrational notion that there is something in the very flow of time that will inevitably cure all ills. Actually, time itself is neutral; it can be used either destructively or constructively. More and more I feel that the people of ill will have used time much more effectively than have the people of good will. We will have to repent in this generation not merely for the hateful words and actions of the bad people but for the appalling silence of the good people. Human progress never rolls in on wheels of inevitability; it comes through the tireless efforts of men willing to be co-workers with God, and without this hard work, time itself becomes an ally of the forces of social stagnation. We must use time creatively, in the knowledge that the time is always ripe to do right. Now is the time to make real the promise of democracy and transform our pending national elegy into a creative psalm of brotherhood. Now is the time to lift our national policy from the quicksand of racial injustice to the solid rock of human dignity.

You speak of our activity in Birmingham as extreme. At first I was rather   27
disappointed that fellow clergymen would see my nonviolent efforts as those of an extremist. I began thinking about the fact that I stand in the middle of two opposing forces in the Negro community. One is a force of complacency, made up in part of Negroes who, as a result of long years of oppression, are so drained of self-respect and a sense of "somebodiness" that they have adjusted to segregation; and in part of a few middle-class Negroes who, because of a degree of academic and economic security and because in some ways they profit by segregation, have become insensitive to the problems of the masses. The other force is one of bitterness and hatred, and it comes perilously close to advocating violence. It is expressed in the various black nationalists groups that are springing up across the nation, the largest and best-known being Elijah Muhammad's Muslim movement. Nourished by the Negro's frustration over the continued existence of racial discrimination, this movement is made up of people who have lost faith in America, who have absolutely repudiated Christianity, and who have concluded that the white man is an incorrigible "devil."

I have tried to stand between these two forces, saying that we need emulate   28
neither the "do-nothingism" of the complacent nor the hatred and despair of the black nationalist. For there is the more excellent way of love and nonviolent protest. I am grateful to God that, through the influence of the Negro church, the way of

nonviolence became an integral part of our struggle.

If this philosophy had not emerged, by now many streets of the South would, I am convinced, be flowing with blood. And I am further convinced that if our white brothers dismiss as "rabble-rousers" and "outside agitators" those of us who employ nonviolent direct action, and if they refuse to support our nonviolent efforts, millions of the Negroes will, out of frustration and despair, seek solace and security in black-nationalist ideologies—a development that would inevitably lead to a frightening racial nightmare. 29

Oppressed people cannot remain oppressed forever. The yearning for freedom eventually manifests itself, and that is what has happened to the American Negro. Something within has reminded him of his birthright of freedom, and something without has reminded him that it can be gained. Consciously or unconsciously, he has been caught up by the Zeitgeist, and with his black brothers of Africa and his brown and yellow brothers of Asia, South America, and the Caribbean, the United States Negro is moving with a sense of great urgency toward the promised land of racial justice. If one recognizes this vital urge that has engulfed the Negro community, one should readily understand why public demonstrations are taking place. The Negro has many pent-up resentments and latent frustrations, and he must release them. So let him march; let him make prayer pilgrimages to the city hall; let him go on freedom rides—and try to understand why he must do so. If his repressed emotions are not released in nonviolent ways, they will seek expression through violence; this is not a threat but a fact of history. So I have not said to my people: "Get rid of your discontent." Rather, I have tried to say that this normal and healthy discontent can be channeled into the creative outlet of nonviolent direct action. And now this approach is being termed extremist. 30

But although I was initially disappointed at being categorized as an extremist, as I continued to think about the matter I gradually gained a measure of satisfaction from the label. Was not Jesus an extremist for love: "Love your enemies, bless them that curse you, do good to them that hate you, and pray for them which despitefully use you, and persecute you." Was not Amos an extremist for justice: "Let justice roll down like waters and righteousness like an ever-flowing stream." Was not Paul an extremist for the Christian gospel: "I bear in my body the marks of the Lord Jesus." Was not Martin Luther an extremist: "Here I stand; I cannot do otherwise, so help me God." And John Bunyan: "I will stay in jail to the end of my days before I make a butchery of my conscience." And Abraham Lincoln: "This nation cannot survive half slave and half free." And Thomas Jefferson: "We hold these truths to be self-evident, that all men are created equal...." So the question is not whether we will be extremists, but what kind of extremists we will be. Will we be extremists for hate or for love? Will we be extremists for the preservation of injustice or for the extension of justice? In that dramatic scene on Calvary's hill three men were crucified. We must never forget that all three were crucified for the same crime—the crime of extremism. Two were extremists for immorality, and thus fell below their environment. The other, Jesus Christ, was an extremist for love, truth and goodness, and thereby rose above his environment. Perhaps the South, the nation and the world are in dire need of creative extremists. 31

I had hoped that the white moderate would see this need. Perhaps I was too optimistic; perhaps I expected too much. I suppose I should have realized that few members of the oppressor race can understand the deep groans and passionate yearnings of the oppressed race, and still fewer have the vision to see that injustice must be rooted out by stong, persistent, and determined action. I am thankful, however, that some of our white brothers in the South have grasped the meaning of this social revolution and committed themselves to it. They are still all too few in quantity, but they are big in quality. Some—such as Ralph McGill, Lillian Smith, Harry Golden, James McBride Dabbs, Ann Braden, and Sarah Patton Boyle—have written about our struggle in eloquent and prophetic terms. Others have marched with us down nameless streets of the South. They have languished in filthy, roach-infested jails, suffering the abuse and brutality of policemen who view them as "dirty nigger-lovers." Unlike so many of their moderate brothers and sisters, they have recognized the urgency of the moment and sensed the need for powerful "action" antidotes to combat the disease of segregation.

32

Let me take note of my other major disappointment. I have been so greatly disappointed with the white church and its leadership. Of course, there are some notable exceptions. I am not unmindful of the fact that each of you has taken some significant stands on this issue. I commend you, Reverend Stallings, for your Christian stand on this past Sunday, in welcoming Negroes to your worship service on a nonsegregated basis. I commend the Catholic leaders of this state for integrating Spring Hill College several years ago.

33

But despite these notable exceptions, I must honestly reiterate that I have been disappointed with the church. I do not say this as one of those negative critics who can always find something wrong with the church. I say this as a minister of the gospel, who loves the church; who was nurtured in its bosom; who has been sustained by its spiritual blessings and who will remain true to it as long as the cord of life shall lengthen.

34

When I was suddenly catapulted into the leadership of the bus protest in Montgomery, Alabama, a few years ago, I felt we would be supported by the white church. I felt that the white ministers, priests, and rabbis of the South would be among our strongest allies. Instead, some have been outright opponents, refusing to understand the freedom movement and misrepresenting its leaders; all too many others have been more cautious than courageous and have remained silent behind the anesthetizing security of stained-glass windows.

35

In spite of my shattered dreams, I came to Birmingham with the hope that the white religious leadership of this community would see the justice of our cause and, with deep moral concern, would serve as the channel through which our just grievances could reach the power structure. I had hoped that each of you would understand. But again I have been disappointed.

36

I have heard numerous southern religious leaders admonish their worshipers to comply with a desegregation decision because it is the law, but I have longed to hear white ministers declare: "Follow this decree because integration is morally right and because

37

the Negro is your brother." In the midst of blatant injustices inflicted upon the Negro, I have watched white churchmen stand on the sideline and mouth pious irrelevancies and sanctimonious trivialities. In the midst of a mighty struggle to rid our nation of racial and economic injustice, I have heard many ministers say: "Those are social issues, with which the gospel has no real concern." And I have watched many churches commit themselves to a completely otherworldly religion which makes a strange, un-Biblical distinction between body and soul, between the sacred and the secular.

I have traveled the length and breadth of Alabama, Mississippi, and all the other southern states. On sweltering summer days and crisp autumn mornings I have looked at the South's beautiful churches with their lofty spires pointing heavenward. I have beheld the impressive outlines of her massive religious-education buildings. Over and over I have found myself asking: "What kind of people worship here? Who is their God? Where were their voices when the lips of Governor Barnett dripped with words of interposition and nullification? Where were they when Governor Wallace gave a clarion call for defiance and hatred? Where were their voices of support when bruised and weary Negro men and women decided to rise from the dark dungeons of complacency to the bright hills of creative protest?" 38

Yes, these questions are still in my mind. In deep disappointment I have wept over the laxity of the church. But be assured that my tears have been tears of love. There can be no deep disappointment where there is not deep love. Yes, I love the church. How could I do otherwise? I am in the rather unique position of being the son, the grandson, and the great-grandson of preachers. Yes, I see the church as the body of Christ. But, oh! How we have blemished and scarred that body through neglect and through fear of being nonconformists. 39

There was a time when the church was very powerful—in the time when the early Christians rejoiced at being deemed worthy to suffer for what they believed. In those days the church was not merely a thermometer that recorded the ideas and principles of popular opinion; it was a thermostat that transformed the mores of society. Whenever the early Christians entered a town, the people in power became disturbed and immediately sought to convict the Christians for being "disturbers of the peace" and "outside agitators." But the Christians pressed on, in the conviction that they were "a colony of heaven," called to obey God rather than man. Small in number, they were big in commitment. They were too God-intoxicated to be "astronomically intimidated." By their effort and example they brought an end to such ancient evils as infanticide and gladiatorial contests. 40

Things are different now. So often the contemporary church is a weak, ineffectual voice with an uncertain sound. So often it is an archdefender of the status quo. Far from being disturbed by the presence of the church, the power structure of the average community is consoled by the church's silent—and often even vocal—sanction of things as they are. 41

But the judgment of God is upon the church as never before. If today's church does not recapture the sacrificial spirit of the early church, it will lose its authenticity, forfeit the loyalty of millions, and be dismissed as an irrelevant social club with 42 no meaning for the twentieth century. Every day I meet young people whose disappointment with the church has turned into outright disgust.

Perhaps I have once again been too optimistic. Is organized religion too inextricably bound to the status quo to save our nation and the world? Perhaps I must turn my faith to the inner spiritual church, the church within the church, as the true *ekklesia* and the hope of the world. But again I am thankful to God that some noble souls from the ranks of organized religion have broken loose from the paralyzing chains of conformity and joined us as active partners in the struggle for freedom. They have left their secure congregations and walked the streets of Albany, Georgia, with us. They have gone down the highways of the South on tortuous rides for freedom. Yes, they have gone to jail with us. Some have been dismissed from their churches, have lost the support of their bishops and fellow ministers. But they have acted in the faith that right defeated is stronger than evil triumphant. Their witness has been the spiritual salt that has preserved the true meaning of the gospel in these troubled times. They have carved a tunnel of hope through the dark mountain of disappointment. 43

I hope the church as a whole will meet the challenge of this decisive hour. But even if the church does not come to the aid of justice, I have no despair about the future. I have no fear about the outcome of our struggle in Birmingham, even if our motives are at present misunderstood. We will reach the goal of freedom in Birmingham and all over the nation, because the goal of America is freedom. Abused and scorned though we may be, our destiny is tied up with America's destiny. Before the pilgrims landed at Plymouth, we were here. Before the pen of Jefferson etched the majestic words of the Declaration of Independence across the pages of history, we were here. For more than two centuries our forebears labored in this country without wages; they made cotton king; they built the homes of their masters while suffering gross injustice and shameful humiliation—and yet out of a bottomless vitality they continued to thrive and develop. If the inexpressible cruelties of slavery could not stop us, the opposition we now face will surely fail. We will win our freedom because the sacred heritage of our nation and the eternal will of God are embodied in our echoing demands. 44

Before closing I feel impelled to mention one other point in your statement that has troubled me profoundly. You warmly commended the Birmingham police force for keeping "order" and "preventing violence." I doubt that you would have so warmly commended the police force if you had seen its dogs sinking their teeth into unarmed, nonviolent Negroes. I doubt that you would so quickly commend the policemen if you were to observe their ugly and inhumane treatment of Negroes here in the city jail; if you were to see them slap and kick old Negro men and young boys; if you were to observe them, as they did on two occasions, refuse to give us food because we wanted to sing our grace together. I cannot join you in your praise of the Birmingham police department. 45

It is true that police have exercised a degree of discipline in handling the demonstrators. In this sense they have conducted themselves rather "nonviolently" 46 in public. But for what purpose? To preserve the evil system of segregation. Over the past few years I have consistently preached that nonviolence demands that the means we use must be as pure as the ends we seek. I have tried to make clear that it is wrong to use immoral means to attain moral ends. But now I must affirm that it is just as wrong, or perhaps even more so, to use moral means to preserve immoral ends. Perhaps Mr. Connor and his policemen have been rather nonviolent in public, as was Chief Pritchett in Albany, Georgia, but they have used the moral means of nonviolence to maintain the immoral end of racial injustice. As T.S. Eliot has said: "The last temptation is the greatest treason: To do the right deed for the wrong reason."

I wish you had commended the Negro sit-inners and demonstrators of   47
Birmingham for their sublime courage, their willingness to suffer and their amazing discipline in the midst of great provocation. One day the South will recognize its heroes. They will be the James Merediths, with the noble sense of purpose that enables them to face jeering and hostile mobs, and with the agonizing loneliness that characterizes the life of the pioneer. They will be old, oppressed, battered Negro women, symbolized in a seventy-two-year old woman in Montgomery, Alabama, who rose up with a sense of dignity and with her people decided not to ride segregated buses, and who responded with ungrammatical profundity to one who inquired about her weariness: "My feets is tired, but my soul is at rest." They will be the young high school and college students, the young ministers of the gospel and a host of their elders, courageously and nonviolently sitting in at lunch counters and willingly going to jail for conscience' sake. One day the South will know that when these disinherited children of God sat down at lunch counters, they were in reality standing up for what is best in the American dream and for the most sacred values in our Judaeo-Christian heritage, thereby bringing our nation back to those great wells of democracy which were dug deep by the founding fathers in their formulation of the Constitution and the Declaration of Independence.

Never before have I written so long a letter. I'm afraid it is much too long to take   48
your precious time. I can assure you that it would have been much shorter if I had been writing from a comfortable desk, but what else can one do when he is alone in a narrow jail cell, other than write long letters, think long thoughts, and pray long prayers?

If I have said anything in this letter that overstates the truth and indicates   49
an unreasonable impatience, I beg you to forgive me. If I have said anything that understates the truth and indicates my having a patience that allows me to settle for anything less than brotherhood, I beg God to forgive me.

I hope this letter finds you strong in faith. I also hope that circumstances will soon   50
make it possible for me to meet each of you, not as an integrationist or a civil-rights leader but as a fellow clergyman and a Christian brother. Let us all hope that the dark clouds of racial prejudice will soon pass away and the deep fog of misunderstanding will be lifted from our fear-drenched communitites, and in some not too distant tomorrow the radiant stars of love and brotherhood will shine over our great nation

with all their scintillating beauty.

Yours for the cause of Peace and Brotherhood,

Martin Luther King Jr.

Analyzing the Persuasive Elements in King's Letter

Before you move further toward your persuasive response to King, read the student response below, a persuasive essay that grew from the same questions you just answered in your journal. More specifically, the student analyzed King's blending of ethos, logos, and pathos in the "Letter," focusing on one of King's claims: that the Christian church has failed to support his cause. As you read this essay, observe his careful analysis of King's techniques for blending these elements of persuasion, a process that builds the student's own ethos. Following the essay, you will find a full description of the reasoning processes the student applied in drafting his essay, ways of thinking that you will practice as you draft your persuasive paper.

Student Analysis of King's Ethos, Logos, and Pathos: "An Ecclesiastical Fall from Grace"

Joshua McCormick

Dr. Martin Luther King, Jr. wrote his "Letter from Birmingham Jail" in response to various clergy who spoke out against his methods. Though intended to counter the clergymen's views, the letter functions more as a discourse on the history of the non-violent direct action movement in Birmingham and on Dr. King's frustration with various elements that inhibited his movement directly—the racists and segregationists—and indirectly—the good people who did nothing. Among the latter group, his own Christian church frustrated King the most. As a Baptist minister, King, of course, held the church in the highest regard; therefore, its lack of support truly shocked him. Accordingly, Dr. King felt that the Christian church failed in its responsibility by not sufficiently supporting the anti-segregation movement; he provided strong support for this view by establishing his credibility, reasoning carefully on the evidence, and offering impassioned pleas for joining the cause.

To understand and thus fully respect King's views, the reader must first ascertain the credibility of his word as a Christian civil rights leader. To build that believability, King insists that he is not someone who "can always find something wrong with the church." Instead, he is someone who "loves the church; who was nurtured in its bosom; who has been sustained by its spiritual blessings and who will remain true to it as long as the cord of life shall lengthen." Further, King views the church as "the body of Christ." Support of the church seems almost hereditary for King, "the son, the grandson, and the great-grandson of preachers." King also holds impressive credentials as a preacher. In addition to earning a PhD in religious studies and pastoring a church, King has "the honor of serving as president of the Southern Christian Leadership Conference, an organization operating in every Southern state" and serving "eighty-five affiliated organizations across the South." Clearly, by sharing his credentials, Dr. King depicts himself as a man of respectable standing within the church. Given his credentials, the reader, King hopes, will see his views not as opportunistic jabs at an institution held in contempt, but as the views of one of the church's staunchest supporters. As Dr. King simply states, "Yes, I love the church."

Though King has built this credible ethos, his reputation alone is not sufficient to make his case against the church. He must also provide rational thought on the evidence. He does so first by citing multiple circumstances in which the church stood by doing nothing and remained "silent behind the anesthetizing security of stained-glass windows" while others marched for justice, an image that suggests the numbing effect of the church's cowardice. King further describes instances when he watched "churchmen stand on the sideline and mouth pious irrelevancies and sanctimonious trivialities" while the Civil Rights movement challenged the racism the church should condemn. Instead of joining the cause of liberty, most of his fellow clergymen, King says, have dismissed these "social issues, with which the gospel has no real concern." Indeed, King has "watched many churches commit themselves to a completely otherworldly religion which makes a strange un-Biblical distinction between body and soul, between the sacred and the secular." King is further shocked by the lack of understanding by the church. After all, he reasons, there are Biblical precedents for King's actions, such as Jesus' resistance of the corrupt temple leaders, the "refusal of Shadrach, Meshach, and Abednego to obey the Laws of Nebuchadnezzar," and the defiance of early Christians against "such ancient evils as infanticide and gladiatorial contests." Such strong evidence, King hopes, will persuade his fellow clergymen that they have no rational basis for their criticism of his movement.

While such logos builds King's ethos, he recognizes that he must also appeal to his readers' emotions if he hopes to persuade them to re-think their stands against him. Thus, he uses emotionally charged language and parallel sentence structure to arouse their Christian feelings. First, he reminds his readers of their commitment to "love thy neighbor"; collectively, they form the body of Christ. Yet his brother clerics have "blemished and scarred that body through social neglect and through fear of being nonconformists." Certainly, Dr. King does take note of those valued few among the clergy who have broken away from "the paralyzing chains of conformity." It is important to note the use of "paralyzing," for King uses it to suggest that the "chains" of the church make its members *incapable* of action. Dr. King finally warns that if the church does not "recapture the sacrificial spirit of the early church, it will loose its authenticity, forfeit the loyalty of millions, and be dismissed as an irrelevant social club." Appealing to readers' fears as well as their guilt with these parallel verbs of loss, King warns of the church's moral decay, its becoming an empty husk that will inevitably collapse into nothingness.

Dr. Martin Luther King, Jr. led a nonviolent campaign against racism in the South. In his mission, he faced great opposition from segregationists and racists entrenched in the legal system. Yet the most vexing concern King faced was the silence from those he expected to rally with him. The lack of action by his comrades in the church was perhaps more morally outrageous than the hostility of those segregationists who opposed King. Though King had no doubt that his goals would eventually be reached and segregation would fall, he suffered great frustration when those he expected to help did nothing. By making use of ethos, logos, and pathos, King was able to prove that the church had moved away from its moral tenets into social complacency. Perhaps this lack of action against segregationist ideas expressed systemic moral decay. If so, King concluded, the church must find itself or ultimately lose itself.

As you read this student's essay, you may have noticed that, whether talking about King's ethos, logos, or pathos, he quoted sentences that blend all three elements of persuasion, a wise rhetorical strategy on his part and on King's. In the paragraph on King's logos, for example, the student provides examples (logos) of the church's betrayal of their mission of brotherhood: failing to support King's demonstrations with their sermons and with their participation. In the same paragraph, the student quotes King's blending of metaphorical language and parallel sentence structure to infuse his logos with emotion (pathos): Instead of preaching on behalf of brotherhood and justice, many clergymen, King asserted, remain "silent behind the anesthetizing security of stained-glass windows"; instead of joining in the dangerous marches for freedom, King further charges, many "churchmen stand on the sideline and mouth pious irrelevancies and sanctimonious trivialities." In other words, by using the "anesthesia" metaphor (implied comparison), King creates an image of ministers using the beauty of the church's stained-glass windows to drug themselves, to become oblivious to the suffering of the segregated. When these same ministers climb down from their "silent" pulpits, they suddenly find their voices on the sidelines, where their words sound both hypocritical and cowardly, as underscored by these rhythmical parallel phrases: "*pious* irrelevancies," "*sanctimonious* trivialities."

Though these fiery words, by themselves, sound almost hostile, you no doubt noticed, within the context of the student's whole essay, that King seems far less interested in defeating his critics than in persuading his fellow clergymen—and all Americans, black and white—to join his cause. As the student notes, King speaks of loving the same church that his critics serve, of being "nurtured in its bosom." King understands the fear of his critics but reminds them that they can draw courage, as he does, from the same cast of Biblical heroes, Shadrach, Meshach, and Abednego. In short, King conveys the ethos of a peacemaker.

In other words, King's famous "Letter" serves as model not only of the "elements of persuasion" described in ancient rhetoric but also of **mediational discourse**, persuasive writing intended to make peace or, as Catherine Lamb puts it in the epigraph to his chapter, to bring opponents together to solve common problems. Interestingly, too, King's mediations illustrate his blending of the two kinds of reasoning stressed in Aristotle's

Rhetoric: **induction**, the process of drawing conclusions from analysis of evidence, and **deduction**, the process of reasoning from premises to conclusions.

In the next sections, then, you will analyze the workings of induction and deduction within King's "Letter," and then explore how the inter-connection of these two modes of reasoning supports King's mediational purpose. You will see, too, how King uses pathos to further his work as mediator. In working through these sections, you will become fully prepared to write your own essay in response to King's essay.

Blending the Inductive and Deductive Processes

While you cannot make your readers accept your view, adopt your recommendations, or change their minds, you can mediate your way toward common ground by ensuring that your logos derives from sound reasoning, that your inductive analysis and your deductive thinking weave together seamlessly. Let me illustrate, first with a simple example, then with a serious one, which will take you back to Dr. King's efforts to persuade.

Induction

Consider this scenario: You're a first-semester college student who hopes to do well in Composition I. Your hope grows from news that your university has just opened a Writing Center staffed with trained graduate student interns who, according to your professor, can help you grow as a writer. As you set out for your first visit to the Writing Center, you have a **hypothesis** in mind, a guess—based on your assumption that tutors edit papers—about how the interns will receive you: Graduate interns will gladly correct my errors for me and tell me what to do to improve my papers.

Fortified by this hypothetical conviction, you ask Emily, the first tutor you meet, to "fix" your draft. Result: Emily responds, "No, I can't." Shocked but undeterred by Emily's apparent rudeness or incompetence, you make the same request of Ed and Ashleigh, two other interns on duty. Result: They both say that "We can't do your work for you; we're here to help you to think about your problems and to find your own solutions." Baffled by their refusal and, even more so, by their explanation, you draw an inductive conclusion based on your sampling of the evidence:

Hypothesis: Graduate interns will gladly correct my errors for me and tell me
   what to do to improve my papers.

Results of testing the hypothesis:

   Experiment #1: Emily refused my request.

   Experiment #2: Ed refused my request.

   Experiment #3: Ashleigh refused my request.

Conclusion: Graduate interns lack competence.

This use of cause-effect analysis and experimentation illustrates the inductive process, a way of thinking that has shaped our view of the world since our infancies, sometimes quite reliably. In this case, however, logicians would quickly point out the **logical fallacy** here: The new college writer has thought inductively but has sampled too little evidence. In other words, though the inductive process shown above is valid, the conclusion is not true because the experimenter has taken the inductive leap prematurely. Logicians often label this fallacy the **sweeping generalization**: the Comp student has assumed that *all* tutors resemble Emily, Ed, Ashleigh, lacking the competence to offer meaningful help with writing.

Even more fundamentally, the Comp student has built an initial hypothesis on a false assumption about the work of tutors, who function as one-on-one teachers, not as proofreaders. In other words, the experiments have revealed the student's lack of understanding about the mission of Writing Centers, not the incompetence of the interns.

Deduction

Unaware of your false assumption, disappointed and angry, you gather your papers and head for the door, only to be interrupted by Leah, the fourth intern on duty, who offers to explain in more detail what Ed and Ashleigh meant when they offered to help you "think about problem" and "find solutions." Though tempted to listen to Leah, you grumble "no thanks" and reach for the door, knowing that you have no need for another experiment, having reached the inductive conclusion that "graduate interns lack competence." Notice, now, how the inductive process blends with and sustains the deductive process, the process of moving from (supposedly) proven or self-evident premises to a conclusion based on those premises:

Major Premise: All graduate interns are incompetent.

Minor Premise: Leah is a graduate intern.

Conclusion: Leah lacks competence.

Logicians call this three-part deductive statement a **syllogism**: the major premise makes a statement about a class or *genus* (in this case, graduate interns); the minor premise makes a statement about a particular member (Leah) of the family named in the major premise; then the conclusion makes a statement about Leah based on the assumed truth of both premises. In other words, if all interns lack competence, and if Leah is an intern, then it necessarily follows that Leah lacks competence.

Once again, however, our logician would remind us that this valid syllogism has generated a falsehood, not a truth, because the major premise rests on insufficient evidence and mistaken assumptions about the intern's job. Had you, our new college writer, given Leah a chance to explain about strategies for discovering ideas, organizing drafts, revising content, and diagnosing and correcting one's own errors, you would have instantly embraced a more reliable major premise: Graduate interns guide students through the writing process. After this explanatory session with Leah, you would find yourself thinking like this:

Major Premise: Graduate interns guide students through the writing process.

Minor Premise: Leah is a graduate intern.

Conclusion: Leah can guide students through the writing process.

Blending Deduction and Induction

Though simplistic, this story about Writing Centers has demonstrated the interconnection between our inductive and deductive thinking processes. Just as important, the story has also reminded us that the persuasiveness of our claims rests on the range and depth of our evidence, and that our own credibility, our ethos, depends on our care in phrasing our claims and in pointing to the evidence that supports them. If you have asked Emily, Ed, and Ashleigh to do your work for you, you can't expect a fair-minded reader to accept your sweeping conclusion about "all graduate interns" or your dubious claims about Leah.

Now let's read paragraph 16 of Martin Luther King's "Letter from Birmingham Jail" to trace his deductive reasoning, his use of major and minor premises to lead his readers toward his conclusion:

> How does one determine whether a law is just or unjust? A just law is a man-made code that squares with the moral law or the law of God. An unjust law is a code that is out of harmony with the moral law. To put it in the terms of St. Thomas Aquinas: An unjust law is a human law that is not rooted in eternal law and natural law. Any law that uplifts human personality is just. Any law that degrades human personality is unjust. All segregation statutes are unjust because segregation distorts the soul and damages the personality. It gives the segregator a false sense of superiority and the segregated a false sense of inferiority. Segregation, to use the terminology of the Jewish philosopher Martin Buber, substitutes an "I-it" relationship for an "I-thou" relationship and ends up relegating persons to the status of things. Hence segregation is not only politically, economically, and sociologically unsound, it is morally wrong and sinful. Paul Tillich has said that sin is separation. Is not segregation an existential expression of man's tragic separation, his awful estrangement, his terrible sinfulness? Thus it is that I can urge men to obey the 1954 decision of the Supreme Court, for it is morally right; and I can urge them to disobey segregation ordinances, for they are morally wrong.

Notice that King begins with a premise which, he assumes, his fellow clergymen, the primary readers, will accept without challenge: human law must be consistent with moral law and, by implication, with the laws of the church. He then summarizes this self-evident truth in a major premise that sets up his syllogism:

Major Premise: All laws that degrade the human personality are unjust.

Minor Premise: Segregation laws degrade the human personality.

Conclusion: Segregation laws are unjust.

He then supports his minor premise, the premise in contention here, by alluding to theologians and philosophers, both Christian and Jewish, whom he knows his readers will respect. More than just dropping their names—St. Thomas Aquinas, Martin Buber, Paul Tillich—King paraphrases their passionate opposition to legalizing racism.

But where, one might fairly ask, has King provided his proof—beyond these allusions to famous theologians—that his minor premise is true, that all segregation laws degrade the human personality? Where does he display the inductive process that leads to the truth of his minor premise? The inductive proofs, as you saw when you read Dr. King's letter, can be found throughout his work but emerge most graphically and memorably in paragraph 14, two paragraphs before the one quoted above. We will analyze the pathos of this paragraph in chapter six in our discussion of "style"; let's limit ourselves here to King's inductive process, his "experiments" with segregation laws, each one offering proof that supports his inductive conclusion that the "stinging darts" of segregation bloody the body and tear the soul, "degrading the human personality":

Hypothesis: Segregation laws degrade the human personality.

Results of Testing the Hypothesis:

Experiment #1: "Vicious mobs" lynch family members.

Experiment #2: "Hate-filled policemen...kick...brothers and sisters."

Experiment #3: Twenty million African Americans live in an "airtight cage of poverty."

Experiment #4: African American children are excluded from amusement parks, and fathers have no explanation.

Experiment #5: African American adults are barred from motels.

Experiment #6: African American women and men are never accorded respect, never called by their names; they suffer, therefore, a "degenerating sense of nobodiness."

Conclusion: Segregation laws degrade the human personality.

Once again, note that the inductive conclusion becomes the major premise for King's syllogism above. This blending shows that our minds work inductively, helping us interpret experience, and that our minds also work deductively, helping us reason from our discovered premises to further conclusions.

Good persuasive writing, then, as you saw in King's letter, makes transparent this blending of inductive and deductive thought. To put it negatively, had Dr. King omitted paragraph 14, with all its examples—proofs—of the degrading effect of segregation laws, then his minor premise in paragraph 16, that segregation laws degrade the human personality, would be another logical fallacy. That is, King would have been guilty of **begging the question,** the fallacy of assuming as proven the very idea that needs to be demonstrated.

Blending Pathos with Sound Reasoning to Achieve Mediational Goals

As you examined King's deductive reasoning in paragraph 16, then his inductive reasoning in paragraph 14, you saw King trying to build his ethos by offering his readers cool logic and sound evidence to persuade them that they cannot ask his followers to "wait" any longer for freedom. Yet King also strives to bridge the gap between "you," the clergymen who have criticized him and the racists who have jailed him, and "we," the victims of segregation. King constructs this peacemaking bridge with the materials of pathos: parallel sentence structure, metaphorical language, and climactic arrangement.

At the simplest level, **parallel structure** creates clarity, not emotional intensity. If you write, for example, that "I love skiing and to skate," you have written an awkward sentence because the two activities are not worded in identical (parallel) grammatical forms:

skiing (a gerund)

to skate (an infinitive)

You can quickly convert this confusion to clarity by changing the infinitive to the gerund form: "I love skiing and skating." Alternatively, you can change the first gerund to the infinitive form: "I love to ski and to skate." Either way, you have expressed the two equally loved activities in equal or parallel grammatical forms; either revision, then, creates clarity.

But strong persuasive writers know that the rhythms of parallel sentence structures create emotional intensity as well as clarity. Notice, for example, the parallel structure in this sentence from King's fourth paragraph:

We are caught in an inescapable network of mutuality,
tied in a single garment of destiny

First, King has given us parallel *verbs,* ("caught" and "tied,") both attached to the subject noun ("we"); he also has given us parallel *metaphors,* ("network" and "garment"), vivid images of our connectedness, each made more emphatic by the parallel *adjectives,* ("inescapable" and "single.") As your eyes see these parallel images of unity, your ears hear the parallel rhythms of the *prepositional phrases* ("of mutuality" and "of destiny"), stressing our "mutual destiny." Clearly, King's images and sounds of brotherhood lend an emotional charge to the concept of "interrelatedness," his main point in paragraph four and the heart of his mediational plea.

Similarly, when King praises those clergymen who have joined in his cause, he writes this sentence in paragraph 43:

They have carved a *tunnel of hope* through the *dark mountain of disappointment*.

Once again, our ears hear the parallel phrases; simultaneously, we see the parallel images, a "dark mountain of disappointment" penetrated by "they," the white and black Americans who have "carved a tunnel of hope" together. This image of brotherhood movingly conveys King's hope that his critics will accept his invitation to join the cause, particularly after they read the last paragraph, where he invites them to share his hope that "in some not too distant tomorrow the radiant stars of love and brotherhood will shine over our great nation with all their scintillating beauty." By saving this inspiring image for the end of his letter, the point where he hopes to have won supporters, not vanquished opponents, King has shown that arrangement works together with parallelism and metaphoric language to *move* his readers toward embracing a positive common destiny.

Prewriting on King's Letter

Though you have already answered journaling prompts on King's "Letter," try answering the following questions, which will allow you to apply what you learned above about deductive, inductive, and mediational logic:

1. In paragraphs 6–11, where do you find evidence of his intent to mediate between his movement and his critics?

2. Extract a syllogism from the material in paragraphs 15–19. Be sure to state the deductive reasoning in syllogistic form: major premise, minor premise, conclusion. Where does the essay provide evidence to support the premises of the syllogism?

3. Do paragraphs 25 and 45 further his mediational purpose, or do they seem confrontational? Explain.

Having answered these questions, you're ready now to write your own persuasive essay. You'll find a suggested topic below, but if you follow the following steps first, you will feel more certainty in choosing a topic or devising your own:

1. Re-read your answers to the journaling questions above. Next, find a subject—perhaps King's comments on white moderates—that grabs your attention.

2. Focusing on that subject, try some of the prewriting techniques discussed in chapters one and two—listing, freewriting, tree-outlining—to refine your focus.

3. Now try some of the invention techniques discussed in chapter three—conjecture, definition, comparison, cause-effect analysis, problem-solving—to develop a preliminary organization and a sense of audience and purpose.

Choosing a Topic for Your Persuasive Essay

Dr. King presents many reasons to support his claim that America has not lived up to its promise of brotherhood: the inappropriateness of "waiting" for freedom, the duty to violate unjust laws, the counter-productivity of support from "white moderates," the hypocrisy and brutality of the city officials. Choosing one of these reasons, discuss the effectiveness of King's blending of ethos, logos, and pathos to achieve his persuasive purpose.

Revising to Reveal Sound Reasoning

Once you have written your rough draft, share it with your Writing Group or with an intern at your campus Writing Center, addressing particularly the strength of your reasoning, essential in persuasive writing.

As you read through the draft, be sure to study closely—and skeptically—the relationship between your claims and the evidence that supports them. Be sure, too, that your draft has led your reader carefully and patiently from your hypothesis, to your evidence, to your conclusion. Doing so will ensure that you avoid the two most common and most serious fallacies mentioned above: making sweeping generalities and begging the question. These fallacies occur often if we remain writer-centered, embracing our long-held and probably unexamined assumptions. As a result of this uncritical thought, we forget that our readers need evidence before they can share our beliefs, a lapse that undercuts our credibility, our ethos, making persuasion impossible.

Notice how these other common fallacies reveal the same kind of sloppy thinking, linking dubious assertions with scant or biased evidence:

The Either/Or Fallacy

You commit this error when you force your reader to choose A or B when at least one other choice exists.

> Example: Anyone who opposes the President's policy on Iraq is un-American.

As the 2004 election results indicate, many patriotic Americans support President Bush's policy on Iraq; just as clearly, equally patriotic Americans oppose that policy. In other words, one can be patriotic and support the policy, be unpatriotic and oppose the policy, or be patriotic and oppose the policy. The sentence above would deprive us of this third choice.

The sentence above also exhibits another common fallacy: the ***ad hominem* attack**. This Latin phrase translates literally as "at the man." In other words, when we indulge in labels and name-calling—un-American—we offer a cheap emotional appeal but not a substantive, reasonable statement.

The Red Herring

You commit this fallacy when you distract your reader with examples or statements irrelevant to the issue at hand.

> Example: John Edwards has made millions of dollars prosecuting large corporations. Obviously, we cannot support his ideas on reducing the deficit.

The truth of the first sentence has been documented by Edwards' own tax returns. However, does his success as a trial lawyer have anything to do with his ideas of fiscal responsibility? If so, the writer would have to demonstrate a connection. As it stands, the first sentence is a red-herring, a distracting irrelevancy.

Once again, more than one fallacy can lurk in a single sentence, just as we saw above in the Iraq example. In the Edwards example, we also have a suppressed premise. Typically, when we state the premise that the original implies, the fallacy leaps out at us:

Major Premise: All trial lawyers are corrupt

Minor Premise: John Edwards is a trial lawyer.

Conclusion: John Edwards is corrupt.

Surely, we can find many corrupt trial lawyers in the world—and many corrupt legislators, judges, scientists, merchants, and teachers. But just as surely, we know that the "all" above creates a sweeping generalization that no one could ever defend; therefore, the conclusion does not follow from the premises.

Your Writing Center has guidelines on logical fallacies, as well as exercises to develop your skill in identifying and correcting such careless or manipulative thinking. If your professor assigns these exercises, please don't dismiss the assignment as busy-work. You will need to use these analytical skills in assessing the soundness of the reasoning in your peer's drafts (if you're working in a Writing Group) and your own. Again, you cannot make your reader agree with you, but you can avoid having your argument rejected because you haven't reasoned persuasively.

Writing an Editorial Essay: A Case for Mediation

Nearly 50 years before Dr. King wrote on the injustice of stifling African Americans, Susan Glaspell wrote her one-act play *Trifles* to expose the injustices suffered by another group of Americans: women. First staged at Glaspell's Cape Cod playhouse in 1916, *Trifles* dramatizes the aftermath to the apparent murder of one Mr. Wright, a "good" man who smothered Mrs. Wright for 30 years with his severity, silencing her soul, her song.

Journaling on Susan Glaspell's Play

As you read this disturbing play, printed below, answer the following questions in your journal. Your answers will prepare you to write a mediational essay in response to the arrest of Mrs. Wright.

1. What do you conclude about Mrs. Wright's mental condition, judging from Mr. Hale's report (paragraphs 19, 23)?

2. The Sheriff and Attorney find no motive for the murder in Mrs. Wright's "kitchen things," mere women's "trifles" such as dirty towels and half-wiped tables. What conclusions do the women draw from these "trifles" (paragraphs 31, 32, 40, 68)? What conclusions do they draw from the description of John Wright (44, 56, 102)?

3. What does Mrs. Hale realize about her own role in this domestic tragedy (98, 100, 135)?

4. Why does Mrs. Hale look with "horror" (115) at the strangled bird? Why does she lie about the bird (119, 120)?

5. What are your own thoughts on the murder and on Mrs. Hale's cover-up?

Trifles

Susan Glaspell

SCENE: The kitchen in the now abandoned farmhouse of JOHN WRIGHT, a gloomy kitchen, and left without having been put in order—unwashed pans under the sink, a loaf of bread outside the breadbox, a dish towel on the table—other signs of incompleted work. At the rear the outer door opens, and the SHERIFF comes in, followed by the county ATTORNEY and HALE. The SHERIFF and HALE are men in middle life, the COUNTY ATTORNEY is a young man; all are much bundled up and go at once to the stove. They are followed by the two women—the SHERIFF'S WIFE first; she is a slight wiry woman, a thin nervous face. MRS. HALE is larger and would ordinarily be called more comfortable looking, but she is disturbed now and looks fearfully about as she enters. The women have come in slowly and stand close together near the door.

COUNTY ATTORNEY (rubbing his hands): This feels good. Come up to the fire, ladies.   1

MRS. PETERS (after taking a step forward): I'm not—cold.   2

SHERIFF (unbuttoning his overcoat and stepping away from the stove as if to the beginning of official business): Now, Mr. Hale, before we move things about, you explain to Mr. Henderson just what you saw when you came here yesterday morning.   3

COUNTY ATTORNEY: By the way, has anything been moved? Are things just as you left them yesterday?   4

SHERIFF (looking about). It's just the same: When it dropped below zero last night, I thought I'd better send Frank out this morning to make a fire for us—no use getting pneumonia with a big case on; but I told him not to touch anything except the stove— and you know Frank. 5

COUNTY ATTORNEY: Somebody should have been left here yesterday. 6

SHERIFF: Oh—yesterday: When I had to send Frank to Morris Center for that man who went crazy—I want you to know I had my hands full yesterday. I knew you could get back from Omaha by today, and as long as I went over everything here myself— 7

COUNTY ATTORNEY: Well, Mr. Hale, tell just what happened when you came here yesterday morning. 8

HALE: Harry and I had started to town with a load of potatoes. We came along the road from my place; and as I got here, I said, "I'm going to see if I can't get John Wright to go in with me on a party telephone!" I spoke to Wright about it once before, and he put me off, saying folks talked too much anyway, and all he asked was peace and quiet—I guess you know about how much he talked himself; but I thought maybe if I went to the house and talked about it before his wife, though I said to Harry that I didn't know as what his wife wanted made much difference to John. 9

COUNTY ATTORNEY: Let's talk about that later, Mr. Hale. I do want to talk about that, but tell now just what happened when you got to the house. 10

HALE: I didn't hear or see anything; I knocked at the door, and still it was all quiet inside. I knew they must be up; it was past eight o'clock. So I knocked again, and I thought I heard somebody say, "Come in!" I wasn't sure. I'm not sure yet, but I opened the door—this door (indicating the door by which the two women are still standing), and there in that rocker—(pointing to it) sat Mrs. Wright. (They all look at the rocker.) 11

COUNTY ATTORNEY: What—was she doing? 12

HALE: She was rocking back and forth. She had her apron in her hand and was kind of— pleating it. 13

COUNTY ATTORNEY: And how did she—look? 14

HALE: Well, she looked queer. 15

COUNTY ATTORNEY: How do you mean—queer? 16

HALE: Well, as if she didn't know what she was going to do next. And kind of done up. 17

COUNTY ATTORNEY: How did she seem to feel about your coming? 18

HALE: Why, I don't think she minded—one way or other. She didn't pay much attention. I said, "How do, Mrs. Wright, it's cold, ain't it?" And she said, "Is it?"—and went on kind of pleating at her apron. Well, I was surprised; she didn't ask me to come up to the stove, or to set down, but just sat there, not even looking at me, so I said, "I want to see John!" And then she—laughed. I guess you would call it a laugh. I thought 19 of Harry and the team outside, so I said a little sharp: "Can't I see John?" "No," she says, kind o' dull like. "Ain't he home?" says I. "Yes," says she, "he's home!" "Then why can't I see him?" I asked her, out of patience. "'Cause he's dead," says she. "Dead?" says I. She just nodded her head, not getting a bit excited, but rockin' back and forth. "Why—where is he?" says I, not knowing what to say. She just pointed upstairs—like that (himself pointing to the room above). I got up, with the idea of going up there. I walked from there to here—then I says, "Why, what did he die of?" "He died of a rope around his neck," says she, and just went on pleatin' at her apron. Well, I went out and called Harry. I thought I might—need help. We went upstairs, and there he was lyin'—

COUNTY ATTORNEY: I think I'd rather have you go into that upstairs, where you can point it all out. Just go on now with the rest of the story. [20]

HALE: Well, my first thought was to get that rope off. I looked (Stops, his face twitches.)... but Harry, he went up to him, and he said, "No, he's dead all right, and we'd better not touch anything!" So we went back downstairs. She was still sitting that same way. "Has anybody been notified?" I asked. "No," says she, unconcerned. "Who did this, Mrs. Wright?" said Harry. He said it businesslike—and she stopped pleatin' of her apron. "I don't know," she says. "You don't know?" says Harry. "No," says she. "Weren't you sleepin' in the bed with him?" says Harry. "Yes," says she, "but I was on the inside." "Somebody slipped a rope round his neck and strangled him, and you didn't wake up?" says Harry. "I didn't wake up," she said after him. We must 'a looked as if we didn't see how that could be, for after a minute she said, "I sleep sound." Harry was going to ask her more questions, but I said maybe we ought to let her tell her story first to the coroner, or the sheriff, so Harry went fast as he could to Rivers' place, where there's a telephone. [21]

COUNTY ATTORNEY: And what did Mrs. Wright do when she knew that you had gone for the coroner? [22]

HALE: She moved from that chair to this over here... (Pointing to a small chair in the corner.)... and just sat there with her hands held together and looking down. I got a feeling that I ought to make some conversation, so I said I had come in to see if John wanted to put in a telephone, and at that she started to laugh, and then she stopped and looked at me—scared. (The COUNTY ATTORNEY, who has had his notebook out, makes a note.) I dunno, maybe it wasn't scared. I wouldn't like to say it was. Soon Harry got back, and then Dr. Lloyd came, and you, Mr. Peters, and so I guess that's all I know that you don't. [23]

COUNTY ATTORNEY: (looking around). I guess we'll go upstairs first—and then out to the barn and around there. (To the SHERIFF.) You're convinced that there was nothing important here—nothing that would point to any motive? [24]

SHERIFF: Nothing here but kitchen things. (The COUNTY ATTORNEY, after again looking around the kitchen, opens the door of a cupboard closet. He gets up on a chair and looks on a shelf. Pulls his hand away, sticky.) [25]

COUNTY ATTORNEY: Here's a nice mess. (The women draw nearer.) 26

MRS. PETERS (to the other woman): Oh, her fruit; it did freeze. (To the LAWYER.) 27
She worried about that when it tuned so cold. She said the fir'd go out and her jars
would break.

SHERIFF: Well, can you beat the women! Held for murder and worryin' about her 28
preserves.

COUNTY ATTORNEY: I guess before we're through she may have something more 29
serious than preserves to worry about.

HALE: Well, women are used to worrying over trifles. (The two women move a little 30
closer together.)

COUNTY ATTORNEY (with the gallantry of a young politician): And yet, for all 31
their worries, what would we do without the ladies? (The women do not unbend.
He goes to the sink, takes a dipperful of water from the pail and, pouring it into a
basin, washes his hands. Starts to wipe them on the roller towel, turns it for a cleaner
place.) Dirty towels! (Kicks his foot against the pans under the sink.) Not much of a
housekeeper, would you say, ladies?

MRS. HALE (stiffly): There's a great deal of work to be done on a farm. 32

COUNTY ATTORNEY: To be sure. And yet... (With a little bow to her)... I know 33
there are some Dickson county farmhouses which do not have such roller towels. (He
gives it a pull to expose its full length again.)

MRS. HALE: Those towels get dirty awful quick. Men's hands aren't always as clean as 34
they might be.

COUNTY ATTORNEY: Ah, loyal to your sex, I see. But you and Mrs. Wright were 35
neighbors. I suppose you were friends, too.

MRS. HALE (shaking her head): I've not seen much of her of late years. I've not been in 36
this house—it's more than a year.

COUNTY ATTORNEY: And why was that? You didn't like her? 37

MRS. HALE: I liked her all well enough. Farmers' wives have their hands full, Mr. 38
Henderson. And then.

COUNTY ATTORNEY: Yes? 39

MRS. HALE (looking about): It never seemed a very cheerful place. 40

COUNTY ATTORNEY: No—it's not cheerful. I shouldn't say she had the homemaking 41
instinct.

MRS. HALE: Well, I don't know as Wright had, either. 42

COUNTY ATTORNEY: You mean that they didn't get on very well? 43

MRS. HALE: No, I don't mean anything. But I don't think a place'd be any cheerfuler for 44

John Wright's being in it.

COUNTY ATTORNEY: I'd like to talk more of that a little later. I want to get the lay of things upstairs now. (He goes to the left, where three steps lead to a stair door.) 45

SHERIFF: I suppose anything Mrs. Peters does'll be all right. She was to take in some clothes for her, you know, and a few little things. We left in such a hurry yesterday. 46

COUNTY ATTORNEY: Yes, but I would like to see what you take, Mrs. Peters, and keep an eye out for anything that might be of use to us. 47

MRS. PETERS: Yes, Mr. Henderson. (The women listen to the men's steps on the stairs, then look about the kitchen) 48

MRS. HALE: I'd hate to have men coming into my kitchen, snooping around and criticizing. (She arranges the pans under the sink which the LAWYER had shoved out of place.) 49

MRS. PETERS: Of course, it's no more than their duty. 50

MRS. HALE: Duty's all right but I guess that deputy sheriff that came out to make the fire might have got a little of this on. (Gives the roller towel a pull.) Wish I'd thought of that sooner. Seems mean to talk about her for not having things slicked up when she had to come away in such a hurry. 51

MRS. PETERS (who has gone to a small table in the left rear corner of the room, and lifted one end of a towel that covers a pan): She had bread set. (Stands still.) 52

MRS. HALE (eyes fixed on a loaf of bread beside the breadbox, which is on a low shelf at the other side of the room. Moves slowly toward it): She was going to put this in there. (Picks up loaf then abruptly drops it. In a manner of returning to familiar things.) It's a shame about her fruit. I wonder if it's all gone. (Gets up on the chair and looks.) I think there's some here that's all right, Mrs. Peters. Yes—here; (Holding it toward the window.) This is cherries, too. (Looking again.) I declare I believe that's the only one. (Gets down, bottle in her hand. Goes to the sink and wipes it off on the outside.) She'll feel awful bad after all her hard work in the hot weather. I remember the afternoon I put up my cherries last summer. (She puts the bottle on the big kitchen table, center of the room, front table. With a sigh, is about to sit down in the rocking chair. Before she is seated realizes what chair it is; with a slow look at it, steps back. The chair, which she has touched, rocks back and forth.) 53

MRS. PETERS: Well, I must get those things from the front room closet. (She goes to the door at the right, but after looking into the other room steps back.) You coming with me, Mrs. Hale? You could help me carry them. (They go into the other room; reappear, MRS. PETERS carrying a dress and skirt, MRS. HALE following with a pair of shoes.) 54

MRS. PETERS: My, it's cold in there. (She puts the cloth on the big table, and hurries to the stove.) 55

MRS. HALE (examining the skirt): Wright was close. I think maybe that's why she kept 56 so much to herself. She didn't even belong to the Ladies' Aid. I suppose she felt she couldn't do her part, and then you don't enjoy things when you feel shabby. She used to wear pretty clothes and be lively, when she was Minnie Foster, one of the town girls singing in the choir. But that—oh, that was thirty years ago. This all you was to take in?

MRS. PETERS: She said she wanted an apron. Funny thing to want, for there isn't much to get you dirty in jail, goodness knows. But I suppose just to make her feel more natural. She said they was in the top drawer in this cupboard. Yes, here. And then her little shawl that always hung behind the door (Opens stair door and looks.) Yes, here it is. (Quickly shuts door leading upstairs.)   57

MRS. HALE (abruptly moving toward her): Mrs. Peters?   58

MRS. PETERS: Yes, Mrs. Hale?   59

MRS. HALE: Do you think she did it?   60

MRS. PETERS (in a frightened voice): Oh, I don't know.   61

MRS. HALE: Well, I don't think she did. Asking for an apron and her little shawl. Worrying about her fruit.   62

MRS. PETERS (starts to speak, glances up, where footsteps are heard in the room above. In a low voice): Mr. Peters says it looks bad for her. Mr. Henderson is awful sarcastic in speech, and he'll make fun of her sayin' she didn't wake up.   63

MRS. HALE: Well, I guess John Wright didn't wake when they was slipping that rope under his neck.   64

MRS. PETERS: No, it's strange. It must have been done awful crafty and still. They say it was such a—funny way to kill a man, rigging it all up like that.   65

MRS. HALE: That's just what Mr. Hale said. There was a gun in the house. He says that's what he can't understand.   66

MRS. PETERS: Mr. Henderson said coming out that what was needed for the case was a motive; something to show anger, or—sudden feeling.   67

MRS. HALE (who is standing by the table): Well, I don't see any signs of anger around here. (She puts her hand on the dish towel which lies on the table, stands looking down at the table, one half of which is clean, the other half messy.) It's wiped here. (Makes a move as if to finish work, then turns and looks at loaf of bread outside the breadbox. Drops towel. In that voice of coming back to familiar things.) Wonder how they are finding things upstairs? I hope she had it a little more ready—up there. You know, it seems kind of sneaking. Locking her up in town and then coming out here and trying to get her own house to turn against her!   68

MRS. PETERS: But, Mrs. Hale, the law is the law.   69

MRS. HALE: I s'pose 'tis. (Unbuttoning her coat.) Better loosen up your things, Mrs. Peters. You won't feel them when you go out.   70

(MRS. PETERS takes off her fur tippet, goes to hang it on hook at the back of room, stands looking at the under part of the small corner table.)

MRS. PETERS: She was piecing a quilt. (She brings the large sewing basket, and they look at the bright pieces.)

MRS. HALE: It's log cabin pattern. Pretty, isn't it? I wonder if she was going to quilt or just knot it? (Footsteps have been heard coming down the stairs. The SHERIFF enters, followed by HALE and the COUNTY ATTORNEY.)

SHERIFF: They wonder if she was going to quilt it or just knot it. (The men laugh, the women look abashed.)

COUNTY ATTORNEY (rubbing his hands over the stove): Frank's fire didn't do much up there, did it? Well, let's go out to the barn and get that cleared up. (The men go outside.)

MRS. HALE (resentfully): I don't know as there's anything so strange, our takin' up our time with little things while we're waiting for them to get the evidence. (She sits down at the big table, smoothing out a block with decision.) I don't see as it's anything to laugh about.

MRS. PETERS (apologetically): Of course they've got awful important things on their minds. (Pulls up a chair and joins MRS. HALE at the table.)

MRS. HALE (examining another block): Mrs. Peters, look at this one. Here, this is the one she was working on, and look at the sewing! All the rest of it has been so nice and even. And look at this! It's all over the place! Why, it looks as if she didn't know what she was about! (After she has said this, they look at each other, then started to glance back at the door. After an instant MRS. HALE has pulled at a knot and ripped the sewing.)

MRS. PETERS: Oh, what are you doing, Mrs. Hale?

MRS. HALE (mildly): Just pulling out a stitch or two that's not sewed very good. (Threading a needle.) Bad sewing always made me fidgety.

MRS. PETERS (nervously): I don't think we ought to touch things.

MRS. HALE: I'll just finish up this end. (Suddenly stopping and leaning forward.) Mrs. Peters?

MRS. PETERS: Yes, Mrs. Hale?

MRS. HALE: What do you suppose she was so nervous about?

MRS. PETERS: Oh—I don't know. I don't know as she was nervous. I sometimes sew awful queer when I'm just tired. (MRS. HALE starts to say something, looks at MRS. PETERS, then goes on sewing.) Well, I must get these things wrapped up. They may be through sooner than we think. (Putting apron and other things together.) I wonder where I can find a piece of paper, and string.

71

72

73

74

75

76

77

78

79

80

81

82

83

84

85

MRS. HALE: In that cupboard, maybe. 86

MRS. PETERS (looking in cupboard): Why, here's a birdcage. (Holds it up.) Did she have a bird, Mrs. Hale? 87

MRS. HALE: Why, I don't know whether she did or not—I've not been here for so long. There was a man around last year selling canaries cheap, but I don't know as she took one; maybe she did. She used to sing real pretty herself. 88

MRS. PETERS (glancing around): Seems funny to think of a bird here. But she must have had one, or why should she have a cage? I wonder what happened to it? 89

MRS. HALE: I s'pose maybe the cat got it. 90

MRS. PETERS: No, she didn't have a cat. She's got that feeling some people have about cats—being afraid of them. My cat got in her room, and she was real upset and asked me to take it out. 91

MRS. HALE: My sister Bessie was like that. Queer, ain't it? 92

MRS. PETERS (examining the cage): Why look at this door. It's broke. One hinge is pulled apart. 93

MRS. HALE (looking, too): Looks as if someone must have been rough with it. 94

MRS. PETERS: Why, yes. (She brings the cage forward and puts it on the table.) 95

MRS. HALE: I wish if they're going to find any evidence they'd be about it. I don't like this place. 96

MRS. PETERS: But I'm awful glad you came with me, Mrs. Hale. It would be lonesome for me sitting here alone. 97

MRS. HALE: It would, wouldn't it? (Dropping her sewing.) But I tell you what I do wish, Mrs. Peters. I wish I had come over sometimes when she was here. I—(Looking around the room.)—wish I had. 98

MRS. PETERS: But of course you were awful busy, Mrs. Hale—your house and your children. 99

MRS. HALE: I could've come. I stayed away because it weren't cheerful—and that's why I ought to have come. I—I've never liked this place. Maybe because it's down in a hollow, and you don't see the road. I dunno what it is, but it's a lonesome place and always was. I wish I had come over to see Minnie Foster sometimes. I can see now— 100

(Shakes her head.)

MRS. PETERS: Well, you mustn't reproach yourself, Mrs. Hale. Somehow we just don't see how it is with other folks until—something comes up. 101

MRS. HALE: Not having children makes less work—but it makes a quiet house, and Wright out to work all day and no company when he did come in. Did you know John Wright, Mrs. Peters? 102

MRS. PETERS: Not to know him; I've seen him in town. They say he was a good man. 103

MRS. HALE: Yes—good; he didn't drink, and kept his word as well as most, I guess, and paid his debts. But he was a hard man, Mrs. Peters. Just to pass the time of day with him. (Shivers.) Like a raw wind that gets to the bone. (Pauses, her eye falling on the cage.) I should think she would 'a wanted a bird. But what do you suppose went with it? 104

MRS. PETERS: I don't know, unless it got sick and died. (She reaches over and swings the broken door, swings it again; both women watch it.) 105

MRS. HALE: You weren't raised round here, were you? (MRS PETERS shakes her head.) You didn't know—her? 106

MRS. PETERS: Not till they brought her yesterday. 107

MRS. HALE: She—come to think of it, she was kind of like a bird herself—real sweet and pretty, but kind of timid and—fluttery. How—she—did—change. (Silence; then as if struck by a happy thought and relieved to get back to everyday things.) Tell you what, Mrs. Peters, why don't you take the quilt in with you? It might take up her mind. 108

MRS. PETERS: Why, I think that's a real nice idea, Mrs. Hale. There couldn't possible be any objection to it, could there? Now, just what would I take? I wonder if her patches are in here—and her things. (They look in the sewing basket.) 109

MRS. HALE: Here's some red. I expect this has got sewing things in it. (Brings out a fancy box.) What a pretty box. Looks like something somebody would give you. Maybe her scissors are in here. (Opens box. Suddenly puts her hand to her nose.) Why—(MRS . PETERS bends nearer, then turns her face away.) There's something wrapped up in this piece of silk. 110

MRS. PETERS: Why, this isn't her scissors. 111

MRS. HALE (lifting the silk): Oh, Mrs. Peters—it's—(MRS. PETERS bends closer.) 112

MRS. PETERS: It's the bird. 113

MRS. HALE (jumping up): But, Mrs. Peters—look at it. Its neck! Look at its neck! It's all—other side to. 114

MRS. PETERS: Somebody—wrung—its neck. (Their eyes meet. A look of growing comprehension of horror. Steps are heard outside. MRS. HALE slips box under quilt pieces, and sinks into her chair. Enter SHERIFF and COUNTY ATTORNEY. MRS. PETERS rises.) 115

COUNTY ATTORNEY (as one turning from serious things to little pleasantries): Well, ladies, have you decided whether she was going to quilt it or knot it? 116

MRS. PETERS: We think she was going to—knot it. 117

COUNTY ATTORNEY: Well, that's interesting, I'm sure. (Seeing the birdcage.) Has the bird flown? 118

MRS. HALE (putting more quilt pieces over the box).:We think the—cat got it. 119

COUNTY ATTORNEY (preoccupied): Is there a cat? 120

(MRS. HALE glances in a quick covert way at MRS. PETERS.)

MRS. PETERS: Well, not now. They're superstitious, you know. They leave. 121

COUNTY ATTORNEY (to SHERIFF PETERS, continuing an interrupted 122
conversation). No sign at all of anyone having come from the outside. Their own rope.
Now let's go up again and go over it piece by piece. (They start upstairs.) It would
have to have been someone who knew just the— (MRS. PETERS sits down. The
two women sit there not looking at one another, but as if peering into something and
at the same time holding back. When they talk now, it is the manner of feeling their
way over strange ground, as if afraid of what they are saying, but as if they cannot
help saying it.)

MRS. HALE: She liked the bird. She was going to bury it in that pretty box. 123

MRS. PETERS (in a whisper): When I was a girl—my kitten—there was a boy took 124
a hatchet, and before my eyes—and before I could get there— (Covers her face an
instant.) If they hadn't held me back, I would have— (Catches herself, looks upstairs
where steps are heard, falters weakly.)—hurt him.

MRS. HALE (with a slow look around her): I wonder how it would seem never to have 125
had any children around. (Pause.) No, Wright wouldn't like the bird—a thing that
sang. She used to sing. He killed that, too.

MRS. PETERS (moving uneasily): We don't know who killed the bird. 126

MRS. HALE: I knew John Wright. 127

MRS. PETERS: It was an awful thing was done in this house that night, Mrs. Hale. 128
Killing a man while he slept, slipping a rope around his neck that choked the life out
of him.

MRS. HALE: His neck. Choked the life out of him (Her hand goes out and rests on the 129
birdcage.)

MRS. PETERS (with a rising voice): We don't know who killed him. We don't know. 130

MRS. HALE (her own feeling not interrupted): If there'd been years and years of 131
nothing, then a bird to sing to you, it would be awful—still, after the bird was still.

MRS. PETERS (something within her speaking): I know what stillness is. When we 132
homesteaded in Dakota, and my first baby died—after he was two years old, and me
with no other then—

MRS. HALE (moving): How soon do you suppose they'll be through, looking for 133
evidence?

MRS. PETERS: I know what stillness is. (Pulling herself back.) The law has got to 134
punish crime, Mrs. Hale.

MRS. HALE (not as if answering that). I wish you'd seen Minnie Foster when she wore 135
a white dress with blue ribbons and stood up there in the choir and sang. (A look
around the room.) Oh, I wish I'd come over here once in a while! That was a crime!
That was a crime! Who's going to punish that?

MRS. PETERS (looking upstairs): We mustn't—take on. 136

MRS. HALE: I might have known she needed help! I know how things can be—for 137
women. I tell you, it's queer, Mrs. Peters. We live close together and we live far apart.
We all go through the same things—it's all just a different kind of the same thing.
(Brushes her eyes, noticing the bottle of fruit, reaches out for it.) If I was you, I
wouldn't tell her her fruit was gone. Tell her it ain't. Tell her it's all right. Take this in
to prove it to her. She—she may never know whether it was broke or not.

MRS. PETERS (takes the bottle, looks about for something to wrap it in; takes petticoat 138
from the clothes brought from the other room, very nervously begins winding this
around the bottle. In a false voice): My, it's a good thing the men couldn't hear us.
Wouldn't they just laugh! Getting all stirred up over a little thing like a—dead canary.
As if that could have anything to do with—with—wouldn't they laugh! (The men are
heard coming downstairs.)

MRS. HALE (under her breath): Maybe they would—maybe they wouldn't. 139

COUNTY ATTORNEY: No, Peters, it's all perfectly clear except a reason for doing 140
it. But you know juries when it comes to women. If there was some definite thing.
Something to show—something to make a story about—a thing that would connect
up with this strange way of doing it.

(The women's eyes meet for an instant. Enter HALE from outer door.)

HALE: Well, I've got the team around. Pretty cold out there. 141

COUNTY ATTORNEY: I'm going to stay here awhile by myself. (To the SHERIFF.) 142
You can send Frank out for me, can't you? I want to go over everything. I'm not
satisfied that we can't do better

SHERIFF: Do you want to see what Mrs. Peters is going to take in? (The LAWYER 143
goes to the table, picks up the apron, laughs.)

COUNTY ATTORNEY: Oh, I guess they're not very dangerous things the ladies have 144
picked up. (Moves a few things about, disturbing the quilt pieces which cover the box.
Steps back.) No, Mrs. Peters doesn't need supervising. For that matter, a sheriff's wife
is married to the law. Ever think of it that way, Mrs. Peters?

MRS. PETERS: Not—just that way. 145

SHERIFF (chuckling): Married to the law. (Moves toward the other room.) I just want 146
you to come in here a minute, George. We ought to take a look at these windows.

COUNTY ATTORNEY (scoffingly): Oh, windows! 147

SHERIFF: We'll be right out, Mr. Hale. (HALE goes outside. The SHERIFF follows 148 the COUNTY ATTORNEY into the other room. Then MRS. HALE rises, hands tight together, looking intense at MRS. PETERS, whose eyes take a slow turn, finally meeting MRS. HALE'S. A moment MRS. HALE holds her, then her own eyes point the way to where the box is concealed. Suddenly MRS. PETERS throws back quilt pieces and tries to put the box in the bag she is wearing. It is too big. She opens box, starts to take the bird out, cannot touch it, goes to pieces, stands there helpless. Sound of a knob turning in the other room. MRS. HALE snatches the box and puts it in the pocket of her big coat. Enter COUNTY ATTORNEY and SHERIFF.)

COUNTY ATTORNEY (facetiously): Well, Henry, at least we found out that she was not going to quilt it. She was going to—what is it you call it, ladies?   149

MRS. HALE (her hand against her pocket): We call it—knot it, Mr. Henderson.   150

Using Role-Playing to Write the Editorial Essay

Write a role-playing editorial in response to *Trifles*. Your editorial essay aims to make peace between the outraged men and the saddened women of Mrs. Wright's town; it also aims to secure more merciful justice for Mrs. Wright, who has, in fact, murdered her husband, and for Mrs. Hale, who has obstructed justice:

Situation: Mrs. Wright has just been sentenced to death for the murder of her husband; Mrs. Hale has been found guilty of perjury. The all-male jury reached this verdict after the prosecuting attorney pressured Mrs. Hale on the witness stand, pushing her to admit to hiding the strangled bird.

Having witnessed the trial and interviewed Mrs. Hale in her cell, you have decided to write an editorial defending both Mrs. Wright for her murder and Mrs. Hale for her obstruction of justice and perjury. You hope to stir public sentiment to re-try Mrs. Wright and to forgive the disgraced Mrs. Hale. Use evidence from the play to make your case.

Works Cited

Augustine. "On Christian Doctrine." *The Rhetorical Tradition: Readings from Classical Times to the Present.* Eds. Patricia Bizzell and Bruce Herzberg. Boston: St. Martin's, 1990. 386–416.

Cooper, Lane, ed. *The Rhetoric of Aristotle.* New York: Appleton, 1960.

Glaspell, Susan. *Trifles. Conversations: Readings for Writing.* 3rd ed. Ed. Jack Selzer. New York: Allyn and Bacon, 1997.

King, Martin Luther, Jr. "Letter from Birmingham Jail." *The Essay Connection.* 6th ed. Ed. Lynn Z. Bloom. Boston: Houghton Mifflin, 2001. 597–614.

Kinneavy, James L. *A Theory of Discourse.* New York: Norton, 1971.

Lamb, Catherine E. "Beyond Argument in Feminist Composition." *College Composition and Communication* 42.1 (February 1991): 11–24

McCormick, Joshua. "An Ecclesiastical Fall from Grace." Student essay.

CHAPTER 5

Finding Answers
to Your Questions:
Research and Documentation

"Scientists ask one more question once their research is complete: 'Are we done yet, or can we improve our understanding of the problem?' When the answer is that more remains to be known, the scientist digs deeper."
GEOFFREY J. S. HART, "The Scientific Method: Learning from Scientists"

"Those who cannot reliably do research or evaluate the research of others will find themselves on the sidelines in a world that increasingly depends on sound ideas based on good information produced by trustworthy inquiry."
WAYNE BOOTH, *The Craft of Research*

Understanding the Research Process

In the first four chapters, you learned to find a strong sense of purpose for your writing by exploring your own experiences, and then finding an audience that will benefit from reading your narrated memories, your responses on others' writings, or your persuasive reflections on social problems. In all four chapters, you also practiced rhetorical analysis of writing by professionals and by students to learn the strategies that writers can employ to discover their ideas, to organize and develop their claims, to build their credibility—in other words, to achieve their purpose and to meet the needs of their readers.

In this fifth chapter, you will learn to enrich your writing by drawing on secondary sources: scholarly articles, books, and websites. Such secondary sources will help you to frame your own questions on problems you want to solve; they will also help you to find answers to those questions and to shape persuasive solutions to meet the challenges of skeptical readers.

To begin this transformation from writer to writer-researcher, you will first read Flannery O'Connor's famous short story "Greenleaf," a work that raises innumerable questions about the dangers of intellectual arrogance and the importance of spiritual growth. After using your journal to explore your responses to O'Connor's themes, you will next explore the rhetorical strategies practiced by Richard Giannone in his work on this same startling story. Next, you will encounter a student's research on the same topic. That research work includes the student's **proposal memo**, a practical kind of writing used every day in the world of work. In examining her proposal, you will see that the memo allows you to use your knowledge of your audience and purpose to plan your research and to forecast the organization of the research paper that will grow from your research. After studying the proposal memo, you will examine her **research paper** on "Greenleaf," the fruit of her proposal.

Before and after you write your own proposal for research, you will be reading books and journals as well as visiting websites. Therefore, this chapter will also examine effective documentation and note-taking practices. In doing so, we will also consider academic integrity issues, focusing particularly on ways to avoid unintentional plagiarism as well as the temptations to cheat.

Following this discussion of documentation, you will read a chapter from Azar Nafiri's *Reading* Lolita *in Tehran*, an engaging memoir that raises questions about access to higher education and the value of interactive learning, as well as the role of literature in awakening readers and effecting social change. After you respond to Nafiri's piece in your journal, you will find suggestions for your own research project. This process will begin with finding a topic, an interpretive problem that needs solving; you will then explore secondary sources, prepare a research proposal memo, and write the research paper itself.

Journaling on Flannery O'Connor's Short Story

As you read O'Connor's story below, answer the following questions in your journal. This process, as you recall from similar work in the first four chapters, will concentrate your reading, prepare you for class discussion, and gather material from which you may eventually draw your research paper. In pondering each question, you will notice in the phrasing the influence of Burke's pentad (chapter one) and stasis theory (chapter three), ways of 'inventing' your response to your reading.

1. Mrs. May thinks of herself as "a good Christian woman" who has spent 15 years running a dairy, raising her sons, and supporting her hired help, the Greenleaf family. List here as many examples as you can find of what Mrs. May would consider as proof of her hard work, her motherly nurture, and her neighborliness. Do you agree with her self-assessment? Why or why not?

2. Mrs. May resents the success of the Greenleaf sons. Cite examples of her resentment and explain the source of her feelings.

3. Given Mrs. May's pride in her Christianity, what comment would you make about her view of Mrs. Greenleaf's faith? Explain.

4. Given Mrs. May's pride in her parenting, what comment would you make about the violent behavior of her sons Wesley and Scofield and their delight in annoying their mother? Why is Mrs. May so disappointed in her sons?

5. Looking back over the story, how has O'Connor prepared you for Mrs. May's violent death? Notice, too, in the beginning and the end, the narrator refers to the bull as a God and a lover. How do these image patterns affect your interpretation of Mrs. May's facial expressions, just before the goring and just after?

"Greenleaf"

FLANNERY O'CONNOR

Mrs. May's bedroom window was low and faced on the east and the bull, silvered in the moonlight, stood under it, his head raised as if he listened—like some patient god come down to woo her—for a stir inside the room. The window was dark and the sound of her breathing too light to be carried outside. Clouds crossing the moon blackened him and in the dark he began to tear at the hedge. Presently they passed and he appeared again in the same spot, chewing steadily, with a hedge-wreath that he had ripped loose for himself caught in the tips of his horns. When the moon drifted into retirement again, there was nothing to mark his place but the sound of steady chewing. Then abruptly a pink glow filled the window. Bars of light slid across him as the venetian blind was slit. He took a step backward and lowered his head as if to show the wreath across his horns.

For almost a minute there was no sound from inside, then as he raised his crowned head again, a woman's voice, guttural as if addressed to a dog, said, "Get away from here, Sir!" and in a second muttered, "Some nigger's scrub bull."

The animal pawed the ground and Mrs. May, standing bent forward behind the blind, closed it quickly lest the light make him charge into the shrubbery. For a second she waited, still bent forward, her nightgown hanging loosely from her narrow shoulders. Green rubber curlers sprouted neatly over her forehead and her face beneath them was smooth as concrete with an egg-white paste that drew the wrinkles out while she slept.

She had been conscious in her sleep of a steady rhythmic chewing as if something were eating one wall of the house. She had been aware that whatever it was had been eating as long as she had the place and had eaten everything from the beginning of her fence line up to the house and now was eating the house and calmly with the same steady rhythm would continue through the house, eating her and the boys, and then on, eating everything but the Greenleafs, on and on, eating everything until nothing was left but the Greenleafs on a little island all their own in the middle of what had been her place. When the munching reached her elbow, she jumped up and found herself, fully awake, standing in the middle of her room. She identified the sound at once: a cow was tearing at the shrubbery under the window. Mr. Greenleaf had left the lane gate open and she didn't doubt that the entire herd was on her lawn. She turned on the dim pink table lamp and then went to the window and slit the blind. The bull, gaunt and long-legged, was standing about four feet from her, chewing calmly like an uncouth country suitor.

For fifteen years, she thought as she squinted at him fiercely, she had been having shiftless people's hogs root up her oats, their mules wallow on her lawn, their scrub bulls breed her cows. If this one was not put up now, he would be over the fence, mining her herd before morning—and Mr. Greenleaf was soundly sleeping a half mile down the road in the tenant house. There was no way to get him unless she dressed and got in her car and rode down there and woke him up. He would come but his expression, his whole figure, his every pause, would say: "Hit looks to me like one or both of them boys would not make their maw ride out in the middle of the night this away. If hit was my boys, they would have got the bull up theirself."

The bull lowered his head and shook it and the wreath slipped down the base of his horns where it looked like a menacing prickly crown. She closed the blind then; in a few seconds she heard him move off heavily.

Mr. Greenleaf would say, "If hit was my boys they would never have allowed their maw to go after the hired help in the middle of the night. They would have did it theirself." Weighing it, she decided not to bother Mr. Greenleaf. She returned to bed thinking that if the Greenleaf boys had risen in the world it was because she had given their father employment when no one else would have him. She had had Mr. Greenleaf fifteen years but no one else would have him five minutes. Just the way he approached an object was enough to tell anybody with eyes what kind of a worker he was. He walked with a high shouldered creep and he never appeared to come directly forward. He walked on the perimeter of some invisible circle and if you wanted to look him in the face, you had to move and get in front of him. She had not fired him because she had always doubted she could do better. He was too shiftless to go out and look for another job; he didn't have the initiative to steal, after she had told him three or four times to do a thing, he did it; but he never told her about a sick cow until it was too late to call the veterinarian and if her barn had caught fire, he would have called his wife to see the flames before he began to put them out. And of the wife, she didn't even like to think. Beside the wife, Mr. Greenleaf was an aristocrat.

"If hit had been my boys," he would have said, "they would have cut off their right arm before they would have allowed their maw to. . . ."   8

"If your boys had any pride, Mr. Greenleaf," she would like to say to him some day, "there are many things that they would not allow their mother to do."   9

The next morning as soon as Mr. Greenleaf came to the back door, she told him there was a stray bull on the place and that she wanted him penned at once.   10

"Done already been here three days," he said, addressing his right foot which he held forward, turned slightly as if he were trying to look at the sole. He was standing at the bottom of the three back steps while she leaned out the kitchen door, a small woman with pale near-sighted eyes and grey hair that rose on top like the crest of some disturbed bird.   11

"Three days!" she said in the restrained screech that had become habitual with her.   12

Mr. Greenleaf, looking into the distance over the near pasture, removed a package of cigarets from his shirt pocket and let one fall into his hand. He put the package back and stood for a while looking at the cigaret. "I put him in the bull pen but he torn out of there," he said presently. "I didn't see him none after that." He bent over the cigaret and lit it and then turned his head briefly in her direction. The upper part of his face sloped gradually into the lower which was long and narrow, shaped like a rough chalice. He had deep-set fox-colored eyes shadowed under a grey felt hat that he wore slanted forward following the line of his nose. His build was insignificant.   13

"Mr. Greenleaf," she said, "get the bull up this morning before you do anything else. You know he'll ruin the breeding schedule. Get him up and keep him up and the next time there's a stray bull on this place, tell me at once. Do you understand?"   14

"Where do you want him put at?" Mr. Greenleaf asked.   15

"I don't care where you put him," she said. "You are supposed to have some sense. Put him where he can't get out. Whose bull is he?"   16

For a moment Mr. Greenleaf seemed to hesitate between silence and speech. He studied the air to the left of him. "He must be somebody's bull," he said after a while.   17

"Yes, he must!" she said and shut the door with a precise little slam.   18

She went into the dining room where the two boys were eating breakfast and sat   19 down on the edge of her chair at the head of the table. She never ate breakfast but she sat with them to see that they had what they wanted. "Honestly!" she said, and began to tell about the bull, aping Mr. Greenleaf saying, "It must be somebody's bull."

Wesley continued to read the newspaper folded beside his plate but Scofield interrupted his eating from time to time to look at her and laugh. The two boys never had the same reaction to anything. They were as different, she said, as night and day. The only thing they did have in common was neither of them cared what happened on the place. Scofield was a business type and Wesley was an intellectual. 20

Wesley, the younger child, had had rheumatic fever when he was seven and Mrs. May thought that this was what had caused him to be an intellectual. Scofield, who had never had a day's sickness in his life, was an insurance salesman. She would not have minded his selling insurance if he had sold a nicer kind but he sold the kind that only Negroes buy. He was what Negroes call a "policy man." He said there was more money in nigger-insurance than any other kind, and before company, he was very loud about it. He would shout, "Mama don't like to hear me say it but I'm the best nigger-insurance salesman in this county!" 21

Scofield was thirty-six and he had a broad pleasant face but he was not married. "Yes," Mrs. May would say, "and if you sold decent insurance, some nice girl would be willing to marry you. What nice girl wants to marry a nigger-insurance man? You'll wake up some day and it'll be too late." 22

And at this Scofield would yodel and say, "Why Mamma, I'm not going to marry until you're dead and gone and then I'm going to marry me some nice fat girl that can take over this place!" And once he had added, "—some nice lady like Mrs. Greenleaf." When he had said this Mrs. May had risen from her chair, her back stiff as a rake handle, and had gone to her room. There she had sat down on the edge of her bed for some time with her small face drawn. Finally she had whispered, "I work and slave, I struggle and sweat to keep this place for them and as soon as I'm dead, they'll marry trash and bring it in here and ruin everything. They'll marry trash and ruin everything I've done," and she had made up her mind at that moment to change her will. The next day she had gone to her lawyer and had had the property entailed so that if they married, they could not leave it to their wives. 23

The idea that one of them might marry a woman even remotely like Mrs. Greenleaf was enough to make her ill. She had put up with Mr. Greenleaf for fifteen years, but the only way she had endured his wife had been by keeping entirely out of her sight. Mrs. Greenleaf was large and loose. The yard around her house looked like a dump and her five girls were always filthy; even the youngest one dipped snuff. Instead of making a garden or washing their clothes, her preoccupation was what she called "prayer healing." 24

Every day she cut all the morbid stories out of the newspaper—the accounts of women who had been raped and criminals who had escaped and children who had been burned and of train wrecks and plane crashes and the divorces of movie stars. She took these to the woods and dug a hole and buried them and then she fell on the 25

181

ground over them and mumbled and groaned for an hour or so, moving her huge arms back and forth under her and out again and finally just lying down flat and, Mrs. May suspected, going to sleep in the dirt.

She had not found out about this until the Greenleafs had been with her a few months. One morning she had been out to inspect a field that she wanted planted in rye but that had come up in clover because Mr. Greenleaf had used the wrong seeds in the grain drill. She was returning through a wooded path that separated two pastures, muttering to herself and hitting the ground methodically with a long stick she carried in case she saw a snake. "Mr. Greenleaf," she was saying in a low voice, "I cannot afford to pay for your mistakes. I am a poor woman and this place is all I have. I have two boys to educate. I cannot…" 26

Out of nowhere a guttural agonized voice groaned, "Jesus! Jesus!" In a second it came again with a terrible urgency. "Jesus! Jesus!" 27

Mrs. May stopped still, one hand lifted to her throat. The sound was so piercing that she felt as if some violent unleashed force had broken out of the ground and was charging toward her. Her second thought was more reasonable: somebody had been hurt on the place and would sue her for everything she had. She had no insurance. She rushed forward and turning a bend in the path, she saw Mrs. Greenleaf sprawled on her hands and knees off the side of the road, her head down. 28

"Mrs. Greenleaf!" she shrilled, "what's happened?" 29

Mrs. Greenleaf raised her head. Her face was a patchwork of dirt and tears and her small eyes, the color of two field peas, were red-rimmed and swollen, but her expression was as composed as a bulldog's. She swayed back and forth on her hands and knees and groaned, "Jesus, Jesus." 30

Mrs. May winced. She thought the word, Jesus, should be kept inside the church building like other words inside the bedroom. She was a good Christian woman with a large respect for religion, though she did not, of course, believe any of it was true. "What is the matter with you?" she asked sharply. 31

"You broke my healing," Mrs. Greenleaf said, waving her aside. "I can't talk to you until I finish." 32

Mrs. May stood, bent forward, her mouth open and her stick raised off the ground as if she were not sure what she wanted to strike with it. 33

"Oh, Jesus, stab me in the heart!" Mrs. Greenleaf shrieked. "Jesus, stab me in the heart!" and she fell back flat in the dirt, a huge human mound, her legs and arms spread out as if she were trying to wrap them around the earth. 34

Mrs. May felt as furious and helpless as if she had been insulted by a child. 35

"Jesus," she said, drawing herself back, "would be ashamed of you. He would tell you to get up from there this instant and go wash your children's clothes!" and she had turned and walked off as fast as she could. 36

Whenever she thought of how the Greenleaf boys had advanced in the world, she had only to think of Mrs. Greenleaf sprawled obscenely on the ground and say to herself, "Well, no matter how far they go, they came from that."

She would like to have been able to put in her will that when she died, Wesley and Scofield were not to continue to employ Mr. Greenleaf. She was capable of handling Mr. Greenleaf; they were not. Mr. Greenleaf had pointed out to her once that her boys didn't know hay from silage. She had pointed out to him that they had other talents, that Scofield was a successful businessman and Wesley a successful intellectual. Mr. Greenleaf did not comment, but he never lost an opportunity of letting her see, by his expression or some simple gesture, that he held the two of them in infinite contempt. As sub-human as the Greenleafs were, he never hesitated to let her know that in any like circumstance in which his own boys might have been involved, they—O. T. and E. T. Greenleaf —would have acted to better advantage.

38

The Greenleaf boys were two or three years younger than the May boys. They were twins and you never knew when you spoke to one of them whether you were speaking to O. T. or E. T., and they never had the politeness to enlighten you. They were long-legged and raw-boned and red-skinned, with bright grasping fox-colored eyes like their father's. Mr. Greenleaf's pride in them began with the fact they were twins. He acted, Mrs. May said, as if this were something smart they had thought of themselves. They were energetic and hard-working and she would admit to anyone that they had come a long way—and that the Second World War was responsible for it.

39

They had both joined the service and, disguised in their uniforms, they could not be told from other people's children. You could tell, of course, when they opened their mouths but they did that seldom. The smartest thing they had done was to get sent overseas and there to marry French wives. They hadn't married French trash either. They had married nice girls who naturally couldn't tell that they murdered the king's English or that the Greenleafs were who they were.

40

Wesley's heart condition had not permitted him to serve his country but Scofield had been in the army for two years. He had not cared for it and at the end of his military service, he was only a Private First Class. The Greenleaf boys were both some kind of sergeants, and Mr. Greenleaf, in those days, had never lost an opportunity of referring to them by their rank. They had both managed to get wounded and now they both had pensions. Further, as soon as they were released from the army, they took advantage of all the benefits and went to the school of agriculture at the university— the tax-payers meanwhile supporting their French wives. The two of them were living now about two miles down the highway on a piece of land that the government had helped them to buy and in a brick duplex bungalow that the government had helped to build and pay for. If the war had made anyone, Mrs. May said, it had made the Greenleaf boys. They each had three little children apiece, who spoke Greenleaf English and French, and who, on account of their mothers' background, would be sent to the convent school and brought up with manners. "And in twenty years," Mrs. May asked Scofield and Wesley, "do you know what those people will be?

41

"Society," she said blackly. 42

She spent fifteen years coping with Mr. Greenleaf and, by now, handling him had 43
become second nature with her. His disposition on any particular day was as much a
factor in what she could and couldn't do as the weather was, and she had learned to
read his face the way real country people read the sunrise and sunset.

She was a country woman only by persuasion. The late Mr. May, a businessman, 44
had bought the place when land was down, and when he died it was all he had to leave
her. The boys had not been happy to move to the country to a broken-down farm, but
there was nothing else for her to do. She had the timber on the place cut and with the
proceeds had set herself up in the dairy business after Mr. Greenleaf had answered her
ad. "i seen yor add and i will come have 2 boys," was all his letter said, but he arrived
the next day in a pieced-together truck, his wife and five daughters sitting on the floor
in the back, himself and the two boys in the cab.

Over the years they had been on her place, Mr. and Mrs. Greenleaf had aged 45
hardly at all. They had no worries, no responsibilities. They lived like the lilies of the
field, off the fat that she struggled to put into the land. When she was dead and gone
from overwork and worry, the Greenleafs, healthy and thriving, would be just ready to
begin draining Scofield and Wesley.

Wesley said the reason Mrs. Greenleaf had not aged was because she released all 46
her emotions in prayer healing. "You ought to start praying, Sweetheart," he had said in
the voice that, poor boy, he could not help making deliberately nasty.

Scofield only exasperated her beyond endurance but Wesley caused her real 47
anxiety. He was thin and nervous and bald and being an intellectual was a terrible
strain on his disposition. She doubted if he would marry until she died but she was
certain that then the wrong woman would get him. Nice girls didn't like Scofield but
Wesley didn't like nice girls. He didn't like anything. He drove twenty miles every day
to the university where he taught and twenty miles back every night, but he said he
hated the twenty-mile drive and he hated the second-rate university and he hated the
morons who attended it. He hated the country and he hated the life he lived; he hated
living with his mother and his idiot brother and he hated hearing about the damn
dairy and the damn help and the damn broken machinery. But in spite of all he said,
he never made any move to leave. He talked about Paris and Rome but he never went
even to Atlanta.

"You'd go to those places and you'd get sick," Mrs. May would say. "Who in Paris 48
is going to see that you get a salt-free diet? And do you think if you married one of
those odd numbers you take out that she would cook a salt-free diet for you? No
indeed, she would not!" When she took this line, Wesley would turn himself roughly
around in his chair and ignore her. Once when she had kept it up too long, he had
snarled, "Well, why don't you do something practical, Woman? Why don't you pray for
me like Mrs. Greenleaf would?"

"I don't like to hear you boys make jokes about religion," she had said. "If you 49
would go to church, you would meet some nice girls."

But it was impossible to tell them anything. When she looked at the two of them now, sitting on either side of the table, neither one caring the least if a stray bull ruined her herd—which was their herd, their future—when she looked at the two of them, one hunched over a paper and the other teetering back in his chair, grinning at her like an idiot, she wanted to jump up and beat her fist on the table and shout, "You'll find out one of these days, you'll find out what Reality is when it's too late!" 50

"Mamma," Scofield said, "don't you get excited now but I'll tell you whose bull that is." He was looking at her wickedly. He let his chair drop forward and he got up. Then with his shoulders bent and his hands held up to cover his head, he tiptoed to the door. He backed into the hall and pulled the door almost to so that it hid all of him but his face. "You want to know, Sugar-pie?" he asked. 51

Mrs. May sat looking at him coldly. 52

"That's O. T. and E. T.'s bull," he said. "I collected from their nigger yesterday and he told me they were missing it," and he showed her an exaggerated expanse of teeth and disappeared silently. 53

Wesley looked up and laughed. 54

Mrs. May turned her head forward again, her expression unaltered. "I am the only adult on this place," she said. She leaned across the table and pulled the paper from the side of his plate. "Do you see how it's going to be when I die and you boys have to handle him?" she began. "Do you see why he didn't know whose bull that was? Because it was theirs. Do you see what I have to put up with? Do you see that if I hadn't kept my foot on his neck all these years, you boys might be milking cows every morning at four o'clock?" 55

Wesley pulled the paper back toward his plate and staring at her full in the face, he murmured, "I wouldn't milk a cow to save your soul from hell." "I know you wouldn't," she said in a brittle voice. She sat back and began rapidly turning her knife over at the side of her plate. "O. T. and E. T. are fine boys," she said. "They ought to have been my sons." The thought of this was so horrible that her vision of Wesley was blurred at once by a wall of tears. All she saw was his dark shape, rising quickly from the table. "And you two," she cried, "you two should have belonged to that woman!" 56

He was heading for the door. 57

"When I die," she said in a thin voice, "I don't know what's going to become of you." 58

"You're always yapping about when-you-die," he growled as he rushed out, "but you look pretty healthy to me." 59

For some time she sat where she was, looking straight ahead through the window across the room into a scene of indistinct grays and greens. She stretched her face and her neck muscles and drew in a long breath but the scene in front of her flowed together anyway into a watery gray mass. "They needn't think I'm going to die any time soon," she muttered, and some more defiant voice in her added: I'll die when I get good and ready. 60

She wiped her eyes with the table napkin and got up and went to the window and gazed at the scene in front of her. The cows were grazing on two pale green pastures across the road and behind them, fencing them in, was a black wall of trees with a sharp sawtooth edge that held off the indifferent sky. The pastures were enough to calm her. When she looked out any window in her house, she saw the reflection of her own character. Her city friends said she was the most remarkable woman they knew, to go, practically penniless and with no experience, out to a rundown farm and make a success of it. "Everything is against you," she would say, "the weather is against you and the dirt is against you and the help is against you. They're all in league against you. There's nothing for it but an iron hand!" 61

"Look at Mamma's iron hand!" Scofield would yell and grab her arm and hold it up so that her delicate blue-veined little hand would dangle from her wrist like the head of a broken lily. The company always laughed. 62

The sun, moving over the black and white grazing cows, was just a little brighter than the rest of the sky. Looking down, she saw a darker shape that might have been its shadow cast at an angle, moving among them. She uttered a sharp cry and turned and marched out of the house. 63

Mr. Greenleaf was in the trench silo, filling a wheelbarrow. She stood on the edge and looked down at him. "I told you to get up that bull. Now he's in with the milk herd." 64

"You can't do two thangs at oncet," Mr. Greenleaf remarked. 65

"I told you to do that first." 66

He wheeled the barrow out of the open end of the trench toward the barn and she followed close behind him. "And you needn't think, Mr. Greenleaf," she said, "that I don't know exactly whose bull that is or why you haven't been in any hurry to notify me he was here. I might as well feed O. T. and E. T.'s bull as long as I'm going to have him here ruining my herd." 67

Mr. Greenleaf paused with the wheelbarrow and looked behind him. "Is that them boys' bull?" he asked in an incredulous tone. 68

She did not say a word. She merely looked away with her mouth taut. 69

"They told me their bull was out but I never known that was him," he said. 70

"I want that bull put up now," she said, "and I'm going to drive over to O. T. and E. T.'s and tell them they'll have to come get him today. I ought to charge for the time he's been here—then it wouldn't happen again." 71

"They didn't pay but seventy-five dollars for him," Mr. Greenleaf offered. 72

"I wouldn't have had him as a gift," she said. 73

"They was just going to beef him," Mr. Greenleaf went on, "but he got loose and run his head into their pickup truck. He don't like cars and trucks. They had a time 74 getting his horn out the fender and when they finally got him loose, he took off and they was too tired to run after him—but I never known that was him there."

"It wouldn't have paid you to know, Mr. Greenleaf," she said. "But you know now. Get a horse and get him." 75

In a half hour, from her front window she saw the bull, squirrel-colored, with jutting hips and long light horns, ambling down the dirt road that ran in front of the house. Mr. Greenleaf was behind him on the horse. "That's a Greenleaf bull if I ever saw one," she muttered. She went out on the porch and called, "Put him where he can't get out." 76

"He likes to bust loose," Mr. Greenleaf said, looking with approval at the bull's rump. "This gentleman is a sport." 77

"If those boys don't come for him, he's going to be a dead sport," she said. "I'm just warning you." 78

He heard her but he didn't answer. 79

"That's the awfullest looking bull I ever saw," she called but he was too far down the road to hear. 80

It was midmorning when she turned into O. T. and E. T.'s driveway. The house, a new red-brick, low-to-the-ground building that looked like a warehouse with windows, was on top of a treeless hill. The sun was beating down directly on the white roof of it. It was the kind of house that everybody built now and nothing marked it as belonging to Greenleafs except three dogs, part hound and part spitz, that rushed out from behind it as soon as she stopped her car. She reminded herself that you could always tell the class of people by the class of dog, and honked her horn. While she sat waiting for someone to come, she continued to study the house. All the windows were down and she wondered if the government could have air-conditioned the thing. No one came and she honked again. Presently a door opened and several children appeared in it and stood looking at her, making no move to come forward. She recognized this as a true Greenleaf trait—they could hang in the door, looking at you for hours. 81

"Can't one of you children come here?" she called. 82

After a minute they all began to move forward, slowly. They had on overalls and were barefooted but they were not as dirty as she might have expected. There were two or three that looked distinctly like Greenleafs; the others not so much so. The smallest child was a girl with untidy black hair. They stopped about six feet from the automobile and stood looking at her. 83

"You're mighty pretty," Mrs. May said, addressing herself to the smallest girl. 84

There was no answer. They appeared to share one dispassionate expression between them. 85

"Where's your Mamma?" she asked. There was no answer to this for some time. 86

Then one of them said something in French. Mrs. May did not speak French.

"Where's your daddy?" she asked.   87

After a while, one of the boys said, "He ain't hyar neither."   88

"Ahhhh," Mrs. May said as if something had been proven. "Where's the colored   89
man?"

She waited and decided no one was going to answer. "The cat has six little   90
tongues," she said. "How would you like to come home with me and let me teach you
how to talk?" She laughed and her laugh died on the silent air. She felt as if she were
on trial for her life, facing a jury of Greenleafs. "I'll go down and see if I can find the
colored man," she said.

"You can go if you want to," one of the boys said.   91

"Well, thank you," she murmured and drove off.   92

The barn was down the lane from the house. She had not seen it before but   93
Mr. Greenleaf had described it in detail for it had been built according to the latest
specifications. It was a milking parlor arrangement where the cows are milked from
below. The milk ran in pipes from the machines to the milk house and was never
carried in no bucket, Mr. Greenleaf said, by no human hand. "When you gonter get
you one?" he had asked.

"Mr. Greenleaf," she had said, "I have to do for myself. I am not assisted hand and   94
foot by the government. It would cost me $20,000 to install a milking parlor. I barely
make ends meet as it is."

"My boys done it," Mr. Greenleaf had murmured and then—"but all boys ain't   95
alike."

"No indeed!" she had said. "I thank God for that!"   96

"I thank Gawd for ever-thang," Mr. Greenleaf had drawled.   97

You might as well, she had thought in the fierce silence that followed; you've never   98
done anything for yourself.

She stopped by the side of the barn and honked but no one appeared. For several   99
minutes she sat in the car, observing the various machines parked around, wondering
how many of them were paid for. They had a forage harvester and a rotary hay baler.
She had those too. She decided that since no one was here, she would get out and have
a look at the milking parlor and see if they kept it clean.

She opened the milking room door and stuck her head in and for the first second   100
she felt as if she were going to lose her breath. The spotless white concrete room was
filled with sunlight that came from a row of windows head-high along both walls.
The metal stanchions gleamed ferociously and she had to squint to be able to look at
all. She drew her head out the room quickly and closed the door and leaned against it,
frowning. The light outside was not so bright but she was conscious that the sun was

directly on top of her head, like a silver bullet ready to drop into her brain.

A Negro carrying a yellow calf-feed bucket appeared from around the corner of the machine shed and came toward her. He was a light yellow boy dressed in the cast-off army clothes of the Greenleaf twins. He stopped at a respectable distance and set the bucket on the ground.   101

"Where's Mr. O. T. and Mr. E. T.?" she asked.   102

"Mist O. T. he in town, Mist E. T. he off yonder in the field," the Negro said, pointing first to the left and then to the right as if he were naming the position of two planets.   103

"Can you remember a message?" she asked, looking as if she thought this doubtful.   104

"I'll remember it if I don't forget it," he said with a touch of sullenness.   105

"Well, I'll write it down then," she said. She got in her car and took a stub of pencil from her pocket book and began to write on the back of an empty envelope. The Negro came and stood at the window. "I'm Mrs. May," she said as she wrote. "Their bull is on my place and I want him off today. You can tell them I'm furious about it."   106

"That bull lef here Sareday," the Negro said, "and none of us ain't seen him since. We ain't knowed where he was."   107

"Well, you know now," she said, "and you can tell Mr. O. T. and Mr. E. T. that if they don't come get him today, I'm going to have their daddy shoot him the first thing in the morning. I can't have that bull ruining my herd." She handed him the note.   108

"If I knows Mist O. T. and Mist E. T.," he said, taking it, "they goin to say go ahead on and shoot him. He done busted up one of our trucks already and we be glad to see the last of him."   109

She pulled her head back and gave him a look from slightly bleared eyes. "Do they expect me to take my time and my worker to shoot their bull?" she asked. "They don't want him so they just let him loose and expect somebody else to kill him? He's eating my oats and ruining my herd and I'm expected to shoot him too?"   110

"I speck you is," he said softly. "He done busted up..."   111

She gave him a very sharp look and said. "Well, I'm not surprised. That's just the way some people are," and after a second she asked, "Which is boss, Mr. O. T. or Mr. E. T.?" She had always suspected that they fought between themselves secretly.   112

"They never quarls," the boy said. "They like one man in two skins."   113

"Hmp. I expect you just never heard them quarrel."   114

"Nor nobody else heard them neither," he said, looking away as if this insolence were addressed to someone else.   115

"Well," she said, "I haven't put up with their father for fifteen years not to know a few things about Greenleafs."   116

The Negro looked at her suddenly with a gleam of recognition. "Is you my policy man's mother?" he asked.   117

"I don't know who your policy man is," she said sharply. "You give them that note and tell them if they don't come for that bull today, they'll be making their father shoot it tomorrow," and she drove off.   118

She stayed at home all afternoon waiting for the Greenleaf twins to come for the bull. They did not come. I might as well be working for them, she thought furiously. They are simply going to use me to the limit. At the supper table, she went over it again for the boys' benefit because she wanted them to see exactly what O. T. and E. T. would do. "They don't want that bull," she said, "—pass the butter—so they simply turn him loose and let somebody else worry about getting rid of him for them. How do you like that? I'm the victim. I've always been the victim."   119

"Pass the butter to the victim," Wesley said. He was in a worse humor than usual because he had had a flat tire on the way home from the university.   120

Scofield handed her the butter and said, "Why, Mamma, ain't you ashamed to shoot an old bull that ain't done nothing but give you a little scrub strain in your herd? I declare," he said, "with the Mamma I got it's a wonder I turned out to be such a nice boy!"   121

"You ain't her boy, Son," Wesley said.   122

She eased back in her chair, her fingertips on the edge of the table.   123

"All I know is," Scofield said, "I done mighty well to be as nice as I am seeing what I come from."   124

When they teased her they spoke Greenleaf English but Wesley made his own particular tone come through it like a knife edge. "Well lemme tell you one thang, Brother," he said, leaning over the table, "that if you had half a mind you would already know."   125

"What's that, Brother?" Scofield asked, his broad face grinning into the thin constricted one across from him.   126

"That is," Wesley said, "that neither you nor me is her boy," but he stopped abruptly as she gave a kind of hoarse wheeze like an old horse lashed unexpectedly. She reared up and ran from the room.   127

"Oh, for God's sake," Wesley growled. "what did you start her off for?"   128

"I never started her off," Scofield said. "You started her off."   129

"She's not as young as she used to be and she can't take it."   130

"She can only give it out," Wesley said. "I'm the one that takes it."   131

His brother's pleasant face had changed so that an ugly family resemblance showed between them. "Nobody feels sorry for a lousy bastard like you," he said and grabbed across the table for the other's shirtfront.   132

From her room she heard a crash of dishes and she rushed back through the kitchen into the dining room. The hall door was open and Scofield was going out of it. Wesley was lying like a large bug on his back with the edge of the overturned table cutting him across the middle and broken dishes scattered on top of him. She pulled the table off him and caught his arm to help him rise but he scrambled up and pushed her off with a furious charge of energy and flung himself out the door after his brother. 133

She would have collapsed but a knock on the door stiffened her and she swung around. Across the kitchen and back porch, she could see Mr. Greenleaf peering eagerly through the screenwire. All her resources returned in full strength as if she had only needed to be challenged by the devil himself to regain them. "I heard a thump," he called, "and I thought the plastering might have fell on you." 134

If he had been wanted someone would have had to go on a horse to find him. She crossed the kitchen and the porch and stood inside the screen and said, "No, nothing happened but the table turned over. One of the legs was weak," and without pausing, "the boys didn't come for the bull so tomorrow you'll have to shoot him." 135

The sky was crossed with thin red and purple bars and behind them the sun was moving down slowly as if it were descending a ladder. Mr. Greenleaf squatted down on the step, his back to her, the top of his hat on a level with her feet. "Tomorrow I'll drive him home for you," he said. 136

"Oh no, Mr. Greenleaf," she said in a mocking voice, "you drive him home tomorrow and next week he'll be back here. I know better than that." Then in a mournful tone, she said, "I'm surprised at O.T. and E.T. to treat me this way. I thought they'd have more gratitude. Those boys spent some mighty happy days on this place, didn't they, Mr. Greenleaf?" 137

Mr. Greenleaf didn't say anything. 138

"I think they did," she said. "I think they did. But they've forgotten all the nice little things I did for them now. If I recall, they wore my boys' old clothes and played with my boys' old toys and hunted with my boys' old guns. They swam in my pond and shot my birds and fished in my stream and I never forgot their birthday and Christmas seemed to roll around very often if I remember it right. And do they think of any of those things now?" she asked. "NOOOOO," she said. 139

For a few seconds she looked at the disappearing sun and Mr. Greenleaf examined the palms of his hands. Presently as if it had just occurred to her, she asked, "Do you know the real reason they didn't come for that bull?" 140

"Naw I don't," Mr. Greenleaf said in a surly voice. 141

"They didn't come because I'm a woman," she said. "You can get away with anything when you're dealing with a woman. If there were a man running this place..." 142

Quick as a snake striking Mr. Greenleaf said, "You got two boys. They know you got two men on the place." 143

The sun had disappeared behind the tree line. She looked down at the dark crafty 144 face, upturned now, and at the wary eyes, bright under the shadow of the hatbrim. She waited long enough for him to see that she was hurt and then she said, "Some people learn gratitude too late, Mr. Greenleaf, and some never learn it at all," and she turned and left him sitting on the steps.

Half the night in her sleep she heard a sound as if some large stone were grinding a hole on the outside wall of her brain. She was walking on the inside, over a succession of beautiful rolling hills, planting her stick in front of each step. She became aware after a time that the noise was the sun trying to burn through the tree line and she stopped to watch, safe in the knowledge that it couldn't, that it had to sink the way it always did outside of her property. When she first stopped it was a swollen red ball, but as she stood watching it began to narrow and pale until it looked like a bullet. Then suddenly it burst through the tree line and raced down the hill toward her. She woke up with her hand over her mouth and the same noise, diminished but distinct, in her ear. It was the bull munching under her window. Mr. Greenleaf had let him out. 145

She got up and made her way to the window in the dark and looked out through the slit blind, but the bull had moved away from the hedge and at first she didn't see him. Then she saw a heavy form some distance away, paused as if observing her. This is the last night I am going to put up with this, she said, and watched until the iron shadow moved away in the darkness. 146

The next morning she waited until exactly eleven o'clock. Then she got in her car and drove to the barn. Mr. Greenleaf was cleaning milk cans. He had seven of them standing up outside the milk room to get the sun. She had been telling him to do this for two weeks. "All right, Mr. Greenleaf," she said, "go get your gun. We're going to shoot that bull." 147

"I thought you wanted theseyer cans…" 148

"Go get your gun, Mr. Greenleaf," she said. Her voice and face were expressionless. 149

"That gentleman torn out of there last night," he murmured in a tone of regret and bent again to the can he had his arm in. 150

"Go get your gun, Mr. Greenleaf," she said in the same triumphant toneless voice. "The bull is in the pasture with the dry cows. I saw him from my upstairs window. I'm going to drive you up to the field and you can run him into the empty pasture and shoot him there." 151

He detached himself from the can slowly. "Ain't nobody ever ast me to shoot my boys' own bull!" he said in a high rasping voice. He removed a rag from his back pocket and began to wipe his hands violently, then his nose. 152

She turned as if she had not heard this and said, "I'll wait for you in the car. Go get your gun." 153

She sat in the car and watched him stalk off toward the harness room where he kept a gun. After he had entered the room, there was a crash as if he had kicked something out of his way. Presently he emerged again with the gun, circled behind the 154 car, opened the door violently and threw himself onto the seat beside her. He held the gun between his knees and looked straight ahead. He'd like to shoot me instead of the bull, she thought, and turned her face away so that he could not see her smile.

The morning was dry and clear. She drove through the woods for a quarter of a mile and then out into the open where there were fields on either side of the narrow road. The exhilaration of carrying her point had sharpened her senses. Birds were screaming everywhere, the grass was almost too bright to look at, the sky was an even piercing blue. "Spring is here!" she said gaily. Mr. Greenleaf lifted one muscle somewhere near his mouth as if he found this the most asinine remark ever made. When she stopped at the second pasture gate, he flung himself out of the car door and slammed it behind him. 155

Then he opened the gate and she drove through. He closed it and flung himself back in, silently, and she drove around the rim of the pasture until she spotted the bull, almost in the center of it, grazing peacefully among the cows. 156

"The gentleman is waiting on you," she said and gave Mr. Greenleaf's furious profile a sly look. "Run him into that next pasture and when you get him in, I'll drive in behind you and shut the gate myself." 157

He flung himself out again, this time deliberately leaving the car door open so that she had to lean across the seat and close it. She sat smiling as she watched him make his way across the pasture toward the opposite gate. He seemed to throw himself forward at each step and then pull back as if he were calling on some power to witness that he was being forced. "Well," she said aloud as if he were still in the car, "it's your own boys who are making you do this, Mr. Greenleaf." O. T. and E. T were probably splitting their sides laughing at him now. She could hear their identical nasal voices saying, "Made Daddy shoot our bull for us. Daddy don't know no better than to think that's a fine bull he's shooting. Gonna kill Daddy to shoot that bull!" 158

"If those boys cared a thing about you, Mr. Greenleaf," she said, "they would have come for that bull. I'm surprised at them." 159

He was circling around to open the gate first. The bull, dark among the spotted cows, had not moved. He kept his head down, eating constantly. Mr. Greenleaf opened the gate and then began circling back to approach him from the rear. When he was about ten feet behind him, he flapped his arms at his sides. The bull lifted his head indolently and then lowered it again and continued to eat. Mr. Greenleaf stooped again and picked up something and threw it at him with a vicious swing. She decided it was a sharp rock for the bull leapt and then began to gallop until he disappeared over the rim of the hill. Mr. Greenleaf followed at his leisure. 160

"You needn't think you're going to lose him!" she cried and started the car straight across the pasture. She had to drive slowly over the terraces and when she reached the gate, Mr. Greenleaf and the bull were nowhere in sight. This pasture was smaller than the last, a green arena, encircled almost entirely by woods. She got out and closed the gate and stood looking for some sign of Mr. Greenleaf but he had disappeared completely. She knew at once that his plan was to lose the bull in the woods. 161

Eventually, she would see him emerge somewhere from the circle of trees and come limping toward her and when he finally reached her, he would say, "If you can find that gentleman in them woods, you're better than me."

She was going to say, "Mr. Greenleaf, if I have to walk into those woods with you and stay all afternoon, we are going to find that bull and shoot him. You are going to shoot him if I have to pull the trigger for you." When he saw she meant business, he would return and shoot the bull quickly himself. 162

She got back into the car and drove to the center of the pasture where he would not have so far to walk to reach her when he came out of the woods. At this moment she could picture him sitting on a stump, making lines in the ground with a stick. She decided she would wait exactly ten minutes by her watch. Then she would begin to honk. She got out of the car and walked around a little and then sat down on the front bumper to wait and rest. She was very tired and she lay her head back against the hood and closed her eyes. She did not understand why she should be so tired when it was only mid-morning. Through her closed eyes, she could feel the sun, red-hot overhead. She opened her eyes slightly but the white light forced her to close them again. 163

For some time she lay back against the hood, wondering drowsily why she was so tired. With her eyes closed, she didn't think of time as divided into days and nights but into past and future. She decided she was tired because she had been working continuously for fifteen years. She decided she had every right to be tired, and to rest for a few minutes before she began working again. Before any kind of Judgment seat, she would be able to say: I've worked, I have not wallowed. At this very instant while she was recalling a lifetime of work, Mr. Greenleaf was loitering in the woods and Mrs. Greenleaf was probably flat on the ground, asleep over her holeful of clippings. The woman had got worse over the years and Mrs. May believed that now she was actually demented. "I'm afraid your wife has let religion warp her," she said once tactfully to Mr. Greenleaf. "Everything in moderation, you know." 164

"She cured a man oncet that half his gut was eat out with worms," Mr. Greenleaf said, and she had turned away, half-sickened. Poor souls, she thought now, so simple. For a few seconds she dozed. 165

When she sat up and looked at her watch, more than ten minutes had passed. She had not heard any shot. A new thought occurred to her; suppose Mr. Greenleaf had aroused the bull chunking stones at him and the animal had turned on him and run him up against a tree and gored him? The irony of it deepened: O. T. and E. T. would then get a shyster lawyer and sue her. It would be the fitting end to her fifteen years with the Greenleafs. She thought of it almost with pleasure as if she had hit on the perfect ending for a story she was telling her friends. Then she dropped it, for Mr. Greenleaf had a gun with him and she had insurance. 166

She decided to honk. She got up and reached inside the car window and gave three sustained honks and two or three shorter ones to let him know she was getting impatient. Then she went back and sat down on the bumper again. 167

In a few minutes something emerged from the tree line, a black heavy shadow that tossed its head several times and then bounded forward. After a second she saw it was the bull. He was crossing the pasture toward her at a slow gallop, a gay almost rocking gait as if he were overjoyed to find her again. She looked beyond him to see if Mr. Greenleaf was coming out of the woods too but he was not. "Here he is, Mr. Greenleaf!" she called and looked on the other side of the pasture to see if he could be coming out there but he was not in sight. She looked back and saw that the bull, his head lowered, was racing toward her. She remained perfectly still, not in fright, but in a freezing disbelief. She stared at the violent black streak bounding toward her as if she had no sense of distance, as if she could not decide at once what his intention was, and the bull had buried his head in her lap, like a wild tormented lover, before her expression changed. One of his horns sank until it pierced her heart and the other curved around her side and held her in an unbreakable grip. She continued to stare straight ahead but the entire scene in front of her had changed—the tree line was a dark wound in a world that was nothing but sky—and she had the look of a person whose sight has been suddenly restored but who finds the light unbearable. 168

Mr. Greenleaf was running toward her from the side with his gun raised and she saw him coming though she was not looking in his direction. She saw him approaching on the outside of some invisible circle, the tree line gaping behind him and nothing under his feet. He shot the bull four times through the eye. She did not hear the shots but she felt the quake in the huge body as it sank, pulling her forward on its head, so that she seemed, when Mr. Greenleaf reached her, to be bent over whispering some last discovery into the animal's ear. 169

Analyzing Richard Giannone's Scholarly Article

Having recorded your first impressions of "Greenleaf" in your journal, you're ready now to consider the questions raised by Richard Giannone in his published research on O'Connor's story, printed below. As you read Giannone's article, see if you can identify the question that generated his research and the problem that emerged from his question. Also, pay close attention to how Giannone uses evidence from the story to support his thesis, that O'Connor has written a "story of Lent." Following the story, you will find an analysis of Giannone's rhetorical strategies and of his care in documenting his research.

*I am grateful to NEH for a travel grant to study the material in The Flannery O'Connor Collection at Georgia College and to the staff of the Russell Library at Georgia College for their hospitality.
1. Flannery O'Connor, *The Habit of Being*, ed. Sally Fitzgerald (New York:Farrar, Straus and Giroux, 1979), p. 146.
2. Ibid, p. 129.
3. Ibid., p. 149.

"'Greenleaf': A Story of Lent"

Richard Giannone

Save me from the mouth of the lion,
my afflicted soul from the horns of
the wild oxen!

—Psalm 22

Among the nine stories that Flannery O'Connor chose for her final volume *Everything That Rises Must Converge* (1965), "Greenleaf" was the first to appear in print. *Kenyan Review* published "Greenleaf" in the summer of 1956. The 0. Henry Awards in the following year honored O'Connor with the first prize for the story, and "Greenleaf" has continued to make its way into prize collections and anthologies for study ever since. The interest accorded the story over the years confirms O'Connor's own judgment of "Greenleaf" as a "good story."[1]

A good story for O'Connor is a well-crafted story. On those rare occasions when she says that her art meets her standards, O'Connor draws satisfaction not from some startling event, for which her writing is famous, but from the way in which the action fulfills the requirements of form so that a concealed skill creates a necessary action. "I am very happy right now writing a story ["Greenleaf"] in which I plan for the heroine, aged 63, to be gored by a bull," she writes in January, 1956, to her friend "A"; and she goes on to say that "it is going to take some doing to do it and it may be the risk that is making me happy."[2] The peril lies in resorting to manipulation to make the bizarre seem inevitable. With "Greenleaf" the danger of contrivance besets O'Connor to the end. She repeats her concern to "A" in late March of 1956: "My preoccupations are technical. My preoccupation is how I am going to get this bull's horn into this woman's ribs."[3]

Scholars do not share O'Connor's enthusiasm for "Greenleaf." The critical consensus is that she does not master the technical challenge that she perceives and therefore that she fails to embody her fundamental meaning in the physical action.

4. Kathleen Feeley, *Flannery O'Connor: Voice of the Peacock*, 2nd ed. (New York: Fordham University Press, 1982), p. 98.
5. Josephine Hendin, *The World of Flannery O'Connor* (Bloomington: Indiana University Press, 1970), p. 115.
6. Robert Drake, *Flannery O'Connor: A Critical Essay* (Grand Rapids: William B. Eerdmans, 1966), p. 28.
7. Melvin J. Friedman, "Introduction," *The Added Dimension: The Art and Mind of Flannery O'Connor*, eds. Melvin J. Friedman and Lewis A. Lawson (New York: Fordham University Press, 1966), p. 19.
8. Leon V. Driskell and Joan T. Brittain, *The Eternal Crossroads: The Art of Flannery O'Connor* (Lexington: University of Kentucky Press, 1971), p. 125.
9. Dorothy Walters, *Flannery O'Connor* (New York: Twayne, 1973), p. 138.
10. Melvin J. Friedman, *The Added Dimension*, p. 18.
11. The earliest record of Flannery O'Connor's reading Pierre Teilhard de Chardin is her copy of Teilhard's *The Divine Milieu*, (New York: Harper, 1960), in which she wrote "1960" after her signature. Four of the nine stories in *Everything That Rises Must Converge* were published before she read Teilhard. The chronology confirms what O'Connor's writing suggests: her enthusiasm for Teilhard's scientific and autobiographical essays derives from her meeting a kindred mind. The spirituality of the French Jesuit expands and authenticates theological ideas that O'Connor herself has been working with all along.

Even a reader who is sympathetic to the spiritual thrust of "Greenleaf" finds "an unsettling ambiguity in the story's end" because the heroine's discovery suggests both "the illumination of grace and the rejection of it."[4] Less congenial discussions do not pause to consider the possibility of value, either ambiguous or explicit, in the ending. One reader turns O'Connor's theology into its opposite: the bull "may be Christ . . . yet his crucifixion of the lady on his horns results in a perception of nothingness."[5] Another reader goes a step further to say that the goring does not convey "the obvious Christian implications" that pervade O'Connor's stories.[6] Then—there is the usual reduction of her complexity into another "grotesque" ending which turns on a "dreadful stroke of irony."[7] The grander evasions distill "Greenleaf" into allegory, making it either a tract on "the Jansenist doctrines of original sin and carnality"[8] or a Snopesian tale of the political transformation of the postwar South.[9]

By and large, "Greenleaf" receives short shrift from critics. The most generous estimate is a passing remark calling the story a bridge between O'Connor's first collection, *A Good Man Is Hard To Find* (1955), and her last, published ten years later.[10] The idea of approaching "Greenleaf" through its contribution to O'Connor's growth is well taken, so long as one does not remand the story to the harmless irrelevancy of place in her canon. "Greenleaf"' is a watershed, in point of fact. If we begin with O'Connor's judgment that "Greenleaf" is a fully realized story, we can not only inquire into the special passion of its drama, but also see how its perplexing conclusion is the earliest expression of O'Connor's valedictory proposal that everything that rises must converge.[11] She gets the bull's horns into the woman's ribs in a way that joins the sixty-three year old heroine with the raising power of God.

The woman is Mrs. May. Until the ending, she remains unaware of having any special appointment with God. The story begins with the intrusion of the latest of many nuisances in her weary life. The steady sound of a bull chewing grass outside Mrs. May's bedroom window interrupts her sleep, and she is annoyed. But the animal is no ordinary stray. The bull stands "silvered in the moonlight. . . his head raised as if he listened—like some patient god come down to woo her—for a stir inside the room."[12] The intruder comes dressed to court. A prickly hedge-wreath crowns his horns, which he tips to the lady in her boudoir. For her part, Mrs. May has nothing but scorn for the bull; and yet she also seems to be getting herself ready for him. Bending forward to peek at him through the venetian blind, Mrs. May can be seen with her hair set with curlers surrounding her face made up with egg-white astringent to smooth her wrinkles. Her bovine face suggests that the bull has come to the right mate to make his suit. Even her outworn coquetry seems fitting for this admirer. The bull himself is old and scrawny. "'Some nigger's scrub bull" (25), mutters the fine Mrs. May. If the situation is a cartoon version of some ancient cultus, romance is nevertheless in the air. O'Connor brings them together in the end locked in an embrace. One horn of the "wild tormented lover" (52) pierces Mrs. May's heart, and his other horn hugs her around her side.

---

12. *Everything That Rises Must Converge* (1965; Noonday ed., New York: Farrar, Straus and Giroux, 1968), p. 24. Hereafter pages are cited within the body of the text

O'Connor's undercutting the noble with the earthy tells us a great deal about   6
the way in which Mrs. May lands in her lover's grip. She must unlearn her disdain
to remove the impediments to the kind of grace that she is experiencing with the
mongrel bull. What justifies her attitude of superiority is her property. Mrs. May is the
very example of the proprietress, and she is proud of it. Another of O'Connor's hard-
working widows, she has labored fifteen years to make a go of her marginal dairy farm
and to raise and educate her sons, Scofield and Wesley. Turning the broken-down farm
that Mr. May left her into a profitable operation is accomplished against great odds.
The failing land, two hostile sons, debt, nature's vagary, and a shiftless employee named
Mr. Greenleaf conspire against Mrs. May. Her effort, nevertheless, remains undaunted
because her fear remains unabated. Loss of property is not, of course, the real threat,
as she thinks it is; nor is survival an issue. Mrs. May is much closer to the end of her
struggle than she is to the beginning of it; and even without the help of her selfish
sons, she has more than enough to see her through. Some deeper uncertainty than
money stalks her, some sharper alienation than being a city woman running a farm
makes her cling to the land. And because she is incapable of being grateful for what
she does have, Mrs. May heightens her anxiety by internalizing her fear and thereby
dooms herself to feeling singled out for abuse. "I'm the victim. I'm always the victim"
(44), she sighs to Scofield and Wesley at supper, simply because the bull's owners do
not immediately obey her order to remove it. Her practiced self-sorrow elicits only her
sons' bored loathing, and Mrs. May can feel used to the limit.

It does not occur to Mrs. May that the need for security and the desire to go   7
beyond oneself—for transcendence, really—are common to human striving. She
feels alone and defends her cherished uniqueness by projecting her very human
but altogether unexamined fear onto others, especially those who impose upon her
hospitality without sharing in the cost involved. Her incessant grievances crystallize
in the name Greenleaf. Greenleaf stands for all the last straws piled on her back. Mr.
Greenleaf's sons own the scrub bull which reminds Mrs. May of all the hogs of other
people that destroy "her oats," of their mules that roam on "her lawn," and of their
bulls that breed "her cows" (26). Creation exists as so many objects to which she can
affix the adjective *her*. She clutches her possession as though her entire life were bound
in her little house and acreage. From her besieged shelter, Mrs. May, when distressed,
can look out any window to draw solace from her pastures; but the calm she finds
comes less from the pastures' vital freshness than from "the reflection" she sees "of her
own character" (37).

The bull is a messenger sent to invade the fortress that Mrs. May has built around   8
her narcissistic rule. No person or power has yet overcome her defense, so the mission is
hard. But the bull has only to be itself, and Mrs. May's paranoia will complete the task of
destruction. Her fear turns anything not under her control into a threat. It even shapes
the message of the night. As she sleeps, an animal's chewing becomes an enemy "eating
one wall of the house" (25), an encroachment which swells into the inimical power that
has been devouring her effort since she moved to the farm. She can control what is not
hers by turning it into a symbol and dealing with the meaning she assigns to it. The bull,

---

13. *The Habit of Being*, p. 148.

in this instance, whose stud days seem behind him, is more interested in grass than Mrs. May's cows; but as a symbol, he is the menace of fifteen years with horn.

If Mrs. May is the victim she claims to be, she exacts a price for her pains. She believes that nature and people owe her acquiesence as repayment for her hardship. When her due is not forthcoming, she demands it. "'All right, Mr. Greenleaf,'" she declares at her wit's end, "'go get your gun. We're going to shoot that bull'" (47). Behind her command lies the assumption that she is the injured one trying to keep order and prosperity and a breeding schedule, while others are living on her industry and causing chaos. She sits in the judgment seat. The world and its freeloading inhabitants stand guilty before her. When taking matters into her already full hands, Mrs. May approaches the bull with the zeal of an exterminator on pest control. One does not trifle, of course, even with a scarecrow of a bull. Nor does one toy with imposing guilt on others. No one submits to Mrs. May's tactics. Mr. Greenleaf in particular ducks the false guilt that Mrs. May tries to place on him. The story of her fight to oust the bull is the story of her demands denounced and reversed so that she takes the bull and her guilt for bullying others into her bosom.

Mrs. May browbeats people with her property and assails them with debasing images. Seen through her "pale near-sighted eyes" (27), Mr. Greenleaf is a charity case. His sons O.T. and E.T. may have done more than their father, but they could not have risen in the world without Mrs. May's keeping their father on her payroll. Moreover, her taxes paid for the war in which they fought and supported their French wives while the boys took advantage of the government's veteran benefits to study agriculture at the state-funded university. Their mother is even worse. She is a prayer healer. Everyday she clips newspaper articles of disasters and prays for the salvation of the victims. Whatever motivates Mrs. Greenleaf to intercede for these unknown sufferers is of no interest to Mrs. May. She dismisses Mrs. Greenleaf as the kind who neglects washing clothes to sprawl and scream in the woods. Her carrying on about Jesus repels Mrs. May, "a good Christian woman with a large respect for religion, though she did not, of course, believe any of it was true" (31). Of course. Belief costs, and Mrs. May is unwilling to pay. Her violent dislike of Mrs. Greenleaf, whom O'Connor calls "a sympathetic character" in her letters,[13] is not a matter of principle but a strategy of self-defense. Mrs. Greenleaf pays the price of her faith. "'Oh Jesus, stab me in the heart!'"(31) she shrieks. She heals by assuming the affliction of the victims. As a living reminder of the sacrifice that Mrs. May tries to shun, Mrs. Greenleaf can best repay the good Christian woman for her largesse to the Greenleafs by staying out of her sight.

Mrs. May sees her own sons as traitors. They could at least lend an ear to her travails. After raising them through childhood and boarding both in adulthood (not to mention seeing to Wesley's salt-free diet), she has a right to ask that they be respectful and be successful. At the very least, they should show her a grateful disposition. The price of filial piety, however, is so exorbitant that Scofield and Wesley go out of their way to mock her expectations. Scofield is a policy man, an embarrassment for whom Mrs. May must supply excuses. Wesley, the emaciated academic, strains her with his hateful temper. When not brawling, they can share in the fun of taunting her. Telling

9

10

11

her, for example, that the detested bull belongs to the hated Greenleaf boys gives them particular delight. Mrs. May shows a knowledge of their emotional maturity in imagining that her sons will marry "'trash'"(29) just to destroy everything that she has done. Spite is synonymous with May. Even if the suspicion proves untrue, it justifies Mrs. May's having the lawyer entail her property so that the spectral trash-wives will not inherit her farm.

Fearful at times to the point of personal cowardice, Mrs. May nevertheless demonstrates stubborn courage to act openly in defending what she takes to be the principles of justice. She storms O.T. and E.T.'s place to leave a message that they promptly remove the bull from her farm. As the grandiosity of her rage meets the reality of others' indifference over a lost scrub bull, her confidence dwindles. Before a "jury" (40) of six nonplussed Greenleaf children, her commotion dissipates into an impertinent scrutiny of how the Greenleafs live. She snoops around their farm to find fault and discovers instead a showplace of efficiency. The advanced technology and spotless milking room distress her anew. Her surfacing awareness that the Greenleaf boys, sons of her hired hand and that prayer healer, are rising above her lays bare the greed behind her tenacity. Again, people have only to be themselves for Mrs. May to feel used. Any advantage or liberty enjoyed by another gives Mrs. May pain, which she turns into self-sorrow. More for others means less for her. And she pays for her covetousness. Envy of the Greenleaf boys drives her into a self-lacerating reminiscence of all that she did for those grasping ingrates—gave them her sons' old clothes, old toys and old guns, gave them "'my pond'" to swim in, gave them "'my birds'"to shoot (46). Her egotism swells into a screech of Creation herself spurned by those to whom she distributed her bounty.

The more Mrs. May is ignored, the sooner her dictatorial impulse hardens into satanic resolve. Her last despairing effort at control is to order Mr. Greenleaf to kill his sons' bull. Her excuse is the safety of the dry cow herd, but the motive is to get at the Greenleaf boys for forgetting that she remembered all their birthdays and Christmases with gifts and for their temerity in surpassing her as a manager of a dairy farm. She does not think twice about using Mr. Greenleaf for her end. The atonement of the bull through the father's hands for his sons' transgressions will be received with gloating pleasure by Mrs. May, who can disclaim responsibility for the killing by ascribing her vengeance to the indifference of the Greenleaf boys. "If those boys cared a thing about you, Mr. Greenleaf,' she said, 'they would have come for that bull. I'm surprised at them'" (49).

A real surprise is in store for Mrs. May when she accompanies Mr. Greenleaf for the slaughter. The black scrub bull that called to her the other moonlit night frolics out of the woods "as if he were overjoyed to find her again." Before Mrs.May comprehends the danger, the "black streak" romps to her and buries "his head in her lap, like a wild tormented lover" (52). The animal's smooth, natural kill drives into Mrs. May the truth about her culpability that reverses her relation to her struggle and to the cosmos. O'Connor captures her heroine's amazing turnabout through a mere shift in facial expression, by which the reader can detect the brightening of Mrs. May's inner light. As the animal bounds toward her, she stares in "freezing unbelief"; when the bull

12

13

14

spears her heart, her face opens into a look of quaking illumination, which changes again into a cooing repose when the bull, shot at last by Mr. Greenleaf for goring Mrs. May, pulls her head close to his ear. In the moment of death, Mrs. May's sight is "suddenly restored." For this restoration she must endure an "unbearable" (52) light.

A new vision is a new morality, and the light is insupportable because things are put back into their original perspective and ownership. With the grievous black bull over her, the pasture she claims and for which she would spill blood, is blotted from her sight: "the tree line was a dark wound in a world that was nothing but sky" (52). The value of her work changes now. She expects nature to assist her in accumulating material wealth, when she should be helping to build the earth for a larger good. She wants to use the earth and ends by injuring it. She thinks that she is increasing order when in actuality she divides and isolates herself from others, and separates others from their dignity. The new light corrects her selfishness to reveal that productive work gains value by sharing. 15

The notable feature of Mrs. May's restored sight is, of course, that it arises out of an erotic embrace between the woman and the bull. O'Connor discerns a connection between sexuality and death that is impressive for all of its triteness. Here she equates the fact of love with the expression of death. One always follows the other. The Christian character of this fusion comes through Mrs. Greenleaf's outcry, "'Oh Jesus, stab me in the heart!'" In the dark woods she abandons herself to personal sacrifice for the anonymous hordes of victims in train wrecks, plane crashes, and rapes. Such self-donation bespeaks an unusual love. She believes that only a pierced heart communicates the strength of her mission, so she asks to be pierced by a love that admits the world's disasters and that is pleased to conquer only in death. That the answer to her exclamation falls on Mrs. May is not a technical trick or a literary irony but O'Connor's incarnation of the belief that the growth of love that builds the earth toward convergence depends upon the response, willing or inadvertent, of one person for another. If others must suffer because of Mrs. May's fear and oppression, then she too must endure anguish in the larger interest of charity. 16

Being subject to affliction should not take Mrs. May unawares, since she tells everyone that she has "'always been the victim.'" On the horns of the bull, she becomes the sufferer she pretends to be. And for all of its self-indulgence, the image conveys the dignity of a woman who insists that her troubles count. The problem, however, is her myopia. Those "pale near-sighted eyes" see material things as holding value for and relief from pain. Her final victimship reveals the loving truth hidden within the conception of herself as sufferer. The intimacy with the bull explains that the yearning and guilt that Mrs. May feels all of her life could have drawn others in union, as the bull comes to her, had she understood that those whom she injures share in her desire for security and in her need to rise and prosper. The many real adversities of her life are not reasons for tyranny or causes for despair; her conflicts are the tribulations of ascent. 17

The amatory embrace also tells us that love is the way of ascent; and along with the cruelty and violence, the action gives definite signs of upsurge. Bloom lies in Mrs. May's name. It abides in her capacity for love awaiting release, which occurs through 18 a refinement of her nature. Until the moment she dies, her name underscores her magisterial manner of giving permission to do this or that; but the story concludes by bringing out the May quality of spring-flowering. Here O'Connor's skill exerts its assured power as she allows nature to vivify the heroine's transformation. The sun, the celestial body manifesting divine love as the source of life, shows how grace seeks out Mrs. May in the diurnal course of things. As the sun sets on the day before her death, it moves "down slowly as if it were descending a ladder" (45). Upon touching the ground, the solar energy seems to enter the bull, for the next day in the pasture the black animal appears to Mrs. May as the shadow of the sun. Then the sun infuses the whole earth to make the morning of Mrs. May's death a shimmering sapphire of a day. Birds are so much with song that they are "screaming everywhere." The grass is "almost too bright to look at," and the sky is "an even piercing blue" (48). The glory of the day seizes Mrs. May. As she drives Mr. Greenleaf through the woods into the open fields to slaughter the bull, she marvels, "Spring is here!" (42)

Spring heralds the greenleafing of Mrs. May. Its ultimate power penetrates her when the bull, the shadow emissary of the sun, pierces her heart. Spring not only coincides with the cycle of new life and with Lent; Lent also means spring. On the horns of the bull, the heroine enters the season of rebirth. In fact, O'Connor's most striking development of the final scene is to embody one of the pleas for deliverance expressed in the psalm that epitomizes passiontide. "My God, my God, why hast thou forsaken me?" begins Psalm 22; and two-thirds (line 21) through the lament, the psalmist sings:

> *Save me from the mouth of the lion,*
> *my afflicted soul from the horns of the wild oxen!*

Psalm 22 is a prayer for deliverance from mortal affliction. The oxen and other animals express to the singer the conduct of her or his enemies who see misery as a sign of God's abandonment, just as Mrs. May sees prosperity as due reward for her troubles. The psalm gains its Christian meaning through Jesus' evoking it in his hour of death. While his association would be congenial to Mrs. May's exaggerated notion of her labor, O'Connor does not use the psalm to sum up a life's work to show how failure justifies God's punishment or how success indicates God's blessing. Neither "Greenleaf" nor Psalm 22 concerns prophecy. Both offer, rather, a presentation of the biblical precedent of the suffering servant, fulfilled for the Christian in transcendent form in Jesus, who will find consolation in God. In the end, love requires that Mrs. May carry the suffering ideal in her heart.

The woman with a pierced heart is not a metaphor for Flannery O'Connor. Heart in her writing is never a figure derived from an anatomical organ or an abstract code. In her stories, heart retains the biblical designation of the inborn center of the human person where one stands before God as a bodily whole, the center where eternity dwells and occurs. Nor is the heart ever sweet. O'Connor knows it to be terrible in its dark death throes. The bull plunges Mrs. May into a starker desolation than any

19

20

21

22

poverty she imagined. She is pierced by her own wretchedness and transience. Her heart feels her essential insufficiency. All of those years of toil, Mrs. May is threatened, usually vulnerable, and thus always guarded and lacking in any more real power than her self-pity could generate. Union with the bull cuts through the defensive stamina to real endurance. To surrender in her long, futile warfare is to prepare Mrs. May for lasting victory and for the future. What supernature calls for is performed by the bull and, more than that, comes by his nature. The achieved union both comes from above and rises out of the ground. The toilworn woman with the pierced heart finds rest.

What gives Mrs. May peace comes not in return for her years of being put upon, 23 as she supposes it would, but arises from the new way in which she is known. The bull's horn spiking Mrs. May's heart is O'Connor's way of showing that the bull knows the heroine as God knows her—as frail and needy and without the protective myths she spends her life cultivating. Such raw exposure would account for the intolerable light and would be sufficient reason to seek being spared the knowledge that comes from the horn. Still, mercy softens the puncture. Mrs. May is loved at last. She no longer needs to assault anyone who tries to compromise her vision of herself because her felt lovableness is unassailable. The last words of "Greenleaf" describe a tremor of joy as Mrs. May seems "to be bent over whispering some last discovery into the animal's ear." As her blessed alarm passes, Mrs. May leans over gently uttering in grateful recognition of finding herself loved. Their attachment is the presence of God.

Now that you have read the results of Giannone's research on "Greenleaf," consider the following analysis of his rhetorical strategies:

Introduction: the Question and the Problem

Like any good literary research paper, Giannone's article begins by identifying the story he will discuss, the author of that story, and the author's purpose: "to make the bizarre seem inevitable" as Mrs. May undergoes her transformation. Just as important, Giannone's introduction (first four paragraphs) provides information that Professor Wayne Booth's *The Craft of Research* describes as essential: the question that motivated Giannone's research and the problem that grew from his question (Booth 10). First, in paragraph three, Giannone raises his question: If O'Connor pronounced her story successful in making Mrs. May's violent death "seem inevitable," why have critics failed to see that success? Then in paragraph four, Giannone states the problem that became his purpose: to show that other critics have missed O'Connor's artistry in planting "the bull's horns into the woman's ribs in a way that joins the sixty-three year old heroine with the raising power of God."

Arrangement

In supporting his claim, Giannone must trace the inevitability of the goring. To begin this process, Giannone provides that long fifth paragraph, an overview of the plot, emphasizing the bull as "patient god" with a crown of thorns, and Mrs. May as willing recipient of "this wild tormented lover." Though Mrs. May offers contemptuous remarks about the "scrub bull," this god-and-lover imagery, Giannone suggests, reveals Mrs. May's intense unconscious longing for this lover and his life-giving spiritual message. In paragraph six, Giannone next analyzes Mrs. May's smug self-approval as widowed dairy farmer and mother, forms of pride that blind her to "some deeper uncertainty" that has nothing to do with her struggle to make economic ends meet, everything to do with her spiritual needs.

Having established Mrs. May's blindness to her spiritual needs and her sense of victimization as farmer and mother, in the next six paragraphs, seven through twelve, Giannone explores Mrs. May's hostility toward the Greenleafs and her sons, those who make her struggle for success a torment. First, Giannone stresses those who fail to appreciate Mrs. May's goodness: Mr. Greenleaf, whose incorrigible carelessness explains how the bull has come to her window; her "traitorous" sons, who repay her nurture with shiftlessness and mockery. He also examines those who annoy Mrs. May—those who actually believe in God, Mrs. Greenleaf, and those who succeed, Sergeants O.T. and E.T. and their high-tech dairy operation. Alienated by her own "narcissistic rule," Mrs. May, Giannone explains, declares war against the bull, the "symbol" of all who have tormented her for fifteen years. At the same time, Giannone notes, the bull munches away at her egotistical "fortress," determined to have her.

Then in paragraphs thirteen and fourteen, Giannone moves to the consequences of Mrs. May's "santanic" assault on the bull, coming first in the form of an order to the Greenleafs to kill their persistent bull, just repayment, she thinks, for 15 years of annoyance and for "surpassing her as a manager of a dairy farm." In turn, that order and her decision to witness the "slaughter" allow the bull to drive his "truth" into Mrs. May's heart, transforming her dying moment into a "quaking illumination" that restores her spiritual sight and her ability to love those she has loathed.

The enormity of O'Connor's revelation, Giannone thinks, merits four additional paragraphs to stress its significance. After stressing the "new light that corrects her selfishness," Giannone notes the irony of Mrs. Greenleaf's prayer for Jesus to "stab [her] in the heart," then the "myopia" that prevented Mrs. May from uttering the same prayer. Throughout the story, Giannone asserts, O'Connor prepares her readers as well as Mrs. May for the necessarily violent "amatory embrace," the only way to cure her willful blindness, the only way to teach her that "love is the way of ascent."

Finally, Giannone concludes his article with four more paragraphs, which place O'Connor's story and Mrs. May's transformation in the larger tradition of Lent, the solemn rite of spring that reminds us that transcendent love begins and ends in suffering.

Logos and Pathos: Building Ethos with Examples and Quotations

Within Giannone's cause-and-effect arrangement, he consistently provides examples and quotations from O'Connor's story—the logos intended to persuade you that his reading makes good sense. In doing so, Giannone also blends pathos, emotional appeal, with his logos to underscore the intensity of his Lenten argument. If you think that he succeeds in this blending, then you probably agree that Giannone has built his ethos, his credibility as a researcher and critic.

Because you must build your ethos through the same blending of logos and pathos when you write your research papers, you might want to review the discussion of these terms in chapter four. Additionally, in the paragraphs below, you will find analysis of Giannone's ways of blending logos and pathos and documenting his indebtedness to O'Connor and to other critics.

Notice that in the first three paragraphs Giannone quotes primarily from O'Connor herself, to stress her concern with plausibility, and then from her critics, to stress their misreading of O'Connor's intent and their giving "short shrift" to her achievement in "Greenleaf." Remember this strategy. If you agree with the critics you have read, you can quote them in your introduction to prepare your reader for your thesis and to "borrow" from their ethos, their credibility as published researchers. Conversely, as in Giannone's case, you can quote critics in your introduction to stress your purpose in writing, your intention to challenge the reading of one or more critics. Such a strategy greatly strengthens your ethos by underscoring your independent thinking.

Notice, too, that Giannone documents his use of critics by including footnotes four through nine, each one identifying the author, the title of his or her book, information on the publisher, and the page on which the quote can be found. Doing so underscores Giannone's ethos, his believability as a researcher. You will have to provide the same kind of documentation in your research paper to build your ethos—and to avoid **plagiary** (see discussion of academic integrity below). However, instead of requiring you to use Giannone's footnoting method, your professor will probably ask you to use parenthetical references to your critics, then a Works Cited page at the end. You will find illustrations of this simpler method of documentation in the student research paper below.

You probably noted, as your read Giannone's support for his claim on the inevitability of the goring and the Lenten theme of purifying pain, that he uses three methods of quoting from "Greenleaf" to help us to hear and see Mrs. May's arrogance, the bull's relentless pursuit, and then her sudden acquisition of sight. You might call these quoting strategies the splicing method, the speaker-tag method, and the colon method, each illustrated below.

The Splicing Method of Quoting: To emphasize the relentless pursuit of Mrs. May's four-legged "lover," Giannone splices "eating one wall of the house" into his own sentence on the significance of the bull's determined gnawing:

> As she sleeps, an animal's chewing becomes an enemy "eating one wall of the house" (25).

Grammatically, Giannone has spliced an adjective (participle) phrase ("eating…") into his own sentence, with "eating" describing the noun "enemy." This method of quoting will allow you to prove the validity of your comments (logos) and to add vivid intensity to that support (pathos); it will also prevent you from falling into a common error in research-paper writing: over-quoting. If your paper strings together numerous lengthy quotations, your voice will grow silent, and your essay will read like a cut-and-paste job. With the splicing method, in other words, as Giannone has shown here, you will be quoting a single key word or phrase, not an entire sentence or several sentences; as a result, you prevent the author's voice from silencing your own. Consider another example of Giannone's spliced quoting:

> Before Mrs. May comprehends the danger, the "black streak" romps to her and buries "his head in her lap, like a wild tormented lover" (52).

Once again, Giannone has supported his claim about this inevitable union, and the spliced language—"black streak," "tormented lover" in her "lap"—captures O'Connor's unforgettable image of the passionate force that opens Mrs. May's eyes. Observe, too, that Giannone follows the quote with a page reference in parentheses (just as he did in the example above), letting his readers know where they may find this language in O'Connor's story. This courteous gesture also builds his ethos, assuring readers that they may check the original text to validate Giannone's reading.

The Speaker-Tag Method of Quoting: This method can also add believability and intensity to your discussion, but it emphasizes dialogue, the exchange between characters, by preceding (or following) a quotation with a verb phrase that indicates who does the talking. Consider this example from Giannone's article:

> "I'm the victim. I'm always the victim" (44), *she sighs* to Scofield and Wesley at supper, simply because the bull's owners do not immediately obey her order to remove it.

Here, Giannone has included a quotation that stresses Mrs. May's self-pity, and the speaker tag (she sighs) allows Giannone to introduce her audience and to emphasize her whining arrogance.

The Colon Method of Quoting: Sometimes, you will want to quote an entire sentence (or more); you will also want to stress its significance by introducing the quoted sentence with your own sentence. Consider this example from Giannone:

> With the grievous black bull over her, the pasture she claims and for which she would spill blood, is blotted from her sight: "the tree line was a dark wound in a world that was nothing but sky" (52).

Here Giannone includes a sentence from the story that mirrors the action: a wound that opens up Mrs. May to endless light. To prepare his readers for this image, Giannone introduces the quotation with his own sentence, stressing her demonic arrogance and the price of her grasping, death. The entire story, Giannone has argued, has built toward this violent, liberating image, a powerful example of logos blending with pathos—and of the need to make your quotations count. Once again, Giannone follows this thesis-clinching quotation with the parenthetical reference to O'Connor's page.

Writing a Proposal Memo on a Literary Topic

In this section, you will find a research proposal memo written by a student who had read O'Connor's "Greenleaf."

Finding a Research Question

The student finding a research question answered the same journaling questions you answered above, a process that helped her to find her **research question**: How does O'Connor use imagery to help us to understand the nature and the cure of Mrs. May's spiritual illness? To answer this question, the student drew not only on her journaling but also on her reading of Giannone and other critics.

Shaping a Research Problem

The paragraphs below will describe in detail the process the student used to find her sources and to use them to shape her sense of the **research problem** that needs solving: What is the significance of the goring, the "inevitable" conclusion of her story? You will then read her proposal memo to discover how this piece of writing prepared her to write the research paper itself. The next section will feature that research paper, as well as the note-taking procedures she followed before and after writing her proposal memo.

Journaling and Freewriting

In addition to the journaling, as mentioned above, the student freewrote on Mrs. May, focusing on her attitude toward the bull, the Greenleafs, and her sons. Recognizing from this process the contradiction between Mrs. May's hostility to those around her and her sense of self as a "good Christian woman," the student began searching for secondary sources, hoping to find professional commentary on O'Connor's purposes and methods in writing on the theme of blindness and awakening.

Searching for Secondary Sources

She started this search electronically, using the databases available on her university's library website. In Figure 5.1, you'll see one of seven pages of sources that popped up on her computer screen after she typed "Greenleaf" and "Flannery O'Connor" and "Religious

Imagination" in the "find" boxes and chose to search the *Modern Language Association International Bibliography*; you'll also see selection #12, "'Greenleaf': A Story of Lent," one of the articles she actually used in her paper. Note, too, that, simply by clicking on "Find It," she could read Giannone's article in "full text" online, as either a pdf or html file. See your Handbook for a full discussion of finding and evaluating secondary sources online or in the library. Of course, your professor and your reference librarian can also help you get started gathering secondary materials.

Having taken notes (see discussion below on note-taking) on several secondary sources, she then used the invention and arrangement strategies you learned in chapter three to begin shaping her project. For example, given the arrogance of Mrs. May, the student worked with the topic of definition and the stasis of conjecture: What is a "good Christian woman"? Does O'Connor want us to see Mrs. Greenleaf's faith as ridiculous or admirable? As she continued her reading in secondary sources, she used the topics of comparison and causation: How do the Greenleafs' sons differ from Mrs. Mays' sons? To what extent does Mrs. May contribute to the Greenleafs' successes and her sons' failures?

These secondary readings also enriched her invention with the testimony of experts and their debate on the stasis of quality: What is great fiction? Does O'Connor succeed in making the goring plausible, "inevitable"? Of course, in reading these debates, the student also began to develop a clear sense of what counts as logos (chapter 4) in persuasive essays on literature, as you will see when you read her research paper below.

Think of this student's proposal memo, then, as a summary of what she has read, what she has thought about the short story, why she cares about doing research to find reliable answers to her questions about O'Connor's work. You may also think of her memo as a piece of persuasive writing. Though the memo format differs from the essays you read in chapter four, she establishes clear purposes here: to persuade her professor

- That she has done considerable prewriting in the process of shaping her questions on the novel

- That she has begun her reading of secondary sources and used them to create a tentative arrangement for her research paper.

- That she actually does care about the short story and the issues it raises.

As you read the memo printed below, see if you can locate where she addresses these interrelated purposes. Also, focusing on the memo format, see if you can determine how the "Purpose" section and the "Summary" section differ in their intent. Finally, try to determine how the student builds her "ethos" in the sections on "Procedures," "Credentials," and "Task Schedule."

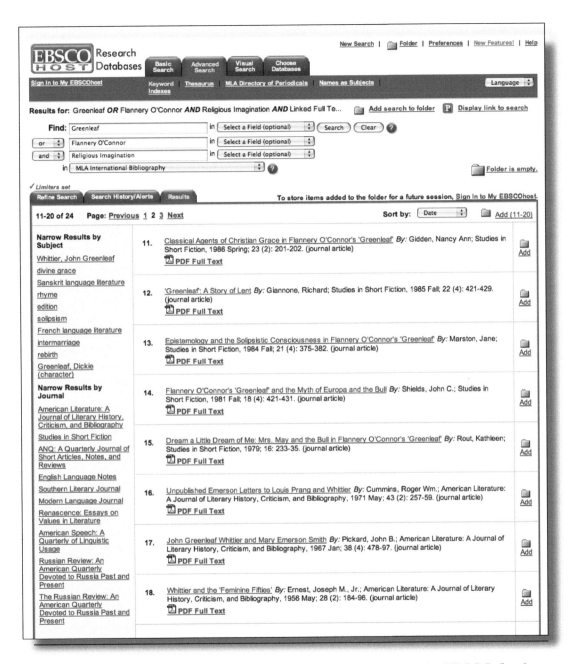

Figure 5.1 EBSCO database

Student Proposal Memo on Literary Topic

Memo

To: Dr. Rich Raymond

From: Leigh-Ann Sallis

Date: June 26, 2006

Subject: Study of Flannery O'Connor's "Greenleaf"

Purpose: The purpose of my paper is to study O'Connor's "Greenleaf" in order to expand my knowledge of her purpose and technique in writing on the theme of spiritual awakening. I also hope to persuade my readers that the ending of "Greenleaf" is masterfully executed.

Summary: My paper will focus on Mrs. May, stressing the causes and effects of her repressed spirituality and the significance of her violent awakening. After demonstrating Mrs. May's scoffing at the Greenleafs, the paper will contrast her failed parenting with the successes of the Greenleafs. Next, the paper will discuss Mrs. May's self-victimizing revenge on the Greenleafs and the spiritual awakening made inevitable by her malice.

Procedures: The following works compose a preliminary bibliography of secondary sources that I have looked at for this paper. At this point, I have other sources that I have yet to examine fully but may prove useful in the evolution of my paper:

Giannone, Richard. "'Greenleaf': A Story of Lent." *Studies in Short Fiction* 22 (1985): 421–29.

Giannone argues that O'Connor succeeds in making the goring of Mrs. May inevitable. He also looks at the story in the context of spiritual purification associated with the season of Lent.

Johansen, Ruthann Knechel. *The Narrative Secret of Flannery O'Connor: the Trickster as Interpreter.* Tuscaloosa: U of Alabama P, 1994.

Johansen examines O'Connor's usage of "trickster activity" in her stories to reveal truth that is often hidden in darkness and misinformation. He argues that her writings work to upset traditional ideas in both the literary and religious fields.

Kilcourse, George A. *Flannery O'Connor's Religious Imagination: a World with Everything off Balance.* New York: Paulist, 2001.

Kilcourse looks at the religious implications of O'Connor's stories, especially when concerning the ideas of salvation through Jesus Christ. He argues that her works use Christianity to attack the status quo and throw off the balance of everyday life.

O'Connor, Flannery. "Greenleaf." *The Complete Stories.* New York: Farrar, 1971.

O'Gorman, Farrell. "Flannery O'Connor." Mississippi State University lecture, June 20 and 22, 2006.

Rout, Kathleen. "Dream a Little Dream of Me: Mrs. May and the Bull in Flannery O'Connor's 'Greenleaf.'" *Studies in Short Fiction* 16 (1979): 233–35.

Rout examines the imagery associated with Mrs. May's conscious and unconscious obsession with the bull.

Smith, Peter A. "Flannery O'Connor's Empowered Women." *Southern Literary Journal* 26 (1994): 35–47.

Smith discusses the irony of power acquired in power lost in several of O'Connor's female main characters.

Credentials: I was exposed to O'Connor's "Greenleaf" in my first literature course at the college level. I was struck by the irony in "Greenleaf" and other stories and hoped for another opportunity to study the story in its critical contexts. This research paper will give me that opportunity.

Task Schedule:

June 5	Research Proposal due
June 6–18	Complete research: reading, note-taking
June 19–22	Write rough draft
June 22	Meet with Dr. Raymond with questions
June 23–30	Revise and produce final draft
June 30	Turn in Research Paper

If your professor requires you to write a proposal memo as a preface to your research paper, please do not regard the assignment as busy-work. On the contrary, you will come to appreciate this short assignment, for it pushes you to clarify your purpose, without which your work will seem like pointless busy-work, indeed. Notice that the purpose statement above clearly announces the student's intention to explore the significance of Mrs. May's awakening.

Nearly twice as long as the purpose statement, the summary above repeats that intent, stressing the self-repression that precedes and necessitates the spiritual awakening. Notice, too, that the summary section forecasts, at least tentatively, the structure of the research paper: the student will trace the causes and effects of Mrs. May's arrogance to the ironic consequences of her attempted revenge on the Greenleafs.

If you read the student's memo from the point of view of her first reader, her professor, then you no doubt noticed how her procedures section builds her credibility by listing her secondary sources and her primary source, O'Connor's story. Note, too, that she follows each listing with a brief **annotation**, a sentence or two that identifies the value of the selection relative to the topic. Such annotations will help you decide exactly how you will use a source in your paper; they will also convince your professor that you have done more than pick up possible sources in the library, that you have actually begun your reading of those materials. In other words, the annotations—never more than two or three sentences—build your ethos as a serious researcher.

The final two sections of the proposal also serve the purpose of building your ethos. In the **credentials** section, the student tells her reader that she has picked this topic because she has studied O'Connor before and grown fascinated with O'Connor and critical approaches to her work. In short, she cares about the topic and wants to share her learning with her readers, her professor and her peers. When you write a similar proposal for a research project, you will want your credentials to announce to your readers that you're just the right person to be writing on this topic. Additionally, the **task schedule**, like the one above, will show your maturity: you have thought through the project, estimating the interim deadlines—researching, drafting, revising—that you'll have to meet in order to meet your final deadline. Professors, just like employers, almost always say "yes" to such thoughtful proposals.

Documenting Your Research

If your professor asks you to prepare a proposal memo, you should follow the model above to persuade your readers that you have actually put your hands on some sources and have begun your reading of those sources, at least enough reading to compose a 1–3 sentence annotation, telling your reader why you believe that particular source will be valuable in making your case. In other words, at the proposal stage, you probably will not have gathered all the sources you will use in your essay, and you may not have completed your reading in the sources you have secured from the library and the internet. However, your professor will not expect to see completed research in your proposal to pursue a research project; instead, she or he will expect to see that you have read enough to clarify your purpose, to narrow the scope of your inquiry, and to know what informational holes you need to fill to make your case persuasively.

To make sure that your Procedures section achieves this persuasive purpose, always document your research by preparing bibliography cards and note cards. Indeed, you should write these cards, illustrated below, before you prepare your proposal memo and after you submit your memo and continue your work. Doing so will ensure that you have complete information about your sources at your finger tips, just where you'll need such information as you're writing your essay.

Bibliography Cards

Let's look first at Figure 5.2, a sample bibliography card documenting the use of a book:

0817307176

Johansen, Ruthann Knechel. *The Narrative Secret of Flannery O'Connor: the Trickster as Interpreter.* Tuscaloosa: U of Alabama P, 1994.

Focuses on O'Connor as "trickster" who awakens both characters and readers blinded by traditional thinking.

Figure 5.2: Bibliography Card on a book

Before we discuss the information and formatting on this card, let's address the question on the tip of your tongue: "Why bother with cards?" Think of your stack of bibliography cards—one source per card—as the time-saving device that will allow you to type your "Works Cited" page (see research paper below) quickly: simply arrange the cards alphabetically and type the name of the author, the title of the chapter, the title of the book, and the publication information, as indicated above.

Of course, you can write electronic cards if you don't want to use 3" x 5" or 4" x 6" cards and have software that will keep track of your bibliographic information for you. In fact, if you go online to *Wikipedia,* you can find free software such as "Keynote" and "WikedPad"; either program will help you to manage your information. Better yet, visit the instructional media center at your university library to learn how to use "EndNote," software which will help you to manage all your notes, sources, and bibliographic information. Another alternative, a bit more old-fashioned: You may record your bibliographic information in a notebook.

Whichever note-taking method you choose, be sure to keep accurate records of your sources. You will need all this information when you're typing your paper, and you certainly don't want to have to look up bibliographic information twice.

Now let's consider the information on the card above, one prepared by the student whose paper you will read below. First, she has placed the book catalog number in the upper-left corner so that she may find the book later if she needs to consult it further. Next, she has written "Johansen, Ruthann Knechel" instead of "Ruthann Knechel Johansen" to make typing easier when she prepares the Works Cited page, which will list sources alphabetically by last name. Please do likewise when you record your bibliography cards: you might as well write the information exactly as you will have to type it later. For the same reason, to highlight the last name, she has indented the second line five spaces, making "Johansen" jump out at the eye. Whether you're a writer arranging bibliography cards prior to typing them, or a reader scanning a Works Cited page for a specific source, you will be grateful for this "hanging" indentation.

Notice, too, that a period separates each major piece of information: author, period; book title, period; publication information, period. Because she is using the Modern Language Association or MLA style, the same style almost always used in English and other humanities disciplines, she has also placed the the book title in italic print (you may use underlining instead of italics if you wish). Following the book title, she has listed the place of publication (Tuscaloosa), then a colon separating the place from the publisher (U of Alabama P—no need to type University of Alabama Press). Finally, a comma separates the publisher from the date of publication, followed by a period. Again, you will follow precisely this format—with the exceptions noted below in Figure 5.3—when entering a journal title on your Works Cited page for your research paper.

Finally, note the annotation. Think of these annotations as notes to yourself, reminders of the probable relevance of a given source to your project. In this case, the fragment (you don't have to use complete sentences on a bibliography card) will help her to remember that this source analyzes O'Connor's concern with readers as well as with plausible characters. You may be thinking, "What's the point of annotations? I'm using just a handful of sources; I don't need such reminders." That may be true, particularly when you're writing that first short research paper with, say, half a dozen sources; however, when your professor requires annotations, she hopes to instill good research habits in you. Can you imagine writing a major research project, perhaps in your senior year, a project based on fifty sources? Wouldn't you be glad to have annotated bibliography cards to help you remember why you thought a particular book, when you picked it off the shelf and scanned it, might be useful to making your case?

Consider now another bibliography card, this one based on a journal article:

Giannone, Richard. "'Greenleaf': A Story of Lent." *Studies in Short Fiction* 22 (1985): 421–29.

Refutes critics who give "short shrift" to O'Connor's purpose and craft. Provides a close reading of Mrs. May's transformation from arrogance to enlightment, an awakening which ends her life in its first moment, embraced by the bull.

Figure 5.3: Bibliography Card on a Journal Article

This card resembles the card in Figure 5.2, differing only in the publication information. Instead of a place of publication and publisher after the title of the journal, you see the volume number for the journal (22), followed by the date (in parentheses) and a colon, which separates the date from the range of pages where the article can be found in volume 22 of *Studies in Short Fiction*. You will use this same format when entering a journal title on your Works Cited page for your research paper.

Note Cards

Next, let's look at a sample note card based on the source described in the bibliography card in Figure 5.3:

Mrs. May's unconscious need   Giannone, 421–24

Giannone describes "Greenleaf" as an award-winning story, which O'Connor placed last in her 1965 collection of stories *Everything that Rises Must Converge* but published in 1956, before any of the other stories. Like O'Connor, he considers "Greenleaf" a "good story," one that makes "the bizarre seem inevitable," even when Mrs. May gets gored by a bull (421). Therefore, he sets out to refute critics who find Mrs. May's awakening ambiguous or inconsistent with Christian theology. He claims instead that this story represents a "watershed" in the development of O'Connor's fiction, the "earliest expression" of her theme on the "raising power of God" (422). He then undertakes a detailed analysis of the bull as the divine messenger drawn toward her by her pride in her business skills and her contempt for the Greenleafs and her own sons. The bull's horns, Giannone argues, must inevitably deflate her pride but also fill the "deeper uncertainty" she has been too busy to discover (423).

Figure 5.4: Combination Note Card

I call this kind of card a "Combo Card" because it combines three methods of note-taking: paraphrasing, quoting, and summarizing. The first sentence illustrates *paraphrasing*, the act of deriving a key idea from a source but expressing that idea in one's own language. Paraphrases, therefore, usually have approximately the same number of words as the original. *Caution*: Paraphrasing does not mean just "changing a couple of words" to synonyms in an otherwise quoted passage. Such verbal games constitute plagiary (see discussion below).

Sentences two, three, and four also illustrate paraphrasing of Giannone's text, but notice that these sentences include quoted key phrases from Giannone, where he stresses the inevitability of Mrs. May's transformation and the success of O'Connor's characterization and plot. This "splicing" or blending technique, as you discovered above, allows you to build your ethos as a researcher by letting your reader hear the authoritative voice of your source; this note-taking strategy also helps you to resist the temptation to over-quote, a common error of beginning research writers. Consider this: If most of your note cards contain long passages of quotations, usually unblended with your own language, then when you transcribe those notes into your paper, your reader will rarely hear your voice. Instead, as noted above, your reader will experience your paper as a cut-and-paste construct of other people's ideas, apparently with no modulation from your voice, your thoughts.

The fifth and sixth sentences then summarize that lengthy sixth paragraph, which begins on 423 and ends on 424. The difference between paraphrasing and summarizing, then, lies with the degree of synthesis in moving from the source to your own writing. Remember that paraphrasing always nearly matches the source material in length; the summary, in contrast, condenses far more information.

Notice, too, that an effective note card also includes a subject heading in the top left-hand corner (Figure 5.3). This phrase will allow the researcher to sort this card with other notes on the subject of Mrs. May's unconscious needs. Typically, your essay will explore at least several subjects or subdivisions of your topic. Think of organizing a deck of cards: the hearts go with the hearts, the clubs with the clubs, and so on. This same simple organizational principle will help you move from notes to essay with far less pain than the writer who took random notes and gave no thought to categories of information.

Opposite your subject heading, on the top right-hand corner of the note card, you will want to provide an author/page heading just like the one in Figure 5.4. "Giannone" will suffice, since we already have full bibliographic information on Richard Giannone on the bibliography card (Figure 5.3). Also, the citing of "421–24" tells us that all the information on this particular card can be found on those pages in Giannone's article. Three weeks after taking this note, when the researcher has begun writing, she will be most grateful that this simple header prevents a return trip to the library to find a page reference.

Finally, notice that within the note card (Figure 5.4) parenthetical page references ensure that the paraphrasing, quoting, and summarizing receive accurate documentation in the research paper. If, for example, the writer decides to use the "watershed" quote in her essay, she has at her finger tips the page (422) on which that phrase occurs in Giannone's article. If she wants to refer her reader to Giannone's emphasis on Mrs. May's "deeper uncertainty," she will know to cite page 423. Such attention to detail at the note-taking stage will save hours of frustration and duplicated efforts at the writing stage.

Writing Summaries

Most of your note cards, whether you write them on 4" x 6" cards or on your computer, will involve primarily **summarizing**. Sometimes, you will be condensing one page of an article or book to a single note card; other times, as in Figure 5.4, you'll be synthesizing several pages or more on a single card. Unless you've already had considerable experience writing summaries, you'll find the process quite demanding intellectual work: identifying key claims, major supporting reasons for holding those claims, essentials facts and examples that validate those supporting reasons.

Because summary writing requires such deep thought, students sometimes choose to write extended "quote cards" instead. It's easy, not much thinking involved, just careful transcription. Doing so, however, forces you to write many more note cards than you need, so you're not really saving time. Consider, too, that transcribing quotations, because it requires little thought, means that you're not internalizing your reading, not finding your position relative to your secondary sources. As a result, when the time comes to begin writing, you will find that you have huge stacks of quote-cards but no ideas. You've been reading but not really thinking. The panic that comes with such realizations sometimes leads to thoughts of plagiary, as we'll discuss below. First, let's consider some well-tested guidelines for writing summaries, for doing your own thinking:

1. Read the title of the article or book chapter, then the introduction, then the headings. This three-step process will give you an overview of the piece and a clear sense of the writer's thesis, purpose, and organizational plan.

2. With your purpose in mind, scan the article or chapter, jotting down which paragraphs or sections seem relevant to your project.

3. Beginning with the first section that looks relevant to your work, read it carefully, then write in your own words a one-sentence summary of each paragraph. If the section has ten paragraphs, you will end up with a ten-sentence summary of those paragraphs.

4. Read your sentences aloud. Most likely, they will sound choppy and repetitive; they can probably be condensed to four or five mature sentences connected by appropriate words or phrases that point out relationships in sequence (e. g., first, next, then, etc.), in space (e. g., above, below, etc.), and in logic (e.g., therefore, consequently, as a result, however, etc.).

5. Write your condensed note card, looking back now to your source to find key words or phrases that can be blended with your language to preserve the voice of your source and to make your sentences more emphatic (see Figure 5.4). Of course, any key words or phrases from your source must be spliced into your sentences via quotation marks and page references. Leaving them out, deliberately or accidentally, constitutes plagiary.

If you consider yourself a rooky when it comes to summary writing, go ahead and write a summary of the first ten paragraphs in Giannone's article, above. You might want to share your summary with your professor to make sure you're getting the key ideas and the key supports.

After you've practiced this five-step technique, you can skip step three, moving directly from scanning to note-taking. Though this process takes time and requires work, you'll be pleased not only by your notes, clear in their concepts and rich in their detail, but also by your sense of engagement with your sources. In fact, such note-taking constitutes prewriting: your first draft will grow quite naturally from your thoughtful note cards.

Avoiding Academic Dishonesty

I've already mentioned above the most common manifestation of academic dishonesty: presenting someone else's words and ideas as your own. Such practices constitute illegal and unethical behavior because they amount to theft. You may confirm this assertion by checking out copyright law at www.copyright.gov, or by consulting the ethics code of any profession. See, for example, the website of the Society for Technical Communication: www.stc.org . Other examples of plagiary—writing a paper for a friend, turning in a paper you wrote in one class to a professor in another class, never acknowledging the earlier work or asking permission to "double-dip"—do not involve theft, but they do involve deception. Deception, in turn, breeds distrust and destroys the credible ethos you have tried to build.

Of course, writers sometimes accidentally violate these laws and codes protecting intellectual property. However, when our violation results from ignorance—not knowing how to paraphrase, for example—or from carelessness—leaving out quotation marks, for instance—we have still undercut our ethos. We have sent our readers the message that we couldn't be bothered to learn the correct procedures.

Clearly, you never want to send such a message. Most professors, recognizing the lesser offense, impose relatively light penalties on students who have violated honesty codes out of haste, typically a "zero" on the assignment. Conversely, when professors uncover evidence of intentional plagiary—represented most egregiously by the essay lifted off the internet—they will typically assign an F in the course; repeat offenses usually lead to dismissal from the university.

Given the severity of such penalties, faculty often marvel that so many students commit plagiary. Their marveling, however, never lasts long, as they recall the seemingly endless parade of perjurers on our witness stands, homerun heroes on steroids, congressional leaders under indictment, CEOs in jail—and college professors fired for plagiary. While such widespread dishonesty corrupts our culture, as a student and writer you must resist the cynical conclusions that "everyone cheats," that you should only avoid getting caught. This resistance centers on your obligation to your readers, to whom you owe your truth (see quote from Anne Lamott among the epigraphs to chapter 1). You must base your resistance, too, on the realization that when you cheat, you have failed to learn, that when you fail to learn, you have cheated yourself.

Analyzing a Literary Research Paper in MLA Style

With this information on the process of research fresh in your mind, you'll fully appreciate another product of this process, specifically, the research paper which grew from the proposal on O'Connor's "Greenleaf". As you read the student's paper, answer the following ten questions: the first four questions focus on her introduction; questions 5–9 focus on her analysis of Mrs. May's interaction with the Greenleafs, her sons, and the bull; question 10 focuses on her conclusion. Answering these questions will allow you to review your earlier reading on "purpose," "invention," and "arrangement"; it will also help you to see the research process as an act of "persuasion."

1. In the first sentence of the introduction, how does the student try to arouse your interest in this disturbing story? Does she succeed? Why or why not? Can you find any other sentences in the introduction that might work well as lead sentences?

2. Sentences two, three and four of the introduction paraphrase O'Connor's purpose in contrasting Mrs. May and the Greenleafs. How does sentence five connect the student's purpose to O'Connor's purpose? What literary and spiritual problems will she try to solve?

3. What claims does the student make in sentences six through twelve concerning Mrs. May, her sons, the Greenleafs, and the bull? Do these sentences effectively forecast the organization of the paper? Could that forecast have been written more clearly?

4. How do the quotes from Professor O'Gorman (sentences eight and ten) reinforce her claims?

5. Paragraphs two and three focus on Mrs. May's repressed sexuality and her contempt for Mrs. Greenleaf and her religion. Using terminology you learned in chapter three, especially the "topic" of comparison and the "stasis" of conjecture, discuss how effectively the student uses quotations from the story to establish Mrs. May's prudish arrogance and her weak claim to being Christian.

6. Explain how the student tries to create smooth transitions in moving from paragraph two to three, and from paragraph three to four. Does she succeed? Why or why not?

7. Paragraphs five through nine examine Mrs. May's attitudes toward her sons and the Greenleaf sons. How does the student use the "stasis" of quality to critique Mrs. May's attitudes?

8. Focusing on paragraphs ten through twelve, explain how the student uses the "topics" of definition, comparison, and relationships to clarify the meaning of the bull as well as the causes and effects of the goring.

9. Focusing still on paragraphs ten through twelve, discuss the value of quotations from the story and from critics in building the student's ethos and supporting her claim that the brutal goring also represents a spiritual awakening.

10. In summarizing her analysis of O'Connor's images of fertility, the student closes by contrasting the economic and spiritual poverty of the Mays with the economic and spiritual health of the Greenleafs. Has the student made her case persuasively? Explain.

Student Literary Research Paper:
Saved by the Bull: Grace Versus Repressiveness in O'Connor's "Greenleaf"

LEIGH-ANN SALLIS

1

In the story "Greenleaf," Flannery O'Connor deals with ideas of sexual and spiritual repression and religious disappointment through the character of Mrs. May. Seeing herself as an aristocrat throughout the story, Mrs. May looks down on the Greenleafs, whom she views as simple white trash. However, O'Connor juxtaposes the two in order to display the spiritual shortcomings of the May family against the fruitfulness of the Greenleaf family. Though she constantly mocks the Greenleafs, she also displays a sense of dissatisfaction with their openness and prosperity, things that she cannot experience through either her own actions or those of her children. Thus, O'Connor uses images of fertility to show that the life of Mrs. May is in fact barren when compared to that of the Greenleafs. She rejects the supposed vulgar behavior of the poor family, even though it leads to greater personal rewards than anything she ever experiences. Only in death does Mrs. May realize that she lives the wrong way; at this point, she finally finds the grace that the Greenleafs possess all along. O'Connor said once that "the reality of death has come upon us and a consciousness of the power of God has broken our complacency like a bullet in the side" (O'Gorman 33). Perhaps no character in O'Connor's fiction displays this idea better than Mrs. May. After living a repressed and unsatisfying life, only a shocking death awakens her: "It is no wonder that this highly symbolic violence is central to her fiction, a predictable instrument of distortion to awaken her audience to the higher truth" (O'Gorman lecture). Therefore, Mrs. May is shocked into this state through her violent death, displaying the meaning of a quotation from O'Connor: "It has always seemed necessary to me to throw the weight of circumstances against the character" (quoted in Kilcourse 41). The "weight" of the charging bull and the gruesome violence of the story's conclusion become the key to Mrs. May's enlightenment.

2

Mrs. May represses her own spirituality throughout the story while scoffing at the personal freedoms of the Greenleafs. She despises the poor family because they embrace everything she hates. A perfect example of this contempt comes in her rejection of open religious expression. While Mrs. May feels that certain actions are not appropriate in public, Mrs. Greenleaf participates in a "prayer healing" ritual in which she grovels on the ground: "Mrs. Greenleaf raised her head. Her face was a patchwork of dirt and tears and her small eyes, the color of two field peas, were red rimmed and swollen, but her expression was as composed as a bulldog's" (316). Mrs. May is visibly upset by this open show of faith and "winced" at the verbal use of Jesus, thinking to herself that "the word…should be kept inside the church building like other words inside the bedroom" (316). Significantly, she links together spirituality and sexuality into a relationship of repressiveness. Rather than expressing these two kinds of passion in the open, she would keep both private. Also, Mrs. May shows that she holds little stock in the power of either when she smugly reflects that she "did not, of course, believe any of it was true" (316). Ultimately, as George Kilcourse explains, her "contempt for Mrs. Greenleaf's emotional, Pentecostal religious displays and 'prayer healing' in the woods exposes her cold, methodic self-righteousness" (254). Rather than embracing the emotional spirituality of Mrs. Greenleaf, Mrs. May scoffs at it, foreshadowing her attitude toward everything else in her life.

Mrs. Greenleaf, thus, acts as a direct opposite to the character of Mrs. May, who rejects the actions of Mrs. Greenleaf and describes her as being "large and loose" (315). By employing Mr. Greenleaf as a farmhand, she bitterly accepts the fact that she occasionally has to witness the "trashy" behavior of his wife: "The irascible Mrs. May judges everything as wrong in the Greenleaf family" (Kilcourse 254). The way Mrs. Greenleaf runs her household almost physically disgusts Mrs. May: "The yard around her house looked like a dump and her five girls were always filthy; even the youngest one dipped snuff" (315). It is no small wonder, then, that Mrs. May has only one thought after the prayer healing: "'[Jesus] would tell you to get up from there this instant and go wash your children's clothes'" (317). The most distressing aspect of the entire situation for Mrs. May is how her sons simply accept this behavior to the point where they tease their mother about it. Scofield, to really distress his mother, says that he will one day marry "some nice lady like Mrs. Greenleaf" (315). At this point, she passes on her own sexual repressiveness to her sons through financial force. There is no evidence that her sons would ever marry women like Mrs. Greenleaf; in fact, the story never hints that they will ever get married at all. However, after hearing their carefree attitude about the matter, Mrs. May rushes "to her lawyer and had the property entailed so that if they married, they could not leave it to their wives" (315). The happiness of her sons is not Mrs. May's primary concern. Instead, she must approve of any women they eventually choose to marry not simply as a wife, but as a representative of the feminine legacy she will leave behind after her death. It must be asked whether any woman can be good enough to meet her high standards.

A comparison of the May and Greenleaf sons displays how the attitudes of each family lead to much different fates as adults. While the repressiveness of Mrs. May lives on in her boys, the Greenleaf twins seem to flourish in the openness practiced by their parents and thrive in a manner that infuriates the self-proclaimed aristocrat. As shown in her actions with the will, Mrs. May does not trust her own boys to carry on the business of the farm after her death. She constantly refers to employing Mr. Greenleaf for "fifteen years" and does not trust the boys to manage his actions: "She was capable of handling Mr. Greenleaf; they were not" (317). She displays constant disappointment in the paths the boys have chosen for their lives. Scofield did not live up to her expectations in the military, and, of course, to compound the problem for Mrs. May, he sells "nigger insurance as a living" (315). She refers to Wesley as being an "intellectual," which she blames on his rheumatic fever at age seven, implying that he leads a useless life. With both boys, she laments them as poor prospects for marriage, especially Scofield: "What nice girl wants to marry a nigger-insurance man"? (315).

Though both of Mrs. May's sons are somewhat successful—Wesley's education, Scofield's job—neither lives up to her ideal of what a man should be. To fill this gap, she takes pride in the way her assistance has helped the Greenleaf twins. She even goes so far as to claim responsibility for their success in farming: "'O. T. and E. T. are fine boys,' she said. 'They ought to have been my sons'" (321). In the same paragraph, she exclaims that Wesley and Scofield should belong to Mrs. Greenleaf, and later denies them by never referring to them as her sons. When the Greenleaf twins' hired hand asks, "Is you my policy man's mother," she emphatically replies, "I don't know who your policy man is" (326). At this point, she completely disassociates herself with her own son.

It thus becomes a running joke between the boys, as they strike back by denying the aristocratic nature of their mother in Greenleaf English. Wesley says that "neither you nor me is her boy," in response to Scofield's comment that "I done mighty well to be as nice as I am, seeing what I come from" (327). Considering the disappointment of Mrs. May in her sons, these comments seem especially painful to her because of her earlier thought concerning the origin of the Greenleaf twins. When witnessing one of Mrs. Greenleaf's "prayer healing" sessions, she comments to herself, "Well, no matter how far they go, they came from that" (317). Mrs. May looks down on the Greenleaf actions but is shocked to find out that "they never quarls" and "they like one man in two skins" (326). In contrast, her sons are complete opposites: "The two boys never had the same reaction to anything. They were as different, she said, as night and day. The only thing they did have in common was that neither of them cared what happened on the place" (326). Unlike the Greenleafs, the May boys dissatisfy their mother with their indifference toward her dreams. It is ironic, then, that the Greenleaf boys personify her hopes, while her own boys unite only in the disruption of her aspirations for her farm, her bloodline, and her very legacy.

Though Mrs. May admires the "fine" Greenleaf boys, as mentioned above, she looks jealously on their successes, unable to dispel the fact that O. T. and E. T. were raised by the two people she hates most in the world. Richard Giannone argues, too, that Mrs. May's "surfacing awareness that the Greenleaf boys, sons of her hired hand and that prayer healer, are rising above hers lays bare the greed behind her tenacity" (426). She therefore attributes their present status as owners of a farm to their service in the military. Essentially, they are everything her sons are not: "They were energetic and hard-working and she would admit to anyone that they had come a long way—and that the Second World War was responsible for that" (318). This comment echoes in her sneering comment on how, after the war, the Greenleaf boys took advantage of their service in that "the two of them were living now about two miles down the highway on a piece of land that the government had helped them to buy and in a brick duplex bungalow that the government had helped them pay for" (318). Of course, Mrs. May's negative opinion of the Greenleaf family causes her to paint the twins as a burden to the "taxpayers" of the local economy (318).

Additionally, at no point does Mrs. May fully acknowledge the success of the Greenleaf boys in their farming enterprise. This bitter denial readily appears in her trip to their home where she hopes to complain about the bull loose on her land. When she goes to the milking parlor to find E. T. and O. T., she sees a number of machines and snidely thinks to herself "how many of them were paid for" (325). The advanced milk parlor that the younger Greenleafs install on their land also becomes a symbol of Mrs. May's despair that the Greenleafs are surpassing her own family in the younger generation. In a discussion with Mr. Greenleaf concerning this parlor, she once again belittles the achievements of E. T. and O. T.: "I have to do for myself. I am not assisted hand and foot by the government. It would cost me $20,000 to install a milking parlor. I barely make ends meet as it is" (324). She never considers that the boys are now successful enough to afford milking equipment themselves rather than relying on the government, simply because she cannot afford one herself.

It is humorous, then, that Mr. Greenleaf takes a shot at Mrs. May's sons by commenting, "My boys done it…but all boys ain't alike" (324). Mr. Greenleaf points out the obvious shortcomings of Scofield and Wesley in comparison to his boys. When she eventually looks inside the parlor itself, she cannot stand the brightness of the new machinery and "drew her head out of the room quickly and closed the door and learned against it, frowning" (325). She gradually realizes that the success of the Greenleafs surpasses her own, mainly because of the disparity in the ambitions of the children: "The advanced technology and the spotless milking room distress her anew" (Giannone 426). As Peter Smith observes, deep down, Mrs. May knows that "her sons represent more of a threat to the established order than the Greenleafs" (43). They do not respect her and threaten to end her aristocratic legacy by refusing to follow the same agricultural path as O. T. and E. T. The trip to the Greenleaf farm further affirms this perception, as Mrs. May readily denies, as noted above, any association with Scofield when a worker mentions Scofield's profession. The most distressing realization for her is that the children of the Greenleaf boys will one day serve as "Society," the same position she currently holds (318). Unfortunately, her own sons do not hold the same potential in the life paths they are following. They are unmarried, irresponsible, and essentially hopeless in the eyes of Mrs. May, the opposite of the Greenleaf boys.

The Greenleaf bull, a constant throughout the story, acts as a symbol of this distress and of Mrs. May's need for grace. The opening pages of the story introduce the reader to this bull, which antagonizes Mrs. May in every passage. Her first exclamation concerning the bull is to say, "Some nigger's scrub bull" (311). At this point, she does not know that the bull belongs to the Greenleaf boys, so this racist comment seems relatively innocent. However, her negative opinion of the bull from the very first experience reflects the unfavorable stance she takes toward the entire Greenleaf family. O'Connor uses this bull in a number of ways to describe the fears and anxieties of Mrs. May concerning her threatened social status. As Kathleen Rout observes, "The Greenleaf bull is a complex symbol. The animal combines his social, sexual, and religious identities in a way that allows him to represent everything that Mrs. May rejects, everything unrestrained or lacking in taste" (233). The bull acts as a constant reminder of the repressed life Mrs. May leads. It shows that the Greenleaf boys live in a way that she had hoped her own sons would have. Indeed, the bull serves as "the menace of fifteen years with horns" (Giannone 424), a direct reference to the anxiety she has experienced over Mr. Greenleaf.

The bull also represents the unbridled energy that she hopes Scofield and Wesley [11] will one day possess. Mrs. May worries that the bull may "ruin the breeding schedule" (314) of her cattle, showing that she places sexual energy in a restrictive pattern. Also, Mr. Greenleaf cannot contain the bull with any kind of fence, increasing Mrs. May's worries. The bull's anxiety concerning technology also mirrors that of Mrs. May. The field hand tells her, "[the Greenleafs] goin to say you go ahead on and shoot him. He done busted up one our trucks already and we be glad to see the last of him" (326). The bull reacts strangely to the advancing technology represented by the truck, much in the same way Mrs. May reacts to the new milking parlor of the Greenleafs.

While the bull's presence builds tension throughout the story, that tension reaches [12] a point of climax in the violent scene on the final page of the story. The first night she sees the bull outside her window, the story foreshadows that he may be a source of grace for the prudish aristocrat: "like some patient god come down to woo her…[he] took a step backward and lowered his head as if to show the wreath across his horns" (311). He works as both a possible spiritual and sexual savior for Mrs. May, an entity attempting to end her repressiveness. As Rout puts it, the bull seems "a potential lover not of her cows, but of Mrs. May herself" (234). Clearly, the bull stalks Mrs. May's farm not because of the other animals, but because of her. The final scene, where the bull kills Mrs. May, brings a sense of grace to the story:

> One of his horns sank until it pierced her heart and the other curved around her side [13] and held her in an unbreakable grip. She continued to stare straight ahead but the entire scene in front of her had changed—the tree line was a dark wound in a world that was nothing but sky—and she had the look of a person whose sight has been suddenly restored but finds the light unbearable. (333)

The bull acts as an agent of God, releasing Mrs. May from the constraints she [14] places on others and society forces on her. The horn pierces Mrs. May through the heart, reminding the reader of an earlier prayer by Mrs. Greenleaf: "Jesus, stab me in the heart!" (317). Thus, the bull acts as her savior, the liberator of her proud, self-alienating soul, just as Johansen has argued: "'Greenleaf' [has] non-human agents who function as mediators or agents of grace" (101). It takes a gruesome death for Mrs. May to realize her waywardness, as the end of the story implies: "…she seemed, when Mr. Greenleaf reached her, to be bent over whispering some last discovery into the animal's ear" (334). As in several of O'Connor's works, it takes a shocking ending for Mrs. May to realize what grace truly is.

Mrs. May's repressive nature affects all of those around her. Her sons live with [15] her disappointment every day, and essentially reflect her negative attitude toward the world. The Greenleafs represent the opposite of Mrs. May's spirit-withering pride. While the parents struggle in poverty, O. T and E. T. distinguish themselves through military service, through their ability to run a successful farm, and their proficiency in securing a fruitful bloodline. The Greenleaf name exemplifies the fulfillment of life, youth, and energy. Mrs. May symbolizes none of these things, but rather inverts the traditional meaning of her name, the season of spring. Only in death does Mrs. May realize that the Greenleafs live in the correct manner: "Spring heralds the greenleafing of Mrs. May. Its ultimate power penetrates her when the bull, the shadow emissary of the sun, pierces her heart" (Giannone 428). O'Connor purposely chooses these names to illustrate the disparities between the two families. Mrs. May looks down upon the Greenleafs, making it ironic that the future generations seem secured in an on-going prosperity. Though Mrs. May experiences grace through the bull, there are no guarantees that her children will undergo the same transformation. With the mother gone, however, change becomes possible for Scofield and Wesley. Perhaps her death acts as grace for her and for the sons, freeing them all from her soul-starving obsessions with possessions and place.

Works Cited

Giannone, Richard. "'Greenleaf': A Story of Lent." *Studies in Short Fiction* 22 (1985): 421–29.

Johansen, Ruthann K. *The Narrative Secret of Flannery O'Connor: The Trickster as Interpreter.* Tuscaloosa: U of Alabama P, 1994.

Kilcourse, George A. *Flannery O'Connor's Religious Imagination: A World with Everything Off Balance.* New York: Paulist, 2001.

O'Connor, Flannery. "Greenleaf." *The Complete Stories.* New York: Farrar, 1971.

O'Gorman, Farrell. "Flannery O'Connor." Lecture, Mississippi State University, June 22, 2006.

O'Gorman, Farrell. *Peculiar Crossroads: Flannery O'Connor, Walker Percy, and Catholic Vision in Postwar Southern Fiction.* Baton Rouge: Louisiana State UP, 2004.

Rout, Kathleen. "Dream a Little Dream of Me: Mrs. May and the Bull in Flannery O'Connor's 'Greenleaf.'" *Studies in Short Fiction* 16 (1979): 233–35.

Smith, Peter A. "Flannery O'Connor's Empowered Women." *Southern Literary Journal* 26 (1994): 35–47.

Analyzing Azar Nafisi's Memoir

Your analysis of the research process, as reflected in the student's proposal memo, and your rhetorical analysis of her research product, as reflected in her research paper, have prepared you well to read a selection from Azar Nafisi's research. Her work argues vigorously that literature can reshape lives and that such readers, in turn, may dare to effect social change. After you read the excerpt and reflect on the three questions below, you can begin work on your own literary research.

Azar Nafisi's memoir tells the story of her teaching literature in the Islamic Republic of Iran. In 1995, she resigned her teaching position at the University of Tehran, fed up by the repressive influence of government censors on academic life and by the theocratic leaders who kept women silent and veiled. Still dedicated to teaching, Nafisi invited seven of her best female students to her home, where her students "shed their mandatory veils" (5) and discussed the novels they all agreed to read. Focusing primarily on the works of English novelist Jane Austen, American novelists F. Scott Fitzgerald and Henry James, and Russian poet/novelist Vladimir Nabokov, the courageous teacher and students agreed that they would search for "the epiphany of truth," when "the ordinary pebble of ordinary life could be transformed into a jewel through the magic eye of fiction" (3, 8).

With this context in mind, read the following excerpts from *Reading* Lolita *in Tehran*, focusing particularly on the story of Yassi, Nafisi's youngest student, and the conversation that lured Yassi into this two-year class, one for which the professor earned no pay, and the students received no credit.

1. Notice that Nafisi requires her students to keep a "private diary" in which each student would "record her responses to the novels, as well as the ways in which these works and their discussions related to their personal experiences" (paragraph 70). Can you see a connection between their requirement and Nafisi's brief anecdote on "the nineteen-year-old Nabokov," who wrote poetry in the midst of a bloody revolution?

2. How does Nafisi's summary of *A Thousand and One Nights* clarify what she means by the "transforming" power of "works of imagination"? (71–73)

3. Nafisi writes that "literature became so essential to our lives…not a luxury but a necessity," a way of surviving by poking "fun at our misery" caused by the "tragedy and absurdity of the cruelty to which we were subjected" (91). Explain in detail how the story of Yassi clarifies these statements.

Excerpt from *Reading* Lolita *in Tehran*

Azar Nafisi

In the fall of 1995, after resigning from my last academic post, I decided to indulge myself and fulfill a dream. I chose seven of my best and most committed students and invited them to come to my home every Thursday morning to discuss literature. They were all women—to teach a mixed class in the privacy of my home was too risky, even if we were discussing harmless works of fiction. One persistent male student, although barred from our class, insisted on his rights. So he, Nima, read the assigned material, and on special days he would come to my house to talk about the books we were reading.

I often teasingly reminded my students of Muriel Spark's *The Prime of Miss Jean Brodie* and asked, Which one of you will finally betray me? For I am a pessimist by nature and I was sure at least one would turn against me. Nassrin once responded mischievously, You yourself told us that in the final analysis we are our own betrayers, playing Judas to our own Christ. Manna pointed out that I was no Miss Brodie, and they, well, they were what they were. She reminded me of a warning I was fond of repeating: *do not*, under *any* circumstances, belittle a work of fiction by trying to turn it into a carbon copy real life; what we search for in fiction is not so much a reality but the epiphany of truth. Yet I suppose that if I were to go against my own recommendation and choose a work of fiction that would most resonate with our lives in the Islamic Republic of Iran, it would not be *The Prime of Miss Jean Brodie* or even *1984* but perhaps Nabokov's *Invitation to a Beheading* or better yet, *Lolita*.

A couple of years after we had begun our Thursday-morning seminars, on the last night I was in Tehran, a few friends and students came to say good-bye and to help me pack. When we had deprived the house of all its items, when the objects had vanished and the colors had faded into eight gray suitcases, like errant genies evaporating into their bottles, my students and I stood against the bare white wall of the dining room and took two photographs. 3

I have the two photographs in front of me now. In the first there are seven women, standing against a white wall. They are, according to the law of the land, dressed in black robes and head scarves, covered except for the oval of their faces and their hands. In the second photograph the same group, in the same position, stands against the same wall. Only they have taken off their coverings. Splashes of color separate one from the next. Each has become distinct through the color and style of her clothes, the color and the length of her hair; not even the two who are still wearing their head scarves look the same. 4

The one to the far right in the second photograph is our poet, Manna, in a white T-shirt and jeans. She made poetry out of things most people cast aside. The photograph does not reflect the peculiar opacity of Manna's dark eyes, a testament to her withdrawn and private nature. 5

Next to Manna is Mahshid, whose long black scarf clashes with her delicate features and retreating smile. Mahshid was good at many things, but she had a certain daintiness about her and we took to calling her "my lady." Nassrin used to say that more than defining Mahshid, we had managed to add another dimension to the word *lady*. Mahshid is very sensitive. She's like porcelain, Yassi once told me, easy to crack. That's why she appears fragile to those who don't know her too well; but woe to whoever offends her. As for me, Yassi continued good-naturedly, I'm like good old plastic; I won't crack no matter what you do with me. 6

Yassi was the youngest in our group. She is the one in yellow, bending forward and bursting with laughter. We used to teasingly call her our comedian. Yassi was shy by nature, but certain things excited her and made her lose her inhibitions. She had a tone of voice that gently mocked and questioned not just others but herself as well. 7

I am the one in brown, standing next to Yassi, with one arm around her shoulders. Directly behind me stands Azin, my tallest student, with her long blond hair and a pink T-shirt. She is laughing like the rest of us. Azin's smiles never looked like smiles; they appeared more like preludes to an irrepressible and nervous hilarity. She beamed in that peculiar fashion even when she was describing her latest trouble with 8 her husband. Always outrageous and outspoken Azin relished the shock value of her actions and comments, and often clashed with Mahshid and Manna. We nicknamed her the wild one.

On my other side is Mitra, who was perhaps the calmest among us. Like the pastel colors of her paintings, she seemed to recede and fade into a paler register. Her beauty was saved from predictability by a pair of miraculous dimples, which she could and did use to manipulate many an unsuspecting victim into bending to her will.

Sanaz, who, pressured by family and society, vacillated between her desire for independence and her need for approval, is holding on to Mitra's arm. We are all laughing. And Nima, Manna's husband and my one true literary critic—if only he had had the perseverance to finish the brilliant essays he started to write—is our invisible partner, the photographer.

There was one more: Nassrin. She is not in the photographs—she didn't make it to the end. Yet my tale would be incomplete without those who could not or did not remain with us. Their absences persist, like an acute pain that seems to have no physical sources. This is Tehran for me: its absences were more real than its presences.

When I see Nassrin in my mind's eye, she's slightly out of focus, blurred, somehow distant. I've combed through the photographs my students took with me over the years and Nassrin is in many of them, but always hidden behind something—a person, a tree. In one, I am standing with eight of my students in the small garden facing our faculty building, the scene of so many farewell photographs over the years. In the backgrounds stands a sheltering willow tree. We are laughing, and in one corner, from behind the tallest student, Nassrin peers out, like an imp intruding roguishly on a scene it was not invited to. In another I can barely make out her face in the small V space behind two other girls' shoulders. In this one she looks absentminded; she is frowning, as if unaware that she is being photographed.

How can I describe Nassrin? I once called her the Cheshire cat, appearing and disappearing at unexpected turns in my academic life. The truth is I can't describe her: she was her own definition. One can only say that Nassrin was Nassrin.

For nearly two years, almost every Thursday morning, rain or shine, they came to my house, and almost every time, I could not get over the shock of seeing them shed their mandatory veils and robes and burst into color. When my students came into that room, they took off more than their scarves and robes. Gradually, each one gained an outline and a shape, becoming her own inimitable self. Our world in that living room with its window framing my beloved Elburz Mountains became our sanctuary, our self-contained universe, mocking the reality of black-scarved, timid faces in the city that sprawled below.

The theme of the class was the relation between fiction and reality. We read Persian classical literature, such as the tales of our own lady of fiction, Scheherazade, from *A Thousand and One Nights*, along with Western classics—*Pride and Prejudice, Madame Bovary, Daisy Miller, The Dean's December* and, yes, *Lolita*. As I write the title of each book, memories whirl in with the wind to disturb the quiet of this fall day in another room in another country.

Here and now in that other world that cropped up so many times in our discussions, I sit and reimagine myself and my students, my girls as I came to call them, reading *Lolita* in a deceptively sunny room in Tehran. But to steal the words from Humbert, the poet/criminal of *Lolita*, I need you, the reader, to imagine us, for we won't really exist if you don't. Against the tyranny of time and politics, imagine us the way we sometimes didn't dare to imagine ourselves: in our most private and secret moments, in the most extraordinary ordinary instances of life, listening to music, falling in love, walking down the shady streets or reading *Lolita* in Tehran. And then imagine us again with all this confiscated, driven underground, taken away from us.

16

If I write about Nabokov today, it is to celebrate our reading of Nabokov in Tehran, against all odds. Of all his novels I choose the one I taught last, and the one that is connected to so many memories. It is of *Lolita* that I want to write, but right now there is no way I can write about that novel without also writing about Tehran. This, then, is the story of *Lolita* in Tehran, how *Lolita* gave a different color to Tehran and how Tehran helped redefine Nabokov's novel, turning it into this *Lolita*, our *Lolita*.

17

2

And so it happened that one Thursday in early September we gathered in my living room for our first meeting. Here they come, one more time. First I hear the bell, a pause, and the closing of the street door. Then I hear footsteps coming up the winding staircase and past my mother's apartment. As I move towards the front door, I register a piece of sky through the side window. Each girl, as soon as she reaches the door, takes off her robe and scarf, sometimes shaking her head from side to side. She pauses before entering the room. Only there is no room, just the teasing void of memory.

18

More than any other place in our home, the living room was symbolic of my nomadic and borrowed life. Vagrant pieces of furniture from different times and places were thrown together, partly out of financial necessity, and partly because of my eclectic taste. Oddly, these incongruous ingredients created a symmetry that the other, more deliberately furnished rooms in the apartment lacked.

19

My mother would go crazy each time she saw the paintings leaning against the wall and the vases of flowers on the floor and the curtainless windows, which I refused to dress until I was finally reminded that this was an Islamic country and windows needed to be dressed. I don't know if you really belong to me, she would lament. Didn't I raise you to be orderly and organized? Her tone was serious but she had repeated the same complaint for so many years that by now it was an almost tender ritual. Azi— that was my nickname—Azi, she would say, you are a grown-up lady now; act like one. Yet there was something in her tone that kept me young and fragile and obstinate, and still, when in memory I hear her voice, I know I never lived up to her expectations. I never did become the lady she tried to will me into being.

20

That room, which I never paid much attention to at that time, has gained a different status in my mind's eye now that it has become the precious object of memory. It was a spacious room, sparsely furnished and decorated. At one corner was the fireplace, a fanciful creation of my husband, Bijan. There was a love seat against one wall, over which I had thrown a lace cover, my mother's gift from long ago. A pale peach couch faced the window, accompanied by two matching chairs and a big square glass-topped table.

My place was always in the chair with its back to the window, which opened onto a wide cul-de-sac called Azar. Opposite the window was the former American Hospital, once small and exclusive, now a noisy, overcrowded medical facility for wounded and disabled veterans of the war. On "weekends"—Thursdays and Fridays in Iran—the small street was crowded with hospital visitors who came as if for a picnic, with sandwiches and children. The neighbor's front yard, his pride and joy, was the main victim of their assaults, especially in summer, when they helped themselves to his beloved roses. We could hear the sound of children shouting, crying and laughing, and, mingled in, their mother's voices, also shouting, calling out their children's names and threatening them with punishments. Sometimes a child or two would ring our doorbell and run away, repeating their perilous exercise at intervals.

From our second-story apartment—my mother occupied the first floor, and my brother's apartment, on the third floor, was often empty since he had left for England—we could see the upper branches of a generous tree and, in the distance, over the buildings, the Elburz Mountains. The street, the hospital and its visitors were censored out of sight. We felt their presence only through the disembodied noises emanating from below.

I could not see my favorite mountains from where I sat, but opposite my chair, on the far wall of the dining room, was an antique oval mirror, a gift from my father, and in its reflection, I could see the mountains capped with snow, even in summer, and watch the trees change color. That censored view intensified my impression that the noise came not from the street below but from some far-off place, a place whose persistent hum was our only link to the world we refused, for those few hours, to acknowledge.

That room, for all of us, became a place of transgression. What a wonderland it was! Sitting around the large coffee table covered with bouquets of flowers, we moved in and out of the novels we read. Looking back, I am amazed at how much we learned without even noticing it. We were, to borrow from Nabokov, to experience how the ordinary pebble of ordinary life could be transformed into a jewel through the magic eye of fiction.

3

Six A.M.: The first day of class. I was already up. Too excited to eat breakfast, I put the coffee on and then took a long, leisurely shower. The water caressed my neck, my back, my legs, and I stood there both rooted and light. For the first time in many years, I felt a sense of anticipation that was not marred by tension: I would not need to go through the torturous rituals that had marked my days when I taught at the university—rituals governing what I was forced to wear, how I was expected to act, the gestures I had to remember to control. For this class, I would prepare differently.

Life in the Islamic Republic was as capricious as the month of April, when short periods of sunshine would suddenly give way to showers and storms. It was unpredictable: the regime would go through cycles of some tolerance, followed by a crackdown. Now, after a period of relative calm and so-called liberalization, we had again entered a time of hardships. Universities had once more become the targets of attack by the cultural purists who were busy imposing stricter sets of laws, going so far as to segregate men and women in classes and punishing disobedient professors. 27

The University of Allameh Tabatabai, where I had been teaching since 1987, had been singled out as the most liberal university in Iran. It was rumored that someone in the Ministry of Higher Education had asked, rhetorically, if the faculty at Allameh thought they lived in Switzerland. *Switzerland* had somehow become a byword for Western laxity: any program or action that was deemed un-Islamic was reproached with a mocking reminder that Iran was by no means Switzerland. 28

The pressure was hardest on the students. I felt helpless as I listened to their endless tales of woe. Female students were being penalized for running up the stairs when they were late for classes, for laughing in the hallways, for talking to members of the opposite sex. One day Sanaz had barged into class near the end of the session, crying. In between bursts of tears, she explained that she was late because the female guards at the door, finding blush in her bag, had tried to send her home with a reprimand. 29

Why did I stop teaching so suddenly? I had asked myself this question many times. Was it the declining quality of the university? The ever-increasing indifference among the remaining faculty and students? The daily struggle against arbitrary rules and restrictions? 30

I smiled as I rubbed the coarse loofah over my skin, remembering the reaction of the university officials to my letter of resignation. They had harassed and limited me in all manner or ways, monitoring my visitors, controlling my actions, refusing a long-overdue tenure; and when I resigned, they infuriated me by suddenly commiserating and refusing to accept my resignation. The students had threatened to boycott classes, and it was of some satisfaction to me to find out later that despite threats of reprisals, they in fact did boycott my replacement. Everyone thought I would break down and eventually return. 31

It took two more years before they finally accepted my resignation. I remember a friend told me, You don't understand their mentality. They won't accept your resignation because they don't think you have the right to quit. *They* are the ones who decide how long you should stay and when you should be dispensed with. More than anything else, it was this arbitrariness that had become unbearable. 32

What will you do? my friends had asked. Will you just stay home now? Well, I could write another book, I would tell them. But in truth I had no definite plans. I was 33 still dealing with the aftershocks of a book on Nabokov I had just published, and only vague ideas, like vapors, formed when I turned to consider the shape of my next book. I could, for a while at least, continue the pleasant task of studying Persian classics, but one particular project, a notion I had been nurturing for years, was uppermost on my mind. For a long time I had dreamt of creating a special class, one that would give me the freedoms denied me in the classes I taught in the Islamic Republic. I wanted to teach a handful of select students wholly committed to the study of literature, students who were not handpicked by the government, who had not chosen English literature simply because they had not been accepted in other fields or because they thought an English degree would be a good career move.

Teaching in the Islamic Republic, like any other vocation, was subservient to politics and subject to arbitrary rules. Always, the joy of teaching was marred by diversions and considerations forced on us by the regime—how well could one teach when the main concern of university officials was not the quality of one's work but the color of one's lips, the subversive potential of a single strand of hair? Could one really concentrate on one's job when what preoccupied the faculty was how to excise the word *wine* from a Hemingway story, when they decided not to teach Brontë because she appeared to condone adultery? 34

I was reminded of a painter friend who had started her career by depicting scenes from life, mainly deserted rooms, abandoned houses and discarded photographs of women. Gradually, her work became more abstract, and in her last exhibition, her paintings were splashes of rebellious color, like the two in my living room, dark patches with little droplets of blue. I asked her about her progress from modern realism to abstraction. Reality has become so intolerable, she said, so bleak, that all I can paint now are the colors of my dreams. 35

The colors of my dreams, I repeated to myself, stepping out of the shower and onto the cool tiles. I liked that. How many people get a chance to paint the colors of their dreams? I put on my oversize bathrobe—it felt good to move from the security of the embracing water to the protective cover of a bathrobe wrapped around my body. I walked barefoot into the kitchen, poured some coffee into my favorite mug, the one with red strawberries, and sat down forgetfully on the divan in the hall. 36

This class was the color of my dreams. It entailed an active withdrawal from a reality that had turned hostile. I wanted very badly to hold on to my rare mood of jubilance and optimism. For in the back of my mind, I didn't know what awaited me at the end of this project. You are aware, a friend had said, that you are more and more withdrawing into yourself, and now that you have cut your relations with the university, your whole contact with the outside world will be mainly restricted to one room. Where will you go from here? he had asked. Withdrawal into one's dreams could be dangerous, I reflected, padding into the bedroom to change; this I had learned from Nabokov's crazy dreamers, like Kinbote and Humbert. 37

In selecting my students, I did not take into consideration their ideological or religious backgrounds. Later, I would count it as the class's great achievement that such 38 a mixed group, with different and at times conflicting backgrounds, personal as well as religious and social, remained so loyal to its goals and ideals.

One reason for my choice of these particular girls was the peculiar mixture of 39
fragility and courage I sensed in them. They were what you would call loners, who did not belong to any particular group or sect. I admired their ability to survive not despite but in some ways because of their solitary lives. We can call the class "a space of our own," Manna had suggested, a sort of communal version of Virginia Woolf's room of her own.

I spent longer than usual choosing my clothes that first morning, trying on 40
different outfits, until I finally settled on a red-striped shirt and black corduroy jeans. I applied my makeup with care and put on bright red lipstick. As I fastened my small gold earrings, I suddenly panicked. What if it doesn't work? What if they won't come?

Don't, don't do that! Suspend all fears for the next five or six hours at least. Please, 41
please, I pleaded with myself, putting on my shoes and going into the kitchen.

4

I was making tea when the doorbell rang. I was so preoccupied with my thoughts 42
that I didn't hear it the first time. I opened the door to Mahshid. I thought you weren't home, she said, handing me a bouquet of white and yellow daffodils. As she was taking off her black robe, I told her, There are no men in the house—you can take that off, too. She hesitated before uncoiling her long black scarf. Mahshid and Yassi both observed the veil, but Yassi of late had become more relaxed in the way she wore her scarf. She tied it with a loose knot under her throat, her dark brown hair, untidily parted in the middle, peeping out from underneath. Mahshid's hair, however, was meticulously styled and curled under. Her short bangs gave her a strangely old-fashioned look that struck me as more European than Iranian. She wore a deep blue jacket over her white shirt, with a huge yellow butterfly embroidered on its right side. I pointed to the butterfly: did you wear this in honor of Nabokov?

I no longer remember when Mahshid first began to take my classes at the 43
university. Somehow, it seems as if she had always been there. Her father, a devout Muslim, had been an ardent supporter of the revolution. She wore the scarf even before the revolution, and in her class diary, she wrote about the lonely mornings when she went to a fashionable girls' college, where she felt neglected and ignored— ironically, because of her then-conspicuous attire. After the revolution, she was jailed for five years because of her affiliation with a dissident religious organization and banned from continuing her education for two years after she was out of jail.

I imagine her in those pre-revolutionary days, walking along the uphill street 44
leading to the college on countless sunny mornings. I see her walking alone, her head to the ground. Then, as now, she did not enjoy the day's brilliance. I say "then, as now" because the revolution that imposed the scarf on others did not relieve Mahshid of her loneliness. Before the revolution, she could in a sense take pride in her isolation. At that time, she had worn the scarf as a testament to her faith. Her decision was

a voluntary act. When the revolution forced the scarf on others, her action became meaningless.

Mahshid is proper in the true sense of the word: she has grace and a certain dignity. Her skin is the color of moonlight, and she has almond-shaped eyes and jet-black hair. She wears pastel colors and is soft-spoken. Her pious background should have shielded her, but it didn't. I cannot imagine her in jail. 45

Over the many years I have known Mahshid, she has rarely alluded to her jail experiences, which left her with a permanently impaired kidney. One day in class, as we were talking about our daily terrors and nightmares, she mentioned that her jail memories visited her from time to time and that she had still not found a way to articulate them. But, she added, everyday life does not have fewer horrors than prison. 46

I asked Mahshid if she wanted some tea. Always considerate, she said she'd rather wait for the others and apologized for being a little early. Can I help? she asked. There's really nothing to help with. Make yourself at home, I told her as I stepped into the kitchen with the flowers and searched for a vase. The bell rang again. I'll get it Mahshid cried out from the living room. I heard laughter; Manna and Yassi had arrived. 47

Manna came into the kitchen holding a small bouquet of roses. It's from Nima, she said. He wants to make you feel bad about excluding him from the class. He says he'll carry a bouquet of red roses and march in front of your house during class hours, in protest. She was beaming; a few bright sparks flashed in her eyes and died down again. 48

Putting the pastries onto a large tray, I asked Manna if she envisioned the words to her poems in colors. Nabokov writes in his autobiography that he and his mother saw the letters of the alphabet in color, I explained. He says of himself that he is a painterly writer. 49

The Islamic Republic coarsened my taste in colors, Manna said, fingering the discarded leaves of her roses. I want to wear outrageous colors, like shocking pink or tomato red. I feel too greedy for colors to see them in carefully chosen words of poetry. Manna was one of those people who would experience ecstasy but not happiness. Come here, I want to show you something, I said, leading her into our bedroom. When I was very young, I was obsessed with the colors of places and things my father told me about in his nightly stories. I wanted to know the color of Scheherazade's dress, her bedcover, the color of the genie and the magic lamp, and once I asked him about the color of paradise. He said it could be any color I wanted it to be. That was not enough. Then one day when we had guests and I was eating my soup in the dining room, my eyes fell on a painting I had seen on the wall ever since I could remember, and I instantly knew the color of my paradise. And here it is, I said, proudly pointing to a small oil painting in an old wooden frame: a green landscape of lush, leathery leaves with two birds, two deep red apples, a golden pear and a touch of blue. 50

My paradise is swimming-pool blue! Manna shot in, her eyes still glued to the painting. We lived in a large garden that belonged to my grandparents, she said, 51 turning to me. You know the old Persian gardens, with their fruit trees, peaches, apples, cherries, persimmons and a willow or two. My best memories are of swimming in our huge irregularly shaped swimming pool. I was a swimming champion at our school, a fact my dad was very proud of. About a year after the revolution, my father died of a heart attack, and then the government confiscated our house and our garden and we moved into an apartment. I never swam again. My dream is at the bottom of that pool. I have a recurring dream of diving in to retrieve something of my father's memory and my childhood, she said as we walked to the living room, for the doorbell had rung again.

Azin and Mitra had arrived together. Azin was taking off her black kimonolike robe—Japanese-style robes were all the rage at the time—revealing a white peasant blouse that made no pretense of covering her shoulders, big golden earrings and pink lipstick. She had a branch of small yellow orchids—from Mitra and myself, she said in that special tone of hers that I can only describe as a flirtatious pout. 52

Nassrin came in next. She had brought two boxes of nougats: presents from Isfahan, she declared. She was dressed in her usual uniform—navy robe, navy scarf and black heelless shoes. When I had last seen her in class, she was wearing a huge black chador, revealing only the oval of her face and two restless hands, which, when she was not writing or doodling, were constantly in motion, as if trying to escape the confines of the thick black cloth. More recently, she had exchanged the chador for long, shapeless robes in navy, black or dark brown, with thick matching scarves that hid her hair and framed her face. She had a small, pale face, skin so transparent you could count the veins, full eyebrows, long lashes, lively eyes (brown), a small straight nose and an angry mouth: an unfinished miniature by some master who had suddenly been called away from his job and left the meticulously drawn face imprisoned in a careless splash of dark color. 53

We heard the sound of screeching tires and sudden brakes. I looked out the window: a small old Renault, cream-colored, had pulled up on the curb. Behind the wheel, a young man with fashionable sunglasses and a defiant profile rested his black-sleeved arm on the curve of the open window and gave the impression that he was driving a Porsche. He was staring straight in front of him as he talked to the woman beside him. Only once did he turn his head to his right, with what I could guess was a cross expression, and that was when the woman got out of the car and he angrily slammed the door behind her. As she walked to our front door, he threw his head out and shouted a few words, but she did not turn back to answer. The old Renault was Sanaz's; she had bought it with money saved from her job. 54

I turned towards the room, blushing for Sanaz. That must be the obnoxious brother, I thought. Seconds later the doorbell rang and I heard Sanaz's hurried steps and opened the door to her. She looked harassed, as if she had been running from a stalker or a thief. As soon as she saw me, she adjusted her face into a smile and said breathlessly: I hope I am not too late? 55

There were two very important men dominating Sanaz's life at the time. The first was her brother. He was nineteen years old and had not yet finished high school and 56 was the darling of their parents, who, after two girls, one of whom had died at the age of three, had finally been blessed with a son. He was spoiled, and his one obsession in life was Sanaz. He had taken to proving his masculinity by spying on her, listening to her phone conversations, driving her car around and monitoring her actions. Her parents had tried to appease Sanaz and begged her, as the older sister, to be patient and understanding, to use her motherly instincts to see him through this difficult period.

The other was her childhood sweetheart, a boy she had known since she was eleven. Their parents were best friends, and their families spent most of their time and vacations together. Sanaz and Ali seemed to have been in love forever. Their parents encouraged this union and called it a match made in heaven. When Ali went away to England six years ago, his mother took to calling Sanaz his bride. They wrote to each other, sent photographs, and recently, when the number of Sanaz's suitors increased, there were talks of engagement and a reunion in Turkey, where Iranians did not require entrance visas. Any day now it might happen, an event Sanaz looked forward to with some fear and trepidation. 57

I had never seen Sanaz without her uniform, and stood there almost transfixed as she took off her robe and scarf. She was wearing an orange T-shirt tucked into tight jeans and brown boots, yet the most radical transformation was the mass of shimmering dark brown hair that now framed her face. She shook her magnificent hair from side to side, a gesture that I later noticed was a habit with her; she would toss her head and run her fingers through her hair every once in a while, as if making sure that her most prized possession was still there. Her features looked softer and more radiant—the black scarf she wore in public made her small face look emaciated and almost hard. 58

I'm sorry I'm a little late, she said breathlessly, running her fingers through her hair. My brother insisted on driving me, and he refused to wake up on time. He never gets up before ten, but he wanted to know where I was going. I might be off on some secret tryst, you know, a date or something. 59

I have been worrying in case any of you would get into trouble for this class, I said, inviting them all to take their seats around the table in the living room. I hope your parents and spouses feel comfortable with our arrangement. 60

Nassrin, who was wandering around the room, inspecting the paintings as if seeing them for the first time, paused to say offhandedly, I mentioned the idea very casually to my father, just to test his reaction, and he vehemently disapproved. 61

How did you convince him to let you come? I asked. I lied, she said. You lied? What else can one do with a person who's so dictatorial he won't let his daughter, at *this age*, got to an all-female literature class? Besides, isn't this how we treat the regime? Can we tell the Revolutionary Guards the truth? We lie to them; we hide our satellite dishes. We tell them we don't have illegal books and alcohol in our houses. Even my venerable father lies to them when the safety of his family is at stake, Nassrin added defiantly. 62

What if he calls me to check on you? I said, half teasingly. He won't. I gave a brilliant alibi. I said Mahshid and I had volunteered to help translate Islamic texts 63 into English. And he believed you? Well, he had no reason not to. I hadn't lied to him before—not really—and it was what he wanted to believe. And he trusts Mahshid completely.

So if he calls me, I should lie to him? I persisted. It's up to you, Nassrin said after a pause, looking down at her twisting hands. Do *you* think you should tell him? By now I could hear a note of desperation in her voice. Am I getting you into trouble? 64

Nassrin always acted so confident that sometimes I forgot how vulnerable she really was under that tough-girl act. Of course I would respect your confidence, I said more gently. As you said, you are a big girl. You know what you're doing. 65

I had settled into my usual chair, opposite the mirror, where the mountains had come to stay. It is strange to look into a mirror and see not yourself but a view so distant from you. Mahshid, after some hesitation, had taken the chair to my right. On the couch, Manna settled to the far right and Azin to the far left; they instinctively kept their distance. Sanaz and Mitra were perched on the love seat, their heads close together as they whispered and giggled. 66

At this point Yassi and Nassrin came in and looked around for seats. Azin patted the empty part of the couch, inviting Yassi with her hand. Yassi hesitated for a moment and then slid between Azin and Manna. She slumped into place and seemed to leave little room for her two companions, who sat upright and a little stiff in their respective corners. Without her robe, she looked a little overweight, as if she had not yet lost her baby fat. Nassrin had gone to the dining room in search of a chair. We can squeeze you in here, said Manna. No, thank you, I actually prefer straight-backed chairs. When she returned, she placed her chair between the couch and Mahshid. 67

They kept that arrangement, faithfully, to the end. It became representative of their emotional boundaries and personal relations. And so began our first class. 68

5

"Upsilamba!" I heard Yassi exclaim as I entered the dining room with a tray of tea. Yassi loved playing with words. Once she told us that her obsession with words was pathological. As soon as I discover a new word, I have to use it, she said, like someone who buys an evening gown and is so eager that she wears it to the movies, or to lunch. 69

Let me pause and rewind the reel to retrace the events leading us to Yassi's exclamation. This was our first session. All of us had been nervous and inarticulate. We were used to meeting in public, mainly in classrooms and in lecture halls. The girls had their separate relationships with me, but except for Nassrin and Mahshid, who were intimate, and a certain friendship between Mitra and Sanaz, the rest were not close; in many cases, in fact, they would never have chosen to be friends. The collective intimacy made them uncomfortable. 70

I had explained to them the purpose of the class: to read, discuss and respond to works of fiction. Each would have a private diary, in which she should record her responses to the novels, as well as ways in which these works and their discussions 71 related to her personal and social experiences. I explained that I had chosen them for this class because they seemed dedicated to the study of literature. I mentioned that one of the criteria for the books I had chosen was their authors' faith in the critical and almost magical power of literature, and reminded them of the nineteen-year-old Nabokov, who, during the Russian Revolution, would not allow himself to be diverted by the sound of bullets. He kept on writing his solitary poems while he heard the guns and saw the bloody fights from his window. Let us see, I said, whether seventy years later our disinterested faith will reward us by transforming the gloomy reality created of this other revolution.

The first work we discussed was *A Thousand and One Nights*, the familiar tale of the cuckolded king who slew successive virgin wives as revenge for his queen's betrayal, and whose murderous hand was finally stayed by the entrancing storyteller Scheherazade. I formulated certain general questions for them to consider, the most central of which was how these great works of imagination could help us in our present trapped situation as women. We were not looking for blueprints, for an easy solution, but we did hope to find a link between the open spaces the novels provided and the closed ones we were confined to. I remember reading to my girls Nabokov's claim that "readers were born free and ought to remain free." 72

What had most intrigued me about the frame story of *A Thousand and One Nights* were the three kinds of women it portrayed—all victims of a king's unreasonable rule. Before Scheherazade enters the scene, the women in the story are divided into those who betray and then are killed (the queen) and those who are killed before they have a chance to betray (the virgins). The virgins, who, unlike Scheherazade, have no voice in the story, are mostly ignored by the critics. Their silence, however, is significant. They surrender their virginity, and their lives, without resistance or protest. They do not quite exist, because they leave no trace in their anonymous death. The queen's infidelity does not rob the king of his absolute authority; it throws him off balance. Both types of women—the queen and the virgins—tacitly accept the king's public authority by acting within the confines of his domain and by accepting its arbitrary laws. 73

Scheherazade breaks the cycle of violence by choosing to embrace different terms of engagement. She fashions her universe not through physical force, as does the king, but through imagination and reflection. This gives her the courage to risk her life and sets her apart from the other characters in the tale. 74

Our edition of *A Thousand and One Nights* came in six volumes. I, luckily, had bought mine before it was banned and only sold on the black market, for exorbitant prices. I divided the volumes among the girls and asked them, for the next session, to classify the tales according to the types of women who played central roles in the stories. 75

Once I'd given them their assignment, I asked them each to tell the rest of us why they had chosen to spend their Thursday mornings here, discussing Nabokov and Jane Austen. Their answers were brief and forced. In order to break the ice, I suggested the calming distraction of cream puffs and tea. 76

This brings us to the moment when I enter the dining room with eight glasses of 77

239

tea on an old and unpolished silver tray. Brewing and serving tea is an aesthetic ritual in Iran, performed several times a day. We serve tea in transparent glasses, small and shapely, the most popular of which is called slim-wasted: round and full at the top, narrow in the middle and round and full at the bottom. The color of the tea and its subtle aroma are an indication of the brewer's skill.

I step into the dining room with eight slim-waisted glasses whose honey-colored liquid trembles seductively. At this point, I hear Yassi shout triumphantly, "Upsilamba!" She throws the word at me like a ball, and I take a mental leap to catch it. **78**

Upsilamba!—the word carries me back to the spring of 1994, when four of my girls and Nima were auditing a class I was teaching on the twentieth-century novel. The class's favorite book was Nabokov's *Invitation to a Beheading*. In this novel, Nabokov differentiates Cincinnatus C., his imaginative and lonely hero, from those around him through his originality in a society where uniformity is not only the norm but also the law. Even as a child, Nabokov tells us, Cincinnatus appreciated the freshness and beauty of language, while other children "understood each other at the first word, since they had no words that would end in an unexpected way, perhaps in some archaic letter, and upsilamba, becoming a bird or catapult with wondrous consequences." **79**

No one in class had bothered to ask what the word meant. No one, that is, who was properly taking the class—for many of my old students just stayed on and sat in on my classes long after their graduation. Often, they were more interested and worked harder than my regular students, who were taking the classes for credit. Thus it was that those who audited the class—including Nassrin, Manna, Nima, Mahshid and Yassi—had one day gathered in my office to discuss this and a number of other questions. **80**

I decided to play a little game with the class, to test their curiosity. On the midterm exam, one of the questions was "Explain the significance of the word *upsilamba* in the context of *Invitation to a Beheading*. What does the word mean, and how does it relate to the main theme of the novel?" Except for four or five students, no one had any idea what I could possibly mean, a point I did not forget to remind them of every once in a while throughout the rest of that term. **81**

The truth was that *upsilamba* was one of Nabokov's fanciful creations, possibly a word he invented out of *upsilon*, the twentieth letter in the Greek alphabet, and *lambda*, the eleventh. So that first day in our private class, we let our minds play again and invented new meanings of our own. **82**

I said I associated *upsilamba* with the impossible joy of a suspended leap. Yassi, who seemed excited for no particular reason, cried out that she always thought it would be the name of a dance—you know, "C'mon, baby, do the Upsilamba with me." I proposed that for the next time, they each write a sentence or two explaining what the word meant to them. **83**

Manna suggested that *upsilamba* evoked the image of small silver fish leaping in and out of a moonlit lake. Nima added in parentheses, Just so you won't forget me, **84** although you have barred me from your class: an upsilamba to you too! For Azin it was a sound, a melody. Mahshid described an image of three girls jumping rope and shouting "Upsilamba!" with each leap. For Sanaz, the world was a small African boy's secret magical name. Mitra wasn't sure why the word reminded her of the paradox of a blissful sigh. And to Nassrin it was the magic code that opened the door to a secret cave filled with treasures.

Upsilamba became part of our increasing repository of coded words and   85
expressions, a repository that grew over time until gradually we had created a secret language of our own. That word became a symbol, a sign of the vague sense of joy, the tingle in the spine Nabokov expected his readers to feel in the act of reading fiction; it was a sensation that separated the good readers, as he called them, from the ordinary ones. It also became the code word that opened the secret cave of remembrance.

6

In his foreward to the English edition of *Invitation to a Beheading* (1959),   86
Nabokov reminds the reader that his novel does not offer "*tout pour tous.*" Nothing of the kind. "It is," he claims, "a violin in the void." And yet, he goes on to say, "I know…a few readers who will jump up, ruffling their hair." Well, absolutely. The original version, Nabokov tells us, was published in installments in 1935. Almost six decades later, in a world unknown and presumably unknowable to Nabokov, in a forlorn living room with windows looking out towards distant white-capped mountains, time and again I would stand witness to the unlikeliest of readers as they lost themselves in a madness of hair-ruffling.

Invitation to a Beheading begins with the announcement that its fragile hero,   87
Cincinnatus C., has been sentenced to death for the crime of "gnostic turpitude": in a place where all citizens are required to be transparent, he is opaque. The principal characteristic of this world is its arbitrariness; the condemned man's only privilege is to know the time of his death—but the executioners keep even this from him, turning every day into a day of execution. As the story unfolds, the reader discovers with increasing discomfort the artificial texture of this strange place. The moon from the window is fake; so is the spider in the corner, which, according to convention, must become the prisoner's faithful companion. The director of the jail, the jailer and the defense lawyer are all the same man, and keep changing places. The most important character, the executioner, is first introduced to the prisoner under another name and as a fellow prisoner: M'sieur Pierre. The executioner and the condemned man must learn to love each other and cooperate in the act of execution, which will be celebrated in a gaudy feast. In this staged world, Cincinnatus's only window to another universe is his writing.

The world of the novel is one of empty rituals. Every act is bereft of substance   88
and significance, and even death becomes a spectacle for which the good citizens buy tickets. It is only through these empty rituals that brutality becomes possible. In another Nabokov novel, *The Real Life of Sebastian Knight*, Sebastian's brother discovers two seemingly incongruous pictures in his dead brother's library: a pretty, curly-haired

child playing with a dog and a Chinese man in the act of being beheaded. The two pictures remind us of the close relation between banality and brutality. Nabokov had a special Russian term for this: *poshlust*.

Poshlust, Nabokov explains, "is not only the obviously trashy but mainly the falsely important, the falsely beautiful, the falsely clever, the falsely attractive." Yes, there are many examples you can bring from everyday life, from the politicians' sugary speeches to certain writers' proclamations to chickens. Chickens? You know, the ones street vendors sell nowadays—if you lived in Tehran, you couldn't possibly miss them. The ones they dip in paint—shocking pink, brilliant red or turquoise blue—in order to make them more attractive. Or the plastic flowers, the bright pink-and-blue artificial gladiolas carted out at the university both for mourning and for celebration. 89

What Nabokov creates for us in *Invitation to a Beheading* is not the actual physical pain and torture of a totalitarian regime but the nightmarish quality of living in an atmosphere of perpetual dread. Cincinnatus C. is frail, he is passive, he is a hero without knowing or acknowledging it: he fights with his instincts, and his acts of writing are his means of escape. He is a hero because he refuses to become like all the rest. 90

Unlike in other utopian novels, the forces of evil here are not omnipotent; Nabokov shows us their frailty as well. They are ridiculous and they can be defeated, and this does not lessen the tragedy—the waste. *Invitation to a Beheading* is written from the point of view of the victim, one who ultimately sees the absurd sham of his persecutors and who must retreat into himself in order to survive. 91

Those of us living in the Islamic Republic of Iran grasped both the tragedy and absurdity of the cruelty to which we were subjected. We had to poke fun at our own misery in order to survive. We also instinctively recognized poshlust—not just in others, but in ourselves. This was one reason that art and literature became so essential to our lives: they were not a luxury but a necessity. What Nabokov captured was the texture of life in a totalitarian society, where you are completely alone in an illusory world full of false promises, where you can no longer differentiate between your savior and your executioner. 92

We formed a special bond with Nabokov despite the difficulty of his prose. This went deeper than our identification with his themes. His novels are shaped around invisible trapdoors, sudden gaps that constantly pull the carpet from under the reader's feet. They are filled with mistrust of what we call everyday reality, an acute sense of that reality's fickleness and frailty. 93

There was something, both in his fiction and in his life, that we instinctively related to and grasped, the possibility of a boundless freedom when all options are taken away. I think that was what drove me to create the class. My main link with the outside world had been the university, and now that I had severed that link, there on the brink of the void, I could invent the violin or be devoured by the void. 94

Choosing a Topic for Your Research Writing

In the second epigraph to this chapter, Wayne Booth warns that you will be left "on the sidelines" of academic and professional life if you "cannot reliably do research or evaluate the research of others" (9). Echoing Geoffrey Hart, who exhorts all researchers to dig "deeper" (first epigraph), Booth also urges you to find a topic about which you truly care, for legitimate research must grow from your questions and from your sense of an audience that needs to hear your answers (20–26).

If you have worked through the first and second chapters, you have already learned how to find your true topic, one that grows from your interests and concerns. You have also learned how to frame your questions and follow them to a clear sense of audience and purpose. Using those same strategies—listing, freewriting, journaling, tree-outlining—can help you to find your topic. But on what subject areas might you apply these prewriting strategies? For starters, why not consider some of the subjects you have explored here in your analysis of other writers' research?

Consider these literary subjects:

1. Did the article and research paper above stir any interest in Flannery O'Connor? If so, consider working with another story dealing with same theme, our need to wake up and to see beyond our prejudices. Suggestions: "Good Country People," "A Good Man Is Hard to Find," "Revelation," or "The Lame Shall Enter First." Though you could write a substantial essay on any one of these stories—and find plenty of secondary sources on each—you might also consider comparing two or three of these stories. In each, you will find characters who will remind you of Mrs. May and the Greenleafs. Consider, too, working with O'Connor's powerful long short story, "The Displaced Person," or with one of her short novels: *The Violent Bear It Away* or *Wise Blood*.

2. Did the excerpts from Nafisi's memoir inspire you? If so, why not write a research paper on the whole book? You'll find plenty of secondary sources on this *New York Times* best-seller.

3. Consider, too, writing your research paper on a work by a chosen author, using Nafisi's theories on fiction (see your answers to questions 1–3 above) as ways of measuring the power of your chosen novel, story, play, or poem. Does your chosen work demonstrate the "transforming" power that Nafisi's describes? Does your experience of your chosen work empower you to understand, face, even resist the "absurdities" and "cruelties" of "real life," as portrayed in the fiction? Of course, your secondary sources, literary critics, could help you answer these questions about your chosen author's work.

Whatever true topic you find, whether found among these subjects or not, the strategies described and illustrated in this chapter, once applied, will keep you off the academic and professional "sidelines" that Booth urged you to avoid.

Works Cited

Booth, Wayne *et al*. *The Craft of Research*. 2nd ed. Chicago: U of Chicago P, 2003.

Giannone, Richard. "'Greenleaf': A Story of Lent." *Studies in Short Fiction* 22 (1985): 421–29.

Hart, Geoffrey J. S. "The Scientific Method: Learning from Scientists." *Intercom* March 2005: 14–17.

Nafisi, Azar. *Reading* Lolita *in Tehran*. New York: Random House, 2004.

O'Connor, Flannery. "Greenleaf." *The Complete Stories of Flannery O'Connor*. New York: Ferrar, Straus, and Giroux, 1991.

Sallis, Leigh-Ann. Proposal Memo.

Sallis, Leigh-Ann. Student research paper.

CHAPTER 6

Revising and Proofing

"Only when a writer's task has come to the end does [he or she] set to work in earnest."

STEPHEN WHITE, *The Written Word*

"With a word processor you can play with your writing on the screen until you get it right....To me this is God's gift, or technology's gift, to good writing, because the essence of writing is rewriting."

WILLIAM ZINSSER, *On Writing Well*

"Read over your compositions, and where ever you meet with a passage which you think is particularly fine, strike it out."

DR. SAMUEL JOHNSON, Boswell's *Life of Johnson*

"La facultad is the capacity to see in surface phenomena the meaning of deeper realities, to see the structure below the surface....It ...causes the depths to open up, causes a shift in perception."

GLORIA ANZALDUA, "Entering into the Serpent"

Understanding Style

You learned in chapter five to write proposal memos, using your knowledge of your readers to refine your sense of purpose, to describe the literary problem you want to solve, and to locate the paths of research you will follow. You also learned to document your research by compiling bibliography cards and note cards, the building blocks for your research papers. Having studied the fruit of this process, the research paper itself, you then found your own literary topic and wrote a documented essay.

In this chapter, you will broaden your strategies for revising your essays, moving beyond peer response groups to a study of **style**. Through this study, you will learn to think of style as the sum total of all the choices writers make to achieve their purposes, to serve their readers, and to do so with a distinctive voice.

To give continuity to this study of style, you will read fiction and nonfiction selections, all focused on a single theme: parents and children. First, you will learn to listen for Jane Austen's voice in the first chapter of her *Pride and Prejudice*, a novel which explores the conflicts between parents and their grown-up children over the topic of marriage. Next, you will read a student's essay on *Pride and Prejudice*, focusing on her efforts to revise her rough draft by enriching her content.

After considering these macro-issues of revision raised by the student's essay, you will learn to address micro-issues of revision by reading a close analysis of style in paragraph 14 of King's "Letter from Birmingham Jail," which you read in chapter four. As you re-examine the choices that King made to achieve his purpose in this paragraph, you will re-discover the destructive effects of racism on parents and children.

This discussion will prepare you to analyze Barack Obama's style displayed in an excerpt from his *Dreams from My Father*. Following the Obama selection, you will find three more readings on parents and children: an excerpt from Frank McCourt's memoir *Angela's Ashes*; Sherwood Anderson's short story, "The Egg"; and Alice Walker's essay "In Search of Our Mothers' Gardens." Before each of these selections you will find some journaling questions that will strengthen your ability to analyze others' style; after the selections, you will find an invitation to write on this same theme, parents and children, and to polish your own style.

Following this study of style, you will consider ways to proofread your paper to ensure correctness.

Identifying Jane Austen's Voice

In *Understanding Style*, Joe Glaser defines **voice** as a "blend of the grammar, diction, and sound qualities" that inform a piece of writing and shape the writer's persona (4). In reading the first chapter of Jane Austen's *Pride and Prejudice* below, you will hear a distinctive voice emerging from these elements as Austen opens the door to the Bennet family, a late-eighteenth-century English family wrestling with Mrs. Bennet's all-consuming problem: finding husbands for five daughters. As you enjoy this brief introduction to Mr. and Mrs. Bennet, see if you can identify places where Austen's voice rings most clearly.

Chapter One of *Pride and Prejudice*

It is a truth universally acknowledged, that a single man in possession of a good fortune, must be in want of a wife.   1

However little known the feelings or views of such a man may be on his first entering a neighbourhood, this truth is so well fixed in the minds of the surrounding families, that he is considered as the rightful property of some one or other of their daughters.   2

"My dear Mr. Bennet," said his lady to him one day, "have you heard that Netherfield Park is let at last?"   3

Mr. Bennet replied that he had not.   4

"But it is," returned she; "for Mrs. Long has just been here, and she told me all about it."   5

Mr. Bennet made no answer.   6

"Do you not want to know who has taken it?" cried his wife impatiently.   7

"*You* want to tell me, and I have no objection to hearing it."   8

This was invitation enough.   9

"Why, my dear, you must know, Mrs. Long says that Netherfield is taken by a young man of large fortune from the north of England; that he came down on Monday in a chaise and four to see the place, and was so much delighted with it that he agreed with Mr. Morris immediately; that he is to take possession before Michaelmas, and some of his servants are to be in the house by the end of next week."   10

"What is his name?"   11

"Bingley."   12

"Is he married or single?"   13

"Oh! single, my dear, to be sure! A single man of large fortune; four or five thousand a year. What a fine thing for our girls!"   14

"How so? how can it affect them?"   15

"My dear Mr. Bennet," replied his wife, "how can you be so tiresome! You must know that I am thinking of his marrying one of them."   16

"Is that his design on settling here?"   17

"Design! nonsense, how can you talk so! But it is very likely that he *may* fall in love with one of them, and therefore you must visit him as soon as he comes." 18

"I see no occasion for that. You and the girls may go, or you may send them by themselves, which perhaps will be still better, for as you are as handsome as any of them, Mr. Bingley might like you the best of the party." 19

"My dear, you flatter me. I certainly *have* had my share of beauty, but I do not pretend to be any thing extraordinary now. When a woman has five grown up daughters, she ought to give over thinking of her own beauty." 20

"In such cases, a woman has not often much beauty to think of." 21

"But, my dear, you must indeed go and see Mr. Bingley when he comes into the neighbourhood." 22

"It is more than I engage for, I assure you." 23

"But consider your daughters. Only think what an establishment it would be for one of them. Sir William and Lady Lucas are determined to go, merely on that account, for in general you know they visit no new comers. Indeed you must go, for it will be impossible for *us* to visit him, if you do not." 24

"You are over scrupulous surely. I dare say Mr. Bingley will be very glad to see you; and I will send a few lines by you to assure him of my hearty consent to his marrying which ever he chooses of the girls; though I must throw in a good word for my little Lizzy." 25

"I desire you will do no such thing. Lizzy is not a bit better than the others; and I am sure she is not half so handsome as Jane, nor half so good humoured as Lydia. But you are always giving *her* the preference." 26

"They have none of them much to recommend them," replied he; "they are all silly and ignorant like other girls; but Lizzy has something more of quickness than her sisters." 27

"Mr. Bennet, how can you abuse your own children in such a way? You take delight in vexing me. You have no compassion on my poor nerves." 28

"You mistake me, my dear. I have a high respect for your nerves. They are my old friends. I have heard you mention them with consideration these twenty years at least." 29

"Ah! you do not know what I suffer." 30

"But I hope you will get over it, and live to see many young men of four thousand a year come into the neighbourhood." 31

"It will be no use to us, if twenty such should come since you will not visit them." 32

"Depend upon it, my dear, that when there are twenty, I will visit them all." 33

Mr. Bennet was so odd a mixture of quick parts, sarcastic humour, reserve, and caprice, that the experience of three and twenty years had been insufficient to make 34 his wife understand his character. *Her* mind was less difficult to develop. She was a woman of mean understanding, little information, and uncertain temper. When she was discontented she fancied herself nervous. The business of her life was to get her daughters married; its solace was visiting and news.

Analyzing Austen's Voice

As you read this chapter, you heard primarily dialogue, the voices of Mr. and Mrs. Bennet, not the voice of their creator, Jane Austen. Yet Austen's first and constant concern as novelist must be to give each of her characters a voice. First, you heard Mrs. Bennet's excitement as she announces the most recent gossip, straight from "Mrs. Long," that the fashionable estate Netherfield has been rented by young Mr. Bingley. Notice in the passage below that Austen's stringing together of noun clauses—"that" clauses—conveys the breathless excitement of Mrs. Bennet:

> Why, my dear, you must know, Mrs. Long says that Netherfield is taken by a young man of large fortune from the north of England; that he came down on Monday is a chaise [carriage] and four [horses] to see the place, and was so much delighted with it that he agreed with Mr. Morris immediately; that he is to take possession before Michaelmas [September 29], and some of his servants are to be in the house by the end of the week.

This series of "that" clauses conveys Mrs. Bennet's excitement; the series also has a child-like sound, the effect of all those "and" conjunctions. This impression of her childishness receives reinforcement when we hear her conclude that this "single man of large fortune" must necessarily be "a fine thing for our girls."

Mr. Bennet's voice carries a far different sound. His first response to his wife's gossip takes the form of silence, which only stokes her eagerness to blurt out the good news. He finally speaks with playful sarcasm: "*You* want to tell me, and I have no objection to hearing it." Notice here that Austen's italicizing the pronoun *you* makes it impossible for us not to hear his gentle mockery of his childish wife. Continuing to tease her, Mr. Bennet pretends to see no connection between Bingley's arrival and his daughters' marriage prospects. Of course, Bingley truly has no such "design," but after twenty-three years of marriage, Bennet knows well his wife's silly illogic and finds sport in egging her on. He does so here by refusing to visit Bingley on his daughters' behalf; we find out in chapter two that he has already made the introductory visit. We hear yet more teasing in Bennet's voice when he assures his wife that she remains as "handsome" as any of her daughters, and that Bingley will no doubt "like you" better than the young Bennet sisters. Though such teasing seems harmless and perhaps deserved, we also hear an edge in his mockery, suggesting his disrespect for women, not just for his gossipy wife: "[Our daughters] have none of them much to recommend them...; they are all silly and ignorant like other girls; but Lizzy has something more of quickness than her sisters."

Having heard these childish and mocking voices, we can readily hear Austen's own amused yet critical voice when we re-read the first two paragraphs:

> It is a truth universally acknowledged, that a single man in possession of a good fortune, must be in want of a wife.
>
> However little known the feelings or views of such a man may be on his first entering a neighbourhood, this truth is so well fixed in the minds of the surrounding families, that he is considered as the rightful property of some one or other of their daughters.

Notice how the second paragraph undercuts the "universal truth" "acknowledged" in the first by stressing the illogic of "surrounding families" who claim the wealthy young man for their daughters without knowing anything of his "feelings or views." In other words, we hear an ironic voice here: this truth may in fact be "universally acknowledged," but this "truth" rests on illogic, not on reality.

At this point, Austen's ironic voice seems playful, much like Mr. Bennet's voice when he claims Mrs. Bennet's "nerves" as his "old friends." However, the last paragraph adds a stinging sound to the playfulness, as Austen's narrator sums up the portraits created by the dialogue:

> Mr. Bennet was so odd a mixture of quick parts, sarcastic humour, reserve, and caprice, that the experience of three and twenty years had been insufficient to make his wife understand his character. *Her* mind was less difficult to develop. She was a woman of mean understanding, little information, and uncertain temper. When she was discontented she fancied herself nervous. The business of her life was to get her daughters married; its solace was visiting and news.

Consider Austen's word choices here as she describes these two parents. By crediting Mr. Bennet with "quick parts" (witiness, intelligence) and "sarcastic humour," Austen aptly summarizes the playfulness we have heard, a playfulness made even more entertaining by its "odd" blending with "reserve," a quality rarely associated with a jokester. Yet when Austen selects the word "caprice" to complete her description of Bennet, she hints at the potential destructiveness of a father, however well intentioned, who capriciously—impulsively— participates in his daughters' lives. Indeed, as you will learn in the student's essay below, Mr. Bennet's capriciousness endangers one daughter's life and the entire family's reputation.

The oddity of Mr. Bennet's nature, the narrator says, makes it impossible for Mrs. Bennet, even after 23 years, to "understand his character." Notice that the italicized pronoun *her* jokingly underlines Mrs. Bennet's weak "mind," but the playful voice becomes harsh in the parallel adjective-noun combinations that follow in the next sentence, describing Mrs. Bennet as a woman with "mean understanding, little information, and uncertain temper."

Though these qualities have entertained us in the first chapter as we listened to her illogic and gossip, the edge in Austen's voice here alerts us to the potential danger of such a woman presuming to arrange her daughters' lives. To be fair, we must acknowledge that many eighteenth-century English mothers considered it their "business" to arrange their daughters' marriages. After all, young women rarely had access to university education or to the professions; therefore, marriage became a matter of survival. However, Mrs. Bennet seems ill-equipped for such serious "business," and her pleasure in "visiting and news" forewarns of her destructively self-centered nature.

Reading a Revised Response to Austen's Novel

Printed below you will find "The Parents' Guilt in *Pride and Prejudice*," an essay that attends to the warnings of Austen's voice, as noted above. The student devised this topic after examining her journal. Having re-read her answers to several questions on Elizabeth Bennet's parents, the student noticed that their parenting affected not only their daughters' personalities but also their choices concerning men and marriage.

After writing her rough draft, the student met with her two writing group members, who offered high praise for her choices in arrangement: she first discusses the Bennets' failure to regulate their youngest daughter's inappropriate flirtatiousness, then Mr. Bennet's guilt in letting one teenage daughter travel with little supervision to Brighton, a resort town full of soldiers. Finally, the student contrasts Mr. Bennet's remorse with Mrs. Bennet's shameless delight, when their disgraced daughter shows up married to Wickham, the money-grubbing soldier with whom she ran off. In other words, given the student's purpose to critique the Bennets' irresponsible parenting, her peers recognized the wisdom of her cause-effect organization and the final emphasis on contrast: one parent learns; the other does not.

However, arrangement represents just one of the macro-concerns you should consider in revising a draft. Just as important, you should consider the range and depth of the evidence you offer to support your claim. After praising the organization, the writing group members stressed this other macro-issue in revision, suggesting that she splice in more quotations from the novel. Doing so, they explained, would allow readers to hear Mr. Bennet's capriciousness, then his remorse, as well as Mrs. Bennet's dangerous obsession with money and good looks and her indifference to the foundations of marriage: love, equality, honesty, and trust.

Before you read the student's revision dealing with her lack of evidence, consider these few facts that will help you follow her analysis of a novel you may not have read:

- Elizabeth Bennet has an older sister, Jane, and three younger sisters: Lydia, Kitty, and Mary.

- Though Darcy's "pride" and Elizabeth's "prejudice" prevent their quickly falling in love, they eventually do so: Elizabeth recognizes his integrity and kindness; Darcy falls for her intelligence and "fine eyes."

- Mr. Bingley is Mr. Darcy's best friend and, eventually, Jane Bennet's husband. Bingley hosts a dance at his rented local estate, called Netherfield, which you read about in chapter one.

- Brighton was a fashionable town where young eighteenth- and nineteenth-century British soldiers often enjoyed leave. Wickham and fifteen-year-old Lydia Bennet meet in Brighton and run off to London, where they live together—unmarried— until Darcy, proving his love for Elizabeth, uses his money to persuade Wickham to marry Lydia, thus salvaging the respectability of the Bennet family.

STUDENT ESSAY ON AUSTEN:

"The Parents' Guilt in *Pride and Prejudice*"

Elizabeth Coggins

Jane Austen's *Pride and Prejudice* vividly records the frailty of women's reputations in early nineteenth-century society. In this genteel society where the Bennet family lives, the responsibilities of parents of young, unmarried women are both crucial and numerous, for the female "reputation is no less brittle than it is beautiful" (Austen 215). Marriages were often not completely determined by affection alone but also by economic security where entails and dowries were involved. Mr. Bennet and Mrs. Bennet are guilty of neglecting their duties to all of their daughters by allowing one daughter's unchecked "exuberant spirits" to nearly ruin the chance of all five daughters to marry well (173). Mr. Bennet's indolence and Mrs. Bennet's encouragement of their daughters' flirtatious, wild behavior cause the family's reputation and livelihood to be nearly destroyed. After watching their reputations reach the brink of disgrace, Mr. Bennet realizes his faults as a parent and strives to amend them; in contrast, Mrs. Bennet never perceives her flaws and consequently does nothing to rectify her character.

Mr. and Mrs. Bennet both make critical errors by not censoring the manners and behaviors of their daughters. Mr. Bennet takes a passive approach to disciplining his daughters. While he is intelligent enough to realize how "uncommonly foolish" his three youngest daughters are, he does nothing to correct their self-indulgence and immaturity (21). Instead, Mr. Bennet prefers spending most of his time in his library where he is "always sure of leisure and tranquility" (53). On the other hand, Mrs. Bennet is immersed in every detail of the town news, and her chief occupation "[is] to get her daughters married" (3). Mrs. Bennet serves as a source of encouragement for her daughters' unpardonable public spectacles and often contributes to the embarrassment. At the Netherfield ball, for example, Mrs. Bennet loudly discusses the probability of eldest daughter Jane's impending engagement to Mr. Bingley, much to the dismay of sensible sister Elizabeth, who "blushed and blushed again with shame and vexation" (75). Appalled by the "folly and indecorum" of the Bennets at Netherfield, Mr. Darcy dissuades Bingley from making an offer of marriage to Jane (160), thus preventing a marriage which could have been extremely advantageous not only for Jane but also for the rest of the family. Even when Darcy first proposes to Elizabeth, he alludes to the "inferiority of [her] relations" (145). This lack of manners displayed by the Bennet family costs Jane and her family both happiness and economic security; both parents must share the blame.

Perhaps the most conspicuous example of Mr. and Mrs. Bennet's lapse in judgment arises when they allow young Lydia to go to Brighton, a fashionable town and temporary residence of many handsome young soldiers. Despite Elizabeth's warnings against allowing Lydia to go because of her "wild volatility," Mr. Bennet once again demonstrates his indolence, failing to check his daughter's wild behavior. Indeed, he ignores Elizabeth's advice, deciding that he would rather pay for the "little expense or inconvenience" of Lydia's trip than to suffer the loss of "peace" in his home, which her remaining would inevitably cause (172-73). Mrs. Bennet likewise encourages Lydia to go to Brighton and "not miss the opportunity of enjoying" herself (174). Lydia's subsequent elopement with the disreputable officer Mr. Wickham very nearly causes not only the demise of her reputation but also those of her sisters, as Reverend Collins observes: "This false step in one daughter will be injurious to the fortunes of all the others, for who…will connect themselves to such a family" (221). It is clear that Elizabeth credits Lydia's fall more to Mr. Bennet's "indolence" than to her mother's encouraging her to chase soldiers (210). Elizabeth also acknowledges that her father "might at least have preserved the respectability of his daughters, even if incapable of encouraging the mind of his wife" (177). Instead, the two irresponsible parents nearly cause the collapse of the family's reputation.

After nearly ruining their family, both Mr. and Mrs. Bennet have the chance to correct their flaws in their parenting. Mr. Bennet has a chance to become a more active father in regulating the manners and behavior of his daughters, and Mrs. Bennet has the opportunity to become more sensible in the way she encourages her daughters. Mr. Bennet realizes and accepts his role in Lydia's incredible error in judgment. He admits that the family's loss of honor was his "own doing," and by accepting the blame he can evaluate how grossly he underestimated the behaviors of his younger daughters and what effect those behaviors could have on the whole family (222). Therefore, Mr. Bennet resolves to correct his mistakes by telling Lydia's sister Kitty that he has "at last learnt to be cautious" (223), a lesson that will limit Kitty's social freedoms considerably. Although Mr. Bennet sees his own faults as a parent and somewhat redeems himself at the end of the novel, Mrs. Bennet does not have quite the same reaction.

Unlike Mr. Bennet, Mrs. Bennet does not comprehend any wrong-doing on her part in her daughter's rash behavior. When Elizabeth returns home after hearing of Lydia's elopement, Mrs. Bennet blames "everybody" but herself, failing to see that her "indulgence" has caused Lydia's collapse of virtue (213). Because she does not accept any blame for her daughter's conduct, Mrs. Bennet cannot become a better parent, just as her husband has. In fact, her "mean understanding" does not allow her to comprehend the gravity of Lydia's actions. Instead of lamenting that her unmarried daughter has been found living in London with Wickham, who agrees to marry her only after being paid to do so, Mrs. Bennet worries about what Lydia will wear at the wedding: "the clothes, the wedding clothes!" (227). Instead of sharing in the shame of Lydia's aborted elopement as the rest of the family does, Mrs. Bennet not only welcomes Lydia with open arms but insists on taking her daughter "visiting about" with her trophy husband in tow (236). When Lydia has the audacity to comment that her sisters might have found husbands had they followed her to Brighton, Mrs. Bennet readily agrees, saying, "if I had my will," they would have gone (236). This inability to see her flaws as a parent prevents Mrs. Bennet from becoming a more responsible parent, as Mr. Bennet has done.

Although Lydia's senselessness and folly cause the family's brush with ruin, Mr. and Mrs. Bennet share her guilt by allowing her to behave recklessly. Marriage was essential for the economic and class security of the Bennet girls, and the parents' disregard of their daughters' behavior could have prohibited their marrying well. In *Pride and Prejudice*, Austen brings the Bennet family to the brink of destruction and, by doing so, depicts the delicacy of the female reputation in nineteenth-century society.

Analyzing the Student Essay

Now that you have read the student's paper, answer the questions below to apply the principles of audience analysis discussed in the first two chapters. In doing so, you will discover the choices she made not only to achieve her purpose but also to meet the expectations of her audience, her professor and peers.

1. Look first at the title of the essay, then at sentence #4. What key word in the title and key phrase in sentence #4 convey the heart of her thesis, her claim about the Bennets' parenting?

2. What phrasing in sentences #4 and #5 announces that the student will focus on the effects of their parenting?

3. What phrasing in sentence #6 stresses the contrast between these guilty parents?

4. What background information does the student provide in the first three sentences to stress the heavy responsibility parents carried in Austen's time?

5. Re-read your answers to questions 1–4. What expectations of the professor has the student tried to satisfy in this introductory paragraph?

6. This assignment did not require research (secondary sources—see chapter five), but the professor did expect the student to select examples and quotations from the novel that support the **topic sentence** (main point) of each body paragraph and, in turn, the thesis (claim) about these guilty parents. Focusing on either paragraph 2 (on their

failure to censor bad manners) or on paragraph 3 (on their poor judgment in letting Lydia go to Brighton), explain how the student's chosen examples and quotations add to her ethos (her credibility—see chapter two). Do you think she has effectively dealt with the "lack of quotes" comment offered by her peers?

7. How successfully did the student provide quotes and examples (logos—see chapter two) in paragraphs 4 and 5 to persuade her professor and peers that Mr. Bennet learns his lesson and that Mrs. Bennet does not?

8. What key words and phrases does the student use in the concluding paragraph to stress the seriousness of her claim about Mr. and Mrs. Bennet?

Having answered these eight questions, you have performed a **rhetorical analysis,** a close study of the choices that the student made to achieve her purpose and to meet her reader's expectations. These questions, however, have focused primarily on macro-issues of revision: arrangement and development. In the section below, you will learn to attend to micro-issues in revision. Remember: your style can be defined as the sum total of all the choices you make in dealing with both macro- and micro-issues.

Revising for Professional Style

This chapter begins with four epigraphs packed with wisdom for writers who want to improve a piece of writing and, more important, to improve as writers. Stephen White stresses the hard work of revision, which begins "in earnest" when that first draft "comes to an end." I've suggested above that the rough draft should be written in good faith before the author has the right to share it with peers, but White reminds us that serious writers regard that draft as only a starting point.

In the second quote, William Zinsser, well-known author of *On Writing Well,* acknowledges the importance of this commitment to re-vise, to see again: "the essence of writing is rewriting." Yet Zinsser joyfully thanks God and technology for the word processor, which has made this demanding work far less daunting than it was 25 years ago, when we had no "screen" on which to "play" with our drafts. Two hundred years before any of us had a screen on which to play, Dr. Samuel Johnson urged writers to search their drafts for their "finest" passage and then to "strike it out." Though Dr. Johnson's advice seems counterintuitive, it rests on his profound knowledge of human nature, including our penchant to think too well of our own words, especially if they cost us some sweat.

Rather than settling for "fine" writing, which often sounds good but says little, Johnson would have us develop what Gloria Anzaldua calls "*la facultad,*" the faculty of looking "below the surface" of words to the "deeper realities" which words, ironically, can never quite express (74). We must embrace a great paradox here. We must revise to get closer to saying what cannot be said.

Having acknowledged this mysterious truth, let's finish this chapter by focusing on practical ways to revise your writing so that you can take your readers closer to that "shift in perception" that Anzaldua describes (75). First, you will examine a check-sheet on the macro-issues related to organization and development, which we discussed above; then, you will look at micro-issues related to sentence structure and diction. Next, you will look at reliable strategies of recognizing and correcting the most common kinds of errors in grammar and punctuation.

Guide to Macro-Issues in Revision

Before attending to the critical issues of sentence structure, word-choice and correctness, most experienced writers prefer to focus on macro-issues: organization and development. If you have shared a rough draft with a writing group, as did the student whose work you considered above, then you can use the "Guidelines for Responding" in chapters 1 and 2 not only to reflect on your peers' suggestions but also to guide your reflections as you revise your work for submission. You would be wise, too, to consult your "Reader Analysis Worksheet" in chapter 3, for we must always assess our organization and development in terms of the reader's needs. Below, you'll find a handy synthesis of the Guide and the Worksheet, a check sheet of questions that you will want to answer "in earnest," as Stephen White suggests.

Introduction

- Have I identified the problem I'm trying to solve or the focus and limits of my study?
- Have I made a claim that moves toward a solution to my problem, or a thesis that takes a stand on the significance of my findings?
- Have I revealed the organization of my essay, my plan for analyzing my problem and my solutions?

Body Paragraphs/Discussion Sections

- Does each body paragraph or section begin with a transition from the previous paragraph or section—a phrase, clause, or sentence that stresses the connection or relationship between the section just concluded and the one just beginning? Sample: Look at the first sentence of this section (Macro-Issues in Revision) and the last two sentences of the previous section.
- Does each body paragraph or section contain a topic sentence, a key reason for accepting the claim or thesis?
- Does each topic sentence receive support from relevant facts, examples, explanations, quoted testimony from experts, and quoted key passages from the primary source? Do these supports seem sufficient to persuade a skeptical or hostile reader? Why?

- Have I blended various rhetorical modes effectively to define and exemplify key terms and to clarify relationships between and among my ideas (e.g., classification, contrast, cause-effect)?

- Have I arranged my key ideas effectively to catch and sustain my reader's interest and to persuade him/her to embrace my claim?

Conclusion

- Does my essay end with a fresh re-statement of the thesis?

- Have I provided a summary of key points?

Guide to Micro-Issues in Revision

Once you've answered the questions above—and dealt with those questions which you first had to answer with "no"—you will be eager to turn your attention to the vehicles which deliver your persuasive arrangement and your thorough analysis: your sentences and your diction or word choice.

Before moving to another guide, a check sheet focused on these micro-issues in revision, let's review these elusive terms, style and voice; then let's watch and listen for their emergence in a passage from King's famous "Letter from Birmingham Jail."

Again, think of your style as the sum of all the choices you make in addressing both the macro- and the micro-issues in revising your work. When you decide to re-order your key ideas, to expand the range of examples or the depth of analysis you must offer to meet your reader's needs and expectations, you contribute to your style. When you re-structure your original sentences to achieve greater emphasis as well as more clarity, you have further shaped your style. When you re-think your word choices, making them more or less formal, depending on your audience, you have made more stylistic choices. When you deliberately revise your word choice to make your diction more vivid, either through concrete nouns or figurative (comparative) language, you have marked your style indelibly. Further, when any of these stylistic choices in sentence structure and diction create audible rhythms, you have given your style its voice.

Analyzing Martin Luther King's Style

You found an analysis of Dr. King's entire letter, as well as the letter itself, in chapter four; let's focus now on paragraph 14 to illustrate the definitions of style and voice above and to observe once again how the writer's awareness of his purpose and his audience guides his choices which, in turn, define his style. To provide some context for this analysis, we must first recall that King wrote the first draft of his letter in the margins of his newspaper as he sat in Birmingham jail, where he and his followers found themselves in 1963 after parading without a permit, the law they knowingly broke to protest the segregationist policies of the city government. He wrote, of course, to us all, to posterity, challenging his church and his country—then and now—to practice the principles of brotherhood and liberty, which they endorsed at the end of the Civil War with the Emancipation Proclamation and, nearly one hundred years before that, in the Declaration of Independence. King's immediate readers, however, were "My Dear Fellow Clergymen," the eight Christian and Jewish clerics who published a letter in the same paper, protesting King's presence in Birmingham, chastising his "unwise and untimely" impatience in staging protest marches for freedom, and urging him to return to Atlanta.

Paragraph 14

We have waited for more than 340 years for our constitutional God-given rights. The nations of Asia and Africa are moving with jetlike speed toward gaining political independence, but we still creep at horse-and-buggy pace toward gaining a cup of coffee at a lunch counter. Perhaps it is easy for those who have never felt the stinging darts of segregation to say, "Wait." But when you have seen vicious mobs lynch your mothers and fathers at will and drown your sisters and brothers at whim; when you have seen hate-filled policemen curse, kick, and even kill your black brothers and sisters; when you see the vast majority of your twenty million Negro brothers smothering in an airtight cage of poverty in the midst of an affluent society; when you suddenly find your tongue twisted and your speech stammering as you seek to explain to your six-year-old daughter why she can't go to the public amusement park that has just been advertised on television, and see tears welling up in her eyes when she is told that Funtown is closed to colored children, and see ominous clouds of inferiority beginning to form in her little mental sky, and see her beginning to distort her personality by developing an unconscious bitterness toward white people; when you have to concoct an answer for a five-year-old son who is asking: "Daddy, why do white people treat colored people so mean?"; when you take a cross-country drive and find it necessary to sleep night after night in the uncomfortable corners of your automobile because no motel will accept you; when you are humiliated day in and day out by nagging signs reading "white" and "colored"; when your first name becomes "nigger," your middle name becomes "boy" (however old you are), and your last name becomes "John," and your wife and mother are never given the respected title "Mrs."; when you are harried by day and haunted by night by the fact that you are a Negro, living constantly at tiptoe stance, never quite knowing what to expect next, and are plagued with inner fears and outer resentments; when you are forever fighting a degenerating sense of "nobodiness"—then you will understand why we find it difficult to wait. There comes a time when the cup of endurance runs over, and men are no longer willing to be plunged into the abyss of despair. I hope, sirs, you can understand our legitimate and unavoidable impatience.

With a passionate sense of his liberatory purpose, stated above, King knew, too, that his audience, his fellow clergymen, considered him a trouble-maker, an outsider. He knew, therefore, that in making the case for liberty and equality he must also make the case for himself, that he must establish a "patient and reasonable" (paragraph 1) ethos of a compassionate man who came to Birmingham because his own organization, the Southern Christian Leadership Conference, invited him (2) and because "injustice anywhere is a threat to justice everywhere" (4).

When King begins in paragraph 14 to answer the clergymen's question why he finds it so difficult to wait a bit longer for freedom, he responds first with a short, simple sentence: "We have waited for more than 340 years for our constitutional and Godgiven rights." Listen. We may hear some understandable anger here, but no hot-headedness, no vengefulness, just a plain statement of outrageous fact. Notice that he follows this statement in sentence two with figurative language that underscores the unreasonableness of waiting any longer for freedom. "Asia and Africa," he writes, have moved "with jetlike speed" toward political rights, but African Americans still "creep at horse-and-buggy pace toward gaining a cup of coffee at a lunch counter." This use of simile and metaphor creates contrasting images, a jet and a horse-drawn wagon, to help his readers *see* the inappropriate lack of speed toward liberty in the United States.

Throughout this paragraph, King continues to use figurative language to create images that blend his reasonable ethos with pathos, appeals to the readers' emotions—and to their sense of family. When he describes, for example, the economic injustice of segregation, he speaks of "twenty million Negro brothers smothering in an airtight cage of poverty in the midst of an affluent society." When he describes the psychological damage suffered by an African American child excluded from amusement parks, he makes sure that we see her under "ominous clouds of inferiority" already forming in her "mental sky." These metaphors imply vivid comparisons—poverty is a cage; inferiority is a cloud—which help us to see the agony caused by "the stinging darts of segregation" (sentence three), another powerful metaphor which explains "why we find it difficult to 'wait'" (end of sentence four). Note, too, that King ends this emotional paragraph with one more example of figurative language, allusion: "There comes a time when the cup of endurance runs over, and men are no longer willing to be plunged into the abyss of despair" (sentence five). Clearly, King's Christian and Jewish colleagues, experts in the New and Old Testaments, would recognize these references (allusions) to the Bible, which describe African Americans as no longer willing to endure the cruelty of racists or to suffer the hell of segregation.

King also carefully crafts his sentences in this paragraph to stress his logos, his evidence of the cruelty of segregation, and his pathos, his emotional appeals to white readers, including the eight clergymen, who have never felt those "stinging darts of segregation." Five of these six sentences achieve the usual average length of sentences written by college-educated writers to college-educated readers: 17.8. Each sentence, as we have already seen in analyzing his diction, offers relatively short (sentence length ranges from 11 words to 31), pithy statements on the unreasonable delays of freedom. However, sentence four reaches the highly unusual length of 311 words. Why would King create such a seemingly endless sentence? Why not break it up into ten or so shorter sentences? The answer to these questions lies in the word voice. In these rhythmical parallel structures—"when you have seen…when you have seen…"—we hear the voice of this passionate Baptist preacher, this son and grandson of Baptist preachers, who grew up hearing these poetic parallel sentence structures from the pulpit each Sunday morning. As we get caught up in these strong rhythms, King's voice and his style become nearly synonymous terms; we discover, too, that clarity has nothing to do with sentence length, everything to do with sentence structure.

But look again at this sentence and the sophistication of King's rhetorical strategies. Each "when" clause gives us an example (logos) of what it feels like to be on the receiving end of one of those "stinging darts" of segregation. After eight or nine "when" clauses, we can imagine his "fellow clergymen" wondering "when will this sentence ever end?" We can then imagine King, with his readers caught in his rhetorical trap, responding, "Brothers, when will *segregation* ever end."

Note, too, the arrangement of King's examples within the parallel "when" clauses. He begins with extremely violent examples of segregation: "vicious mobs" lynching "your mothers and fathers" and drowning "your sisters and brothers." Additionally, he uses other parallel phrases—"at will…at whim"—to stress the impunity of racists whose brutality receives sanction from a segregated culture. Still within this endless sentence, King moves to other examples of physical violence, letting us hear the alliterated outrage in his voice when he speaks of policemen "cursing, kicking, even killing" his "black brothers and sisters." This repetition (alliteration) of the harsh "k" sound (curse, kick, kill) reinforces the violence of the image, another image which he insists that we "see" so that we will understand why he "can't wait" to be free. Finally, King moves from these shocking examples of physical violence to even more outrageous examples of psychological violence inflicted on the segregated: the child excluded from "Funtown," a place for white kids only; a man who must sleep in his car, excluded by his black skin from motels; a mature man called "boy." By placing last these and other examples of the psychological "sting" of segregation, King identifies that "degenerating sense of 'nobodiness'" as the ultimate horror of segregation.

Finally, notice the power of the last eleven words of this extraordinary sentence. The first 300 words, grammatically speaking, represent an extremely long fragment. A "when" clause, more properly an adverbial clause, cannot stand by itself; it must be attached to the independent clause that it describes or modifies. The same rule holds true for nine "when-you-see" clauses, even with their countless "and see" constructions imbedded in some of them. To complete the long fragment, King must add an independent clause, a clause that answers the adverbial and moral question about what will happen "when you see" and feel all these horrors of segregation: "then you will see why we find it difficult to wait."

Professional rhetoricians give this kind of sentence a name: the **periodic sentence**. Linguists describe the typical English sentence as **standard** or **loose,** meaning that the main clause comes up front, with modifying clauses and phrases coming at the end (you just read a standard sentence). In contrast, reversing this standard pattern, giving us the main clause at the end, the opposite of what our ears expect, the periodic sentence creates emphasis (you just read a periodic sentence). Consider the effect of King's choice. He could have easily converted his 311-word periodic sentence into nine standard sentences, each sounding something like this: "You will understand why we can't wait (main or "independent clause"), when you have seen policemen kill your brothers and sisters (adverbial or "dependent" clause). However, by choosing the one periodic sentence instead of the nine standard sentences, King places tremendous rhetorical emphasis on the examples of "stinging darts" and the painful "when-you-have-seen" clause that introduces each dart. Imagine the psychological and spiritual discomfort of his "fellow clergymen" as each "when" clause forces them to feel the dart, to see what they have chosen not to see. Imagine their even greater discomfort—and, by extension, the discomfort of all King's readers—when we finally "understand," in the last eleven words, what we as Americans should have always understood: "we can wait no longer" to be free. Indeed, after this "periodic" intensity, the final standard sentence, only eleven words, achieves a perfect blend of courtesy and moral outrage made all the more powerful by its brevity: "I hope, sirs, you can understand our legitimate and unavoidable impatience."

Please don't conclude from this analysis that your professor expects you to write in the style of Dr. King. On the contrary, she wants you to find and sound your own voice. King's work, however, gives us a particularly striking example of style as choice and voice as the sound of those choices. Style, then, has nothing to do with "flair," everything to do with substance—and the strategies you choose to deliver your substance most emphatically to your reader.

Reading More About Parents and Children

This section contains readings from President Barack Obama, Frank McCourt, Sherwood Anderson, and Alice Walker. Before each selection, you will find brief comments on the context of the selection as well as journaling questions to help you focus on style. Following the readings, you will find an invitation to write your own essay on "parents and children." Then at the end of the chapter, you'll also find two supports for revising that essay: a guide to micro-issues in revision and tips on achieving correctness.

Journaling on Barack Obama's Memoir

Committed to print over 30 years after Dr. King's "Letter," President Obama's dreams resemble those of Dr. King, but you will hear a different voice in the passage from his memoir at the end of this chapter.

Before you read the excerpt from *Dreams*, consider the context in which Obama wrote and the purposes which motivated his writing. In the introduction to the 2004 edition of his memoir (first published in 1995), Obama acknowledges his longing for privacy, the result of seeing so many others search his "eyes," guessing "at my troubled heart," imagining "the mixed blood, the divided soul, the ghostly image of the tragic mulatto trapped between two worlds," the separate worlds of his white mother and his black father (xv). Yet in spite of his wish for privacy, Obama has written this memoir to show that his racial "tragedy" is "not mine alone," that Americans of all colors can witness this public tragedy "on the nightly news"(xv).

This memoir, then, extends from Obama's efforts—first as an Illinois senator, and as a U.S. senator, now as president—to "break down" this "tragic cycle" of discrimination and racial violence (xv). He explains, too, that he writes to clarify his sense of self, a clarity he can reach only by recording his "personal, interior journey—a boy's search for his father, and through that search a workable meaning for [his] life as a black American" (xvi). In recounting that interior journey, Obama also takes his readers on an external journey, form his childhood in New York and Hawaii, to his college days in Los Angeles, to his social work in Chicago, to his law studies at Harvard, to his search for roots in Kenya.

The excerpt below focuses on Occidental College, where Obama discovered his voice and his public mission. As you read this selection, answer the following questions on Obama's style. Doing so will help you to develop the sharp eye you will need to analyze and strengthen your own style as you move from draft to polished essay:

1. This section begins with a thesis: "A single conversation can change you," a lesson he learned from "the power of [his] father's words." Focusing on paragraphs 12–29, explain how Obama uses dialogue to reveal how and why young Obama needs to change, and how Regina initiates that change. As you answer this question, concentrate on the rhythms of their sentences and on individual word choices that reveal his immaturity and her ability to stimulate growth.

2. Obama explains that his campus political activities developed his "hunger for words." Focusing on his speech outside the trustees' meeting (paragraphs 5–8), explain how Obama's parallel sentence structures reveal his delight that he can "carry a message, support an idea" (paragraph 2).

3. Focusing on paragraphs 4 and 9, explain how Obama uses description to reveal the power of language to move people.

4. In paragraph 10, Obama describes the political rally as "a school play without parents." Explain the appropriateness of this metaphor in clarifying his skepticism (at that moment) about the power of language to correct social injustice. Explain, too, how his description of Regina and Marcus (paragraph 10) contradicts young Obama's comments about this "farce."

Excerpt from *Dreams from my Father*

BARACK OBAMA

Strange how a single conversation can change you. Or maybe it only seems that way in retrospect. A year passes and you know you feel differently, but you're not sure what or why or how, so your mind casts back for something that might give that difference shape: a word, a glance, a touch. I know that after what seemed a long absence, I had felt my voice returning to me that afternoon with Regina. It remained shaky afterward, subject to distortion. But entering sophomore year I could feel it growing stronger, sturdier, that constant honest portion of myself, a bridge between my future and my past.

It was around that time that I got involved in the divestment campaign. It had started as something of a lark, I suppose, part of the radical pose my friends and I sought to maintain, a subconscious end run around issues closer to home. But as the months passed and I found myself drawn into a larger role—contacting representatives of the African National Congress to speak on campus, drafting letters to the faculty, printing up flyers, arguing strategy—I noticed that people had begun to listen to my opinions. It was a discovery that made me hungry for words. Not words to hide behind but words that could carry a message, support an idea. When we started planning the rally for the trustees' meeting, and somebody suggested that I open the thing, I quickly agreed. I figured I was ready, and could reach people where it counted. I thought my voice wouldn't fail me.

Let's see, now. What was it that I had been thinking in those days leading up to the rally? The agenda had been carefully arranged beforehand—I was only supposed to make a few opening remarks, in the middle of which a couple of white students would come onstage dressed in their paramilitary uniforms to drag me away. A bit of street theater, a way to dramatize the situation for activists in South Africa. I knew the score, had helped plan the script. Only, when I sat down to prepare a few notes for what I might say, something had happened. In my mind it somehow became more than just a two-minute speech, more than a way to prove my political orthodoxy. I started to remember my father's visit to Miss Hefty's class; the look on Coretta's face that day; the power of my father's words to transform. If I could just find the right words, I had thought to myself. With the right words everything could change—South Africa, the lives of ghetto kids just a few miles away, my own tenuous place in the world.

I was still in that trancelike state when I mounted the stage. For I don't know how long, I just stood there, the sun in my eyes, the crowd of a few hundred restless after lunch. A couple of students were throwing a Frisbee on the lawn; others were standing off to the side, ready to break off to the library at any moment. Without waiting for a cue, I stepped up to the microphone.

"There's a struggle going on," I said. My voice barely carried beyond the first few rows. A few people looked up, and I waited for the crowd to quiet.

"I say, there's a struggle going on!"

6

The Frisbee players stopped.

7

"It's happening an ocean away. But it's a struggle that touches each and every one of us. Whether we know it or not. Whether we want it or not. A struggle that demands we choose sides. Not between black and white. Not between rich and poor. No—it's a harder choice than that. It's a choice between dignity and servitude. Between fairness and injustice. Between commitment and indifference. A choice between right and wrong..."

8

I stopped. The crowd was quiet now, watching me. Somebody started to clap. "Go on with it, Barack," somebody else shouted. "Tell it like it is." Then the others started in, clapping, cheering, and I knew that I had them, that the connection had been made. I took hold of the mike, ready to plunge on, when I felt someone's hands grabbing me from behind. It was just as we'd planned it, Andy and Jonathan looking grim-faced behind their dark glasses. They started yanking me off the stage, and I was supposed to act like I was trying to break free, except a part of me wasn't acting, I really wanted to stay up there, to hear my voice bouncing off the crowd and returning back to me in applause. I had so much left to say.

9

But my part was over. I stood on the side as Marcus stepped up to the mike in his white T-shirt and denims, lean and dark and straightbacked and righteous. He explained to the audience what they had just witnessed, why the administration's waffling on the issue of South Africa was unacceptable. Then Regina got up and testified, about the pride her family had felt in seeing her start at college and the shame she now felt knowing that she was part of an institution that paid for its privilege with the profits of oppression. I should have been proud of the two of them; they were eloquent, you could tell the crowd was moved. But I wasn't really listening anymore. I was on the outside again, watching, judging, skeptical. Through my eyes, we suddenly appeared like the sleek and well-fed amateurs we were, with our black chiffon armbands and hand-painted signs and earnest young faces. The Frisbee players had returned to their game. When the trustees began to arrive for their meeting, a few of them paused behind the glass walls of the administration building to watch us, and I noticed the old white men chuckling to themselves, one old geezer even waving in our direction. The whole thing was a farce, I thought to myself—the rally, the banners, everything. A pleasant afternoon diversion, a school play without the parents. And me and my one minute oration—the biggest farce of all.

10

At the party that night, Regina came up to me and offered her congratulations. I asked what for.

11

"For that wonderful speech you gave."

12

I popped open a beer. "It was short, anyway."

13

Regina ignored my sarcasm. "That's what made it so effective," she said. "You spoke from the heart, Barack. It made people want to hear more. When they pulled you away, it was as if—"

14

"Listen, Regina," I said, cutting her off, "you are a very sweet lady. And I'm happy you enjoyed my little performance today. But that's the last time you will ever hear another speech out of me. I'm going to leave the preaching to you. And to Marcus. Me, I've decided I've got no business speaking for black folks." 15

"And why is that?" 16

I sipped on my beer, my eyes wandering over the dancers in front of us. "Because I've got nothing to say Regina. I don't believe we made any difference by what we did today. I don't believe that what happens to a kid in Soweto makes much difference to the people we were talking to. Pretty words don't make it so. So why do I pretend otherwise? I'll tell you why. Because it makes *me* feel important. Because *I* like the applause. It gives me a nice, cheap thrill. That's all." 17

"You don't really believe that." 18

"That's what I believe." 19

She stared at me, puzzled, trying to figure out whether I was pulling her leg. "Well, you could have fooled me," she said finally, trying to match my tone. "Seemed to me like I heard a man speak who believed in something. A black man who cared. But hey, I guess I'm stupid." 20

I took another swig of beer and waved at someone coming through the door. "Not stupid, Regina. Naive." 21

She took a step back, her hands on her hips. "Naive? *You're* calling *me* naive? Uh-uh. I don't think so. If anybody's naive, it's you. You're the one who seems to think he can run away from himself. You're the one who thinks he can avoid what he feels." She stuck a finger in my chest. "You wanna know what your real problem is? You always think everything's about you. You're just like Reggie and Marcus and Steve and all the other brothers out here. The rally is about you. The speech is about you. The hurt is always your hurt. Well, let me tell you something, Mr. Obama. It's not just about you. It's never just about you. It's about people who need your help. Children who are depending on you. They're not interested in your irony or your sophistication or your ego getting bruised. And neither am I." 22

Just as she was finishing, Reggie wandered out of the kitchen, drunker than I was. He came over and threw his arm around my shoulder. "Obama! Great party, man!" He threw Regina a sloppy grin. "Let me tell you, Regina, Obama and me go way back. Should have seen our parties last year, back at the dorms. Man, you remember that time we stayed up the whole weekend? Forty hours, no sleep. Started Saturday morning and didn't stop till Monday." 23

I tried to change the subject, but Reggie was on a roll. "I'm telling you, Regina, it was wild. When the maids show up Monday morning, we were all sitting in the hallway, looking like zombies. Bottles everywhere. Cigarette butts. Newspapers. That spot where Jimmy threw up..." Reggie turned to me and started to laugh, spilling more beer on the rug. "You remember, don't you, man? Shit was so bad, those little 24 old Mexican ladies started to cry. *'Dios Mio,'* one of 'em says, and the other one starts patting her on the back. Oh shit, we were crazy...." 25

I smiled weakly, feeling Regina stare me down like the bum that I was. When she finally spoke it was as if Reggie weren't there. 26

"You think that's funny?" she said to me. Her voice was shaking, barely a whisper. "Is that what's real to you, Barack—making a mess for somebody else to clean up? That could have been my grandmother, you know. She had to clean up behind people for most of her life. I'll bet the people she worked for thought it was funny, too." 27

She grabbed her purse off the coffee table and headed for the door. I thought about running after her, but I noticed a few people staring at me and I didn't want a scene. Reggie pulled on my arm, looking hurt and confused, like a lost child. 28

"What's her problem?" he said. 29

"Nothing," I said. I took the beer out of Reggie's hand and set it on top of the bookshelf. "She just believes in things that aren't really there." 30

Journaling on Frank McCourt's Memoir

In 1996, one year after Obama published his memories of his parents, Frank McCourt did likewise. His *Angela's Ashes* became an immediate best-seller and brought McCourt the National Book Critics Circle Award, the *Los Angeles Times* Book Award, and the Pulitzer Prize, awards which acknowledge the range and depth of his memoir. In telling his story of growing up in Limerick, Ireland, McCourt vividly paints the poverty generated by his father's alcoholism, but he also resurrects his mother Angela from her ashes, acknowledging her desperation and despair but honoring her endurance and love. In recalling his parents, McCourt also teaches his readers what he has learned: If we would survive, if we would feel whole, we must learn to cry and laugh together. And if we would share these tears and laughter, we must read and write.

As you read the excerpt below, the first eleven pages of *Angela's Ashes*, answer the following questions in your journal. Your answers will help you to hear the laughter as well as the anger in McCourt's voice as he begins to sketch both parents.

1. After the first three paragraphs introduce the unhappiness of his Irish Catholic childhood, McCourt writes paragraph four: "Above all—we were wet." That dash could have been a comma, and the whole sentence could have been attached to the next paragraph, which lists the effects of wetness. What effects does McCourt achieve with the dash, which creates a longer pause than would a comma, and with the one-sentence paragraph, which surrounds "wet" with white space?

2. In paragraph five, what metaphors does McCourt use to help readers see the misery of breathing so much wetness? Why do you think he offers so much detail about cures

for wheezing and sneezing?

3. Explain how McCourt uses action verbs to lend vividness to the concrete nouns of wet misery in paragraphs six, seven, and eight.

4. The next four paragraphs introduce Malachy, McCourt's father. Where does McCourt inject humor in this summary of his father's misspent life?

5. In the remainder of this excerpt, the humorous narrative continues: his mother's birth, his mother and father's premarital adventures, his baptism, his brother's cut tongue, and the story-telling on his father's lap. Where do you find the humor, and why do you think McCourt wants us to laugh as we read this narration of his parents' impoverished history? Do you find any tenderness in his parents?

Excerpt from *Angela's Ashes*

Frank McCourt

My father and mother should have stayed in New York where they met and married and where I was born. Instead, they returned to Ireland when I was four, my brother, Malachy, three, the twins, Oliver and Eugene, barely one, and my sister, Margaret, dead and gone.

When I look back on my childhood I wonder how I survived at all. It was, of course, a miserable childhood: the happy childhood is hardly worth your while. Worse than the ordinary miserable childhood is the miserable Irish childhood, and worse yet is the miserable Irish Catholic childhood.

People everywhere brag and whimper about the woes of their early years, but nothing can compare with the Irish version: the poverty; the shiftless loquacious alcoholic father; the pious defeated mother moaning by the fire; pompous priests; bullying schoolmasters; the English and the terrible things they did to us for eight hundred long years.

Above all—we were wet.

Out in the Atlantic Ocean great sheets of rain gathered to drift slowly up the River Shannon and settle forever in Limerick. The rain dampened the city from the Feast of the Circumcision to New Year's Eve. It created a cacophony of hacking coughs, bronchial rattles, asthmatic wheezes, consumptive croaks. It turned noses into fountains, lungs into bacterial sponges. It provoked cures galore; to ease the catarrh you boiled onions in milk blackened with pepper; for the congested passages you made a paste of boiled flour and nettles, wrapped it in a rag, and slapped it, sizzling on the chest.

From October to April the walls of Limerick glistened with the damp. Clothes never dried: tweed and woolen coats housed living things, sometimes sprouted mysterious vegetations. In pubs, steam rose from damp bodies and garments to be inhaled with cigarette and pipe smoke laced with the stale fumes of spilled stout and whiskey and tinged with the odor of piss wafting in from the outdoor jakes where many a man puked up his week's wages.

The rain drove us into the church—our refuge, our strength, our only dry place. At Mass, Benediction, novenas, we huddled in great damp clumps, dozing through priest drone, while steam rose again from our clothes to mingle with the sweetness of incense, flowers and candles. 7

Limerick gained a reputation for piety, but we knew it was only the rain. 8

My father, Malachy McCourt, was born on a farm in Toome, County Antrim. Like his father before, he grew up wild, in trouble with the English, or the Irish, or both. He fought with the Old IRA and for some desperate act he wound up a fugitive with a price on his head. 9

When I was a child I would look at my father, the thinning hair, the collapsing teeth, and wonder why anyone would give money for a head like that. When I was thirteen my father's mother told me a secret: as a wee lad your poor father was dropped on his head. It was an accident, he was never the same after, and you must remember that people dropped on their heads can be a bit peculiar. 10

Because of the price on the head he had been dropped on, he had to be spirited out of Ireland via cargo ship from Galway. In New York, with Prohibition in full swing, he thought he had died and gone to hell for his sins. Then he discovered speakeasies and he rejoiced. 11

After wandering and drinking in America and England he yearned for peace in his declining years. He returned to Belfast, which erupted all around him. He said, A pox on all their houses, and chatted with the ladies of Andersontown. They tempted him with delicacies but he waved them away and drank his tea. He no longer smoked or touched alcohol, so what was the use? It was time to go and he died in the Royal Victoria Hospital. 12

My mother, the former Angela Sheehan, grew up in a Limerick slum with her mother, two brothers, Thomas and Patrick, and a sister, Agnes. She never saw her father, who had run off to Australia weeks before her birth. 13

After a night of drinking porter in the pubs of Limerick he staggers down the lane singing his favorite song, 14

> Who threw the overalls in Mrs. Murphy's chowder?
> Nobody spoke so he said it all the louder
> It's a dirty Irish trick and I can lick the Mick
> Who threw the overalls in Murphy's chowder. 15

He's in great form altogether and he thinks he'll play a while with little Patrick, one year old. 16

Lovely little fella. Loves his daddy. Laughs when Daddy throws him up in the air. Upsy daisy, little Paddy, upsy daisy, up in the air in the dark, so dark, oh, Jasus, you 17 miss the child on the way down and poor little Patrick lands on his head, gurgles a bit, whimpers, goes quiet. Grandma heaves herself from the bed, heavy with the child in her belly, my mother. She's barely able to lift little Patrick from the floor. She moans a long moan over the child and turns on Grandpa. Get out of it. Out. If you stay here a minute longer I'll take the hatchet to you, you drunken lunatic. By Jesus, I'll swing at the end of a rope for you. Get out.

Grandpa stands his ground like a man. I have a right, he says, to stay in me own house. 18

She runs at him and he melts before this whirling dervish with a damaged child in her arms and a healthy one stirring inside. He stumbles from the house, up the lane, and doesn't stop till he reaches Melbourne in Australia. 19

Little Pat, my uncle, was never the same after. He grew up soft in the head with a left leg that went one way, his body the other. He never learned to read or write but God blessed him in another way. When he started to sell newspapers at the age of eight he could count money better than the Chancellor of the Exchequer himself. No one knew why he was called Ab Sheehan, The Abbot, but all Limerick loved him. 20

My mother's troubles began the night she was born. There is my grandmother in the bed heaving and gasping with the labor pains, praying to St. Gerard Majella, patron saint of expectant mothers. There is Nurse O'Halloran, the midwife, all dressed up in her finery. It's New Year's Eve and Mrs. O'Halloran is anxious for this child to be born so that she can rush off to her parties and celebrations. She tells my grandmother: Will you push, will you, push. Jesus, Mary and holy St. Joseph, if you don't hurry with this child it wont' be born till the New Year and what good is that to me with me new dress? Never mind St. Gerard Majella. What can a man do for a woman at a time like this even if he is a saint? St. Gerard Majella my arse. 21

My grandmother switches her prayers to St. Ann, patron saint of difficult labor. But the child won't come. Nurse O'Halloran tells my grandmother, Pray to St. Jude, patron saint of desperate cases. 22

St. Jude, patron of desperate cases, help me. I'm desperate. She grunts and pushes and the infant's head appears, only the head, my mother, and it's the stroke of midnight, the New Year. Limerick City erupts with whistles, horns, sirens, brass bans, people calling and singing, Happy New Year. Should auld acquaintance be forgot, and church bells all over ring out the Angelus and Nurse O'Halloran weeps for the waste of a dress, that child still in there and me in me finery. Will you come out, child, will you? Grandma gives a great push and the child is in the world, a lovely girl with black curly hair and sad blue eyes. 23

Ah, Lord above, says Nurse O'Halloran, this child is a time straddler, born with her head in the New Year and her arse in the Old or was it her head in the Old Year and her arse in the New. You'll have to write to the Pope, missus, to find out what year this child was born in and I'll save this dress for next year. 24

And the child was named Angela for the Angelus which rang the midnight hour, 25 the New Year, the minute of her coming and because she was a little angel anyway.

> Love her as in childhood
> Though feeble, old and grey.
> For you'll never miss a mother's love
> Till she's buried beneath the clay.

26

At the St. Vincent de Paul School, Angela learned to read, write and calculate and by her ninth year her schooling was done. She tried her hand at being a charwoman, a skivvy, a maid with a little white hat opening doors, but she could not manage the little curtsy that is required and her mother said, You don't have the knack of it. You're pure useless. Why don't you go to America where there's room for all sorts of uselessness? I'll give you the fare.

27

She arrived in New York just in time for the first Thanksgiving Day of the Great Depression. She met Malachy at a party given by Dan MacAdorey and his wife, Minnie, on Classon Avenue in Brooklyn. Malachy liked Angela and she liked him. He had a hangdog look, which came from the three months he had just spent in jail for hijacking a truck. He and his friend John McErlaine believed what they were told in the speakeasy, that the truck was packed to the roof with canned pork and beans. Neither knew how to drive and when the police saw the truck lurch and jerk along Myrtle Avenue they pulled it over. The police searched the truck and wondered why anyone would hijack a truck containing, not pork and beans, but cases of buttons.

28

With Angela drawn to the hangdog look and Malachy lonely after three months in jail, there was bound to be a knee-trembler.

29

A knee-trembler is the act itself done up against a wall, man and woman up on their toes, straining so hard their knees tremble with the excitement that's in it.

30

That knee-trembler put Angela in an interesting condition and, of course, there was talk. Angela had cousins, the MacNamara sisters, Delia and Philomena, married, respectively, to Jimmy Fortune of County Mayo, and Tommy Flynn, of Brooklyn itself.

31

Delia and Philomena were large women, great-breasted and fierce. When they sailed along the sidewalks of Brooklyn lesser creatures stepped aside, respect was shown. The sisters knew what was right and they knew what was wrong and any doubts could be resolved by the One, Holy, Roman, Catholic and Apostolic Church. They knew that Angela, unmarried, had no right to be in an interesting condition and they would take steps.

32

Steps they took. With Jimmy and Tommy in tow they marched to the speakeasy on Atlantic Avenue where Malachy could by found on Friday, payday when he had a job. The man in the speak, Joey Cacciamani, did not want to admit the sisters but Philomena told him that if he wanted to keep the nose on his face and that door on its hinges he'd better open up for they were there on God's business. Joey said, Awright, awright, you Irish? Jeezoz! Trouble, trouble.

33

Malachy, at the far end of the bar, turned pale, gave the great-breasted ones a

34

sickly smile, offered them a drink. They resisted the smile and spurned the offer. Delia said, We don't know what class of a tribe you come from in the North of Ireland.

Philomena said, There is a suspicion you might have Presbyterians in your family, which would explain what you did to our cousin. 35

Jimmy said, Ah, now, ah, now. 'Tisn't his fault if there's Presbyterians in his family. 36

Delia said, You shuddup. 37

Tommy had to join in. What you did to that poor unfortunate girl is a disgrace to the Irish race and you should be ashamed of yourself. 38

Och, I am, said Malachy. I am. 39

Nobody asked you to talk, said Philomena. You done enough damage with your blather, so shut your yap. 40

And while your yap is shut, said Delia, we're here to see you do the right thing by our poor cousin, Angela Sheehan. 41

Malachy said, Och, indeed, indeed. The right thing is the right thing and I'd be glad to buy you all a drink while we have this little talk. 42

Take the drink, said Tommy, and shove it up your ass. 43

Philomena said, Our little cousin no sooner gets off the boat than you are at her. We have morals in Limerick, you know, morals. We're not like jackrabbits from Antrim, a place crawling with Presbyterians. 44

Jimmy said, He don't look like a Presbyterian. 45

You shuddup, said Delia. 46

Another thing we noticed, said Philomena. You have a very odd manner. 47

Malachy smiled. I do? 48

You do, says Delia. I think 'tis one of the first things we noticed about you, that odd manner, and it gives us a very uneasy feeling. 49

'Tis that sneaky little Presbyterian smile, said Philomena. 50

Och, said Malachy, it's just the trouble I have with my teeth. 51

Teeth or no teeth, odd manner or no odd manner, you're gonna marry that girl, said Tommy. Up the middle aisle you're going. 52

Och, said Malachy, I wasn't planning to get married, you know. There's no work and I wouldn't' be able to support... 53

Married is what you're going to be, said Delia. 54

Up the middle aisle, said Jimmy 55

You shuddup, said Delia. 56

Malachy watched them leave. I'm in a desperate pickle, he told Joey Cacciamani.   57

Bet your ass, said Joey. I see them babes comin' at me I jump inna Hudson River.   58

Malachy considered the pickle he was in. He had a few dollars in his pocket   59
from the last job and he had an uncle in San Francisco or one of the other California
Sans. Wouldn't he be better off in California, far from the great-breasted MacNamara
sisters and their grim husbands? He would, indeed, and he'd have a drop of the Irish
to celebrate his decision and departure. Joey poured and the drink nearly took the
lining off Malachy's gullet. Irish, indeed! He told Joey it was a Prohibition concoction
from the devil's own still. Joey shrugged. I don't know nothing. I only pour. Still, it
was better than nothing and Malachy would have another and one for yourself, Joey,
and ask them two decent Italians what they'd like and what are you talking about, of
course, I have the money to pay for it.

He awoke on a bench in the Long Island Railroad Station, a cop rapping on his   60
boots with a nightstick, his escape money gone, the MacNamara sisters ready to eat
him alive in Brooklyn.

On the feast of St. Joseph, a bitter day in March, four months after the knee-   61
trembler, Malachy married Angela and in August the child was born. In November
Malachy got drunk and decided it was time to register the child's birth. He thought he
might name the child Malachy, after himself, but his North of Ireland accent and the
alcoholic mumble confused the clerk so much he simply entered the name Male on the
certificate.

Not until late December did they take Male to St. Paul's Church to be baptized   62
and named Francis after his father's father and the lovely saint of Assisi. Angela
wanted to give him a middle name, Munchin, after the patron saint of Limerick but
Malachy said over his dead body. No son of his would have a Limerick name. It's
hard enough going through life with one name. Sticking on the middle names was
an atrocious American habit and there was no need for a second name when you're
christened after the man from Assisi.

There was a delay the day of the baptism when the chosen godfather, John   63
McErlaine, got drunk at the speakeasy and forgot his responsibilities. Philomena
told her husband, Tommy, he'd have to be godfather. Child's soul in danger, she said.
Tommy put his head down and grumbled. All right. I'll be godfather but I'm not goin'
to be responsible if he grows up like his father causin' trouble and goin' through life
with the odd manner for if he does he can go to John McErlaine at the speakeasy.
The priest said, True for you, Tom, decent man that you are, fine man that never set
foot inside a speakeasy. Malachy, fresh from the speakeasy himself, felt insulted and
wanted to argue with the priest, one sacrilege on top of another. Take off that collar
we'll see who's the man. He had to be held back by the great-breasted ones and their
husbands grim. Angela, new mother, agitated, forgot she was holding the child and
let him slip into the baptismal font, a total immersion of the Protestant type. The altar
boy assisting the priest plucked the infant from the font and restored him to Angela,
who sobbed and clutched him, dripping, to her bosom. The priest laughed, said he had

never seen the likes, that the child was a regular little Baptist now and hardly needed a priest. This maddened Malachy again and he wanted to jump at the priest for calling the child some class of a Protestant. The priest said, Quiet, man, you're in God's house, and when Malachy said, God's house, my arse, he was thrown out on Court Street because you can't say arse in God's house.

After baptism Philomena said she had tea and ham and cakes in her house around the corner. Malachy said, Tea? And she said, Yes, tea, or is it whiskey you want? He said tea was grand but first he'd have to go and deal with John McErlaine, who didn't have the decency to carry out his duties as godfather. Angela said, You're only looking for an excuse to run to the speakeasy, and he said, As God is my witness, the drink is the last thing on my mind. Angela started to cry. Your son's christening day and you have to go drinking. Delia told him he was a disgusting specimen but what could you expect from the North of Ireland. 64

Malachy looked from one to the other, shifted on his feet, pulled his cap down over his eyes, shoved his hands deep in his trouser pockets, said, Och, aye, the way they do in the far reaches of Country Antrim, turned, hurried up Court Street to the speakeasy on Atlantic Avenue where he was sure they'd ply him with free drink in honor of his son's baptism. 65

At Philomena's house the sisters and their husbands ate and drank while Angela sat in a corner nursing the baby and crying. Philomena stuffed her mouth with bread and ham and rumbled at Angela, That's what you get for being such a fool. Hardly off the boat and you fall for that lunatic. You shoulda stayed single, put the child up for adoption, and you'd be a free woman today. Angela cried harder and Delia took up the attack, Oh, stop it, Angela, stop it. You have nobody to blame but yourself for gettin' into trouble with a drunkard from the North, a man that doesn't even look like a Catholic, him with his odd manner. I'd say that...that...Malachy has a streak of the Presbyterian in him right enough. You shuddup, Jimmy. 66

If I was you, said Philomena, I'd make sure there's no more children. He don't have a job, so he don't, an' never will the way he drinks. So...no more children, Angela. Are you listenin' to me? 67

I am, Philomena. 68

A year later another child was born. Angela called him Malachy after his father and gave him a middle name, Gerard, after his father's brother. 69

The MacNamara sisters said Angela was nothing but a rabbit and they wanted nothing to do with her till she came to her senses. 70

Their husbands agreed. 71

I'm in a playground on Classon Avenue in Brooklyn, with my brother, Malachy. He's two, I'm three. We're on the seesaw. 72

Up, down, up, down. 73

Malachy goes up. ⁷⁴

I get off. ⁷⁵

Malachy goes down. Seesaw hits the ground. He screams. His hand is on his mouth and there's blood. ⁷⁶

Oh, God. Blood is bad. My mother will kill me. ⁷⁷

And here she is, trying to run across the playground. Her big belly slows her. ⁷⁸

She says, What did you do? What did you do to the child? ⁷⁹

I don't know what to say. I don't know what I did. ⁸⁰

She pulls my ear. Go home. Go to bed. ⁸¹

Bed? In the middle of the day? ⁸²

She pushes me toward the playground gate. Go. ⁸³

She picks up Malachy and waddles off. ⁸⁴

My father's friend, Mr. MacAdorey, is outside our building. He's standing at the edge of the sidewalk with his wife, Minnie, looking at a dog lying in the gutter. There is blood all around the dog's head. It's the color of the blood from Malachy's mouth. ⁸⁵

Malachy has dog blood and the dog has Malachy blood. ⁸⁶

I pull Mr. MacAdorey's hand. I tell him Malachy has blood like the dog. ⁸⁷

Oh, he does, indeed, Francis. Cats have it, too. And Eskimos. All the same blood. ⁸⁸

Minnie says, Stop that, Dan. Stop confusing the wee fellow. She tells me the poor wee dog was hit by a car and he crawled all the way from the middle of the street before he died. Wanted to come home, the poor wee creature. ⁸⁹

Mr. MacAdorey says, You'd better go home, Francis. I don't know what you did to your wee brother, but your mother took him off to the hospital. Go home, child. ⁹⁰

Will Malachy die like the dog, Mr. MacAdorey? ⁹¹

Minnie says, He bit his tongue. He won't die. ⁹²

Why did the dog die? ⁹³

It was his time, Francis. ⁹⁴

The apartment is empty and I wander between the two rooms, the bedroom and the kitchen. My father is out looking for a job and my mother is at the hospital with Malachy. I wish I had something to eat but there's nothing in the icebox but cabbage leaves floating in the melted ice. My father said never eat anything floating in water for the rot that might be in it. I fall asleep on my parents' bed and when my mother shakes me it's nearly dark. Your little brother is going to sleep a while. Nearly bit his tongue off. Stitches galore. Go into the other room. ⁹⁵

My father is in the kitchen sipping black tea from his big white enamel mug. He lifts me to his lap. 96

Dad, will you tell me the story about Coo Coo? 97

Cuchulain. Say it after me, Coo-hoo-lin. I'll tell you the story when you say the name right. Coo-hoo-lin. 98

I say it right and he tells me the story of Cuchulain, who had a different name when he was a boy, Setanta. He grew up in Ireland where Dad lived when he was a boy in County Antrim. Setanta had a stick and ball and one day he hit the ball and it went into the mouth of a big dog that belonged to Culain and choked him. Oh, Culain was angry and he said, What am I to do now without my big dog to guard my house and my wife and my ten small children as well as numerous pigs, hens, sheep? 99

Setanta said, I'm sorry. I'll guard your house with my stick and ball and I'll change my name to Cuchulain, the Hound of Culain. He did. He guarded the house and regions beyond and became a great hero, the Hound of Ulster itself. Dad said he was a greater hero than Hercules or Achilles that the Greeks were always bragging about and he could take on King Arthur and all his knights in a fair fight which, of course, you could never get with an Englishman anyway. 100

That's my story. Dad can't tell that story to Malachy or any other children down the hall. 101

He finishes the story and let's me sip his tea. It's bitter, but I'm happy there on his lap. 102

Journaling on Sherwood Anderson's Short Story

In moving from Frank McCourt to Sherwood Anderson, you will move once again from nonfiction to fiction, but the line between autobiography and short story becomes particularly murky with Anderson. His stories grow from his small-town Ohio childhood, when his family drifted from failure to failure in the 1880s. His fiction, as you will see in "The Egg," also reflects his search as a man for the rich inner life so often stifled or silenced, he thought, by the early twentieth century, the age of machines and obsessions with progress.

As you read Anderson's story, answer the following questions in your journal. Your responses will help you to understand Anderson as stylist and to reflect on his idea of the "grotesque" as it relates to self-knowledge.

1. The first three paragraphs of Anderson's story introduce the narrator's once happy father and plant the seed for potential conflict, as the mother persuades the father to become "ambitious." Where and why does Anderson inject humor in the next two paragraphs, which narrate the disastrous chicken farm adventure, the experience which gave the narrator his first impressions of "disaster" and made him a "gloomy man"?

2. In the description of the wagon ride down Grigg's Road, what details emphasize the destructive effects of the mother's ambition on the narrator's father? How does the comical description of the father's bald head reveal the longings of the narrator as a boy?

3. After describing his father's obsession with the "grotesques," the deformed chickens floating in bottles of alcohol, the narrator describes his own ridiculous "hopping," then his father's even more ridiculous "ambition." Why do the father's efforts to entertain Joe Kane with egg tricks seem ridiculous?

4. How does Anderson use description to stir our sympathy for the narrator's father after Joe Kane's mocking laughter?

5. Can you empathize (identify) as well as sympathize with the narrator's father? Why or why not?

6. Notice that the narrator concludes his story with mystified reflections on the "final triumph of the egg." Can you infer a thematic statement here on the subject of striving? Does the story imply that we're foolish to strive for any success? Given the symbolic association of eggs with hope and new life, what "problem remains unsolved" at the end, and how can such a problem become part of one's "blood"?

"The Egg"

SHERWOOD ANDERSON

My father was, I am sure, intended by nature to be a cheerful, kindly man. Until he was thirty-four years old he worked as a farm-hand for a man named Thomas Butterworth whose place lay near the town of Bidwell, Ohio. He had then a horse of his own and on Saturday evenings drove into town to spend a few hours in social intercourse with other farm-hands. In town he drank several glasses of beer and stood about in Ben Head's saloon—crowded on Saturday evenings with visiting farm-hands. Songs were sung and glasses thumped on the bar. At ten o'clock father drove home along a lonely country road, made his horse comfortable for the night and himself went to bed, quite happy in his position in life. He had at that time no notion of trying to rise in the world.

It was in the spring of his thirty-fifth year that father married my mother, then a country school-teacher, and in the following spring I came wriggling and crying into the world. Something happened to the two people. They became ambitious. The American passion for getting up in the world took possession of them.

It may have been that mother was responsible. Being a school-teacher she had no doubt read books and magazines. She had, I presume, read of how Garfield, Lincoln, and other Americans rose from poverty to fame and greatness and as I lay beside her—in the days of her lying-in—she may have dreamed that I would some day rule men and cities. At any rate she induced father to give up his place as a farm-hand, sell his horse and embark on an independent enterprise of his own. She was a tall silent woman with a long nose and troubled grey eyes. For herself she wanted nothing. For father and myself she was incurably ambitious.

The first venture into which the two people went turned out badly. They rented ten acres of poor stony land on Grigg's Road, eight miles from Bidwell, and launched into chicken raising. I grew into boyhood on the place and got my first impressions of life there. From the beginning they were impressions of disaster and if, in my turn, I am a gloomy man inclined to see the darker side of life, I attribute it to the fact that what should have been for me the happy joyous days of childhood were spent on a chicken farm.

One unversed in such matters can have no notion of the many and tragic things that can happen to a chicken. It is born out of an egg, lives for a few weeks as a tiny fluffy thing such as you will see pictured on Easter cards, then becomes hideously naked, eats quantities of corn and meal bought by the sweat of your father's brow, gets diseases called pip, cholera, and other names, stands looking with stupid eyes at the sun, becomes sick and dies. A few hens, and now and then a rooster, intended to serve God's mysterious ends, struggle through to maturity. The hens lay eggs out of which come other chickens and the dreadful cycle is thus made complete. It is all unbelievably complex. Most philosophers must have been raised on chicken farms. One hopes for so much from a chicken and is so dreadfully disillusioned. Small chickens, just setting out on the journey of life, look so bright and alert and they are in fact so dreadfully stupid. They are so much like people they mix one up in one's judgments of life. If disease does not kill them they wait until your expectations are thoroughly aroused and then walk under the wheels of a wagon—to go squashed and dead back to their maker. Vermin infest their youth, and fortunes must be spent for curative powders. In later life I have seen how a literature has been built up on the subject of fortunes to be made out of raising chickens. It is intended to be read by the gods who have just eaten of the tree of the knowledge of good and evil. It is a hopeful literature and declares that much may be done by simple ambitious people who own a few hens. Do not be led astray by it. It was not written for you. Go hunt for gold on the frozen hills of Alaska, put your faith in the honesty of a politician, believe if you will that the world is daily growing better and that good will triumph over evil, but do not read and believe the literature that is written concerning the hen. It was not written for you.

I, however, digress. My tale does not primarily concern itself with the hen. If correctly told it will centre on the egg. For ten years my father and mother struggled to make our chicken farm pay and then they gave up that struggle and began another. They moved into the town of Bidwell, Ohio and embarked in the restaurant business. After ten years of worry with incubators that did not hatch, and with tiny—and in their own way lovely—balls of fluff that passed on into semi-naked pullethood and from that into dead henhood, we threw all aside and packing our belongings on a wagon drove down Grigg's Road toward Bidwell, a tiny caravan of hope looking for a new place from which to start on our upward journey through life.

We must have been a sad looking lot, not, I fancy, unlike refugees fleeing from a battlefield. Mother and I walked in the road. The wagon that contained our goods had been borrowed for the day from Mr. Albert Griggs, a neighbor. Out of its sides stuck the legs of cheap chairs and at the back of the pile of beds, tables, and boxes filled with kitchen utensils was a crate of live chickens, and on top of that the baby carriage in which I had been wheeled about in my infancy. Why we stuck to the baby carriage I don't know. It was unlikely other children would be born and the wheels were broken. People who have few possessions cling tightly to those they have. That is one of the facts that make life so discouraging. [7]

Father rode on top of the wagon. He was then a bald-headed man of forty-five, a little fat and from long association with mother and the chickens he had become silent and discouraged. All during our ten years on the chicken farm he had worked as a laborer on neighboring farms and most of the money he had earned had been spent for remedies to cure chicken diseases, on Wilmer's White Wonder Cholera Cure or Professor Bidlow's Egg Producer or some other preparations that mother found advertised in poultry papers. There were two little patches of hair on father's head just above his ears. I remember that as a child I used to sit looking at him when he had gone to sleep in a chair before the stove on Sunday afternoons in the winter. I had at that time already begun to read books and have notions of my own and the bald path that led over the top of his head was, I fancied, something like a broad road, such a road as Caesar might have made on which to lead his legions out of Rome and into the wonders of an unknown world. The tufts of hair that grew above father's ears were, I thought, like forests. I fell into a half-sleeping, half-waking state and dreamed I was a tiny thing going along the road into a far beautiful place where there were no chicken farms and where life was a happy eggless affair. [8]

One might write a book concerning our flight from the chicken farm into town. Mother and I walked the entire eight miles—she to be sure that nothing fell from the wagon and I to see the wonder of the world. On the seat of the wagon beside father was his greatest treasure. I will tell you of that. [9]

On a chicken farm where hundreds and even thousands of chickens come out of eggs surprising things sometimes happen. Grotesques are born out of eggs as out of people. The accident does not often occur—perhaps once in a thousand births. A chicken is, you see, born that has four legs, two pairs of wings, two heads or what not. The things do not live. They go quickly back to the hand of their maker that has for a moment trembled. The fact that the poor little things could not live was one of the tragedies of life to father. He had some sort of notion that if he could but bring into henhood or roosterhood a five-legged hen or a two-headed rooster his fortune would be made. He dreamed of taking the wonder about to county fairs and of growing rich by exhibiting it to other farm-hands. [10]

At any rate he saved all the little monstrous things that had been born on our chicken farm. They were preserved in alcohol and put each in its own glass bottle. These he had carefully put into a box and on our journey into town it was carried on the wagon seat beside him. He drove the horses with one hand and with the other [11] clung to the box. When we got to our destination the box was taken down at once and the bottles removed. All during our days as keepers of a restaurant in Bidwell, Ohio, the grotesques in their little glass bottles sat on a shelf back of the counter. Mother sometimes protested but father was a rock on the subject of his treasure. The grotesques were, he declared, valuable. People, he said, liked to look at strange and wonderful things.

Did I say that we embarked in the restaurant business in the town of Bidwell, Ohio? I exaggerated a little. The town itself lay at the foot of a low hill and on the shore of a small river. The railroad did not run through the town and the station was a mile away to the north at a place called Pickleville. There had been a cider mill and pickle factory at the station, but before the time of our coming they had both gone out of business. In the morning and in the evening busses came down to the station along a road called Turner's Pike from the hotel on the main street of Bidwell. Our going to the out of the way place to embark in the restaurant business was mother's idea. She talked of it for a year and then one day went off and rented an empty store building opposite the railroad station. It was her idea that the restaurant would be profitable. Traveling men, she said, would be always waiting around to take trains out of town and town people would come to the station to await the incoming trains. They would come to the restaurant to buy pieces of pie and drink coffee. Now that I am older I know that she had another motive going. She was ambitious for me. She wanted me to rise in the world, to get into a town school and become a man of the towns. [12]

At Pickleville father and mother worked hard as they always had done. At first there was the necessity of putting our place into shape to be a restaurant. That took a month. Father built a shelf on which he put tins of vegetables. He painted a sign on which he put his name in large red letters. Below his name was the sharp command— "EAT HERE"—that was so seldom obeyed. A show case was bought and filled with cigars and tobacco. Mother scrubbed the floors and the walls of the room. I went to school in the town and was glad to be away from the farm and from the presence of the discouraged, sad-looking chickens. Still I was not very joyous. In the evening I walked home from school along Turner's Pike and remembered the children I had seen playing in the town school yard. A troop of little girls had gone hopping about and singing. I tried that. Down along the frozen road I went hopping solemnly on one leg. "Hippity Hop To The Barber Shop," I sang shrilly. Then I stopped and looked doubtfully about. I was afraid of being seen in my gay mood. It must have seemed to me that I was doing a thing that should not be done by one who, like myself, had been raised on a chicken farm where death was a daily visitor. [13]

Mother decided that our restaurant should remain open at night. At ten in the evening a passenger train went north past our door followed by a local freight. The freight crew had switching to do in Pickleville and when the work was done they came to our restaurant for hot coffee and food. Sometimes one of them ordered a fried egg. In the morning at four they returned north-bound and again visited us. A little trade began to grow up. Mother slept at night and during the day tended the restaurant and fed our boarders while father slept. He slept in the same bed mother had occupied during the night and I went off to the town of Bidwell and to school. During the long [14] nights, while mother and I slept, father cooked meats that were to go into sandwiches for the lunch baskets of our boarders. Then an idea in regard to getting up in the world came into his head. The American spirit took hold of him. He also became ambitious.

In the long nights when there was little to do father had time to think. That was his undoing. He decided that he had in the past been an unsuccessful man because he had not been cheerful enough and that in the future he would adopt a cheerful outlook on life. In the early morning he came upstairs and got into bed with mother. She woke and the two talked. From my bed in the corner I listened. 15

It was father's idea that both he and mother should try to entertain the people who came to eat at our restaurant. I cannot remember now his words, but he gave the impression of one about to become in some obscure way a kind of public entertainer. When people, particularly young people from the town of Bidwell, came into our place, as on very rare occasion they did, bright entertaining conversation was to be made. From father's words I gathered that something of the jolly inn-keeper effect was to be sought. Mother must have been doubtful from the first, but she said nothing discouraging. It was father's notion that a passion for the company of himself and mother would spring up in the breasts of the younger people in the town of Bidwell. In the evening bright happy groups would come singing down Turner's Pike. They would troop shouting with joy and laughter into our place. There would be song and festivity. I do not mean to give the impression that father spoke so elaborately of the matter. He was as I have said an uncommunicative man. "They want some place to go. I tell you they want some place to go," he said over and over. That was as far as he got. My own imagination has filled in the blanks. 16

For two or three weeks this notion of father's invaded our house. We did not talk much, but in our daily lives tried earnestly to make smiles take the place of glum looks. Mother smiled at the boarders and I, catching the infection, smiled at our cat. Father became a little feverish in his anxiety to please. There was no doubt, lurking somewhere in him, a touch of the spirit of the showman. He did not waste much of his ammunition on the railroad men he served at night but seemed to be waiting for a young man or woman from Bidwell to come in to show what he could do. On the counter in the restaurant there was a wire basket kept always filled with eggs, and it must have been before his eyes when the idea of entertaining was born in his brain. There was something pre-natal about the way eggs kept themselves connected with the development of his idea. At any rate an egg ruined his new impulse in life. Late one night I was awakened by a roar of anger coming from father's throat. Both mother and I sat upright in our beds. With trembling hands she lighted a lamp that stood on a table by her head. Downstairs the front door of our restaurant went shut with a bang and in a few minutes father tramped up the stairs. He held an egg in his hand and his hand trembled as though he were having a chill. There was a half insane light in his eyes. As he stood glaring at us I was sure he intended throwing the egg at either mother or me. Then he laid it gently on the table beside the lamp and dropped on his knees beside mother's bed. He began to cry like a boy and I, carried away by his grief, cried with him. The two of us filled the little upstairs room with our wailing voices. It is ridiculous, but of the picture we made I can remember only the fact that 17 mother's hand continually stroked the bald path that ran across the top of his head. I have forgotten what mother said to him and how she induced him to tell her of what happened downstairs. His explanation also has gone out of my mind. I remember only my own grief and fright and the shiny path over father's head glowing in the lamp light as he knelt by the bed.

As to what happened downstairs. For some unexplainable reason I know the story as well as though I had been a witness to my father's discomfiture. One in time gets to know many unexplainable things. On that evening young Joe Kane, son of a merchant in Bidwell, came to Pickleville to meet his father, who was expected on the ten o'clock evening train from the South. The train was three hours late and Joe came into our place to loaf about and wait for its arrival. The local freight train came in and the freight crew were fed. Joe was left alone in the restaurant with father. 18

From the moment he came into our place the Bidwell young man must have been puzzled by my father's actions. It was his notion that father was angry at him for hanging around. He noticed that the restaurant keeper was apparently disturbed by his presence and he thought of going out. However, it began to rain and he did not fancy the long walk to town and back. He bought a five-cent cigar and ordered a cup of coffee. He had a newspaper in his pocket and took it out and began to read. "I'm waiting for the evening train. It's late," he said apologetically. 19

For a long time father, whom Joe Kane had never seen before, remained silently gazing at his visitor. He was no doubt suffering from an attack of stage fright. As so often happens in life he had thought so much and so often of the situation that now confronted him that he was somewhat nervous in its presence. 20

For one thing, he did not know what to do with his hands. He thrust one of them nervously over the counter and shook hands with Joe Kane. "How-de-do," he said. Joe Kane put his newspaper down and stared at him. Father's eye lighted on the basket of eggs that sat on the counter and he began to talk. "Well," he began hesitatingly, "well, you have heard of Christopher Columbus, eh?" He seemed to be angry. "That Christopher Columbus was a cheat," he declared emphatically. "He talked of making an egg stand on its end. He talked, he did, and then he went and broke the end of the egg." 21

My father seemed to his visitor to be beside himself at the duplicity of Christopher Columbus. He muttered and swore. He declared it was wrong to teach children that Christopher Columbus was a great man when, after all, he cheated at the critical moment. He had declared he would make an egg stand on end and then when his bluff had been called he had done a trick. Still grumbling at Columbus, father took an egg from the basket on the counter and began to walk up and down. He rolled the egg between the palms of his hands. He smiled genially. He began to mumble words regarding the effect to be produced on an egg by the electricity that comes out of the human body. He declared that without breaking its shell and by virtue of rolling it back and forth in his hands he could stand the egg on its end. He explained that the warmth of his hands and the gentle rolling movement he gave the egg created a new centre of gravity, and Joe Kane was mildly interested. "I have handled thousands of eggs," father said. "No one knows more about eggs than I do." 22

He stood the egg on the counter and it fell on its side. He tried the trick again and again, each time rolling the egg between the palms of his hands and saying the words regarding the wonders of electricity and the laws of gravity. When after a half hour's effort he did succeed in making the egg stand for a moment he looked up to find that his visitor was no longer watching. By the time he had succeeded in calling Joe Kane's attention to the success of his effort the egg had again rolled over and lay on its side. 23

Afire with the showman's passion and at the same time a good deal disconcerted by the failure of his first effort, father now took the bottles containing the poultry monstrosities down from their place on the shelf and began to show them to his visitor. "How would you like to have seven legs and two heads like this fellow?" he asked, exhibiting the most remarkable of his treasures. A cheerful smile played over his face. He reached over the counter and tried to slap Joe Kane on the shoulder as he had seen men do in Ben Head's saloon when he was a young farmhand and drove to town on Saturday evenings. His visitor was made a little ill by the sight of the body of the terribly deformed bird floating in the alcohol in the bottle and got up to go. Coming from behind the counter father took hold of the young man's arm and led him back to his seat. He grew a little angry and for a moment had to turn his face away and force himself to smile. Then he put the bottles back on the shelf. In an outburst of generosity he fairly compelled Joe Kane to have a fresh cup of coffee and another cigar at his expense. Then he took a pan and filling it with vinegar, taken from a jug that sat beneath the counter, he declared himself about to do a new trick. "I will heat this egg in this pan of vinegar," he said. "Then I will put it through the neck of a bottle without breaking the shell. When the egg is inside the bottle it will resume its normal shape and the shell will become hard again. Then I will give the bottle with the egg in it to you. You can take it about with you wherever you go. People will want to know how you got the egg in the bottle. Don't tell them. Keep them guessing. That is the way to have fun with this trick." 24

Father grinned and winked at his visitor. Joe Kane decided that the man who confronted him was mildly insane but harmless. He drank the cup of coffee that had been given him and began to read his paper again. When the egg had been heated in the vinegar father carried it on a spoon to the counter and going into a back room got an empty bottle. He was angry because his visitor did not watch him as he began to do his trick, but nevertheless went cheerfully to work. For a long time he struggled, trying to get the egg to go through the neck of the bottle. He put the pan of vinegar back on the stove, intending to reheat the egg, then picked it up and burned his fingers. After a second bath in the hot vinegar the shell of the egg had been softened a little but not enough for his purpose. He worked and worked and a spirit of desperate determination took possession of him. When he thought that at last the trick was about to be consummated the delayed train came in at the station and Joe Kane started to go nonchalantly out at the door. Father made a last desperate effort to conquer the egg and make it do the things that would establish his reputation as one who knew how to entertain guests who came into his restaurant. He worried the egg. He attempted to be somewhat rough with it. He swore and the sweat stood out on his forehead. The egg broke under his hand. When the contents spurted over his clothes, Joe Kane, who had stopped at the door, turned and laughed. 25

283

A roar of anger rose from my father's throat. He danced and shouted a string of inarticulate words. Grabbing another egg from the basket on the counter, he threw it, just missing the head of the young man as he dodged through the door and escaped.

Father came upstairs to mother and me with an egg in his hand. I do not know what he intended to do. I imagine he had some idea of destroying it, of destroying all eggs, and that he intended to let mother and me see him begin. When, however, he got into the presence of mother something happened to him. He laid the egg gently on the table and dropped on his knees by the bed as I have already explained. He later decided to close the restaurant for the night and to come upstairs and get into bed. When he did so he blew out the light and after much muttered conversation both he and mother went to sleep. I suppose I went to sleep also, but my sleep was troubled. I awoke at dawn and for a long time looked at the egg that lay on the table. I wondered why eggs had to be and why from the egg came the hen who again laid the egg. The question got into my blood. It has stayed there, I imagine, because I am the son of my father. At any rate, the problem remains unsolved in my mind. And that, I conclude, is but another evidence of the complete and final triumph of the egg—at least as far as my family is concerned.

26

Journaling on Alice Walker's Essay

Born in 1944, three years after the death of Sherwood Anderson, Alice Walker, like Anderson, has written movingly about her childhood, in her case a childhood spent in Georgia, where her parents and seven siblings worked as sharecroppers. Best known for her Pulitzer Prize winning novel *The Color Purple* and several collections of short stories and poems, Walker has also written a memoir, *In Search of Our Mothers' Gardens*, excerpted below. As the title suggests, Walker's reflections celebrate the creativity of women generally and of African American women particularly, most of whom have had the courage to express their creativity in a culture that denied their humanity and their freedom.

As you read the selection below, answer the following questions in your journal. Once again, this rhetorical analysis will give you insight to her use of figurative language, parallel sentence structure, and concrete description, tools Walker uses to show us the daring creativity of these women and to motivate our searches for our own gardens.

1. Walker begins with an epigraph from Jean Toomer's *Cane*, describing an African American woman brimming with creative emotion yet trapped in prostitution. In the first eleven paragraphs, how does Walker use figurative language—similes and metaphors—and parallel sentence structure to clarify the creative potential and the wasting of such women?

2. To clarify what happens to women whose creativity finds no outlet, Walker quotes Virginia Woolf, who has written passionately on the needs of women. How do Walker's parenthetical "inserts" clarify the greater burdens carried by stifled black women?

3. What details does Walker offer concerning the life, work, and writing of eighteenth-century American poet Phillis Wheatley to support her thesis on the daring artistry of enslaved women?

4. To illustrate her idea of women daring to do the "work [their souls] must have," Walker tells the story of her mother's garden. What details does Walker offer, concerning the conditions under which her mother grew her flowers, which clarify the obstacles and the risks that made such gardening almost impossible?

5. In paragraphs 39 and 40, beginning with "Like Mem" and "Whatever she planted," how does Walker use action verbs and concrete nouns to clarify the immense energy behind her mother's artistry?

6. In searching for her mother's garden, Walker says that she "found [her] own." What does she mean? Have Walker's examples helped you to think about where you might "garden"?

"In Search of our Mothers' Gardens"

ALICE WALKER

I described her own nature and temperament. Told how they needed a larger life for their expression. . . . I pointed out that in lieu of proper channels, her emotions had overflowed into paths that dissipated them. I talked, beautifully I thought, about an art that would be born, an art that would open the way for women the likes of her. I asked her to hope, and build up an inner life against the coming of that day. . . . I sang, with a strange quiver in my voice, a promise song.

JEAN TOOMER, "AVEY," *CANE*
The poet speaking to a prostitute who falls asleep while he's talking—

When the poet Jean Toomer walked through the South in the early twenties, he discovered a curious thing: black women whose spirituality was so intense, so deep, so *unconscious*, that they were themselves unaware of the richness they held. They stumbled blindly through their lives: creatures so abused and mutilated in body, so dimmed and confused by pain, that they considered themselves unworthy even of hope. In the selfless abstractions their bodies became to the men who used them, they became more than "sexual objects," more even than mere women: they became "Saints." Instead of being perceived as whole persons, their bodies became shrines: what was thought to be their minds became temples suitable for worship. These crazy Saints stared out at the world, wildly, like lunatics—or quietly, like suicides; and the "God" that was in their gaze was as mute as a great stone. 1

Who were these Saints? These crazy, loony, pitiful women? 2

Some of them, without a doubt, were our mothers and grandmothers. 3

In the still heat of the post-Reconstruction South, this is how they seemed to Jean Toomer: exquisite butterflies trapped in an evil honey, toiling away their lives in an era, a century, that did not acknowledge them, except as "the *mule* of the world." They dreamed dreams that no one knew—not even themselves, in any coherent fashion—and saw visions no one could understand. They wandered or sat about the countryside crooning lullabies to ghosts, and drawing the mother of Christ in charcoal on courthouse walls. 4

They forced their minds to desert their bodies and their striving spirits sought to rise, like frail whirlwinds from the hard red clay. And when those frail whirlwinds fell, in scattered particles, upon the ground, no one mourned. Instead, men lit candles to celebrate the emptiness that remained, as people do who enter a beautiful but vacant space to resurrect a God. 5

Our mothers and grandmothers, some of them: moving to music not yet written. And they waited. 6

They waited for a day when the unknown thing that was in them would be made known; but guessed, somehow in their darkness, that on the day of their revelation they would be long dead. Therefore to Toomer they walked, and even ran, in slow motion. For they were going nowhere immediate, and the future was not yet within their grasp. And men took our mothers and grandmothers, "but got no pleasure from it." So complex was their passion and their calm. 7

To Toomer, they lay vacant and fallow as autumn fields, with harvest time never in sight: and he saw them enter loveless marriages, without joy; and become prostitutes, without resistance; and become mothers of children, without fulfillment. 8

For these grandmothers and mothers of ours were no Saints, but Artists; driven to a numb and bleeding madness by the springs of creativity in them for which there was no release. They were Creators, who lived lives of spiritual waste, because they were so rich in spirituality—which is the basis of Art—that the strain of enduring their unused and unwanted talent drove them insane. Throwing away this spirituality was their pathetic attempt to lighten the soul to a weight their work-worn, sexually abused bodies could bear. 9

What did it mean for a black woman to be an artist in our grandmothers' time? In our great-grandmothers' day? It is a question with an answer cruel enough to stop the blood. 10

Did you have a genius of a great-great-grandmother who died under some ignorant and depraved white overseer's lash? Or was she required to bake biscuits for a lazy backwater tramp, when she cried out in her soul to paint water colors of sunsets, or the rain falling on the green and peaceful pasturelands? Or was her body broken and forced to bear children (who were more often than not sold away from her) eight, ten, fifteen, twenty children—when her one joy was the thought of modeling heroic figures of rebellion, in stone or clay? 11

How was the creativity of the black woman kept alive, year after year and century after century, when for most of the years black people have been in America, it was 12 a punishable crime for a black person to read or write? And the freedom to paint, to sculpt, to expand the mind with action did not exist. Consider, if you can bear to imagine it, what might have been the result if singing, too, had been forbidden by law. Listen to the voices of Bessie Smith, Billie Holiday, Nina Simone, Roberta Flack, and Aretha Franklin among others, and imagine those voices muzzled for life. Then you may begin to comprehend the lives of our "crazy," "Sainted" mothers and grandmothers. The agony of the lives of women who might have been Poets, Novelists, Essayists, and Short Story Writers (over a period of centuries), who died with their real gifts stifled within them.

13

And, if this were the end of the story, we would have cause to cry out in my paraphrase of Okot p'Bitek's great poem:

> O, my clanswomen
> Let us all cry together!
> Come,
> Let us mourn the death of our mother,
> The death of a Queen
> The ash that was produced
> By a great, fire!
> O, this homestead is utterly dead
> Close the gates
> With *lacari* thorns,
> For our mother
> The creator of the Stool is lost!
> And all the young women
> Have perished in the wilderness!

But this is not the end of the story, for all the young women—our mothers and grandmothers, *ourselves*—have not perished in the wilderness. And if we ask ourselves why, and search for and find the answer, we will know beyond all efforts to erase it from our minds, just exactly who, and of what, we black American women are.

14

One example, perhaps the most pathetic, most misunderstood one, can provide a backdrop for our mothers' work: Phillis Wheatley, a slave in the 1700s.

15

Virginia Woolf, in her book *A Room of One's Own*, wrote that in order for a woman to write fiction she must have two things, certainly: a room of her own (with key and lock) and enough money to support herself.

16

What then are we to make of Phillis Wheatley, a slave, who owned not even herself? This sickly, frail black girl who required a servant of her own at times—her health was so precarious—and who, had she been white, would have been easily considered the intellectual superior of all the women and most of the men in the society of her day.

17

Virginia Woolf wrote further, speaking of course not of our Phillis, that "any woman born with a great gift in the sixteenth century [insert "eighteenth century,"

18

insert "black woman," insert "born or made a slave"] would certainly have gone crazed, shot herself, or ended her days in some lonely cottage outside the village, half witch, half wizard [insert "Saint"] feared and mocked at. For it needs little skill and psychology to be sure that a highly gifted girl who had tried to use her gift for poetry would have been so thwarted and hindered by contrary instincts [add "chains, guns, the lash, the ownership of one's body by someone else, submission to an alien religion"], that she must have lost her health and sanity to a certainty."

The key words, as they relate to Phillis, are "contrary instincts." For when we read the poetry of Phillis Wheatley—as when we read the novels of Nella Larsen or the oddly false-sounding autobiography of that freest of all black women writers, Zora Hurston—evidence of "contrary instincts" is everywhere. Her loyalties were completely divided, as was, without question, her mind. 19

But how could this be otherwise? Captured at seven, a slave of wealthy, doting whites who instilled in her the "savagery" of the Africa they "rescued" her from. . . one wonders if she was even able to remember her homeland as she had known it, or as it really was. 20

Yet, because she did try to use her gift for poetry in a world that made her a slave, she was "so thwarted and hindered by. . . contrary instincts, that she. . . lost her health. . . ." In the last years of her brief life, burdened not only with the need to express her gift but also with a penniless, friendless "freedom" and several small children for whom she was forced to do strenuous work to feed, she lost her health, certainly. Suffering from malnutrition and neglect and who knows what mental agonies, Phillis Wheatley died. 21

So torn by "contrary instincts" was black, kidnapped, enslaved Phillis that her description of "the Goddess"—as she poetically called the Liberty she did not have—is ironically, cruelly humorous. And, in fact, has held Phillis up to ridicule for more than a century. It is usually read prior to hanging Phillis's memory as that of a fool. She wrote: 22

> The Goddess comes, she moves divinely fair,
> Olive and laurel binds her *golden* hair.
> Wherever shines this native of the skies,
> Unnumber'd charms and recent graces rise. [My italics]

It is obvious that Phillis, the slave, combed the "Goddess's" hair every morning; prior, perhaps, to bringing in the milk, or fixing her mistress's lunch. She took her imagery from the one thing she saw elevated above all others. 23

With the benefit of hindsight we ask, "How could she?"

But at last, Phillis, we understand. No more snickering when your stiff, struggling, ambivalent lines are forced on us. We know now that you were not an idiot or a traitor; only a sickly little black girl, snatched from your home and country and made a slave; a woman who still struggled to sing the song that was your gift, although in a land of barbarians who praised you for your bewildered tongue. It is not so much what you sang, as that you kept alive, in so many of our ancestors, *the notion of song*. 24 25

Black women are called, in the folklore that so aptly identifies one's status in society, "the mule of the world," because we have been handed the burdens that everyone else—*everyone* else—refused to carry. We have also been called "Matriarchs," "Superwomen," and "Mean and Evil Bitches." Not to mention "Castraters" and "Sapphire's Mama." When we have pleaded for understanding, our character has been distorted; when we have asked for simple caring, we have been handed empty inspirational appellations, then stuck in the farthest corner. When we have asked for love, we have been given children. In short, even our plainer gifts, our labors of fidelity and love, have been knocked down our throats. To be an artist and a black woman, even today, lowers our status in many respects, rather than raises it: and yet, artists we will be.

Therefore we must fearlessly pull out of ourselves and look at and identify with our lives the living creativity some of our great-grandmothers were not allowed to know. I stress *some* of them because it is well known that the majority of our great-grandmothers knew, even without "knowing" it, the reality of their spirituality, even if they didn't recognize it beyond what happened in the singing at church—and they never had any intention of giving it up.

How they did it—those millions of black women who were not Phillis Wheatley, or Lucy Terry or Frances Harper or Zora Hurston or Nella Larsen or Bessie Smith, or Elizabeth Catlett, or Katherine Dunham, either—brings me to the title of this essay, "In Search of Our Mothers' Gardens," which is a personal account that is yet shared, in its theme and its meaning, by all of us. I found, while thinking about the far-reaching world of the creative black woman, that often the truest answer to a question that really matters can be found very close.

In the late 1920s my mother ran away from home to marry my father. Marriage, if not running away, was expected of seventeen-year-old girls. By the time she was twenty, she had two children and was pregnant with a third. Five children later, I was born. And this is how I came to know my mother: she seemed a large, soft, loving-eyed woman who was rarely impatient in our home. Her quick, violent temper was on view only a few times a year, when she battled with the white landlord who had the misfortune to suggest to her that her children did not need to go to school.

She made all the clothes we wore, even my brother's overalls. She made the towels and sheets we used. She spent the summers canning vegetables and fruits. She spent the winter evenings making quilts enough to cover all our beds.

During the "working" day, she labored beside—not behind—my father in the fields. Her day began before sunup, and did not end until late at night. There was never a moment for her to sit down, undisturbed, to unravel her own private thoughts; never a time free from interruption—by work or the noisy inquiries of her many children. And yet, it is to my mother—and all our mothers who were not famous—that I went in search of the secret of what has fed that muzzled and often mutilated, but vibrant, creative spirit that the black woman has inherited, and that pops out in wild and unlikely places to this day.

26

27

28

29

30

31

But when, you will ask, did my overworked mother have time to know or care about feeding the creative spirit?

The answer is so simple that many of us have spent years discovering it. We have constantly looked high, when we should have looked high—and low.

For example: in the Smithsonian Institution in Washington, D.C., there hangs a quilt unlike any other in the world. In fanciful, inspired, and yet simple and identifiable figures, it portrays the story of the Crucifixion. It is considered rare, beyond price. Though it follows no known pattern of quilt-making, and though it is made of bits and pieces of worthless rags, it is obviously the work of a person of powerful imagination and deep spiritual feeling. Below this quilt I saw a note that says it was made by "an anonymous Black woman in Alabama, a hundred years ago."

If we could locate this "anonymous" black woman from Alabama, she would turn out to be one of our grandmothers—an artist who left her mark in the only materials she could afford, and in the only medium her position in society allowed her to use.

As Virginia Woolf wrote further, in *A Room of One's Own*:

Yet genius of a sort must have existed among women as it must have existed among the working class. [Change this to "slaves" and "the wives and daughters of sharecroppers."] Now and again an Emily Brontë or a Robert Burns [change this to "a Zora Hurston or a Richard Wright"] blazes out and proves its presence. But certainly it never got itself on to paper. When, however, one reads of a witch being ducked, of a woman possessed by devils [or "Sainthood"], of a wise woman selling herbs [our root workers], or even a very remarkable man who had a mother, then I think we are on the track of a lost novelist, a suppressed poet, of some mute and inglorious Jane Austen. . . . Indeed, I would venture to guess that Anon, who wrote so many poems without signing them was often a woman. . .

And so our mothers and grandmothers have, more often than not anonymously, handed on the creative spark, the seed of the flower they themselves never hoped to see: or like a sealed letter they could not plainly read.

And so it is, certainly, with my own mother. Unlike "Ma" Rainey's songs, which retained their creator's name even while blasting forth from Bessie Smith's mouth, no song or poem will bear my mother's name. Yet so many of the stories that I write, that we all write, are my mother's stories. Only recently did I fully realize this: that through years of listening to my mother's stories of her life, I have absorbed not only the stories themselves, something of the manner in which she spoke, something of the urgency that involves the knowledge that her stories—like her life—must be recorded. It is probably for this reason that so much of what I have written is about characters whose counterparts in real life are so much older than I am.

But the telling of these stories, which came from my mother's lips as naturally as breathing, was not the only way my mother showed herself as an artist. For stories, too, were subject to being distracted, to dying without conclusion. Dinners must be started, and cotton must be gathered before the big rains. The artist that was and is my mother showed itself to me only after many years. This is what I finally noticed:

290

Like Mem, a character in *The Third Life of Grange Copeland,* my mother adorned with flowers whatever shabby house we were forced to live in. And not just your typical straggly country stand of zinnias, either. She planted ambitious gardens—and still does—with over fifty different varieties of plants that bloom profusely from early March until late November. Before she left home for the fields, she watered her flowers, chopped up the grass, and laid out new beds. When she returned from the fields she might divide clumps of bulbs, dig a cold pit, uproot and replant roses, or prune branches from her taller bushes or trees—until night came and it was too dark to see. 39

Whatever she planted grew as if by magic, and her fame as a grower of flowers spread over three counties. Because of her creativity with her flowers, even my memories of poverty are seen through a screen of blooms—sunflowers, petunias, roses, dahlias, forsythia, spirea, delphiniums, verbena. . . and on and on. 40

And I remember people coming to my mother's yard to be given cuttings from her flowers; I hear again the praise showered on her because whatever rocky soil she landed on, she turned into a garden. A garden so brilliant with colors, so original in its design, so magnificent with life and creativity, that to this day people drive by our house in Georgia—perfect strangers and imperfect strangers—and ask to stand or walk among my mother's art. 41

I notice that it is only when my mother is working in her flowers that she is radiant, almost to the point of being invisible—except as Creator: hand and eye. She is involved in work her soul must have. Ordering the universe in the image of her personal conception of Beauty. 42

Her face, as she prepares the Art that is her gift, is a legacy of respect she leaves to me, for all that illuminates and cherishes life. She has handed down respect for the possibilities—and the will to grasp them. 43

For her, so hindered and intruded upon in so many ways, being an artist has still been a daily part of her life. This ability to hold on, even in very simple ways, is work black women have done for a very long time. 44

This poem is not enough, but it is something, for the woman who literally covered the holes in our walls with sunflowers: 45

> They were women then
> My mama's generation
> Husky of voice—Stout of
> Step
> With fists as well as
> Hands
> How they battered down
> Doors
> And ironed
> Starched white
> Shirts

How they led
Armies
Headragged Generals
Across mined
Fields
Booby-trapped
Kitchens
To discover books
Desks
A place for us
How they knew what we
Must know
Without knowing a page
Of it
Themselves.

Guided by my heritage of a love of beauty and a respect for strength—in search of my mother's garden, I found my own. 46

And perhaps in Africa over two hundred years ago, there was just such a mother; perhaps she painted vivid and daring decorations in oranges and yellows and greens on the walls of her hut; perhaps she sang—in a voice like Roberta Flack's—*sweetly* over the compounds of her village; perhaps she wove the most stunning mats or told the most ingenious stories of all the village storytellers. Perhaps she was herself a poet—though only her daughter's name is signed to the poems that we know. 47

Perhaps Phillis Wheatley's mother was also an artist. 48

Perhaps in more than Phillis Wheatley's biological life is her mother's signature made clear.

Writing a Rhetorical Analysis Essay

1. Now that you have analyzed the style of these authors, draw on your answers to the questions above to write a rhetorical analysis essay on the selection of your choice. As you draft your introductory paragraph, remember the need to restate the author's purpose in this selection and to explain why you care about this story, why you find it compelling or disturbing. Your introduction should also state how effectively, in your view, the author achieved his or her purpose, and then forecast that you will defend your view by analyzing the author's diction, description, sentence structure, and arrangement.

2. Write an essay-length memoir (4–6 pages) narrating one of your own experiences—as a child or as a parent—in struggling to overcome your own or your parents' mistakes. What did you learn? Has the conflict been resolved, or do you remain, like Anderson's narrator, puzzled by the significance of the experience? Did you learn to forgive

others? Did you learn to forgive yourself? Explain.

3. Once you have written a rough draft of this essay, use the guidelines above and below to evaluate the effectiveness of your own diction, description, sentence structure and arrangement. You will find, too, that these same guidelines will help you evaluate your style in any essay, yours or that of a peer in your response group.

Revising for Micro-Issues

Introduction

- In the process of identifying my subject, limiting my focus, stating my claim, and revealing the organization of my analysis, have I also explained why I care about this subject, what I have invested in this subject?

Body Paragraphs: Sentence Structure

- Have I varied the length and structure of my sentences? Though I want an average length of 15–20 words per sentence, depending on the educational level of my readers, I want to reach that average through varied lengths, not through monotonous consistency in length. Have I placed key ideas in emphatically short sentences? Example from King: "Injustice anywhere is a threat to justice everywhere"—eight words.

- Have I used introductory phrases to stress the relationship between sentences and to prevent every sentence from beginning the same way, with the subject and verb? Example from King: In paragraph 34, just after praising white church leaders who have supported his efforts to achieve integration, King writes, "*But despite these exceptions*, I must honestly reiterate that I have been disappointed with the church."

- Have I used parallel sentence structures—within sentences and between sentences— to stress parallel ideas and to energize the rhythms of my sentences? Example from King: "*I doubt that you would* have so warmly commended the police *if you had seen* its dogs sinking their teeth into unarmed, nonviolent Negroes. *I doubt that you would* so quickly commend the policemen *if you were to observe* their ugly and inhumane treatment of Negroes here in the city jail" (paragraph 45).

- Have I occasionally used a periodic sentence to create a climactic build-up to the main clause at the end of the sentence? Example from King: "Before Jefferson etched the majestic words of the Declaration of Independence across the pages of history, *we were here*" (paragraph 44).

- Have I used semicolons effectively to link closely related sentences which, together, stress a key point? Example: After King describes his disappointment with the "white moderate," he writes, "Perhaps I was too optimistic; perhaps I expected too much" (paragraph 32).

Body Paragraphs: Diction

- Whenever appropriate, have I used action verbs instead of "being verbs" (is/are, was/were, etc.) to create vigor and brevity in my writing? Example: "I *study* political science" instead of "I am a student of political science." The second version stretches four words into seven and replaces the action of studying with "am a student."

- To help my readers *see* an abstract concept, have I used figurative language appropriately? Example: To persuade his readers that injustice must never be considered a local matter, King writes, "We are caught in an inescapable *network* of mutuality, tied in a single *garment* of destiny" (paragraph 4). These metaphors (implied comparisons) help us to see our interconnectedness as a net that catches us all, then our destiny as a coat which all Americans wear.

- Have I defined key terms? Sometimes, a clear definition takes plenty of writing. King, for example, requires three paragraphs (6–8) to define what he means by "nonviolent direct action." Other times, a single sentence may be enough. For example, to reinforce his idea of "segregation," King quotes theologian Paul Tillich: "Sin is separation" (paragraph 16). Still other times, you can define a term parenthetically (as I did above after the word "metaphor").

- Have I used courteous language, particularly when I refer to opponents? King, for example, refers to the men who have publicly criticized and dismissed him as "my dear fellow clergymen"; he also addresses them as "sirs." Courtesy, however, doesn't mean false flattery; King, you recall, does not mince words when he describes what he wants his colleagues to see and do.

- Does my diction strike a level of formality or informality appropriate to my subject and my audience? King, a Ph.D. writing to other highly educated men, uses direct but formal diction; the serious situation calls for such formality. On the other hand, if you're writing a light-hearted narrative on your first week at the university, and your readers include your professor, your classmates, and eventually your family, you will use informal diction, though you will probably exclude street-talk in an academic assignment. For example, you might refer to the "hassle" you experienced in the bookstore, but you wouldn't call the clerk who hassled you a "discourteous university employee" (too formal); neither would you call him a "dork" (too slangy).

Conclusion

- In summarizing my key points and repeating my claim, have I written with conviction? Do I sound like I believe strongly in the ideas I have asked my reader to accept? What word choices and sentence structures convey that conviction, that intensity?

This guide limits itself to rhetorical concerns in shaping sentences and choosing words. As you revise your paper, you will want to consult a handbook, too, particularly if you have questions on methods of punctuation and on strategies for eliminating wordy diction. Indeed, you will find whole chapters on these issues as well as exercises to develop your skills. Also, your university probably has a Writing Center, a great place to work on sentence structure and diction and to receive feedback from trained student interns.

Checking for Correctness

That same handbook which can show you how to cut wordiness and punctuate compound sentences, can also refresh your memory on basic grammar and current usage. If your professor has not required such a handbook for this course, then you can find dozens of them in your campus Writing Center. Therefore, I won't duplicate all that material here.

Instead, let's close this chapter by reviewing three kinds of errors: subject-verb disagreement, the comma splice, and the fragment. I have chosen these three because they torment students everywhere—and because most professors consider them serious errors. We will look at examples of each, and, more important, we will examine proofreading strategies that will help you to recognize and correct these common errors.

Subject-Verb Disagreement

When verbs disagree in number with their subjects, we have an error in counting: how can we logically match a plural verb with a singular subject? When we write, for example, *He go*, we have a singular subject (he) and a plural verb (go). Precisely because of this quantitative mismatch, most teachers consider subject-verb disagreement a major error, one that distracts your reader from your ideas and, therefore, weakens your ethos, suggesting that you're not paying much attention to what you write. In Standard American English (SAE), we have a simple solution to this problem: add an "s" or, as in this case, an "es": He go*es*.

Why do students commit this error? Quite often, this problem results from haste: the writer simply hasn't taken the time to proofread carefully. Other times, the error results from the writer mixing a nonstandard dialect with SAE. In African American English, as well as in Appalachian dialects, for example, *He go* is correct. For this reason, most professors of writing do not refer to SAE as right and a dialectical version as wrong; instead, they urge students to use the pattern that fits their audience and purpose. Admittedly, however, college professors almost always expect SAE in academic writing.

If you have a problem with "SV" (the maddening notation teachers sometimes write in the margins of your papers), you have probably suffered enough lowered grades to know that you have a problem with subject-verb disagreement. Before you can correct such errors, however, you have to see them.

Proofreading Solution Slow down. Once you've revised the *content* of your essay, using the procedures described above, then—and only then—go looking for your SVs. Take one sentence at a time: Identify the subject, find the verb that tells what that subject is doing, then check for agreement in number (singular/singular, plural/plural).

In doing so, you will probably unearth another cause of SV: a long phrase separating the subject and verb, causing the writer to loose sight of the subject. Look at this sentence: "The *President* as well as his cabinet secretaries and half of the senators *believe* that invading Iraq has been good for Iraq." At first glance, this sentence looks correct: "senators believe." But notice that the subject is "President," so the verb must be the singular form, "believes." With that long phrase intervening between the subject and verb, however, a writer can easily lose track of the subject noun (President) and align the verb (incorrectly) with the object of the prepositional phrase (of the *senators*). **Note:** If this correct version bothers your ear, you can always exchange "as well as" for the conjunction "and," which functions like a plus-sign, creating a compound (plural) subject: "The President *and* (+) secretaries and senators *believe...*"

Related Problems. Make sure that your pronouns agree in number with their **antecedents**, the words that "go before" the pronouns, the words to which the pronouns refer. Consider this example: "Every *student* should do *their* own proofreading." Do you see that this sentence matches the plural pronoun "their" with the singular antecedent "student"? To correct the problem, you make the pronoun agree with its antecedent: "Every student should do his or her own proofreading." If you would rather not bother with the correct but clumsy "his or her," then change the antecedent to a plural form, as the adjective "every" seems to encourage: "All *students* should do *their* own proofreading."

Comma Splice

Comma splices occur when writers try to use a comma to link two independent clauses, that is, two sentences. The comma can't do such heavy work—unless the two sentences are extremely short, three or four words each. Consider this example: "I'll bring the wine, you bring the cheese." Technically, this sentence fits the definition of a comma splice given above. However, "correcting" this comma splice with a semicolon seems like overkill. Besides, professional writers have grown increasingly fond of comma splices; students rightly want to follow their example. Now re-read the last sentence. Do you see that placing a comma after "splices" would create a confusing sentence? The semicolon allows the writer to combine these related sentences into one compound sentence and to mark clearly where the first idea ends and the second one begins.

Proofreading Solution. If your drafts have been returned with lots of penalties for comma splices, try this: Read each of your sentences (yes, this process takes time, but don't expect an easy cure) aloud, and then ask yourself this question: "How many complete ideas did I just hear? If the answer is "two," and you notice a mere comma between the ideas, you just found a comma splice. Replace the comma with a semicolon. I'm indebted for this common-sense strategy to the best book on tutoring writing I have ever read: Emily Meyer and Louise Z. Smith's *The Practical Tutor*, page 186.

Alternative Solution. If the semicolon seems too formal for your style or your situation, you can always use a comma and a coordinating conjunction (and, but, or, nor, for, so, yet): "Besides, professional writers have grown fond of comma splices, *and students* rightly want to follow their example." **Caution:** If you choose a conjunctive adverb in this situation instead of the coordinating conjunction, you will need to return to the semicolon: "Besides, professional writers have grown fond of comma splices; therefore, students want to follow their example." If these terms "coordinating conjunction" and "conjunctive adverb" confuse you, please see your handbook for more examples and definitions.

Related Problems. The fused sentence occurs when the writer places no punctuation between two complete sentences. Notice the confusion created when we omit punctuation between the independent clauses we just considered: "Professional writers have grown fond of the comma splice students want to follow their example." Such fused sentences—blurred sentences would be a more accurate term—usually result from carelessness; they always disorient the reader. Therefore, they represent a more serious error than the comma splice.

Fragment

The sentence fragment, as the name suggests, occurs when the writer misrepresents a phrase or a dependent clause as a complete idea. Consider this example: "When King wrote his first draft. He sat in Birmingham jail." At first reading, we seem to have two complete sentences here: both have subjects and verbs (King wrote, He sat). However, the adverb at the beginning of the first clause, "when," gives the entire clause a modifying function: it tells what happened when King sat in jail. Therefore, the fragmented sentence should be attached to the independent clause it describes: "When King wrote his first draft, he sat in Birmingham jail." In other words, replace the period with a comma; the fragment disappears.

Proofreading Solution. Read your essay backwards. In other words, start with the last sentence in the essay. Ask yourself this question: Does this sentence express a complete idea? Once it passes inspection, back up, reading the sentence before it. Continue this slow process until you reach the beginning. This process works because it slows you down, forcing you to tune-out to the forward-flow of the essay and, instead, to read each sentence on its own. Also, read out of order, fragments tend to leap off the page. In the example above, for instance, if you were reading backwards, you would have read "He sat in Birmingham jail" before you read "When King wrote his first draft." When you hear this "when" clause by itself, it leaves you asking, "Yes, then what?" Once you hear your fragment, you will usually have little trouble correcting it.

You may well recall committing some of these errors on your earlier essays. If so, use the descriptions above to find your errors in your current draft; then use the correction strategies illustrated here to make necessary repairs.

Works Cited

Anderson, Sherwood. "The Egg." *The Realm of Fiction*. Ed. James B. Hall. New York: McGraw-Hill, 1970.

Anzaldua, Gloria. "Entering into the Serpent." *Ways of Reading: An Anthology for Writers*. Eds. David Bartholomae and Anthony Petrosky. 7th ed. Boston: St. Martin's, 2005. 64–76.

Austen, Jane. *Pride and Prejudice*. Ed. Mark Schorer. Boston: Houghton Mifflin, 1956.

Boswell, James. *Life of Johnson*. Ed. R. W. Chapman. Oxford: Oxford UP, 1980. 528.

Coggins, Elizabeth. "The Parents' Guilt in *Pride and Prejudice*." Student essay.

Glaser, Joe. *Understanding Style: Practical Ways to Improve your Writing*. New York: Oxford UP, 1999.

King, Martin Luther, Jr. "Letter from Birmingham Jail." *The Essay Connection*. 7th ed. Ed. Lynn Z. Bloom. Boston: Houghton Mifflin, 2004. 446–59.

McCourt, Frank. *Angela's Ashes*. New York: Scribner, 1996.

Obama, Barack. *Dreams from my Father: A Story of Race and Inheritance*. New York: Three Rivers, 2004.

Walker, Alice. "In Search of our Mothers' Gardens." *Ways of Reading: An Anthology for Writers*. Eds. David Bartholomae and Anthony Petrosky. 7th ed. Boston: St. Martin's 2005. 676–84.

White, Stephen. *The Written Word: Associated Digressions Concerned with the Writer as Craftsman*. New York: Harper and Row, 1984.

Zinsser, William. *On Writing Well*. 4th ed. New York: Harper, 1990.

CHAPTER 7

Writing About Poetry

"*Reading poetry is an act of reciprocity, and one of the great tasks of the lyric is to bring us into right relationship to each other....The lyric poem is a highly concentrated and passionate form of communication between strangers.*"

EDWARD HIRSCH, *How to Read a Poem*

"*Poetry is a kind of distilled insinuation. It's a way of expanding and talking around an idea or a question. Sometimes, more actually gets said through such a technique than a full frontal assault.*"

YUSEF KOMUNYAKAA, New York University *English Newsletter*

Learning to Read Poetry

If you consult your college or university catalogue and read the descriptions of composition courses, you will likely read the promise that students will learn to write about personal experience, about topics grounded in research, and about literature. You have already learned to write in response to nonfiction, short stories, novels, and plays; in this chapter, you will learn to write in response to poetry by Robert Frost, William Wordsworth, William Shakespeare, Wilfred Owen, Lawrence Ferlinghetti, Elizabeth Bishop, and Seamus Heaney.

To do so, you must first learn how to read poetry. Such reading often seems daunting to many students, especially those who enjoy the directness of essays. In contrast to the comforting clarity of the claim-support patterns of essays, poetry seems, indeed, much more like "distilled insinuation," as poet Yusef Komunyakaa calls it above. In the other epigraph, poet Edward Hirsh echoes Komunyakaa, describing poetry as "highly concentrated and passionate." Annoyed by poetry's complex indirection, and uncomfortable—sometimes even angry—over the requirement to write an essay on poetry, some students wonder, "Why bother?"

The answer to this perfectly valid question lies in the other key words of Hirsch and Komunyakaa. Just like the mediational persuasive essay you learned to write in chapter four, the poem builds what Hirsch calls "reciprocity" between writer and reader, forming a "right relationship" of acceptance, empathy, and trust "between strangers." In fact, throughout this book we have talked about the importance of building your "ethos" as a writer and practiced ways of building a relationship with your readers based on your credibility. In other words, learning to read poetry and to write about your reading will bolster your reader-centeredness, a quality all good writers must develop and sustain. Additionally, you learned in chapter five to root your research writing in your own questions, questions that allowed you to "expand and talk around an idea," as Komunyakaa puts it, before offering a "full frontal assault" on your topic in the research paper. Learning to read and write about poetry, then, will build your courage, your willingness to play with language and ideas, your willingness to follow those ideas wherever they may take you, another key characteristic for writers who would continue to grow.

To put the case another way, though writing an essay about poetry won't make you a poet, the process of writing about your reading will teach you to ask penetrating questions about the power and elusiveness of words. In turn, with your ear better attuned to language, your eyes will grow more perceptive, more likely to see what the busy-ness of our lives often hides. Hearing better, seeing better, you will then care more about that "stranger," that reader whom you want to hear what you hear, see what you see.

Historically, rhetoricians have always been concerned about this power of poetry to shape writers and readers. Sometimes, they have urged caution in reading poems. Most notably, Plato acknowledges the "mimetic" power of poetry, the power to imitate real life and, thereby, to arouse the emotions as well as the mind. Consequently, in his *Republic*, Plato disallows all poetry, except that which praises the gods and the glories of the state. Other poetry, such as Homer's stories of love and war in *The Iliad* and *The Odyssey*, must be silenced, Plato believes, because their vivid images might teach readers to fear battle and to question the government and the gods (G. M. A. Grube, *Plato's Republic*, Book X, 242-51).

Sharing Plato's belief in the imitative or mimetic power of poetry, Aristotle, Plato's student, draws far different conclusions about the validity and truth of poetic pictures. While Plato values "dialectic" or philosophy as the only way to reach the Truth, Aristotle believes that poetry offers instruction in ethical living as well as delight in portrayals of the human heart. Therefore, poetry, Aristotle concludes in his *Poetics*, should be universally read, not silenced; it should be cherished for its beauties and its lessons, not censored for its dangers (31–38). As mentioned in chapter one, Roman rhetoricians Cicero and Quintilian share Aristotle's views about poetry. If you hope to speak or write persuasively on political or judicial matters, they believe, then you must know well the passions of the heart, truths taught by the vivid pictures of the poets.

This shaping power of poetry has inspired similar thoughts in more modern rhetoricians, critics, and poets. For example, Shakespeare's contemporary, Sir Philip Sidney—a rhetorician, poet, and soldier—writes in his *Defense of Poesy* that poetry provides readers "a speaking picture" of human life, one that will "teach and delight" (958). Three other founders of English literary criticism—John Dryden in the seventeenth century, Samuel Johnson in the eighteenth century, and Matthew Arnold in the nineteenth century—echo Sidney's beliefs. In "An Essay on Dramatic Poesy," Dryden argues that the best poetry provides "a just and lively image of human nature…for the delight and instruction" of us all (327). Similarly, in his preface to his edition of *The Works of William Shakespeare*, Dr. Johnson praises Shakespeare's dramatic poetry for its "just representation of general nature," one that offers many "pleasures" but also "the stability of truth" about our mortal condition (420). One hundred years later, Matthew Arnold—a poet, rhetorician of culture, professor, school administrator, and critic—writes in *The Study of Poetry* that "more and more" people "will discover that we have to turn to poetry to interpret life for us" (306).

You have heard two contemporary testimonies to the value of poetry in the epigraphs to this chapter. Listen to two more recent voices on the nature of poetry as sustenance. Christina Crosby, professor of English and women's studies at Wesleyan University, explains that she teaches her students to read and write about poetry so that they can learn how language shapes meaning in a text and, just as important, how poems effect social change by shaping the "past" we remember and the "future" we anticipate (495). Finally, in his influential book *Rhetorics, Poetics, and Cultures*, James Berlin argues that we all need "rhetorical education" and "poetic understanding" for the same reason that Aristotle's students needed such knowledge, the knowledge of citizenship: "Both rhetorical and poetic discourse played crucial roles in fulfilling the ends of Athenian democracy, including the authentic pursuit of the virtuous life....It is as impossible for us to separate literary and rhetorical texts from political life as it as for the citizens of ancient Athens" (xii/xiii). If Berlin, Crosby, and their predecessors make valid points about the power of poetry to shape us as individuals and as cultures, then we owe it to ourselves to hear what the poets have written.

Journaling on Edward Hirsch's Advice on Reading Poetry

To begin our study, read the excerpt below from Edward Hirsh's book *How to Read a Poem*. As you read, reflect on the following questions in your journal. Your answers will help you clarify how you feel about poetry—positively or negatively—and why you feel that way.

1. As a child or as an adult, have you ever read a poem that gave you "spiritual sustenance" or helped you to understand your "inner life"? If so, narrate the experience. Did the "sound of words," the "first primitive pleasure in poetry," play a part in this experience? If you have never had such an experience with a poem, reflect on why you have been deprived of this experience.

2. Hirsch speaks of metaphor as the essence of poetry, the comparisons that bring the poem's picture to life and engage us, the readers, in "making the meaning." List two or three metaphors (implied comparisons: x is y) or similes (stated comparison: x is *like* y) that you might use if you chose to write a poem about your life as a student. After each comparison, explain how the image would help the reader of the poem to "read" you.

Excerpt from *How to Read a Poem*

Edward Hirsch

The Immense Intimacy, the Intimate Immensity

The profound intimacy of lyric poetry makes it perilous because it gets so far under the skin, into the skin. "For poems are not, as people think, simply emotions (one has emotions early enough)—they are experiences," Rilke wrote in a famous passage from *The Notebooks of Malte Laurids Brigge*. I am convinced the kind of experience— the kind of knowledge—one gets from poetry cannot be duplicated elsewhere. The spiritual life wants articulation—it wants embodiment in language. The physical life wants the spirit. I know this because I hear it in the words, because when I liberate the message in the bottle a physical—a spiritual—urgency pulses through the arranged text. It is as if the spirit grows in my hands. Or the words rise in the air. "Roots and wings," the Spanish poet Juan Ramón Jiménez writes, "But let the wings take root and the roots fly."

There are people who defend themselves against being "carried away" by poetry, thus depriving themselves of an essential aspect of the experience. But there are others who welcome the transport poetry provides. They welcome it repeatedly. They desire it so much they start to crave it daily, nightly, nearly abject in their desire, seeking it out the way hungry people seek food. It is spiritual sustenance to them. Bread and wine. A way of transformative thinking. A method of transfiguration. There are those who honor the reality of roots and wings in words, but also want the wings to take root, to grow into the earth, and the roots to take flight, to ascend. They need such falling and rising, such metaphoric thinking. They are so taken by the ecstatic experience—the overwhelming intensity—of reading poems they have to respond in kind. And these people become poets.

2

Emily Dickinson is one of my models of a poet who responded completely to what she read. Here is her compelling test of poetry:

3

If I read a book [and] it makes my whole body so cold no fire can ever warm me I know that is poetry. If I feel physically as if the top of my heard were taken off, I know that is poetry. These are the only ways I know it. Is there any other way?

4

Dickinson recognizes true poetry by the extremity—the actual physical intensity—of her response to it. It's striking that she doesn't say she knows poetry because of any intrinsic qualities of poetry itself. Rather, she recognizes it by contact; she knows it by what it does to her, and she trusts her own response. Of course, only the strongest poetry could effect such a response. Her aesthetic is clear: always she wants to be surprised, to be stunned, by what one of her poems calls "Bolts of Melody."

5

Dickinson had a voracious appetite for reading poetry. She read it with tremendous hunger and thirst—poetry was sustenance to her. Much has been made of her reclusion, but, as her biographer Richard Sewell suggests, "She saw herself as a poet in the company of Poets—and, functioning as she did mostly on her own, read them (among other reasons) for company." He also points to Dickinson's various metaphors for the poets she read. She called them "the dearest ones of time, the strongest friends of the soul," her "Kinsmen of the Shelf," her "enthralling friends, the immortalities." She spoke of the poet's "venerable Hand" that warmed her own. Dickinson was a model of poetic responsiveness because she read with her whole being.

6

One of the books Emily Dickinson marked up, Ik Marvel's *Reveries of a Bachelor* (1850), recommends that people read for "soul-culture." I like that dated nineteenth-century phrase because it points to the depth that can be shared by the community of solitaries who read poetry. I, too, read for soul-culture—the culture of the soul. That's why the intensity of engagement I have with certain poems, certain poets, is so extreme. Reading poetry is for me an act of the most immense intimacy, of intimate intensity. I am shocked by what I see in the poem but also by what the poem finds in me. It activates my secret world, commands my inner life. I cannot get access to that inner life any other way than through the power of the words themselves. The words pressure me into a response, and the rhythm of the poem carries me to another plane of time, outside of time.

7

Rhythm can hypnotize and alliteration can be almost hypnotic. A few lines from Tennyson's *The Princess* can still send me into a kind of trance:

> The moan of doves in immemorial elms
> And murmurings of innumerable bees.

And I can still get lost when Hart Crane links the motion of a boat with an address to his lover in part 2 of "Voyages":

> And onward, as bells off San Salvador
> Salute the crocus lustres of the stars
> In these poinsettia meadows of her tides,—
> Adiagos of islands, O my Prodigal,
> Complete the dark confessions her veins spell.

The words move ahead of the thought in poetry. The imagination loves reverie, the daydreaming capacity of the mind set in motion by words, by images.

As a reader, the hold of the poem over me can be almost embarrassing because it is so childlike, because I need it so much to give me access to my own interior realms. It plunges me into the depths (and poetry is the literature of depths) and gives a tremendous sense of another world growing within. ("There is another world and it is in this one," Paul Éluard wrote.) I need the poem to enchant me, to shock me awake, to shift my waking consciousness and open the world to me, to open me up to the world—to the word—in a new way. I am pried open. The spiritual desire for poetry can be overwhelming, so much do I need it to experience and name my own perilous depths and vast spaces, my own well-being. And yet the work of art is beyond existential embarrassment. It is mute and plaintive in its calling out, its need for renewal. It needs a reader to possess it, to be possessed by it. Its very life depends upon it.

Mere Air, These Words, but Delicious to Hear

I remember once walking through a museum in Athens and coming across a tall-stemmed cup from ancient Greece that has Sappho saying, "Mere air, these words, but delicious to hear." The phrase inscribed into the cup, translated onto a museum label, stopped me cold. I paused for a long time to drink in the strange truth that all the sublimity of poetry comes down in the end to mere air and nothing more, to the sound of these words and no others, which are nonetheless delicious and enchanting to hear. Sappho's lines (or the lines attributed to her) also have a lapidary quality. The phrase has an elegance suitable for writing, for inscription on a cup or in stone. Writing fixes the evanescence of sound. It holds it against death.

The sound of the words is the first primitive pleasure in poetry. "In poetry," Wallace Stevens asserted, "you must love the words, the ideas and images and rhythms with all your capacity to love anything at all" ("Adagia"). Stevens lists the love of the words as the first condition of a capacity to love anything in poetry at all because it is the words that can make things happen. There are times when I read a poem and can feel the syllables coming alive in my mouth, the letters enunciated in the syllables, the syllables coming together as words, the words forming into a phrase, the phrase finding a rhythm in the line, in the lines, in the shape of the words crossing the lines into a sentence, into sentences. I feel the words creating a rhythm, a music, a spell, a mood, a shape, a form. I hear the words coming off the page into my own mouth—in transit, in action. I generate—I re-create—the words incantatory, the words liberated and self-reflexive. Words rising from the body, out of the body. An act of language paying attention to itself. An act of the mind.

"Mere air, these words, but delicious to hear." In poetry the words enact—they make manifest—what they describe. This is what Gerard Manley Hopkins calls "the roll, the rise, the carol, the creation." Indeed, one hears in Hopkins's very phrase the trills or rolled consonants of the letter *r* reverberating through all four words, the voiced vowels, the *r-o-l* of "roll" echoing in the back of "ca*rol*," the alliterative *cs* building a cadence, hammering it in, even as the one-syllable words create a rolling, rising effect that is slowed down by the rhythm of the multisyllabic words, the caroling creation. The pleasure all this creates in the mouth is intense. "The world is charged with the grandeur of God." I read Hopkins's poems and feel the deep joy of the sounds creating themselves ("What is all this juice and all this joy?"), the nearly buckling strain of so much drenched spirit, "the achieve of, the mastery of the thing!" 16

The poem is an act beyond paraphrase because what is being said is always inseparable from the way it is being said. Osip Mandelstam suggested that if a poem can be paraphrased, then the sheets haven't been rumpled, poetry hasn't spent the night. The words are an (erotic) visitation, a means to an end, but also an end in and of themselves. The poet is first of all a language worker. A maker. A shaper of language. With Heinrich Heine, the linguist Edward Sapir affirmed in his book *Language*, "one is under the illusion that the universe speaks German." With Shakespeare, one is under the impression that it speaks English. This is at the heart of the Orphic calling of the poet: to make it seem as if the very universe speaks and reveals itself through the mother tongue. 17

In Plain American Which Cats and Dogs Can Read!

The lyric poem walks the line between speaking and singing. (It also walks the line between the conventions of poetry and the conventions of grammar.) Poetry is not speech exactly—verbal art is deliberately different than the way that people actually talk—and yet it is always in relationship to speech, to the spoken word. "It has to be living, to learn the speech of the place," as Wallace Stevens puts it in his poem "Of Modern Poetry." W. B. Yeats called a poem "an elaboration of the rhythms of common speech and their association with profound feeling" ("Modern Poetry"). W. H. Auden said: "In English verse, even in Shakespeare's grandest rhetorical passages, the ear is always aware of its relation to everyday speech" ("Writing"). I'm reminded of the many poems in the American vernacular—from Walt Whitman to William Carlos Williams ("The Horse Show"), Frank O'Hara ("Having a Coke with You"), and Gwendolyn Brooks ("We Real Cool")—that give the sensation of someone speaking in a texturized version of American English, that create the impression of letters written, as Marianne 18

Moore joyfully puts it, "not in Spanish, not in Greek, not in Latin, not in shorthand, / but in plain American which cats and dogs can read!" A demotic linguistic vitality— what Williams calls "the speech of Polish mothers"—is one of the pleasures of the American project in poetry.

Here is the opening of Randall Jarrell's poem "Next Day": [19] [20]

> Moving from Cheer to Joy, from Joy to All,
> I take a box
> And add it to my wild rice, my Cornish game hens.
> The slacked or shorted, basketed, identical
> Food-gathering flocks
> Are selves I overlook. Wisdom, said William James
>
> Is learning what to overlook. And I am wise [21]
> If that is wisdom

One hears in this poem the plaintive, intelligent voice of a suburban housewife [22] who knows she has become invisible, who wants only to be seen and heard. What particularly marks the poem as a verbal construct is the self-conscious treatment of the words themselves, the way the words behave in rhythmic lines and shapely stanzas. There's the delightful pun on the names of household detergents, the play off "hens" and "flocks," the acute way the woman sums up her companions in the supermarket, how she pivots on the word "overlook" and ruefully quotes William James's pragmatic American notion of "wisdom." I've always been touched by the way Jarrell animates the woman's voice in this poem, how he inscribes his own voice into her voice and captures the reality of someone who is exceptional, commonplace, solitary.

Give a Common Word the Spell

The medium of poetry is language, our common property. It belongs to no one [23] and to everyone. Poetry never entirely loses sight of how the language is being used, fulfilled, debased. We ought to speak more often of the *precision* of poetry, which restores the innocence of language, which makes the language visible again. Language is an impure medium. Speech is public property and words are the soiled products, not of nature, but of society, which circulates and uses them for a thousand different ends.

Poetry charts the changes in the language, but it never merely reproduces or [24] recapitulates what it finds. The lyric poem defamiliarizes words, it wrenches them from familiar or habitual contexts, it puts a spell on them. The lyric is cognate with those childish forms, the riddle and the nursery rhyme, with whatever form of verbal art turns language inside out and draws attention to its categories. As the eighteenth-century English poet Christopher Smart put it, freely translating from Horace's *Art of Poetry*:

> It is exceedingly well [25]
> To give a common word the spell
> To greet you as entirely new.

The poem refreshes language, it estranges and makes it new. ("But if the work be new, / So shou'd the song be too," Smart writes.) There is a nice pun on the word *spell* in Smart's Horatian passage since, as tribal peoples everywhere have believed, the act of putting words in a certain rhythmic order has magical potency. That power can only be released when the spell is changed aloud. I'm reminded, too, that the Latin word *carmen*, which means "song" or "poem," has attracted English poets since Sidney because of its closeness to the word *charm*, and, in fact, in the older Latin texts it also means a magic formula, an incantation meant to make things happen, to cause action (Andrew Welsh, *Roots of Lyric*). And a charm is only effective when it is spoken or sung, incanted.

The lyric poem separates and uproots words from the daily flux and flow of living speech but it also delivers them back—spelled, changed, charmed—to the domain of other people. As Octavio Paz puts it in *The Bow and the Lyre*:

> *Two opposing forces inhabit the poem: one of elevation or uprooting, which pulls the word from the language: the other of gravity, which makes it return. The poem is an original and unique creation, but it is also reading and recitation: participation. The poet creates it; the people, by recitation, re-create it. Poet and reader are two moments of a single reality.*

Metaphor: A Poet Is a Nightingale

The transaction between the poet and the reader, those two instances of one reality, depends upon figurative language—figures of speech, figures of thought. Poetry evokes a language that moves beyond the literal and, consequently, a mode of thinking that moves beyond the literal. "There are many other things I have found myself saying about poetry," Robert Frost confesses in "The Constant Symbol," "but chiefest of these is that it is a metaphor, saying one thing and meaning another, saying one thing in terms of another, the pleasure of ulteriority." Poetry is made of metaphor. It is a collision, a collusion, a compression of two unlike things: A is B. The term *metaphor* comes from the Latin *metaphora*, which in turn derives from the Greek *metapherein*, meaning "to transfer," and, indeed, a metaphor transfers the connotations or elements of one thing (or idea) to another. It is a transfer of energies, a mode of interpenetration, a matter of identity and differences. Each of these propositions about the poem depends upon a metaphor: *The poem is a capsule where we wrap up our punishable secrets* (William Carlos Williams). *A poem is a well-wrought urn* (Cleanth Brooks), *a verbal icon* (W.K. Wimsatt). *A poem is a walk* (A.R. Ammons); *a poem is a meteor* (Wallace Stevens). *A poem might be called a pseudo-person. Like a person it is unique and addresses the reader personally* (W.H. Auden). A poem is a hand, a hook, a prayer. It is a soul in action.

When Paul Celan wrote, "A poem…can be a message in a bottle," he didn't think literally that he would be dropping his poems into the Seine (though he was writing them from Paris) and that someone might find them floating ashore on the banks of the Chicago River (though I was living in Chicago when I first read him). What did he mean then? This book tries to tease out the implications.

31

The language of poetry, Shelley claims in his *Defence of Poetry*, "is vitally metaphorical; that is, it marks the before unapprehended relations of things and perpetuates their apprehension." Shelley is suggesting that the poet creates relations between things unrecognized before, and that new metaphors create new thoughts and thus revitalize language. In his fine book *Poetic Diction*, Owen Barfield remarks that he would like to change one detail in Shelley's phrase, to alter "before unapprehended relations" to "forgotten relations." That's because poetry delivers back an archaic knowledge, an ancient and vitally metaphorical way of thinking, now mostly lost. The poet, by creating anew, is also likely to be "restoring something old."

32

The oldest English poetry, for example (the Anglo-Saxon *Beowulf* and poems written in other old Germanic languages), has a number of poetic tropes that enable the poet to describe things at an angle, without naming them, and thus invite the listener to imaginatively construct them. The most widespread are known as *kennings*; these occur in compounds, such as calling the sea *swanrad* ("swan-road") or *winegeard* ("home of the winds"). The word *ken*, meaning "to know," is still used in Scottish dialects, and indeed such figurative language is a way of knowing.

33

What especially concerns me here is how the reader actively participates in the making of meaning through metaphor, in thinking through the relation of unlike things. How do we apprehend these previously unapprehended or forgotten relations: in ironic tension, in exact correspondence, in fusion? The meaning emerges as part of a collaboration between writer and reader. Out of this interactive process comes the determination to what extent metaphor *works*, where it breaks down, to what extent a poem can be a message in a bottle, or a machine made out of words (Williams), or a derangement of the senses (Rimbaud); to what extent "a book is a cubic piece of burning, smoking conscience—and nothing else" (Boris Pasternak); to what extent, as Shelley writes,

34

> *A poet is a nightingale, who sits in darkness and sings to cheer its own solitude with sweet sounds; his auditors are as men entranced by the melody of an unseen musician, who feel that they are moved and softened, yet know not whence or why.*

35

The singing of a nightingale becomes a metaphor for writing poetry here, and listening to that bird (that natural music) becomes a metaphor for reading it. One of the premises of Shelley's metaphor is that the poet "sings" in "solitude" without any consideration for an audience and that the audience—"his auditors"—responds to the work of an "unseen musician." They can't actually *see* him because they are physically removed from each other. And yet they are brought into mysterious (visionary) relation.

36

The philosopher Ted Cohen suggests that one of the main points of metaphor is "the achievement of intimacy." Cohen argues in "Metaphor and the Cultivation of Intimacy" that the maker and the appreciator of a metaphor are brought into deeper relationship with one other. That's because the speaker issues a concealed invitation through metaphor which the listener makes a special effort to accept and interpret. Such a "transaction constitutes the acknowledgement of a community." This notion perfectly describes how the poet enlists the reader's intellectual and emotive involvement and how the reader actively participates in making meaning in poetry. Through this dynamic and creative exchange the poem ultimately engages us in something deeper than intellect and emotion. And through this ongoing process the reader becomes more deeply initiated into the sacred mysteries of poetry.

Imagining Images: Collaborating on Frost's Poem

To test Hirsch's idea about our role in making meaning as we read a poem, consider this poem by Robert Frost:

> The old dog barks backward without looking up
> I can remember when he was a pup.

You may well be thinking, "You're kidding me. Two lines count as a poem? Two lines about an old dog?" I had precisely the same response the first time I encountered this poem in 1991 at the Coastal Georgia Writing Project, where workshop leaders Pat Fox and Connie Aloise distributed the poem to 20 teachers, kindergarten through college level, who had assembled to learn about "collaborative learning," a strategy for their classrooms. Fox and Aloise also distributed the following instructions to each of the four groups of five teachers:

1. Pull your chairs together and introduce yourselves to one another. Next, choose one person to read the poem and the instructions to the group.

2. Agree on one person to record the views expressed by the group and the decisions the group makes collectively. Agree on another person who will speak for the group.

3. Arrive at a consensus in answer to each question, even if the only consensus you reach is to disagree.

4. Review the recorder's notes to see if they accurately express what the group has done and decided collectively. Record the significant dissent.

These instructions bear a strong resemblance to the procedures you have used in your writing groups, as you probably noticed. Notice, too, the emphasis on working toward consensus, agreement, but also on honoring disagreement in responding to the poem.

At the end of the workshop, Professors Fox and Aloise credited composition theorist John Trimbur for the task design of their workshop; they credited Trimbur, too, for encouraging "dissensus" as well as consensus when groups work together to solve a problem—particularly if that problem involves interpreting a poem. Even a two-line poem stirs disagreement about meaning, precisely because each reader brings his or her own experiences to the poem, to the image of an old dog, head down, barking backward.

As Hirsch might put it, then, each of us collaborates with Frost in making the meaning of the dog poem. But is it a dog poem? Below, you'll see the four interpretive questions that each group of teachers tried to answer. They did not reach consensus:

1. Who is the poem about?

2. What is the poem about?

3. In what ways is this a dog poem?

4. In what ways is this not a dog poem?

Predictably, two or three teachers in each group—perhaps teachers who have owned old dogs—insisted that Frost has written a "dog poem," a simple image of an old dog seen through the eyes of an owner who recalls the dog as a "pup." But other teacher-readers challenged the idea of a "simple" image: How, exactly, they wanted to know, does a dog bark "backward"? The dog can't be barking over his shoulder (one guess at the meaning of "backward") because he barks "without looking up." Others suggested that the speaker of the poem, presumably the dog's owner, projects his own memories of the pup onto the dog, imagining that his head-down bark echoes "backward," to the past. Those teachers arguing this personified view—granting the dog the human capacity to remember the distant past—said that the poem really focuses on the speaker, someone who converts the image of the old dog barking backward into a meditation on the brevity of life, a realization of his own mortality. Other teachers insisted that we don't have to choose, that the poem begins as a "dog poem" but becomes a mortality poem if the image stirs that reflection.

Whichever view you take in helping Frost to make meaning in this poem, notice that all the interpretations stated above begin with the image of the dog. Your own imagination brings sharper detail to the dog: Frost describes the dog as "old" and barking "without looking up"; each of us must color the dog by size, color, breed, and degree of decrepitude, details provided by our imaginations based on our experience with dogs.

In short, without imagery, we have no poem. Consider, for example, the following two-stanza poem:

> Because life bends us, breaks us,
> We long for the joys of youth,
> For escape from pain.
>
> But knowing we can't reverse time,
> We accept our Earth, the right place
> For love, for play, for pain.

What do you see? As you ponder this question, notice that the poem has plenty of nouns—life, joys, youth, pain, time, Earth, place, love, play—but, with the exception of "Earth," we find only abstract nouns, imageless concepts such as "love" and "pain." True, the lines look like a poem—the two-stanza structure, even the poetic sound effect of **alliteration**, the repetition of initial consonant sounds such as **b**ends and **b**reaks, **p**lay and **p**ain—but if the writer provides no image, how can we join the poet in making meaning?

The "poem" above, in other words, does not deserve the venerable label, "poem." As the author of this non-poem, I can tell you that you have read only an imageless paraphrase and summary of another poem by Robert Frost, "Birches." As you read Frost's poem below, see if you can *see* the images that Frost substitutes for my abstractions about "joy" and "pain":

"Birches"

Robert Frost

When I see birches bend to left and right
Across the lines of straighter darker trees,
I like to think some boy's been swinging them.
But swinging doesn't bend them down to stay.
Ice-storms do that. Often you must have seen them
Loaded with ice a sunny winter morning
After a rain. They click upon themselves
As the breeze rises, and turn many-colored
As the stir cracks and crazes their enamel.
Soon the sun's warmth makes them shed crystal shells
Such heaps of broken glass to sweep away
You'd think the inner dome of heaven had fallen.
They are dragged to the withered bracken by the load,
And they seem not to break; though once they are bowed
So low for long, they never right themselves:
You may see their trunks arching in the woods
Years afterwards, trailing their leaves on the ground
Like girls on hands and knees that throw their hair
Before them over their heads to dry in the sun.
But I was going to say when Truth broke in
With all her matter-of-fact about the ice-storm
I should prefer to have some boy bend them
As he went out and in to fetch the cows—
Some boy too far from town to learn baseball,
Whose only play was what he found himself,
Summer or winter, and could play alone.
One by one he subdued his father's trees
By riding them down over and over again
Until he took the stiffness out of them,
And not one but hung limp, not one was left
For him to conquer. He learned all there was
To learn about not launching out too soon
And so not carrying the tree away
Clear to the ground. He always kept his poise

312

To the top branches, climbing carefully
With the same pains you use to fill a cup
Up to the brim, and even above the brim.
Then he flung outward, feet first, with a swish,
Kicking his way down through the air to the ground.
So was I once myself a swinger of birches.
And so I dream of going back to be.
It's when I'm weary of considerations,
And life is too much like a pathless wood
Where your face burns and tickles with the cobwebs
Broken across it, and one eye is weeping
From a twig's having lashed across it open.
I'd like to get away from earth awhile
And then come back to it and begin over.
May no fate willfully misunderstand me
And half grant what I wish and snatch me away
Not to return. Earth's the right place for love;
I don't know where it's likely to go better.
I'd like to go by climbing a birch tree,
And climb black branches up a snow-white trunk
Toward heaven, till the tree could bear no more,
But dipped its top and set me down again.
That would be good both going and coming back.
One could do worse than be a swinger of birches.

Granted, you may like my paraphrase better than Frost's poem if you value directness and clarity, but what price have you had to pay for this instant accessibility? To discover that price, read Frost's poem again, aloud this time, listening for his equivalents to my bending, playing, and hurting.

Did you *see*? Did you see that Frost's boy swinging on birches replaces my "play"; that his pathless wood, with cobwebs tickling and burning the face, the twig lashing the eyeball replaces my "pain"? Did you *hear* the ice-covered branches clicking in the wind, then "shattering and avalanching" on the crusty snow, then forming "heaps of broken glass" below the maimed tree, Frost's double metaphor for the beauty and brutality of nature, a life worth living? If you can answer "yes" to these questions, then you have just experienced the power that lies in poetic pictures, a power no paraphrase or summary can ever capture.

Listening for Your Story, Creating Your Own Images

Now that you have learned to see and hear the difference between vivid poetic language and abstract language, consider the following poem by William Wordsworth, "The world is too much with us," a sonnet that shows us what happens when we starve the imagination fed by poetry. As you read, see if you can pick out the images that reveal the power of our imaginations to keep us connected to the natural world.

"The World Is Too Much With Us"

The world is too much with us; late and soon,
Getting and spending, we lay waste our powers:
Little we see in Nature that is ours;
We have given our hearts away, a sordid boon!
This Sea that bares her bosom to the moon;
The winds that will be howling at all hours,
And are up-gathered now like sleeping flowers;
For this, for every thing, we are out of tune;
It moves us not. Great God! I'd rather be
A Pagan suckled in a creed outworn;
So might I, standing on this pleasant lea,
Have glimpses that would make me less forlorn;
Have sight of Proteus rising from the sea;
Or hear old Triton blow his wreathed horn.

Analyzing the Figurative Language in Wordsworth's Sonnet

Though Wordsworth, one of the great Romantic poets, prided himself on writing about ordinary people and "situations from common life" (446), you may have been puzzled by some of his British words and mythological references. Published in 1807, this poem, for example, refers to our prosperity as a "boon," a word less often used in twenty-first century American English. Meaning "gift," the word "boon" lies at the center of Wordsworth's claim that our obsession with "getting and spending" has proven a "sordid" or lowly gift to ourselves, leaving us blind to "Nature." Then at the end of the poem, Wordsworth's speaker refers to "Proteus" and "Triton," mythological gods of the sea. He does so not to advocate a return to "Pagan" religion but to confess to his "Great God" that we have given up "too much" if we look out at the ocean and see only salt water—and perhaps a dump for the waste of our powerful economy—remaining blind to the deity in the mix of hydrogen, oxygen, and salt.

But so far we have only paraphrased the poem, stressing Wordsworth's warning about living too much in the material world, giving "our hearts away" for comfort and wealth. How does the poem engage our emotions as well as our minds in considering his claim? Read again lines five through nine. Notice, first, that Wordsworth has personified the Sea, now a woman baring "her bosom to the moon." This specialized metaphor, **personification**, humanizes the ocean, revealing a moonlit beauty that "getters and spenders" can never see; neither can they hear the "winds" as the womanly moon gathers them "like sleeping flowers." This simile lets us see as well as hear the moon and the winds—unless, that is, "we are out of tune," blinded and deafened by the mundane, materialistic "boon." Notice here that Wordsworth uses the **rhyme**, words that end with the same sound, to reinforce the meaning of the imagery: we are out of *tune* with the moon because we have accepted the "sordid boon."

Personal Response: Student's Narration

Though Wordsworth has provided you with a moving illustration of the connection between concrete imagery to emotional response, you may still dread the prospect of writing an interpretive essay on a poem. To overcome this anxiety, use your journal to find the feelings and the personal associations which, once discovered, will make writing that analytical essay far more meaningful. You will have a chance to do so at the end of this chapter; for now, just enjoy the example of such journaling below.

To prepare for writing an essay on Wordsworth's sonnet, one student wrote the following narrative, a journal entry in response to the prompt to describe a place in nature that arouses a strong emotional response, using sensory detail and figurative language (comparisons) to recreate for the reader the same feelings:

Though I haven't always lived in Savannah, I have always managed to live near salt water. Last summer, my friend John asked me to join him on a weekend sailing trip with his wife and two children. He'd been teaching me to sail for about ten months on his twenty-five foot boat. Seeing a great opportunity to learn and have fun, I said "yes." My husband and two children were in California and I was in summer school. The trip would be a welcome break from Algebra 101.

I was at the helm when we left the dock on that hot July morning. The air was already steamy, the breeze light and salty. Heading up the Skidaway River was pleasant. The sounds of the breeze tickling the sails as it pushed us along added to the pleasing sight and smell of the river. I was happy as a cat rolling in a sunny patch of grass on a winter day.

Conditions remained so until we neared the Vernon River. I could see rough water ahead, a sure sign of more wind than I had now. After a quick scramble, the sails were changed to accommodate the increased wind. Waves periodically spit spray at us, and soon white caps frolicked on the wave tops as the wind continued to grow stronger. Feeling the weight of responsibility for those on board, I wondered aloud to John if I should give up the helm, though I was eager to see if I could meet the challenging weather conditions. Instead, we took down all of the sails and cranked the outboard motor.

I was at the helm and the wind stepped up the pace again. The bow bore so deeply into the heavy swells that the motor rose completely out of the water. When the bow came up again, it pitched water over us. No one was dry and the cockpit was swamped again and again. Salt water ran in my eyes and burned them. I was cold. It took both hands gripping hard to attempt to maneuver the boat through the pitching river. Yet I was in awe of what surrounded me, not afraid. The very power of nature was upon us all. I felt vibrantly alive. And as the wind whistled through the rigging on this summer day, I felt a wild, idiotic exhilaration being in the wild wind and whirling water, and glad I was at the helm.

As you read about this student's shifting emotions, did you notice how her language reaches toward the poetic? First, to help you feel her pleasure and contentment, she describes the breeze "tickling" the sail, another example of personification; then she describes herself as "happy as a cat rolling in a sunny patch of grass on a winter day," a simile that includes strong appeal to our sense of touch as well as our sense of sight. As the wind grows more vigorous, she uses alliteration to help us hear the "spitting spray" then another animal metaphor to suggest the "frolicking" waves. Finally, when the wind becomes threateningly violent, she describes the mixture of pleasure and pain, as the salty water burns her eyes and chills her skin, leaving her feeling "vibrantly alive" in the "wild wind and whirling water," another "exhilarating" use of alliteration.

Personal Response: Student's Poem

Having successfully created her own imagery, this student took the second step in building her confidence before writing analytically about Wordsworth's poem: She returned to her journal and converted her narrative essay into the following poem:

> When the wind blows leniently
> I think of the summer day
> I was at the helm when it
> tickled the sails with steamy
> salty air as it pushed us up
> the Skidaway River.
>
> It was the same day
> the mischievous wind made the
> waves spit spray on us, while
> white caps frolicked across
> the wave tops that pulled the bow
> deep into the Vernon River.
>
> I fought the tiller the July day
> the wind turned wild and the
> bow shook water over us again
> and again as she wrestled to
> be free of the swells.
>
> Not storm winds, just wicked winds
> as Nature, catlike, flexed her claws,
> and I in reverence, not fear,
> was glad I was at the helm to greet
> the lenient wind
> and the mischievous wind
> and the wild wind
> that summer day.

CELIA MORRETT

In reading this poem, you found the same imagery and sound effects which the student used to bring life to her narrative, but did you notice that her concept of the three winds helped her to shape her poem? First, she writes one stanza for the "lenient" wind, another for the "mischievous" wind, a third for the "wild" wind, then a concluding stanza to express her "reverence" for Nature, which gave her exhilarating pleasure even as it tested her. Notice, too, the new simile: Nature, "catlike," claws at the boat.

At the end of this chapter, you'll try you own hand at creating images and writing a poem. Doing so will deepen your understanding of the power of imagery and build your confidence for writing about poetry.

Listening for the Song

Though the previous sections of this chapter focus primarily on imagery, the visual nature of poetry, you have also heard about alliteration, one of the many sound effects that poets have always used so that, as eighteenth-century poet Alexander Pope puts it, "sound" echoes "sense" (155).

No poet can better illustrate the validity of Pope's observation than William Shakespeare, whose famous sonnet below provides examples in every line of sound echoing sense, of image becoming song. As you read this poem—simultaneously a song of love and a song of death—you will hear the speaker, a man on his death bed, say good-bye to his lover. He tells her, to paraphrase the poem, that "when you look at me, you can see I'm dying; therefore, you love me better, knowing we must soon part forever." Read the poem aloud, listening for the images that lend tremendous emotional power to the flat, rather trite paraphrase I just offered.

"That Time of Year"

That time of year thou mayst in me behold
When yellow leaves, or none, or few do hang
Upon those boughs which shake against the cold,
Bare ruined choirs where late the sweet birds sang.
In me thou seest the twilight of such day
As after sunset fadeth in the west;
Which by and by black night doth take away,
Death's second self that seals up all in rest.
In me thou seest the glowing of such fire
That on the ashes of his youth doth lie,
As the deathbed whereon it must expire,
Consumed with that which it was nourished by.
    This thou perceiv'st, which makes thy love more strong,
    To love that well, which thou must leave ere long.

Like all sonnets, Shakespeare's has 14 lines, and like most of his sonnets, this one can be described structurally as having three four-line units, called **quatrains**, each distinguished by a rhyme in the first and third lines (behold, cold) and a rhyme in the second and fourth lines (hang, sang), then a closing **couplet**, a two-line rhyming unit (strong, long).

Before considering the contribution to meaning that comes from the rhymes and other sound effects, notice the double-image pattern in each quatrain. In the first quatrain, the speaker describes his old age metaphorically as "that time of year" when late-autumn trees bear "yellow leaves" or none on their branches. Before the quatrain ends, Shakespeare transposes a second image on the first: the bare trees, now personified as shaking "against the cold" November wind, become "bare ruined choirs," a church empty of singers, just as the tree branches now hold no "sweet birds."

The next two quatrains follow the same pattern, one image of desolation and loss transposed on another. In the second quatrain, the speaker's lover now sees his old age as a "sunset" fading "in the west"; quickly, the setting sun becomes a corpse, "sealed" in a tomb just as the sunset gets "sealed up" in the night, "Death's second self." Then in the last quatrain, the lover sees the speaker's old age as a flickering "fire" choking on its "ashes," which will soon become the "deathbed" of the flames.

Students often wonder why Shakespeare needs three quatrains to say the same thing: "When you look at me, you can tell I'm dying." This valid question has an equally valid answer: Each image pattern helps us to see what my paraphrase only says. If we can see personified naked trees shaking against the cold, then a vacant church without hymns, then a personified sun entombed, then a personified fire on its "deathbed," then we can feel the emotion of the speaker and imagine that of his lover as they deal with mortality, the ultimate loss. Yet before this most intimate, most painful scene closes, Shakespeare provides a final couplet, a glimmer of joy that lends even more tenderness to their shared grief: she loves him better—and by implication forever—because she has seen that she must leave him "ere long."

But how does Shakespeare use sound effects to deepen the emotions stirred by the images in each quatrain? Though the sonnet form conventionally requires a rhyme scheme, in the hands of a great poet the rhyme will truly reinforce sense. Consider, first, Shakespeare's structural use of the rhymes: though each quatrain conveys the same message about the consequence of her seeing his decline, each quatrain also has its own image patterns. Appropriately, then, the alternating sounds change with each quatrain; they also echo the theme of desolation and death. She can "behold" the trees bare in the "cold"; she can see the "day" taken "away"; she can see the "fire" "expire."

Consider, too, the contribution of rhythm to the emotional intensity of the poem. Conventionally, sonnets must be written in **meter.** Think of meter as simply a model of the rhythmic nature of our language. That phrase I just used, for example, carries a rhythm, a pattern of strong and weak stresses: RHYTHmic, NATure. When a poet writes a sonnet, then he or she must write in a fixed metrical pattern called **iambic pentameter**, meaning that each line will contain ten syllables arranged in a weak-stress/strong-stress pattern. Don't let this technical language deafen your ear. We get the word "iambic" from Latin, originally from Greek, meaning one two-syllable unit or "foot" containing "both" a weak stress, then a strong stress. Then "penta-meter," or a meter with "five" (from the Latin *penta*) two-syllable feet, simply means that each line will have ten syllables following a weak-STRONG pattern, as in Shakespeare's first line:

That TIME of YEAR thou MAYST in ME beHOLD.

So what? Why should you care that Shakespeare alternates weak and strong syllables? Of course, you should *not* care, if simply marking the beat replaces the personal response, the work and the joy of the reader. But once you become aware of Shakespeare's iambic pentameter, you can *hear* where he deliberately *deviates from the iambic pattern* to allow beat to echo sense. Consider, for example, the fourth line of the first quatrain:

BARE RU/ined CHOIRS/ where LATE/ the SWEET/ BIRDS SANG

If you try to read this line in the iambic pattern, you hear nonsense. Though the meter calls for "bare" to be unstressed, you must almost shout "BARE," the adjective that stresses the desolate, suffering trees and the depopulated church. Similarly, the meter calls for "birds" to receive a weak stress, but the personified birds reflect the condition of the dying speaker; they must receive a strong stress.

These rhythmic departures from the iambic pattern have a Greek name: linguists and critics would refer to the first foot and the fifth foot above as *spondees* or spondaic feet, meaning simply two strong stresses in a row. Using your ear, however, matters far more than learning technical jargon. Notice that when you decide how to pronounce a line, much like an actress or actor in a play, you make interpretive decisions. 'How should my *voice* sound when I pronounce this line?' In pronouncing the line above, your voice should sound like the voice of a dying man saying goodbye to the woman he loves. In other words, the rhythmic irregularity of the line, an irregularity resulting from the two spondaic feet, creates a beat that fits the emotional intensity of the line.

Samuel Taylor Coleridge, Wordsworth's friend and fellow poet, spoke of meter as the "pulse" of the poem (*Biographia Literaria*, volume 2, chapter 18, 56). When the speaker's emotions seem calm, then the iambic beat—the beat of a human heart at rest—makes perfect emotional sense: weak-STRONG/ weak-STRONG/ weak-STRONG/ weak-STRONG/ weak-STRONG. But when the speaker's emotions intensify, then the meter *ought* to become irregular so that the beat, like an irregular heart beat, fits the passion of the words. Consider one more sample of this creatively irregular beat, the fourth line of Shakespeare's second quatrain:

DEATH'S SEC/ond SELF/ that SEALS/ UP ALL/ in REST.

Once again, we hear a spondee in the first foot, the noun "death," the focus of the speaker's message, demanding a strong stress. Then in the fourth foot, we hear yet another spondee. Coming after the iambic third foot, this spondee creates three consecutive strong stresses— "seals up all"—marking time with the speaker's emotion as he paints an image of his own tomb. To put it another way, had Shakespeare written this line in a perfect iambic pattern, he would have created a beat, a pulse, which belies the supposed passions of the dying lover.

Analyzing Sound Effects and Imagery in Owen's War Poem

Now that you have seen and heard the rhetorical force of rhyme and rhythm, consider now some other contributors to poetry's song. In the poem below, "Dulce et Decorum Est," World War I veteran Wilfred Owen writes from first-hand experience about the horrors of warfare. Read the poem silently first, then aloud, listening for the shocking merger of sound and sense.

"Dulce et Decorum Est"

Bent double, like old beggars under sacks,
Knock-kneed, coughing like hags, we cursed through sludge,
Till on the haunting flares we turned our backs
And towards our distant rest began to trudge.
Men marched asleep. Many had lost their boots,
But limped on, blood-shod. All went lame; all blind;
Drunk with fatigue; deaf even to the hoots
Of tired, outstripped Five-Nines that dropped behind.
Gas! GAS! Quick, boys!—An ecstasy of fumbling,
Fitting the clumsy helmets just in time;
But someone still was yelling out and stumbling
And flound'ring like a man in fire or lime...
Dim, through the misty panes and thick green light,
As under a green sea, I saw him drowning.
In all my dreams before my helpless sight,
He plunges at me, guttering, choking, drowning.
If in some smothering dreams, you too could pace
Behind the wagon that we flung him in,
And watch the white eyes writhing in his face,
His hanging face, like a devil's sick of sin;
If you could hear, at every jolt, the blood
Come gargling from the froth-corrupted lungs,
Obscene as cancer, bitter as the cud
Of vile, incurable sores on innocent tongues,—

My friend, you would not tell with such high zest
To children ardent for some desperate glory,
The old Lie: *Dulce et decorum est*
Pro patria mori.

You will likely never forget the horrible image in the first two stanzas of these exhausted soldiers as they stumble bare-footed through bloody mud. To help you see the soldiers' exhaustion, Owen uses a simile, comparing them to "old beggars under sacks." But the warrior-poet also uses alliteration to intensify this image of young men crushed under the weight of war, first with the repetition the "b" sound—bent, beggars, backs, blood-shod, blind—then with the "d" sounds—drunk, deaf—all harsh consonants sounding out the brutal song of combat fatigue.

Owen's heavy use of alliteration creates what critics describe as **cacophony**, harsh sounds to underscore, in this case, human suffering. The poet adds to the cacophony noted above with still more alliteration, the initial "n" sound in "knock-kneed," the hacking "k" sound in "coughing" and "cursed," and with the rhyming words and their hard internal consonants: the soldiers carry "sacks" on their "backs"; they tru**dg**e through slu**dg**e, as shells rain all about them.

When the gas bomb hits them in the third stanza, the cacophony increases, not only because of the soldiers' terrified shouting but also, for those who have inhaled too much gas, because of their "guttering" and "choking." These words illustrate the sound effect called **onomatopoeia**, words whose very sounds suggest their meaning. Owen also emphasizes the soldiers' panic when the gas bomb first hits by using other onomatopoetic words: fumbling, flound'ring, stumbling. Then Owen insists that you hear the sound of a dying man vomiting blood, using another onomatopoetic word to intensify the horror of his "gargling" song. To stress the mangling effect of such weaponry, Owen uses another simile, comparing the dying young soldier's face, twisted now by the gas, to the face of the "devil"; and Owen's hissing alliteration—"sick of sin"—and consonance (repetition of internal consonants)—"obscene as cancer," bitter as sores on "innocent tongues"—lets you hear his anger over this brutal, dehumanizing death.

You're probably wondering why Owen ends this frightening poem with the Latin sentence, "Dulce et decorum est pro patria mori." Why not just use the English translation: It is sweet (dulce) and fitting (decorum) to die (mori) for one's country (pro patria). This important question finds an answer in sound effects. Even if you understand no Latin, you can hear the soft, melodic *sounds* of the Latin, particularly when you learn that Latin vowels receive "long" pronunciations—**pah**triah, not pat-ria; **doo**lche, not **dull**che. These long vowels, combined with the *slurring* effect in moving your lips from one word to the other—dulc**e-et**, decoru**m-est**, patria-**m**ori—make sweet music. In other words, the Latin version creates a sound effect called **euphony**, smooth, soothing sounds, the opposite of cacophony. How appropriate to end this cacophonous poem with euphony, the sound of the "old lie" so often told with "high zest" to the "children" who must do the dying. Notice that this soldier-poet, a man who died in these same trenches just before the end of the war, makes no pacifist case against warfare, and he certainly has no criticism for the long-suffering soldiers. But his horrible images and sounds seem to demand that we tell all soldiers the decidedly un-sweet truth about their self-sacrificial work.

Prewriting for an Essay on Poetry

You have already learned one way to respond in writing to poetry: writing a narrative and perhaps even a poem to tell a story that conveys your personal connection to a poem you have read. Discovering that personal connection, as you saw in the narrative and poem about sailing above, makes analysis of poetry seem much more like a meaningful way to explore questions about your own life, and much less like a pointless academic exercise.

Sometimes, however, instructors ask students to follow the personal narrative with an essay that offers *critical commentary* on the poem that inspired the narrative, or on a group of thematically related poems. The word "critical" here does not mean finding fault; instead, it means offering analysis to support your interpretive comments. Consider the assignment below, one that begins with a rhetorical situation:

In a recent editorial in the college newspaper, a student enrolled in Comp II complained bitterly: "Poetry! What a waste of time! The world stands on the brink of regional warfare in the Middle East, millions are starving in Africa, civil wars abound and refuse to go away, yet here we sit reading poems! What's the point?" The student also expressed considerable doubt about his professor's claim that learning the elements of poetry helps us to learn the elements of our own survival.

Convinced that poetry can tell us much about the causes and effects of violence, you have decided to write your own editorial, using three of the following poems to show the relevance of studying poems in the modern, violent world.

Robert Browning's "My Last Duchess"

Thomas Hardy's "The Man He Killed"

Lawrence Ferlinghetti's "In Goya's Greatest Scenes"

John Donne's "Batter My Heart"

William Blake's "London"

Matthew Arnold's "Dover Beach"

Your role here is that of mediator, agreeing with the student's demand for relevance but arguing the value of seeing where violence comes from and what it leaves.

Notice, first, that students who choose to write on this topic also get to choose three of the six poems listed, each of which they had read, journaled on, and discussed in class. In other words, the student will write only about poems that truly captured his or her interest, poems about which the student has found a personal connection. The students also had two other topics from which to choose: one focused on what we can learn about our relationship with nature from poetry that uses figurative language and sound effects; the other assignment allowed students to devise their own topic, one that relates a few of the poems they had studied to some other engaging theme. As you have learned throughout this book, you do your best writing when you feel fully informed and when you care about you topic and your audience. You can count on your professor recognizing that you must write from choice.

Notice, too, that the assignment above does not ask for analysis without a purpose. Instead, it supplies an audience, a skeptical student audience that angrily rejects poetry because they consider it irrelevant to their lives. Those who choose this topic, then, will be writing a persuasive paper, one defined by its mediational purpose. Having studied persuasion and mediation in chapter four, you know that this paper must respectfully acknowledge fellow students' demands for relevance, but then patiently explain how each of the three poems provides valuable lessons about the causes and effects of violence, lessons critical to our collective survival.

Whatever your choice of topics, how should you proceed? Any student who chose the topic above, for example, would have found significant prewriting in his or her journal, where the student would have answered questions assigned by the professor, questions focused, like those above, on the relationship of imagery to sound effects in making meaning. The journal might also include a personal response narrative like the one above, and perhaps a poem derived from the narrative.

Having reviewed the journal, the student would then employ other prewriting techniques, the techniques you learned in chapters one and two. For example, the student might list key figurative language in each poem—metaphors, similes, personifications—and freewrite on the significance of each and its relation to the other figures. The student could then freewrite further on sound effects that intensify the meaning of the images.

Having completed these stages of prewriting, the student would draw on chapter three, sketching an arrangement for the first draft, a plan that would call for moving poem-by-poem, or one that would examine all three poems under the heading of "causes" of violence, followed by another section on "effects." That arrangement might also draw on the common topic of comparison—similar and differing revelations about violence—and on the stasis of conjecture—what we should do to contain the violence. With that rough draft in hand, the student would then begin the process of peer review and revision you have been practicing throughout this book.

Reading A Critical Response to Ferlinghetti's Poem

Before undertaking this process yourself, consider first one of the poems listed in the topic above, "In Goya's Greatest Scenes." Written by American poet Lawrence Ferlinghetti, this poem contrasts terrifying scenes from the canvases of Spanish artist Francisco de Goya with urban scenes from twentieth-century America. As you will see, Goya paints scenes of European warfare in the late-eighteenth and early-nineteenth centuries; Ferlinghetti "paints" the maiming and devouring that occurs in our cities. Both wars, you will see and hear, emerge from Ferlinghetti's blending of imagery and sound effects within a ragged structure that suggests a loss of control, a decent into chaos. Following the poem, you will read a sample of a student's response to Ferlinghetti's poem, a response addressed to the skeptical audience described in the assignment above.

"In Goya's Greatest Scenes"

In Goya's greatest scenes we seem to see
                                    the people of the world
            exactly at the moment when
                        they first attained the title of
                                    'suffering humanity'
        They writhe upon the page
                                in a veritable rage
                                        of adversity
        Heaped up
                Groaning with babies and bayonets
                                        under cement skies
                in an abstract landscape of blasted trees
                    bent statues bats wings and beaks
                            slippery gibbets
                    cadavers and carnivorous cocks
            and all the final hollering monsters
                of the
                            'imagination of disaster'
            they are so bloody real
                            it is as if they really still existed

        And they do

                Only the landscape is changed

        They still are ranged along the roads
                    plagued by legionaires

                            false windmills and demented roosters
        They are the same people
                                only further from home
                on freeways fifty lanes wide

324

> on a concrete continent
> spaced with bland billboards
> illustrating imbecile illusions of happiness
>
> The scene shows fewer tumbrels
> but more maimed citizens
> in painted cars
> and they have strange license plates
> and engines
> that devour America

Excerpt from Student Essay on "In Goya's Greatest Scenes"

With Goya's and Ferlinghetti's nightmarish images fresh in your mind, read this excerpt from a student's paper responding to the topic above, arguing that we need to see and hear what the poets and painters have to teach us about the sources and consequences of our rage. As you read, you will see that she enriches her discussion of Ferlinghetti's imagery with a reference to one of Goya's actual paintings, a war scene entitled "The Executions of the Third of May."

> From "In Goya's Greatest Scenes" we discover that violence often befalls powerless people trapped in a culture run by those who would maintain their own power and wealth. Ferlinghetti imagines these scenes as symbols of "suffering humanity" (5). Beneath the veil of darkness, the people crowd together, "heaped up, groaning with babies and bayonets" (9, 10). This alliteration only emphasizes the horrible images, as the peasants try desperately to defend themselves from the firing squad. Both civilians and soldiers seem to be victims here, caught up in the same madness, the same war declared by their betters.
>
> Ferlinghetti then reveals that though the "landscape is changed" (22), the scene still exists in America, where our "concrete continent" has become littered with "bland billboards," "freeways," and countless "maimed citizens," the consequence of others pursuing "imbecile illusions of happiness" (29, 30, 28, 33, 31). On the one hand, these disturbingly similar scenes suggest that we can do nothing about violence resulting from selfishness. On the other hand, by insisting that we see how little moral progress we have made in our technologically advanced culture, the poet challenges us to admit that our selfish hearts, unchecked, will continue to "devour America" until nothing remains to consume (37). We can all benefit from such a poetic dose of reality.

Notice that the student makes no grandiose or naïve claims about the power of poetry to bring world peace. Instead, she shows her reader a sampling of the imagery and sound effects that the painter and the poet use to persuade us that we might have fewer "maimed citizens" if we acknowledge our capacity to devour one another.

325

Writing on Poetry

Having studied two kinds of written responses to poetry, the personal narrative and the interpretive analysis, you're ready now to write your own responses to a poem or several poems. You may decide to write on one or more of the poems above, or you may choose one or both of the poems printed below: Elizabeth Bishop's mid-twentieth century poem "The Fish," or Seamus Heaney's contemporary poem "Digging." Before each poem, you will find analytical questions which will help you to decide if one or both of these memorable poems insist that you respond.

Journaling on Elizabeth Bishop's Poem

First, read the poem below, Elizabeth Bishop's "The Fish." Published in 1946, this poem and others of equal vividness and power led to the Pulitzer Prize for Poetry and to Bishop's teaching career at Harvard. After you have read the poem twice, once silently, once aloud, read it a third time, answering the following questions in your journal as you read:

1. What is the meaning of "venerable" (line 7), "isinglass" (line 40), and "gunnels" (line 74)? Consult your dictionary for the meaning of these words and any others whose meanings you don't know.

2. If "venerable" denotes "respectable," why do you think that Bishop chose "venerable" instead of "respectable"? What **connotation** or emotional association comes with the word "venerable"?

3. In lines 1–21, what details does Bishop use to help you *see* the condition of the old fish? Where does Bishop use alliteration and onomatopoeia to emphasize the fish's immensity, its willingness to fight, its "battered" condition? What similes and metaphors help you begin to see the beauty of this grotesque fish?

4. Lines 22–40 focus on the fish's anatomy and on the effects of breathing air. Explain how Bishop uses literal details and figurative details (metaphors and similes) to affect your feelings toward the dying fish.

5. The rest of the poem continues this dense description of the fish. Explain how Bishop's use of personification, similes, and metaphors prepare you to see "rainbows" at the end. How did you respond to the last line? Why?

"The Fish"

I caught a tremendous fish   1
and held him beside the boat
half out of water, with my hook
fast in a corner of his mouth.
He didn't fight.

He hadn't fought at all.
He hung a grunting weight,
battered and venerable
and homely. Here and there
his brown skin hung in strips   10
like ancient wall-paper,
and its pattern of darker brown
was like wall-paper:
shapes like full-blown roses
stained and lost through age.
He was speckled with barnacles,
fine rosettes of lime,
and infested
with tiny white sea-lice,
and underneath two or three   20
rags of green weed hung down.
While his gills were breathing in
the terrible oxygen
—the frightening gills,
fresh and crisp with blood,
that can cut so badly—
I thought of the coarse white flesh
packed in like feathers,
the big bones and the little bones,
the dramatic reds and blacks   30
of his shiny entrails,
and the pink swim-bladder
like a big peony.
I looked into his eyes
Which were far larger than mine
but shallower, and yellowed,
the irises backed and packed
with tarnished tinfoil
seen through lenses
of old scratched isinglass.   40
They shifted a little, but not
to return my stare.
—It was more like the tipping
of an object toward the light.
I admired his sullen face,
The mechanism of his jaw,
And then I saw that from his lower lip
—if you could call it a lip—
grim, wet, and weapon-like,
hung five old pieces of fish-line   50

or four and a wire leader
with the swivel still attached,
with all their five big hooks
grown firmly in his mouth.
A green line, frayed at the end
where he broke it, two heavier lines,
and a fine black thread
still crimped from the strain and snap
when it broke and he got away.
Like medals with their ribbons   60
frayed and wavering,
a five-haired beard of wisdom
trailing from his aching jaw.
I stared and stared
and victory filled up
the little boat,
from the pool of bilge
where oil had spread a rainbow
around the rusted engine
to the bailer rusted orange,   70
the sun-cracked thwarts,
the oarlocks on their strings,
the gunnels—until everything
was rainbow, rainbow, rainbow!
And I let the fish go.

Journaling on Seamus Heaney's Poem

Now that Bishop has taught you to see a fish through imaginative eyes, consider the humble act of digging, as described by Irish poet Seamus Heaney, who won the Nobel Prize for Literature in 1995. This poem will introduce you to Heaney's Northern Ireland, but you will also find yourself meditating once again on how you relate to the soil and how you spend your time. As you read, fill your journal with answers to these prompts:

1. Write a one- or two-sentence summary of the poem.

2. What attitude toward his father's and his grandfather's work emerges in the poem? What images, sound effects, and sensory details shape that attitude?

3. The poem begins with a simile focused on Heaney's "pen"; it ends with a metaphor also focused on the pen. Explain how this figurative language helps you to understand Heaney's attitude toward his own work.

"Digging"

Between my finger and my thumb
The squat pen rests; snug as a gun.

Under my window, a clean rasping sound
When the spade sinks into gravelly ground:
My father, digging, I look down

Till his straining rump among the flowerbeds
Bends low, comes up twenty years away
Stooping in rhythm through potato drills
Where he was digging.

The coarse boot nestled on the lug, the shaft
Against the inside knee was levered firmly.
He rooted out tall tops, buried the bright edge deep
To scatter new potatoes that we picked
Loving their cool hardness in our hands.
By God, the old man could handle a spade.
Just like his old man.
My grandfather cut more turf in a day
Than any other man on Toner's bog.
Once I carried him milk in a bottle
Corked sloppily with paper. He straightened up
To drink it, then fell to right away

Nicking and slicing neatly, heaving sods
Over his shoulder, going down and down
For the good turf. Digging.

The cold smell of potato mould, the squelch and slap
Of soggy peat, the curt cuts of an edge
Through living roots awaken in my head.

But I've no spade to follow men like them.
Between my finger and my thumb
The squat pen rests.
I'll dig with it.

Choosing a Topic for Your Essay on Poetry

After reviewing the answers you wrote in your journal, write an essay on one of the following topics:

1. After referring to Bishop's story of "The Fish" in your introduction, write an essay that narrates one of your own experiences in the world of nature, one that changed the way you think about nature and your own place in the natural world. Be sure to include plenty of description and figurative language to help your readers *see* how and why your feelings changed.

2. Write an analytical essay on the second topic mentioned at the beginning of this section: How does Bishop use figurative language and sound effects in "The Fish" to teach us about our relationship to nature. Assume that you're addressing readers who consider poetry a waste of time and nature as a collection of "resources" to be "developed" by human beings.

3. Write on topic two but expand your analysis to include Frost's "Birches," Wordsworth's "The World is Too Much with Us," and Bishop's "The Fish." Assume the same skeptical readers mentioned in topic two.

4. Write an analytical essay on Heaney's "Digging," explaining how he uses sensory detail, figurative language, and sound effects to shape your thinking about meaningful work. Assume that you're addressing readers who consider poetry a waste of time, having nothing important to teach us about how we live our lives.

5. Write a personal narrative or an analytical essay in response to a poem—or several thematically related poems—of your choice. The topic discussed at the beginning of this section, focused on the causes and effects of violence, might give you some ideas. Whatever your choices, be sure to think about your audience and purpose before proceeding.

Once you have selected your topic, follow the procedures summarized in this section and practiced throughout this book, including the processes of revision discussed in chapter six.

Works Cited

Aristotle. *Poetics. The Great Critics: An Anthology of Literary Criticism.* 3rd ed. Eds. James H. Smith and Edd W. Parks. New York: Norton, 1967. 28–61.

Arnold, Matthew. "The Study of Poetry." *Poetry and Criticism of Matthew Arnold.* Ed. A. Dwight Culler. Boston: Houghton Mifflin, 1961.

Berlin, James. *Rhetorics, Poetics, and Cultures: Refiguring College English Studies.* Urbana: NCTE, 1996.

Bishop, Elizabeth. "The Fish."

6th ed. Vol. E. Eds. Nina Baym et al. New York: Norton, 2002. 2715-15.

Coleridge, Samuel Taylor. *Biographers' Literaria*. Ed. J. Shawcross. Oxford: Oxford UP, 1969.

Crosby, Christina. "Why Major in Literature—What Do We Tell Our Students?" *PMLA* 117.3 (2002): 493–95.

Dasher, Dana. Excerpt from student essay on Ferlinghetti.

Dryden, John. "An Essay on Dramatic Poesy." *Selected Works of John Dryden*. Ed. William Frost. New York: Holt, 1967. 321–87.

Ferlinghetti, Lawrence. "In Goya's Greatest Scenes We Seem to See." A Coney Island of the Mind. New Directions Publishing Co., 1958.

Frost, Robert. "Birches."

Grube, G. M. A., trans. *Plato's Republic*. Indianapolis: Hackett, 1974.

Heaney, Seamus. "Digging." Death of a Naturalist. Faber and Faber, 1966.

Hirsch, Edward. *How to Read a Poem: And Fall in Love with Poetry*. New York: Harcourt, 1999.

Johnson, Samuel. "Preface to *The Works of William Shakespeare*." *Samuel Johnson: the Major Works*. Ed. Donald Greene. Oxford: Oxford UP, 1984. 419–56.

Komunyakaa, Yusef. *NYU English Newsletter*. New York University, 2005–2006.

Morrett, Cecilia. Student narrative and poem.

Owen, Wilfred. "Dulce et Decorum Est."

Pope, Alexander. "An Essay on Criticism." The Poems of Alexander Pope. "Ed. John Butt. Yale University Press, 1966. 143-68.

Shakespeare, William. "That Time of Year."

Sidney, Philip. *Defense of Poesy*. *The Norton Anthology of English Literature*. 8th ed. Eds. Stephen Greenblatt *et al*. New York: Norton, 2006. 954–74.

Wordsworth, William. "Preface to the Second Edition of *Lyrical Ballads*. *Selected Poems and Prefaces*. Ed. Jack Stillinger. Boston: Houghton Mifflin, 1965. 445–64.

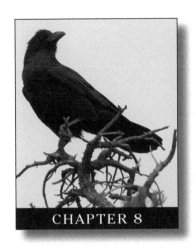

CHAPTER 8

Growing As a Writer:
Portfolios and
Reflective Writing

"Reflecting, or looking back, on the experience of writing a piece is…an integral part of becoming a more accomplished writer."
SANDRA MURPHY, "Assessing Portfolios," *Evaluating Writing*

"To get more trustworthy evidence of a writer's ability, use portfolios."
PETER ELBOW, "Writing Assessment: Do It Better; Do It Less,"
Assessment of Writing: Politics, Policies, Practices

"The concept of portfolios…implies that students' best and most representative pieces are displayed, that students have a choice in selecting what goes into the portfolio, and that their selection is based on knowledgeable reflections about their own work done over a period of time."
WILLA WOLCOTT, "Portfolio Assessment,"
An Overview of Writing Assessment

Practicing Reflective Vision

As you near the end of your composition course, your professor may require you to prepare a portfolio. If so, he or she will provide specific guidelines for this project, one that will ask you to reflect on your reading and writing processes, on the sources of your growth as reader/writer. In preparing your portfolio, you will see that you have done far more than complete a specified number of essays; you have also learned to think like a writer: you know how to analyze your purpose and audience (chapters one and two) as well as your strategies for fulfilling your purpose and serving your reader (chapters three through seven).

Thinking like a writer entails more than forward-looking analysis; it requires **reflection**, looking back on your work and assessing the effectiveness of your choices. If you have already worked through the first seven chapters, you have extensive experience in reflective reading. In chapter one, for example, when you answered questions on Frederick Douglass' *Narrative*, you assessed the effectiveness of the abolitionist in tracing the cause-effect relationships between acquiring literacy and liberty, then between acquiring liberty and maintaining solidarity with one's community. Then in chapter two, you sought the causes of your sympathy and admiration for Hurston's Delia, as she abandons her husband to the snake.

You also read reflectively in chapter three, when you assessed John McCain's use of definition, testimony, contrast, and narration to convince his readers that "courage matters." Your reflective reading continued in chapter four, where you traced King's blending of ethos, logos, and pathos in "Letter from Birmingham Jail" to make his case for justice via non-violent direct action. After reading "Greenleaf" in chapter five, you reflected on O'Connor's care in preparing readers for the revelatory goring, then on the student's efforts to blend ethos and logos in supporting her claims on O'Connor. Finally, in chapter six, you examined Barack Obama's use of dialogue and description to dramatize his painful acquisition of a public voice, and in chapter seven, you reflected on the power of poetic images to stir your emotions, to sound your "depths" (Hirsch 6).

You have also been writing reflectively all semester. In chapters one and two, your reflective readings generated a narrative on acquiring literacy and an expository essay on the elements of fiction, the literary tools that shape the personal development of Jewett's Sylvia or Hurston's Delia. Chapters three and four featured readings that led to writings on ways to overcome our fears of the Other, and on ways to persuade and mediate. In chapter five, your reflections on Nafisi's teaching motivated research on the transformative powers of literature. Then in chapter six, the reading of Obama's memoir sparked analysis of his style, or a memoir on your experiences with parents or parenting. Finally, in chapter seven, your reflective essay traced your experience of reading a poem, of reading beyond analysis to a sense of your own transformation. Whatever your topics, if you have participated in peer-response groups, then devised and followed a plan for revision, you have practiced reflective revision, looking back on your choices and assessing their effectiveness in light of your purpose and your readers' needs.

Journaling on Kevin Brockmeier's Essay

Before proceeding further with your own reflective writing, enjoy reading "A Kind of Mystery," printed below. You'll find in this essay Kevin Brockmeier's reflections on the processes that have generated his prize-winning fiction and nonfiction. As you read the excerpt, answer the questions below in your journal. Once again, doing so will help you discover his rhetorical strategies, his ways of building his credibility as a writer (ethos), his ways of appealing to your mind (logos) and heart (pathos) as he persuades you, through revision and reflection, to pursue the "mystery" of good writing.

1. The first section, "Mustard," serves as Brockmeier's introduction. Why do you think he devotes his first six paragraphs to the "Grey Poupon" mustard story?

2. In paragraph seven, Brockmeier draws two serious points about writing from the humorous mustard story. State the two points and explain how and where he illustrates these points in the mustard story.

3. In paragraph eight, Brockmeier stresses the "revelation" that always comes to writers patient enough to look at their subject closely. What "sensory details" in the mustard story prove that he practices his own principles as a writer?

4. What evidence does Brockmeier provide to support his claims that "writing is work" and that "reading is holy"? Do the examples and revelations clarify exactly what he means by "holy"? What key words and phrases emphasize the spiritual intensity of reading and the ethical applications that grow from the holiness?

5. What does Brockmeier mean by the "strange silence" that writers strive to share with their readers? How do the last two paragraphs clarify the difference between the "desire to be read" and this desire to share the "strange silence"?

6. The title, "A Kind of Mystery," suggests that Brockmeier has written primarily in the narrative mode. Looking back over the piece, find several examples of the descriptive mode and use them to explain why good narration almost always weaves vivid description into the story.

"A Kind of Mystery"

Kevin Brockmeier

Mustard

Here is a true story. When I was sixteen years old and got my first car, I kept a jar of Grey Poupon mustard in the glove compartment. There was a popular commercial running at the time in which an aristocratic fellow in a Rolls-Royce pulls up alongside another aristocratic fellow in a Rolls-Royce and asks, "Pardon me, but do you have any Grey Poupon?" The second aristocrat says, "But of course," and passes a jar of Grey Poupon across the gap on a silver platter. My first car was a boat-like Plymouth Reliant, and I thought it was funny to assume an air of elegance while I was driving it, but I also hoped that someone would eventually stop beside me at a traffic light, ask for some Grey Poupon, and I would be able to hand it over just like the man in the commercial. 1

Years passed. I was a senior in college. Late one night I was driving home from Denny's with a friend when a pickup truck appeared behind me, thundering up to my bumper and backing away, honking its horn and flashing its headlights. When I stopped at a red light, the truck veered alongside me, and I heard shouting and cursing. "I'm not going to look," I told myself. "I'm not going to look." But I did. There were three or four guys in cowboy hats packed into the front seat, obviously drunk. One of them gestured for me to roll down my window. You can probably guess what he said. 2

"Pardon me, do you have any Grey Poupon?" 3

Rarely have I been so delighted. I reached across my friend in the other seat—he knew how long I had been waiting for this, and he was beaming—and I fished the mustard out of the glove compartment. I held it out the window. "But of course," I said. 4

The guys in the pickup truck went wild. I handed the jar to them, the light changed, and they tore away down the street. I don't know what happened after that. The mustard had been in my car for more than six years. If they tried to eat it they must have gotten horribly sick, but it's more likely they threw it at a street sign or a wall somewhere. At any rate, for the rest of the night I had that wonderful feeling of serendipity you get at those rare moments when a pattern of grace seems to be at work in your life. Franz Kafka once said of G.K. Chesterton, "He is so gay, that one might almost believe he had found God." For the next few days I was so gay that I could almost believe I had found God. 5

Now, I've always liked my Grey Poupon story, for two reasons—one, because I'm the hero, and two, because it suggests that even the most absurd faith will be rewarded if you hold to it long enough. 6

This is the same philosophy by which I sit down to write in the morning. My stories come to me very slowly. It would be easy for me to abandon them at any of the half-hundred times when the ledge seems too narrow to maneuver if I didn't trust that 7 they would deliver me where I need to go in the end. It usually takes me a month or two, writing every day for at least several hours, to produce a single short story. I write so slowly because it's important to me that every sentence in my stories be exactly as it should be. If a word feels clumsy or ill-chosen, I'll spend as much time as I can trying to fix it. I believe that if you love a story, you'll be willing to give it as much time as it needs—and you have to love your stories if you're going to ask other people to read them. You have to love your characters so much that you're not willing to say anything false about them. Everything a good story offers us—its ability to create living characters, to help us understand other lives, to move us, and make us dream—is borne up by the words we use to tell it, and if those words aren't chosen with precision then the story will empty out, as anything will do when the air leaks out from around the edges.

That said, much of the time I spend on my stories—an embarrassingly large amount, in fact—I devote to looking for and trying to shape the right sensory details. Which is to say that much of the time I spend on my stories I devote to walking around my apartment and gazing out the windows. I think that if you really take the time to look at something, anything—a stone, a ketchup packet, an ant—you'll experience a quality of revelation. This may sound like a mystical or murky or esoteric idea, but I believe that such an experience of revelation is fairly universal, and somewhat mysterious, and beautiful in its way. Because I'm interested in conveying this experience to my readers, I probably use a little more sensory detail than is strictly necessary.

What's Holy

Another request I sometimes get (particularly from interviewers, but also from people who have just met me) is to name my influences. The responses I give have always seemed disingenuous to me. This is not because I have no influences, of course, but because I have so many—and also, perhaps, because I'm only dimly aware of them. The books I've read have shaped my writing in ways that I've rarely been able to predict or account for. I'm almost never aware of my influences as I'm writing, and if I were I suspect I would find it debilitating. Rather, the writers I admire have an effect on me that is mostly subterranean—which is to say that the rhythms of their language, the ways that they notice, become a part of how I think about the world. This is probably because when I'm really enjoying a book I approach it as a reader seeking a certain richness of perception, rather than as a writer seeking lessons. There are shelves and shelves of writing guidebooks out there dedicated to the notion that writing is holy. I hate this idea. Writing is work. When it's going well, it can make you feel as if you're inhabiting the still center of your life, and this can unquestionably be satisfying. But it isn't holy. What's holy is reading.

Now, all of this does not mean that I cannot discuss the writers who feel the most intimate to me. I can, endlessly. By far the best book I've read in the past year, for instance, is *The Complete Short Stories* by J.G. Ballard (still unpublished in the U.S.; I bought my copy through amazon.com.uk), which is first of all so *big*, and second of all so packed with wonders, that it's like one of those amazing, neverending books you encounter in a dream: an almanac of worlds. And it's easy to name the writers who have meant the most to me over, say, the past five years: William Maxwell and Italo Calvino. Both of them are writers who are better known for their novels than for their short fiction, but I first came to them through their story collections, and that's the work I still love the best.

Italo Calvino writes singular, heartfelt, deeply witty stories that seem like folk or fairy tales—the kind of stories you might almost imagine had been around forever if the subject matter weren't so contemporary. "The Light-Years," from his book *Cosmicomics*, is the one that most clearly illustrates what I'm talking about. Here is the beginning:

> *One night I was, as usual, observing the sky with my telescope. I noticed that a sign was hanging from a galaxy a hundred million light-years away. On it was written: I SAW YOU. I made a quick calculation: the galaxy's light had taken a hundred million years to reach me, and since they saw up there what was taking place here a hundred million years later, the moment when they had seen me must date back two hundred million years.*

> *Even before I checked my diary to see what I had been doing that day, I was seized by a ghastly presentiment: exactly two hundred million years before, not a day more nor a day less, something had happened to me that I had always tried to hide. I had hoped that with the passage of time the episode had been completely forgotten; it was in sharp contrast—at least, so it seemed to me—with my customary behavior before and after that date: so, if ever anybody wanted to dig up that business again, I was ready to deny it quite calmly, and not only because it would have been impossible to furnish proof, but also because an action determined by such exceptional conditions—even if it was really verified—was so improbable that it could be considered untrue in all good faith, even by me. Instead, from a distant celestial body, here was somebody who had seen me, and the story was cropping up again, now of all times.*

This is so charming, so full of whimsy and recognizable human anxiety, that it's hard to imagine the reader who would dislike it.

William Maxwell is a very different writer, but his stories are no less transforming. There's a wistfulness and a humility to his fiction that moves me every time I read him. The one Maxwell story I find myself returning to most often is "The Thistles in Sweden," the last paragraph of which is so lovely that I want to present it whole:

> *Now when I walk past that house I look up at the windows that could be in Leningrad or Innsbruck or Dresden or Parma, and I think of the stairway that led only to the trapdoor in the roof, and of the marble fireplace, the bathroom skylight, and the tiny kitchen, and of what school of Italian painting we would have been if we had been a school of Italian painting, and poor Mrs. Pickering sitting in her bedroom chair with her eyes wide open, waiting for help, and the rainy nights on Thirty-sixth Street, and the grey-and-blue thistles, the brown seashells, the Mills Brothers singing* Shine, little glowworm,

glimmer, glimmer, and the guests who came the wrong night, the guest who was going to die and knew it, the sound of my typewriter, and of a paintbrush clinking in a glass of cloudy water, and Floribunda's adventure, and Margaret's empty days, and how it was settled that, although I wanted to put my head on her breast as I was falling asleep, she needed even more (at that point) to put her head on mine. And of our child's coming, at last, and the black cat who thought she *was our child, and of the two friends who didn't after all get married, and the old woman who found one treasure after another in the trash baskets all up and down Lexington Avenue, and that other old woman, now dead, who was so driven by the need to describe the inner life of very large granite boulders. I think of how Miss Mattie Gressner's face fell and how she closed her notebook and became a stranger to us, who had been so deeply our friend. I think of the oversexed ironer, and the Holmses, and the Venables, and the stranger who meant nobody good and was frightened away by Albertha's cursing, and the hissing of the airbrakes of the Lexington Avenue bus, and the curtains moving at the open window, and the baby crying on the other side of the wall. I think of that happy grocery store run by boys, and the horse-drawn flower cart that sometimes waited on the corner, and the sound of footsteps in the night, and the sudden no-sound that meant it was snowing, and I think of the unknown man or woman who found the blue duffel bag with the manuscript of my novel in it and took it to the police station, and the musical instrument (not a lute, but that's what the artist must have had in mind, only she no longer bothers to look at objects and draws what she remembers them as being like) played in the dark, over our sleeping bodies, while the children flew their kites, and I think if it's true that we are all in the hands of God, what a capacious hand it must be.*

The gentleness of this, and the cadence, and the quality of attention, are all remarkable.

I would love to be able to mingle the flawless oddity of Italo Calvino with the tenderness and wonder of William Maxwell. In fact, if I were to put my aspirations in words, those might be the ones I would use.

We Were Everybody

A truism of writing guidebooks is that the act of writing—or any act of creativity—should be like joyfully giving birth to some part of yourself. This is an old idea that has found its most recent manifestation in the advent of the personal-growth movement. I can't look at personal growth as anything other than an admirable goal, but if I truly believed it were the object of my writing, I would long since have given it up. For this reason: those moments when I feel a jubilant outpouring of my most indispensable self (and I believe that's what the writing guidebooks are asking me to feel) are few and far between (particularly when I set them alongside the sheer labor of envisioning that's involved in writing fiction). But providing such moments for yourself is hardly the point—the point is to offer them to your readers. To put it plainly, it's not when I am writing that I feel the most unbroken, unencumbered, and capable of understanding my life; it's when I am reading my own favorite books. The impulse behind writing a work of fiction is, or should be, essentially a generous one: to duplicate the experience for other people.

Certainly it is the case that when you read a book that has the influence on you 20
it is meant to have, you feel that you are participating in its creation. I think of this
as the difference between reading and deciphering a piece of writing. When you *read*
a book—truly *read* it, rather than simply analyzing it to unlock the words as a set of
symbols—you experience it as a sort of continuous waking dream, and you feel what
Marilynne Robinson refers to as "the physical exhilaration of consciousness." This
might be the deepest pleasure that literature offers, and I can't imagine there is a reader
who doesn't recognize it. (I myself sometimes have the same feeling when I listen to
music, though not, oddly enough, when I watch films or television shows, which, no
matter how beautiful or stirring or even perfect they can be, always seem as though
they are happening *to* me rather than *out* of me.) How often do we have access to
the whole of our own consciousness, or even to the whole of our own memories—to
everything we are capable of being? Almost never, I'd wager. Maybe when we die our
minds will be laid out before us in their entirety and we will know ourselves as we
really were, in all our shades and circumstances, and we will realize we were everybody,
but for now, at least, we see ourselves only in glimpses, as though we were passing
through the forest behind a screen of leaves and branches. Great books show us not
only those parts of ourselves that we know intimately, but also those parts we are only
dimly aware of or have forgotten about completely. They clear some of the branches
away. They remember us to ourselves.

This capacity that fiction has to set us squarely inside the lives of other people, 21
or more completely inside our own lives, strikes me as central to the project of
imaginative writing. It's an endowment beside which everything else becomes
secondary—whether the investigation of social issues or the teasing out of plots and
themes.

Not long ago, I met a man in a bookstore who told me that he would rather read 22
Dostoevsky than Tolstoy because Tolstoy writes about members of the wealthy class,
whereas Dostoevsky writes about members of the working class, and he was more
interested in the problems of the impoverished than in the problems of the wealthy.
I've thought about this a lot since then, probably because I disagreed with the man,
but didn't bother to argue with him at the time. What he said is very roughly true,
I suppose, but I can't help but think that it misses the point. For people who read in
order to feel a sympathetic response in their own consciousness, the great writers have
a significance that goes beyond the cerebral. It seems to me that for those of us who
read as though our lives depended on it, the difference between Tolstoy and Dostoevsky
has little to do with their stance on matters of wealth and privilege, but with the way
they approach the question of how on earth we ought to live. Simply put, Tolstoy writes
about people who find it difficult to be alive because they're sane, whereas Dostoevsky
writes about people who find it difficult to be alive because they're not. That's why
their books are important. That's why they matter. It's not easy to talk about issues
like this in literature classes or reading groups, and so they often go ignored, but they
shouldn't. They are at the very heart of why writers such as Tolstoy and Dostoevsky (and
Shakespeare and Faulkner and Proust and Márquez) ask us to read their books in the
first place. (For what it's worth, by the way, I like Tolstoy better.)

The Strange Silence

One of my favorite quotations is from G.K. Chesterton's book *The Everlasting Man*, in which he writes: "I am concerned rather with an internal than an external truth; and, as I have already said, the internal truth is almost indescribable We have to speak of something of which it is the whole point that people did not speak of it; we have not merely to translate from a strange tongue or speech, but from a strange silence." Chesterton was actually writing here about religious sentiment, but I have sometimes used this quotation to illustrate to my students the aim of the fiction writer—to translate from that strange silence of our innermost lives. 23

It can also be used to illustrate the dilemma of the writer who is newly published or just beginning to submit his work for publication. We write our books and place our manuscripts in the mail, sending them out to agents and editors, magazines and publishing houses, and we wait our weeks and months for a response. We go to the movies and teach our classes and eat in restaurants with friends, filled all the while with this absurd hope. It's as if we've shouted into a canyon, "I'm worth reading!" and then cupped our hands to our ears to listen for an echo. What are we to do, though, if we hear nothing at all? What are we to do with this strange silence? 24

All of us who are struggling to find our footing in the publishing world must grapple with this question. The answer I have come to is only provisional, but I offer it anyway because it's the best that I've got. 25

The real struggle for a writer always takes place on the page. It's not that publishing isn't important: it is, and we know that it is. Moreover, we all know why it is. We write to be read. We write so that we can publish, so that we can make some money, so that we can have the time to write. The process of sending our fiction out into the world and waiting to hear something back can seem like a worthwhile use of our time—can seem, in fact, as if it's as legitimate a part of our work as the writing itself. The thing is, it isn't. What truly matters is what we do when we're sitting at our desks, pen in hand, piecing together our assemblies of words—the stories we tell, the ideas we bring to life, the characters we endow with our humanity. I have learned that when I apply myself to my writing, I quickly become absorbed in the problems of language and storytelling. These are problems I can do something about, and as I struggle with them, that other problem, the problem of publication, recedes from my mind. The silence is still there, but it takes on a different tone, a deeper and more living one. 26

It may be difficult for the established writer to understand, or rather remember, the vehemence of the beginning writer's desire to be read: in time, I suspect, all things come to seem inevitable. But there's another desire, an equal and more persistent one, that we all share in common—the desire to become a better, more generous, more searching writer. This is the true aspiration of every writer of worth, and in times of drought, it's the one that should sustain us. 27

Creating a Portfolio

In summarizing the reflective reading and writing you have completed, as I did above, then in asking you to consider the reflections of a professional writer, I have tried to persuade you that you're ready, should your professor require you to prepare a portfolio. Realize, too, that your professor would never make such an assignment unless you had been practicing reflective reading and writing all semester. Far too difficult and much too important to be tacked-on at the end of a course, a portfolio requires what your psychology professor calls metacognitive thinking: stepping back from your work, looking for the big picture, thinking about your thinking, or, more appropriately here, writing about your writing—work you can do if you've been writing about your writing all semester. Professor Lee Odell acknowledges writing as "an act of discovery, an act of discovering meaning" (7), but he believes that you can best understand your "mind at work" if you can *connect* the hundreds of moments of discovery that take place over a semester, determining where and how growth has occurred. Only portfolios can do such work, as Willa Wolcott implies in the epigraph above, because they examine "work done over a period of time." Theorists Peter Elbow and Sandra Murphy agree with Wolcott and Odell, as the other epigraphs reveal, because portfolios reveal what an objective test or a single piece of writing *never can*:

- What you have learned about critical reading
- What you have learned about your own reading, writing, and researching processes
- What you have learned about solving a problem and writing persuasively about your solution
- What you have learned about revising with your purpose and reader in mind.

Again, because you have read and revised reflectively all semester, you should be ready for this challenging, exciting assignment: creating a portfolio of your work.

Below, you will find guidelines for selecting materials for your portfolio, as well as for writing about your writing. You will also learn about in-class workshopping, a key part of this process, which will keep you moving in the right direction. After considering these guidelines, you will examine more samples of reflective writing. These reflections come from Comp I students examining their strategies and evaluating their successes in their essays on King's "Letter from Birmingham Jail." Finally, you will find suggestions for your own reflective writing, as well as a final sample of reflective writing by a professional writer, Anne Lamott.

Selecting Materials for Your Portfolio

As the epigraph from Willa Wolcott rightly insists, *you*, not your professor, must *choose* the materials that will faithfully represent not only your best work but also the causes and manifestations of your growth. If your professor does the choosing, your thinking stops, and your portfolio becomes a meaningless file of papers. Still, your professor will provide directions to guide you through this challenging process of selection and reflection. In the list below, you'll see a sampling of the kinds of directions you can expect your professor to provide as you begin to build your portfolio:

Your portfolio might include the following items:

- At least three selections from your prewriting: journaling, freewriting, study questions, peer response sheets, revision strategy statements

- One of your first three essays. The essay may be the one that received the highest grade, but look past the grade. Pick the essay that taught you the most about prewriting, writing, and revising, the essay that taught you the most about writing from the heart as well as from the head, the essay where you most clearly hear your own voice.

- A revision of your last essay

- A reflective essay

- All these "might include" statements may seem to violate the principle of student independence in making selections, but look again: choice lies embedded in each item. Prewriting claimed a central place in your work throughout the course: responding to readings, prewriting in class, responding to peers, planning revisions of drafts. In other words, you cannot accurately represent your work or your growth without including selections from your prewriting, but *you* do the choosing. *You* decide where you saw your "mind at work" within the pages of your journal.

- You also determine which essay taught you the most about yourself as reader, prewriter, writer, and reviser. As you will see in the sample reflections below, you will focus a substantial portion of you reflective essay explaining and defending this one choice.

- The revised paper will give you a chance to highlight your growth in personal style and in awareness of your reader's needs.

- The reflective essay—the heart of the portfolio—will give you a forum to explain your choices, to illustrate your growth as reader and writer.

Writing about Your Writing

In addition to providing guidelines for your selections, your professor will also offer guidelines on writing the centerpiece of the portfolio, the reflective essay. Those guidelines may sound something like these:

Your reflective essay should include the following components:

- An appropriate title
- An introductory paragraph, including a thesis that comments on your growth as reader, prewriter, writer, and reviser
- A section (1–3 paragraphs) on the prewriting selections, explaining why/how they helped you in preparing to write a paper
- A paragraph explaining the prewriting techniques that you used in preparing the essay you have selected. You may omit this paragraph if you already covered this material in the journaling section.
- A section (probably at least two paragraphs) explaining the strengths of the essay you chose. Be sure to refer specifically to word choices, sentence structures, examples, quotations, or organization and to explain why they work well.
- A section explaining how revision improved the paper (you may want to blend this material with the section on strengths)
- A section explaining how revision improved your last essay. Again, describe strategies (such as the need to build ethos or add logos/pathos) and refer specifically to the improvements. It's OK to quote yourself!
- A concluding paragraph that summarizes your growth and draws conclusions about where you'll need to focus in your next writing course.

Once again, these guidelines may seem prescriptive in the range of issues to address in the reflective essay; however, notice that you remain completely free to determine points to emphasize in your sections on prewriting and revising. Again, in analyzing these choices, you will come face to face with yourself as writer.

Workshopping on Reflective Writing and Portfolio Organization

To facilitate this reflecting process, your professor may devote several class periods to one-on-one conferences as well as to peer-group discussions. This informal workshop atmosphere will help you get started in selecting materials for your portfolio, a looking-back process that most students enjoy. Workshopping will also help you to evaluate your reflective essay as you move it through the drafting process, sharing your draft with your professor and with writing group members. They will ask you questions like these:

- "Do you think you've explained where or how journaling enriched your essay?
- Have you shown *where* that paragraph has improved through your revision process?
- Have you explained *how* that reorganization will assist the reader in navigating your essay?

- Have you cited examples to support your claim that you learned to use parallel sentence structure effectively?

In answering such questions, you will deepen your analysis of your own writing and, in the process, your understanding of *how and why* you have grown as a reader/writer.

Workshopping will also help you to think about organizing your portfolio. For example, if you received instructions that look like those above, then you might have chosen this simple organizational plan:

1. The reflective essay
2. The three selections from your prewriting
3. The essay chosen from the first three assignments
4. The revision of the last essay

Once you share this plan with your professor or your peer group, you may get questions like these: "Shouldn't you distribute your reflections throughout the portfolio? Won't this placing of the reflective essay at the beginning force the reader to flip back and forth constantly?" As you field these questions, an alternating pattern may emerge:

1. The introductory paragraph of the reflective essay, acting as a preface to the entire portfolio
2. The reflective paragraph(s) on the prewriting selections
3. The prewriting selections
4. The reflective paragraph(s) on prewriting that generated the chosen essay
5. The chosen essay
6. The reflective paragraph(s) on the strengths of the chosen essay and the role of revision in creating those strengths
8. Reflective paragraph(s) on revision strategies in the last essay
9. Last essay
10. Concluding reflective paragraph, summarizing growth as reader/writer

In turn, this outline will generate a debate on whether most readers would prefer to read a *whole* reflective essay at the front of the portfolio, or a *segmented* reflective essay distributed throughout the portfolio. Likely, you will not reach consensus. The *choice remains yours*. But the debate will have been worthwhile because it forces you to think about your reader, to make rhetorical choices instead of arbitrary, coin-flipping choices: heads, it's Plan A; tails, it's Plan B. The debate will also raise other reader-centered questions: Should I create a table of contents? Would tabs be a good idea? Do I need a fancy, expensive binder?

To help you to continue taking such questions seriously, your professor may supply you with a rubric for rating the portfolios. The list below provides a sample of such a 100-point rubric:

Rubric for Rating Portfolios

Completeness and Accessibility—20 points: Are all required elements present and appropriately labeled (headers, tabs, some consistent plan to facilitate reading and navigation)?

- Three selections from Journal—5 points
- One essay chosen from first three essays—5 points
- Revision of Last Essay —5 points
- Reflective Essay—5 points

Reflective Essay—80 points

- Clarity of introduction, thesis, and conclusion on degree of growth in reading, writing, revising—5 points
- Clarity of explanation for choosing each of three prewriting selections—10 points
- Thoroughness in explaining successes and failures in prewriting activities for chosen essay—10 points
- Thoroughness in explaining and describing the strengths of chosen essay—15 points
- Thoroughness in explaining and describing the revisions of chosen essay—15 points
- Thoroughness in explaining and describing revision strategies in the last essay—15 points
- Correctness of Reflective Essay: spelling, punctuation, verb and pronoun forms—10 points

At first glance, you may conclude from this rubric that you would receive 20 automatic points just for submitting all the required material. Notice, however, that the heading stresses "accessibility" as well as "completeness." You will likely receive 20 points, in other words, if you include the prewriting selections, the chosen essay, the last essay, and the reflective essay, *and if* you have also devised some system—headings, sectional tabs, perhaps a table of contents—to make it *immediately* clear to the reader the focus of each section and the arrangement of the material. Though such issues may seem superficial, consider the impression made by materials poorly labeled or haphazardly arranged. Such presentation of your work would suggest carelessness, lack of professionalism, just the kind of negative ethos that you don't want to convey to your readers—ever.

Note, too, that *80* of the 100 points come from the metacognitive analysis that makes reflective essays so difficult yet so rewarding to write: If you can describe the strengths of your documents, if you can explain how those strengths emerged (prewriting activities) and how you turned weaknesses into strengths (revision), then you will have discovered your identity as a writer and taught yourself how to continue your growth.

Predictably, appropriately, you will receive those last 10 points if your reflective essay shows that you have learned to proofread effectively. Additionally, if you had difficulties with correctness throughout the course, you might address those problems in the reflective essay, explaining *how*, for example, you learned to avoid comma splices, and then citing effective examples in your chosen essay or in your last essay, where you have used the semicolon correctly to yoke two closely related independent clauses (see chapter six for discussion of proofreading).

Reading Samples of Reflective Writing

When Comp I student Amanda Beard submitted her portfolio, she titled her reflective essay "I Have Conquered the Comma!: A Semester in Retrospect." She included both a table of contents and sectional headings, making it easy to navigate through her analysis of her selections, which she placed after her five-page reflective essay. She begins her reflective analysis with this introductory overview:

> Many nights of reading, journaling, and writing have brought me to this point in my scholastic career. Throughout this semester in Composition I, I have done prewriting, writing, revising, and rewriting. In spite of all my moaning and groaning about writing another essay, I have learned a great deal about who I am as a writer as well as who I am as a learner. Though I have grown from a tiny acorn into a sapling, I have miles to grow before becoming a giant oak.

To begin substantiating her claim of growth, Amanda reflects on the journaling and freewriting practices that helped her to improve as a writer. Though she acknowledges that her early journaling felt like "prolonged torture," busy-work, she explains that "toward the middle of the semester" she came to understand journaling and freewriting as "precursors to good writing," ways to invent ideas in response to her reading, ideas discovered through close analysis of language.

These analytical skills proved their value again, Amanda says, when she revised her last essay for the portfolio. Titled "Signed, Sealed, and Delivered," that essay responded to Dr. King's "Letter from Birmingham Jail," focusing on his argument against waiting any longer for freedom. In discussing her strategies for improving that paper, Amanda offers this analysis:

In my discussion of ethos I failed to mention the Apostle Paul. By mentioning Paul in my revision, I have given my readers another reason to agree with King's urgent call to action. King borrows Paul's credibility when he states that "just as the Apostle Paul left his village of Tarsus and carried the gospel of Jesus Christ to the far corners of the Greco-Roman world, so am I compelled to carry the gospel of freedom beyond my own home town. Like Paul, I must constantly respond to the Macedonian call for aid." By quoting this allusion, my revision becomes stronger by stressing King's wisdom in citing an authority who would command the respect of his fellow clergymen. Another aspect of King's essay that I left out but inserted during the revision process is the parallel structure that emphasizes King's pathos as he talks about the mistreatment of his people in Birmingham jail. Within my revised version, I provided this explanation: "The phrase 'if you were to' reveals King's compassion for the victims of segregation and stirs the guilt of clergymen who have refused to see."

Amanda's classmate, Josh McCormick, also reflected on the power of revision to improve his work. Consider first the introduction to his reflective essay for the portfolio:

My experience in English Composition has been growth with practice. By writing on various topics, I have been able to develop and further improve skills in forming logical and well founded arguments based on textual evidence from various works. The lessons learned were not so much on how to write, but how to mature my level of writing with proper use of logos, pathos, and ethos along with making sure that the paper remains effective to its stated point. The primary experience I have acquired from this class is how to effectively build a case in writing and how to read into a piece of literature to deduce the intentions and feelings of the author. In this reflective essay, I would like to display some works I have done for journaling, and then explain their significance to my writing. I will then describe some of my prewriting techniques for my selected essay, "Looking for a Champion," and some of the essay's strengths, along with how revision improved the paper. I will then focus on a second essay, "An Ecclesiastical Fall from Grace," taking note of how revisions improved that paper.

You read Josh's essay, "An Ecclesiastical Fall from Grace," in chapter four. Consider now his reflections on how his journaling served him well as a prewriting technique:

I selected my essay on King's "Letter" because of the practical lessons I learned from journaling on his work prior to writing "An Ecclesiastical Fall from Grace." After we framed our study of argument with the concepts of ethos, logos, and pathos, I was able to dissect Dr. King's letter to understand not only his point but also Dr. King as a person. As I journaled on the question about King's disappointment with the church, I gained insight into his frustration over the church's inaction. Looking deeper, I saw a King who was not only frustrated but who also had great anxiety over his membership in a church that failed to act on Christian principles of brotherhood. I saw that it harrowed his mind to love Christianity so much, to be devoted to its moral philosophy, and to see the leaders of that religion stand silent, even resistant to a degree, of that which is right. Further, I saw that he feared the moral decay of the church, the waning of its influence on events, and felt tormented to see the church turn its back on such an important movement for brotherhood. By giving me this insight to King's distress, my journal enabled me to write more persuasively on King's purpose.

As you move toward completing your portfolio, this difficult academic task may begin to feel like something else: the reflective work of a real writer, like Kevin Brockmeier, not just the work of a student competing for a grade. You will have provided—as did Kevin Brockmeier, Amanda Beard, and Josh McCormick—"glimpses of the writing life" which will enrich your learning in Composition if you savor the "mystery" that occurs when words unite writers and readers (114).

Suggestions for Reflective Writing

Whether or not your professor requires a portfolio, you would be wise to write reflectively on the following questions. If your professor does assign a portfolio, answering these questions will provide a powerful prewriting tool, giving you a sense of direction and commitment as you begin your work. If your professor does *not* assign a portfolio, answering these questions becomes even more important: What more fruitful task could you undertake, as you prepare to move on into other courses requiring academic writing, than determining *where you are as a reader and writer*, how you arrived at this point, and where you need to travel for further growth?

Answering Eight Key Reflective Questions

1. **Where do you write?** Do you, like early twentieth-century English novelist Virginia Woolf, need a "room of your own," a special place where your creativity comes to life? What must you have in your writing *space*, whether a particular room or not? Why?

2. **When do you write?** Does it matter? Does your "time to write" have any connection to your "place to write"?

3. **What rituals do you follow?** Perhaps none, but many writers, like many athletes, *must* do certain tasks or gather certain lucky charms before "going to the plate" or "taking the field" as a writer.

4. **What invention strategies** (see chapters two and three) **work best for you?** Does your prewriting differ, depending on the type of writing you're doing? You can answer this question swiftly and in detail if you simply freewrite on the prewriting you have done in each of these chapters.

5. **How effectively have you worked in writing groups?** Have you learned to respond honestly and specifically to your peers? Have you learned to demand (tactfully) the same treatment from your peers when they respond to your drafts? Have you learned to reflect on your peers' suggestions before adopting their ideas for revision? Have you learned how to maintain ownership of your paper?

6. **Have you learned how to revise effectively?** What strategies have worked for you? Which have failed? Why?

7. **Have you learned how to proofread effectively?** What kinds of errors have you conquered? Which kinds of errors baffle you still? What strategies seem to sharpen your proofreader's eye?

8. **Do you feel like a writer?** Why or why not?

Writing About Anne Lamott's Essay

Finally, if you read Anne Lamott's "The Moral Point of View," printed below, you will come face to face with the most important reflective questions you can answer: Have you chosen a topic about which you "care passionately"? Have you told your "truth"? I can think of no richer way to end your course in writing than to read this brief chapter from Anne Lamott's *Bird by Bird: Some Instructions on Writing and Life*, and then to write about your writing in terms of the two questions above.

Excerpt from "The Moral Point of View"

Anne Lamott

If you find that you start a number of stories of pieces that you don't ever bother finishing, that you lose interest or faith in them along the way, it may be that there is nothing at their center about which you care passionately. You need to put yourself at their center, you and what you believe to be true or right. The core, ethical concepts in which you most passionately believe are the language in which you are writing. [1]

These concepts probably feel like givens, like things no one ever had to make up, that they have been true through all cultures and for all time. Telling these truths is your job. You have nothing else to tell us. But needless to say, you can't tell them in a sentence or a paragraph; the truth doesn't come out in bumper stickers. There may be a flickering moment of insight in a one-liner, in a sound bite, but everyday meat-and-potato truth is beyond our ability to capture in a few words. Your whole piece is the truth, not just one shining epigrammatic moment in it. There will need to be some kind of unfolding in order to contain it, and there will need to be layers. We are dealing with the ineffable here—we're out there somewhere between the known and the unknown, trying to reel in both for a closer look. This is why it may take us a whole book. [2]

I'm not suggesting that you want to be an author who tells a story in order to teach a moral or deliver a message. If you have a message, as Samuel Goldwyn said, send a telegram. But we feel morally certain of some things, sure that we're right, even while we know how often we've been wrong, and we need to communicate these things. For instance, I used to think that paired opposites were a given, that love was the opposite of hate, right the opposite of wrong. But now I think we sometimes buy [3] into these concepts because it is so much easier to embrace absolutes than to suffer reality. I don't think anything is the opposite of love. Reality is unforgivingly complex.

When you start off writing, if you are anything like me, you may want to fill the page with witticisms and shimmering insights so that the world will see how uniquely smart and sensitive you are. Over the course of time, as you get the knack of doing some writing every day, what seems to happen almost organically is that you end up wanting your characters to act out the drama of humankind. Much of this drama does not involve witticisms and shimmer. Yet this drama is best couched in moral terms; the purpose of most great writing seems to be to reveal in an ethical light who we are. My favorite moment in Jeanne Moreau's latest movie—a comedy called *The Summer House*—takes place in a kitchen, when she proclaims that every human has something to cry about. When mocked by the owner of the kitchen and pressed to say what it is that we have to cry about, she tosses back her head of flaming read hair and says, "The winds of solitude roaring at the edge of infinity." How do we, as individuals and communities, behave with that wind blowing behind us? Are we well behaved, striving for dignity and compassion, or is it every man for himself? 4

As we live, we begin to discover what helps in life and what hurts, and our characters act this out dramatically. This is moral material. The word *moral* has such bad associations: with fundamentalism, stiff-necked preachers, priggishness. We have to get past that. If your deepest beliefs drive your writing, they will not only keep your work from being contrived but will help you discover what drives your characters. You may find some really good people beneath the packaging and posing—people whom we, your readers, will like, whose company we will rejoice in. We like certain characters because they are good or decent—they internalize some decency in the world that makes them able to take a risk or make a sacrifice for someone else. They let us see that there is in fact some sort of moral compass still at work here, and that we, too, could travel by this compass if we so choose. 5

In good fiction, we have one eye on the hero or the good guy and a fascinated eye on the bad guys, who may be a lot more interesting. The plot leads all of these people (and us) into dark woods where we find, against all odds, a woman or a man with the compass, and it still points true north. That's the miracle, and it's astonishing. This shaft of light, sometimes only a glimmer, both defines and thwarts the darkness. 6

Think of a medieval morality play as the model. We love to hear that goodness will triumph over evil, that the fragile prize—humanity, life—will be saved. In formula fiction, evil wins out until the very end, and then against all odds goodness prevails and the hero gets to kiss the girl with the big bosoms. Life is somewhat more complicated than it was in the Middle Ages, but in many ways it is so much the same—violent, terrifying, full of chaos and plague, murderers and thieves. So the acknowledgment that in the midst of ourselves there is still a good part that hasn't been corrupted and destroyed, that we can tap into and reclaim, is most reassuring. When a more or less ordinary character, someone who is both kind and self-serving, somehow finds that place within where he or she is still capable of courage and goodness, we get to see something true that we long for. This is what helps us connect with your characters and 7 with your book. This is what makes it a book we will foist on our friends, a book we will remember, that will accompany us through life.

But you have to believe in your position, or nothing will be driving your work. If you don't believe in what you are saying, there is no point in your saying it. You might as well call it a day and go bowling. However, if you do care deeply about something—if, for instance, you are conservative in the great sense of the word, if you are someone who is trying to conserve the landscape and the natural world—then this belief will keep you going as you struggle to get your work done. 8

To be a good writer, you not only have to write a great deal but you have to care. You do not have to have a complicated moral philosophy. But a writer always tries, I think, to be a part of the solution, to understand a little about life and to pass this on. Even someone as grim and unsentimental as Samuel Beckett, with his lunatics in garbage cans or up to their necks in sand, whose lives consist of pawing through the contents of their purses, stopping to marvel at each item, gives us great insight into what is true, into what helps. He gets it right—that we're born astride the grave and that this planet can feel as cold and uninhabitable as the moon—and he knows how to make it funny. He smiles an oblique and private smile at us, the most delicious smile of all, and this changes how we look at life. A few small things seem suddenly clear, things to which we can cling, and this makes us feel like part of the solution. (But perhaps we have the same problem with the word *solution* as we do with the word *moral*. It sounds so fixative, and maybe we have gone beyond fixing. Maybe all we can do is to make our remaining time here full of gentleness and good humor.) 9

Or look at the fourteenth Dalai Lama, who is, for my money, the sanest person currently on earth. He says simply, "My true religion is kindness, keeping one's heart open in the presence of suffering." Unfortunately it does not make great literature. You will need to embroider it a little. Otherwise you will have a one-sentence book, and potential agents will look at you as if—as the Texans say—you are perhaps not the brightest porch light on the block. 10

So a moral position is not a message. A moral position is a passionate caring inside you. We are all in danger now and have a new everything to face, and there is no point gathering an audience and demanding its attention unless you have something to say that is important and constructive. My friend Carpenter says we no longer need Chicken Little to tell us the sky is falling, because it already has. The issue now is how to take care of one another. Some of us are interested in any light you might be able to shed on this, and we will pay a great deal extra if you can make us laugh about it. For some of us, good books and beautiful writing are the ultimate solace, even more comforting than exquisite food. So write about the things that are most important to you. Love and death and sex and survival are important to most of us. Some of us are also interested in God and ecology. 11

Maybe what you care most passionately about are fasting and high colonics—cappuccino enemas, say. This is fine, but we do not believe that you are simply spiritualizing your hysteria. There are millions of people already doing this at churches and New Age festivals across the land. 12

Write instead about freedom, freedoms worth fighting for. Human rights begin 13
with and extend to your characters, no matter how horrible they are. You have to
respect the qualities that make them who they are. A moral position is not a slogan, or
wishful thinking. It doesn't come from outside or above. It begins inside the heart of a
character and grows from there. Tell the truth and write about freedom and fight for
it, however you can, and you will be richly rewarded. As Molly Ivins put it, freedom
fighters don't always win, but they are always right.

Works Cited

Beard, Amanda. Excerpt from student reflection essay.

Brockmeier, Kevin. "A Kind of Mystery: Glimpses of the Writing Life." *Oxford American*
48 (Winter 2005): 114–21.

Elbow, Peter. "Writing Assessment: Do It Better; Do It Less." *Assessment of Writing:
Politics, Policies, Practices.* Eds. Edward M. White, William D. Lutz, and Sandra
Kamusikiri. New York: Modern Language Association, 1996. 120–34.

Hirsch, Edward. *How to Read a Poem: And Fall in Love with Poetry.* New York: Harcourt,
1999.

Lamott, Anne. *Bird by Bird: Some Instructions on Writing and Life.* New York: Doubleday,
1994.

McCormick, Joshua. Excerpt from student reflective essay.

Murphy, Sandra. "Assessing Portfolios." *Evaluating Writing: the Role of Teachers'
Knowledge about Text, Learning, and Culture.* Eds. Charles R. Cooper and Lee
Odell. Urbana: NCTE, 1999. 114–35.

Odell, Lee. "Assessing Thinking: Glimpsing a Mind at Work." *Evaluating Writing:
the Role of Teachers' Knowledge about Text, Learning, and Culture.* Eds. Charles R.
Cooper and Lee Odell. Urbana: NCTE, 1999. 7–22.

Wolcott, Willa. "Portfolio Assessment." *An Overview of Writing Assessment: Theory,
Research, and Practice.* Ed. Willa Wolcott. Urbana: NCTE, 1998.

Glossary

Ad hominem attack: a logical error in which a person and not an issue is attacked, 159

Alliteration: the repetition of initial consonant sounds, 311

Allusions: literary and historical references, 15

Annotation: a sentence or two on a bibliography card that identifies the value of the selection relative to the topic, 212

Antagonist: the character whose interests conflict with those of the protagonist, 75

Begging the question: the fallacy of assuming as proven the idea that needs to be demonstrated, 157

Cacophony: harsh sounds used in poetry to emphasize the unpleasant, 323

Ceremonial discourse: discourse that aims to persuade the audience that a person should be honored for her/his virtue or dishonored for her/his vice, 99

Characterization: the process of creating a character for a story, 75, 76

Chronological order: the order of time, 10

Climax: the point in a story at which the conflict reaches its highest pitch and the protagonist stands on the brink of a major choice, 76

Conflict: competing points of view between characters in a story, `10, 75

Confirmatio: the part of an oration in which the orator confirms points of agreement with the opposing speaker, 110

Confutatio: the part of an oration in which the orator refutes other claims and presents instead more compelling points to the contrary, 110

Connotation: emotional association attached to a word or phrase, 326

Couplet: a rhyming two-line unit of poetry, 318

Credentials section of a research proposal memo: the section that explains the reason for choosing the topic and your qualifications for researching the topic, 212

Critical reading: reading that analyzes and interprets, 10

Deduction: the process of reasoning from premises to conclusions, 153

Deliberative discourse: discourse that aims to persuade the audience to adopt one course of action and dissuade them from adopting another, 199

Dialogue: the words spoken by characters in a story, 10, 77

Dispositio: the arrangement of an oration, 110

Divisio: a statement in an oration that makes clear the order of key points to be addressed, 110

Dynamic character: a character who undergoes great change, 76

Either/or fallacy: a logical error in which the audience is forced to choose between only two choices when other choices are also possible, 159

Ethos: credibility, 136

Euphony: smooth, soothing sounds; the opposite of cacophony, 321

Exordium: an introduction in an oration that identifies the deliberative, judicial, or ceremonial issue to be explored, 110

Exposition in a story: the part of the story that orients the reader to the main character and his or her situation, 75

Expository essay: an essay that aims to explain and interpret, 17

Falling action: the part of a story between the climax and the resolution, 76

Figurative language: the language of comparison, 11, 118

Flashback: a movement back in time to show events that shaped the present situation, 75

Freewriting: a writing exercise in which the writer writes for a specified length of time to discover thoughts and feelings, ignoring spelling, punctuation, and grammar issues, 15, 16

Hypothesis: an interpretation of a situation based on assumptions, 153

Iambic pentameter: a kind of meter in which each line of poetry has ten syllables arranged in a weak-stress/strong-stress pattern, 319

Imagery and Symbolism: words that paint a picture and take on significance beyond their face value, 76

Induction: the process of drawing conclusions from analysis of evidence, 153

Invention: methods of discovering information on a topic and ways to organize the information. 102

Irony: a rhetorical device that stresses the difference between what we expect and what we get, 10

Judicial discourse: discourse that aims to persuade the audience of someone's guilt or innocence, 101

Logical fallacy: errors in reasoning, 154

Logos: evidence and reasoning, 136

Mediational discourse: persuasive writing that aims to make peace, 152

Metaphor: an implied comparison, 138

Meter: the pattern of stressed and unstressed syllables in lines of poetry, 318

Narratio: a brief story in an oration that dramatizes the importance of the subject, 110

Narration: story-telling, 3

Narrative essay: an essay that tells a true story, usually in chronological order, 10

Onomatopoeia: a kind of figurative language in which the sound suggests the meaning, 323

Parallel structure: identical grammatical structure of words, phrases, or sentences, 11, 157

Pathos: an appeal to emotion, 136

Periodic sentence: a sentence in which the main point, made in the independent clause, comes at the end of the sentence, 261

Personification: a type of figurative language in which human qualities are ascribed to things that are not human, 314

Peroration: the conclusion of an oration that summarizes key points and urges action, 113

Plagiarism: academic dishonesty, 205

Plot: the pattern of action in a story, 75, 76

Point of view: the perspective from which a story is told, including first-person point of view, third-person point of view, and omniscient point of view, 76

Proposal memo: a proposal, in the form of a memo, for a research topic, 177

Protagonist: the major character in a story, 75

Quatrain: a four-line unit of poetry, 318

Recursiveness: the back-and-forth nature of the writing process, 69

Red herring: a logical error in which attention is drawn to irrelevant examples or statements, 160

Reflection: the process of looking back on your work and assessing the effectiveness of your choices, 335

Research paper: a documented essay that explores a problem and primary texts in light of secondary texts and sources, such as journal articles, books, websites, and interviews of experts, 177

Research problem: the problem that develops from the initial research on the research question, 207

Research question: the question that directs the research, 207

Resolution: the point in a story at which the consequences of the character's choice become clear, 76

Rhetorical analysis: a close study of the choices that the writer made to achieve the purpose and to meet the reader's expectations, 256

Rhyme: words that end with the same sound, 214

Rising action: the section of the story where the conflict begins, when the main character encounters a problem and an opponent, 75

Setting: where and when the action takes place in a story and the range of social values for that historical period, 76

Simile: an explicit comparison, 138

Standard or loose sentence: a sentence in which the main point comes at the beginning of the sentence, 261

Stases: places to "stand" relative to those with opposing views, 100

Static character: a character in a story who undergoes no change, 76

Style: the sum total of all the choices writers make to achieve their purposes, to serve their readers, and to do so with a distinctive voice, 247

Summarizing: the process of condensing and/or synthesizing information from a secondary source and putting it into your own words, 217

Sweeping generalization: a false conclusion based on sampling too little evidence, 154

Syllogism: a deductive statement with three parts—a major premise that makes a statement about a class or genus; a minor premise that makes a statement about a particular member of the class named in the major premise; and a conclusion that makes a statement about the particular member based on the assumed truth of the major and the minor premises, 154

Task schedule in a research proposal memo: the section that specifies the dates that the writer will complete the stages of the research writing process, 212

Theme: the author's implied comment on one of the subjects explored in a story, 76

Thesis: the explicit claim that all essays should include, 12, 46

Topic sentence: the main point of a paragraph, 255

Topoi: the common topics that provide lines of argument for persuasive discourse, 102

Tree outline: a writing exercise in which subtopics branch off from main topic, 16